Read by
Jane Foster 2018

KU-393-798

YOUNG,
BRAVE AND
BEAUTIFUL

Violette inscribed and gave this photo to Aunt Florrie, Charlie Bushell's sister, who lived at The Kennels in Wormelow, Herefordshire, UK. *Author's archives*

YOUNG, BRAVE AND BEAUTIFUL

THE MISSIONS OF SPECIAL OPERATIONS EXECUTIVE
AGENT LIEUTENANT VIOLETTE SZABÓ,
GEORGE CROSS, CROIX DE GUERRE AVEC ÉTOILE DE BRONZE

TANIA SZABÓ

The
History
Press

Violette fondly laughing as Tania upturns the tin of talc. *Author's archives*

First published 2015
Reprinted 2015 (twice)

The History Press
The Mill, Brimscombe Port
Stroud, Gloucestershire, GL5 2QG
www.thehistorypress.co.uk

© Tania Szabó, 2015

The right of Tania Szabó to be identified as the Author
of this work has been asserted in accordance with the
Copyright, Designs and Patents Act 1988.

All rights reserved. No part of this book may be reprinted
or reproduced or utilised in any form or by any electronic,
mechanical or other means, now known or hereafter invented,
including photocopying and recording, or in any information
storage or retrieval system, without the permission in writing
from the Publishers.

British Library Cataloguing in Publication Data.
A catalogue record for this book is available from the British Library.

ISBN 978 0 7509 6209 4

Typesetting by Sparks – www.sparkspublishing.com
Printed by TJ International, Padstow

Dedication

To my mother, Violette Szabó,
in her honour;
to all those who jumped
and to the late Paul E.F. Holley
who found me a safe landing place.

Contents

The book was entitled *Young, Brave and Beautiful* by Seamus Morvan of the Morvan Family Group of Hotels in Jersey who, along with his father, Bill Morvan, is devoted to the memory of Violette.

My Aim

My aim has been to breathe life into Violette. The two existing biographies, although great in their unique way, did not do that for me, the daughter. I hope I have succeeded for you, at least in part.

Some of the people in this book have asked for anonymity; sometimes I have given living people roles they may not have played but fulfilled courageous roles in other ways. Sometimes I have created a fictional Résister carrying out real actions. All the events and dialogue are based on family anecdotes, primary sources in the main, people involved in France and the UK over the years, War Office reports and National Archives PFs and are included to give her the breath of life. An example is that of Philippe explaining to Violette the task of her first mission in Burnley Road which did actually take place in John's miniscule bedroom. The words are taken directly from Philippe's report to the War Office to create an authentic dialogue. This is not a biography in the strict sense of the term, rather an informative and deeply researched reconstruction of the dramatic events of Violette's two real-life missions during 1944, leading up to her fate in January 1945.

Violette's three weeks in Rouen in April 1944, overflowing with Gestapo, German soldiers, French police and Milice – all bristling with weapons – have always been glossed over. It was a long time to spend alone in the most dangerous area in France those few months before D-Day, under enemy eyes and weaponry, to discover what happened to a blown circuit, many of whose members were tortured and killed, their families under constant suspicion and suffering. She gathered intelligence and persuaded those who were perhaps initially unwilling to continue perilous sabotage activities under instruction from London leading to D-Day.

You will note I have used footnotes. First, I was told to get rid of them because they get in the way of reading. I have not done so. Second, it was suggested they go to the end of the chapter so as not to irritate the reader. I have not complied. The reason is simple. Footnotes are the only place for extraneous but interesting detail and it is highly unsatisfactory to have to turn the pages to find where the end of the chapter is, then find the relevant footnote within a page of numbers. I have made the footnotes small in size, and small is the marker beside the object of the footnote.

I do not have one 'idem' but there are some funny anecdotes, comments and notes on language and such like that would not fit in the narrative. Yet they may be of interest to some of you, dear readers.

There are those who have contributed greatly whom I have not mentioned. Some because they wanted it that way, but those others, please forgive me my lapse. I shall blush a thousand blushes when I realise. You know who you are and how much I thank you. I have made copious but careful use of the Internet; have scoured many books and articles; I have used their information with gratitude. The bibliography is a further acknowledgement to those whose written words and images have greatly assisted me. Thank you all.

It is to be understood that all errors, historical or otherwise, as well as intentional and unintentional liberties are mine and mine alone.

Thank you for reading this book. I do hope you enjoy the journey I made and have written here with the kind support of so many.

Lastly, I thank my mother, Violette Szabó, and her mother, Reine Bushell (née Leroy), for without them the world's treasury of courage would have been immeasurably less, and without whom this book would, truly, not have been possible.

Tania Szabó,
Violette's daughter,
Powys, Wales
2015

Foreword by Virginia McKenna

Of all the memories revived and tributes paid to the valiant, selfless — and yes, beautiful — Violette Szabó, none can be more poignant than this biography, written by her daughter, Tania. It is everything one could wish for in a biography. But this one is unique in its factual detail, its brave retelling of Violette's last months and, above all, the author's courage in sharing with us the deep and lasting love of a daughter for an extraordinary mother.

Virginia McKenna

Foreword by Author Jack Higgins

Soon after the debacle of Dunkirk that left Britain standing alone at the edge of a Europe occupied by Nazi forces, Winston Churchill proposed the setting up of an organisation to be known as Special Operations Executive (SOE).

This was to be a unit of secret agents whose job was to penetrate occupied territory and wreak as much havoc as possible.

For logistical reasons, France – directly across the Channel – presented the most obvious target. Set Europe ablaze was Churchill's order and members of the SOE certainly were to do that having arrived by parachute, motor torpedo boats and light aircraft such as the Lysander, a plane capable of landing in a ploughed field and taking off again.

But where were the recruits for such an organisation to come from? People who would have to be capable of jumping into total darkness over unknown territory, armed to the teeth, willing to engage enemy forces in combat and capable of accepting the terrible fate that would face them were they taken prisoner by an enemy who believed that torture of the vilest kind was acceptable.

Where, then, could SOE expect to find the recruits needed? Strangely enough, not from the military, but from the general public and in many cases, women. Women like Violette Szabó.

She was born in Paris to a French mother and an English father. The family moved to England before the war. Violette had grown up into an incredibly beautiful young woman who bore an astonishing resemblance to Ingrid Bergman. She married Étienne Szabó, a French–Hungarian Foreign Legion officer, who was killed at El Alamein. Grief stricken, she offered her services to SOE, making it quite clear that she was seeking personal vengeance.

In April 1944, she parachuted into France a good distance from Rouen, travelled there alone by train, and reorganised an important resistance network that the Nazis had smashed.

She returned by Lysander to England, but about five weeks later arrived back in June 1944 to the Limousin, where she worked with local Maquis in attacks on German communications lines. She and a companion, *Anastasie*, were ambushed by SS soldiers of Das Reich and Deutschland Regiments. Wounded, she held them off with her Sten gun, ordering *Anastasie* to make his escape.

From June to August 1944, she was interrogated by the SS, tortured, and then transferred to Ravensbrück concentration camp where, like other prisoners, her health deteriorated due to severe malnutrition.

Desperate to dispose of her and facing the imminent end of the war, the Nazis got rid of the evidence in their usual way. She was executed and her body probably cremated.

That her George Cross was awarded posthumously in 1946 was all the more poignant when one remembers that it was received by her four-year-old daughter, Tania, who so many years later has produced this totally unique account of her mother's life and work.

Jack Higgins
Channel Islands
April 2007

Introduction by US Wireless Operator Jean-Claude Guiet

I was a little taken aback when I was asked to provide an introduction to *Young, Brave and Beautiful*, never having had any experience in such an undertaking. However, I found it quite satisfying to have the opportunity mentally to review some very old personal feelings and memories in the process.

This is the story of a person with whom I was only briefly acquainted, yet whom I remember clearly and very fondly. Indeed, after being introduced to her and all the other team members, I didn't see her for about three weeks until we all were together at Hazells Hall awaiting departure. We remained there for three days, and intermittently during the days before her capture. There were four of us involved in the *Salesman* team dropped by parachute in the Haute-Vienne of the Limousin.

Firstly, the team leader, *Major Charles Staunton* (real name Philippe Liewer) who selected me after an interview where he spoke perfect British English and without warning switched to perfect Parisian French. I switched languages with him, and he concluded I would meet his requirements and was far better than his other choices. He then invited me to lunch.

It was at that lunch that I met the others. There was the weapons instructor and demolition expert *Bob Mortier* (real name Bob Maloubier), a Canadian captain with his cap at a jaunty angle. The third member was our courier *Corinne* (real name Violette Szabó), a FANY (First Aid Nursing Yeomanry) officer. Finally there was me, the radio operator *Claude* (real name Jean-Claude Guiet). All the other three had had prior field experience: Philippe and Bob in a network Philippe had set up in Normandy and Violette, in the same Normandy area after the net had been blown, to see if anything could be salvaged; a most dangerous task.

I was a neophyte preparing for his first mission. I had just been promoted to second lieutenant, but hadn't yet received a proper uniform. I met them in plain khaki without rank. In spite of their sincere efforts I was not of the group yet, and the lack of uniform and rank did not help. The conversation was primarily directed at finding out more about me. It was a difficult meal for me since they all knew each other and made many references to past common events. Their seeming lack of concern for security appalled me. At Hazells Hall there was joking and friendly banter, but no operational talk of the forthcoming operation.

Violette's previous undercover experience gave her the aura of a veteran. Yet our age difference was slight. I was quite struck by her sense of humour and even her tendency towards practical jokes: in fact, when she awoke us all very early after return from an aborted landing with the news that the invasion had started, we at first refused to believe her; thinking it to be another of her jokes.

When she winked at me on the plane of an aborted flight over our drop zone in France just before we were supposed to jump, I interpreted it as a sort of flirtation. Probably a typical male reaction on my part. As I look back on it, I realise that it was a kind attempt at reassurance on her part.

Once we were in France, I saw her only three times: twice for meals at a restaurant with the others and one time alone, the day before she was captured. This was primarily because, as the American radio operator for the group, I was to be segregated from all operational activities as our sole source of contact with London. On this last occasion Violette walked me to the little house near the watermill I had moved into as my base. She needed to know where to contact me, since she was our courier. She was pushing the bicycle she was to use the next day. Other than telling me she was going on a trip the following day, she volunteered no information. We had a pleasant conversation though we knew nothing about each other except that she was *Corinne* and I was *Claude*. She spoke forcefully of her admiration for our team leader, *Charles Staunton*, and of her determination and belief in duty. I was looking forward to seeing her again often.

Two days later, I was in a flurry of transmissions concerning her capture. I found that I missed her, even though I was very much occupied. It was only after the war that I found out her real name and some of her background, including her mission around the Normandy area. In fact, the feeling that I have missed her for so long is a tribute to the effect her personality, friendliness, concern and efficiency had on me and all the others who knew and dealt with her.

Jean C. Guiet, CdeG★
Tucson, Arizona, US
April 2007

Dramatis Personae

The many SOE and Résistance operatives working in occupied France often had code names to protect their identity. Here, some of them used in *Young, Brave and Beautiful* are explained, along with the brave people who were assigned them. The names in *italics* signify code and cover names.

Atkins, Vera   Buckmaster's assistant in SOE and an Intelligence officer

Bloch, Denise   Denise was an SOE operative and wireless operator for Roger Benoist. She was executed along with Violette at Ravensbrück concentration camp

Boulanger, Henri   Known as *Commandant Fantomas*, Henri ran the Maquis group called the *Diables Noir* with his brother, Raoul, until their arrest

Boulanger, Pascaline   Known as *Calourette*, Pascaline ran the *Diables Noir* after her sons, Henri and Raoul, were captured by the Gestapo

Boulanger, Raoul   Known as *Capitaine Cartouche*, Raoul ran the *Diables Noir* with his brother, Henri, until their arrest

Buckmaster, Maurice   Head of SOE French section in the UK

Clement, George   Known as *Edmond*, *Driver*, *Georges Bourdias* and *Georges Flamand*, George was an SOE operative who first thought Violette would be suitable as an SOE operative

Desvaux, Denise   No known aliases, Denise was a Résistance worker who ran a safe-house in Rouen

Dufour, Jacques   Known as *Anastasie*, Jacques was a Résistance worker involved with *Salesman II*. He ran his own Maquis group called *Soleil*

Liewer, Philippe   Known in London as *Major Charles Staunton*; known in France as *Charles Beauchamp* or *Clément Beauchamp* in the *Salesman* circuit and *Hamlet* and *Capitaine Charles Clément* in the *Hamlet* sub-circuit, among other aliases. Philippe Liewer, a French journalist, was an SOE operative who ran *Salesman* in the Rouen area, *Hamlet* in Le Havre and *Salesman II* in the Haute-Vienne during the Second World War

Maloubier, Bob Known as *Robert* or *Bob Mortier, Robert* or *Bob Mollier, Paco* and as *Dieudonné* – God given! Bob, a Frenchman, was an SOE operative and trained Résistance groups

Malraux, André Known as *Colonel Berger*, André was an author, Résister and much more besides and held an important role directly from de Gaulle who tried to bring together disparate Résistance groups

Malraux, Claude Known as *Cicero* or *Serge*, Claude was a Résister and Philippe Liewer's second-in-command in the Rouen *Salesman* circuit. He was André Malraux's half-brother

Malraux, Roland He was André Malraux's other half-brother and a Résister. He was Harry Peulevé's lieutenant in the *Author* circuit

Mayer, Roger Roger was a Résister and Philippe Liewer's lieutenant in his Le Havre *Hamlet* circuit

Newman, Isidore Known as *Pierre Jacques Nerrault* or *Pepe*. Isidore was an SOE operative, working as a wireless operator further south in France until he became the w/o for *Salesman* and Philippe Liewer

Peulevé, Harry Known as *Paul* in the Author circuit, which he ran, Harry was an SOE operative who trained with Violette and was in love with her

Philippon, George Known as *Jo*, George was an important Résister and hid weapons from London. An external member of the *Diables Noirs*

Pionteck, Bronislaw Known under the nicknames of Broni or Bruni, Broni was a Résistance worker and Isidore Newman's wireless operator and 'bodyguard'

Poirier, Jacques Known as *Nester* or *Captain/Capitaine Jack*. Jacques was a Résister who took over Harry Peulevé's *Author* circuit

Rolfe, Lilian Lilian was an SOE operative and wireless operator for George Wilkinson. She was executed along with Violette at Ravensbrück concentration camp

Samson–Churchill–Hallowes, GC, Odette Known as *Lise*, Odette was an SOE operative who met Violette at Ravensbrück

Southgate, Maurice Known as *Hector*, Maurice was an SOE operative who ran the *Southgate* circuit

Sueur, Florentine Known as *Jeanne* and *Micheline*, Florentine was a Résistance worker and external member of the *Diables Noir* who ran Micheline's store with her husband, Jean

Sueur, Jean Known as *Nénésse, Néné* or *Serge*. Jean was a Résistance worker and external member of the *Diables Noir* who ran Micheline's store with his wife, Florentine

Szabó, Violette Known in London as *Vicky Taylor*; known in France as *Corinne Leroy, Louise Leroy, Madame Marguerite Blanchard*, née *Picardeau*, widow, among other aliases. Violette was an SOE operative, working as courier and liaison officer. She was illegally executed in Ravensbrück concentration camp in 1945

Valois, Lise Lise worked with Jean and Florentine Sueur and kept their Résistance links active after their arrests

List of Organisations

AMF French organisation under de Guélis, which was the duplicate of SOE's F Section. Taken over by Brooks Richards in October 1943, it took on the mantle of the RF, de Gaulle's French Section within SOE

Allied Air Force (AAF) RAF, French, Polish, Dutch, Australian, New Zealand, American & Canadian pilots among others who flew during the Second World War

Bureau Central de Renseignements et d'Action (militaire) BCRA(M) Created under Dewarin, the BCRA eventually became the French intelligence service

Comité départemental de Libération nationale (CDLN) Formed to bring the disparate Résistance groups of Rouen together to co-ordinate sabotage and intelligence gathering within the Seine-Inférieure

Défense contre avions (DCA) French organisation of defence against aircraft

Défense Passive The equivalent of the air raid wardens in London

Diables Noirs A group set up not long after the beginning of the Occupation, formed to receive the first parachute drops of material and to gather intelligence, which later expanded to train young *réfractaires* as fighting units in the Maquis

First Aid Nursing Yeomanry (FANY) Incorporated in 1909 as an unofficial auxiliary of upper-crust women volunteers set up to serve mounted troops. It was later called the WTS – Women's Transport Service – incorporated in 1939 into the ATS (Auxiliary Territorial Service)

Forces Françaises de l'Intérieur (FFI) Groups of Résistance fighters who became organised and worked with the Free French forces

Francs-Tireurs et Partisans (FTP) (armed section of the PCF) Partisans and Sharpshooters, the armed section of the French Communist Party; frequently the final 'F' is excluded, as it is obvious they are French

Free French Charles de Gaulle's military forces who worked with the Allies against German occupation

French Communist Party (PCF) (of which FTP was the armed section) Worked with SOE and OSS to some extent

L'Heure H Group of Résistance fighters

Libé-Nord   Set up by Léon Gonier, a Freemason, among others, in 1941 to work with the Allies against the German occupation of France. A leading member was Raoul Leprettre who worked to bring the Rouen groups under the newly formed réseau

Mouvements d'Unité de la Résistance (MUR)   A single group made up of Combat, Libération and the non-communist Franc-Tireur (FT)

Maquis   Groups of Résistance fighters in occupied France, aiding the Allies and fighting back against the Milice and German occupiers

Navy, Army and Air Force Institute (NAAFI)   Her Majesty's Forces (HMF) official trading organisation, with shops or outlets wherever armed forces are stationed

Office of Strategic Services (OSS)   American counterpart to SOE, which evolved into the CIA after the war

Organisation civile et militaire civil (OCM)   Military organisation that recruited high-ranking and junior French officers into its service along with French professionals in the teaching sector, law and various industries

Secret Intelligence Service (SIS, now often known as MI6)   British organisation that works abroad to collect foreign intelligence

Service du travail obligatoire (STO)   Compulsory work service of French prisoners in Nazi Germany from 26 February 1943

Sicherheitsdienst (SD)   The intelligence agency of the SS and Nazi Party

Special Operations Executive (SOE)   Set up in 1940 to work with often disparate Résistance groups to conduct espionage, sabotage and reconnaissance, among other things

Vagabond Bien-Aimé   Group of Résistants and saboteurs

Part I

1

Dropped Blind

5/6 April 1944 – night of Wednesday/Thursday
Full moon in the week before Easter Sunday

'She stepped from a plane, high in the air, in the darkness of the night'
From 'Ode to Violette' by her father, Charles Bushell, 1946

Tangled in the hedgerows, south of Paris, her parachute lying all around, a mud-spattered Violette froze in her struggle to free herself. Voices. Garbled voices. Voices in the dark. Footsteps closing in. Language – what language were they speaking? French? German? Breath held, sweat prickling her eyes, she listened hard. To be caught on landing before her work had started would be ignominious. As the two men stopped some way off to light a cigarette, they chatted on and Violette could dimly hear and see they were French. Which French? Friend or foe? Peering through the brambles, she first thought that they were farm workers. But her natural instinct and her training told her never to presume. The Nazis are certainly setting up clandestine organisations in France too, thought Violette. Looking again, she saw that the men were armed and in the uniform of the gendarmerie – Pétain's semi-military country police force. Many gendarmes joined the Résistance but many did not. Some infiltrated and reported to their German masters.

The discussion between the two gendarmes was becoming decidedly animated. Violette moved not a muscle, breathing slowly and quietly in the damp cold hedgerow. The moon was at full gleam with the occasional cloud scudding up from the south. There had been a few light April showers during the day and rain was forecast for the morrow.

After a while, the men walked on, still engrossed in their discussion. Perhaps they had heard the dull roar of the aircraft flying from the north to drop 'joes'[1] but they remained unaware of the slim young woman in parachute garb, entangled in a heap of wires and silk, ankle a little sore from the thud of landing. Perhaps on the morrow, seeing the propaganda leaflets dropped on the neighbouring towns, including Châteauroux, they would assume the roar in the night had merely been

---

[1] A 'joe' is the American term for any anonymous agent dropped into enemy territory, also used by the British.

an Allied aircraft dropping its load of leaflets. Scattering such propaganda was frequent and, in fact, used to cover this very kind of operation, parachuting or landing agents in France.

This would make a great gown, thought Violette fleetingly as she extricated herself and hastily gathered up the silk of the parachute, burying it in the shallow hedgerow's ditch under a mass of wet autumn and winter foliage. Her initial fright had died down quickly – this was *her* mission; no more practice runs – and she felt the thrill of the adventure. She inhaled deeply. Her eyes adjusted to the dark and, quickly scanning her surroundings, she searched the night for the reception committee and her commanding officer Philippe Liewer (whose cover name in the UK was *Major Charles Staunton*), who was to accompany her as far as Paris (Philippe was French and had been a journalist for the Havas agency, which in 1944 became a public company, Agence France-Presse (AFP), which rivals Reuters today). She smiled to herself, feeling she had overcome one hurdle – fear of discovery. Fear had been overcome and defeated.

‡

Violette had completed her SOE[2] training with very mixed reports that would not have delighted her had she read them. Reports that showed some instructors were somewhat smug in their clearly superficial understanding of this half-French, half-English young woman.

On completion of her initial training assessment course at Winterfold in August 1943, this FANY Section Leader, Violette Szabó, clearly had leadership qualities, but gave somewhat disappointing results on her mechanical and Morse code abilities which were merely average; an intelligence rating of 5 and general agent grading an unpromising D:

```
A quiet, physically tough, self-willed girl of average
intelligence. Out for excitement and adventure but not
entirely frivolous. Has plenty of confidence in herself and
gets on well with others. Plucky and persistent in her
endeavours. Not easily rattled. In a limited capacity not
calling for too much intelligence and responsibility and
not too boring she could probably do a useful job, possibly
a courier.
```

2 The Special Operations Executive was the undercover group formed on the instructions of Sir Winston Churchill during the Second World War to infiltrate and 'set Europe ablaze'. The other services, e.g. the Secret Intelligence Service (SIS), very often looked on SOE as an 'outfit of amateurs' and were loath to supply it with anything at all.

On 7 September, a first report on her paramilitary course with an illegible signature stated:

> I seriously wonder whether this student is suitable for our
> purpose. She seems lacking in a sense of responsibility and
> although she works well in the company of others, does not
> appear to have any initiative or ideals. She speaks French
> with an English accent.

Violette had been invited to join SOE, where she mixed and trained with people from every stratum of English and European society. She came from a working-class background in England and her life in France had been that of *la petite bourgeoisie*. Her excellent French was accented from the northern regions of France where she had lived and been schooled and where she had travelled every year, working briefly on the Belgian border. Violette had learned to move effortlessly from one social circle to another and had turned out to be exactly the right material – better than SOE could have imagined. She was also extremely athletic and a crack shot with rifle or pistol.

Violette was vivacious and very attractive, and she knew it in a quiet, unpretentious way. She had enjoyed romantic encounters and had fun-loving cousins and friends for dancing, skating and cycling. With her soft French accent and gaiety she was captivating. A free spirit, she loved the cinema, cycling and dancing, attending many dance halls, including the Locarno in Streatham, the Hammersmith Palais and the Trocadero.

With her residual French accent and her gaiety, she was captivating. An accomplished acrobat and dancer, a strong swimmer and skater, especially on ice, she could pedal the pants off her brothers or cousins.

Other successful agents from similar backgrounds to Violette fared no better in their reports. She was conscious that some of her instructors, mostly military, came from a class and educational background vastly different from her own yet they were not able to dampen her spirit of fun or her determination to succeed, no matter what they threw at her. Fortunately, as in every organisation, there were people who could spot and promote agents of real calibre and who also saw in Violette the ability, intelligence and the will to win through to the end of arduous courses.

Violette had often demonstrated both her frivolity and her clear determination as a child, as a teenager, and finally in early adulthood as a young working woman and at the various SOE 'Special Schools' scattered throughout England, Wales and Scotland. Her co-students thoroughly enjoyed her company, especially when she led them on pranks against their superiors. As a youngster she had butted in and sent packing boys who were bullying one of her girlfriends. To my grandmother's very real consternation, Violette would allow her father to put an apple on her head and shoot it off with an air rifle with great giggles from her and chuckles from her father.

‡

During the ten years of the Great Depression in England, the Bushells had at first decided to live in Paris where they tried to carve out a living from Reine's expertise with the needle while Charles ran his one-man private taxi and chauffeuring service. So, at the age of four, Violette had already glimpsed life in the beguiling French capital but as my grandfather did not enjoy learning 'that bloody language French', he would grumble until they reluctantly returned to England.

On their return, it proved very difficult for Violette's English father, Charles Bushell, to get a decent job or maintain his own small business endeavours. In the late 1920s and early '30s, money was increasingly scarce, even with his French wife, Reine,[3] working on commissions of sewing work and her intermittent winnings at whist, at which she excelled.

With great heartache, especially on Reine's side, the couple decided that their children, Roy and Violette, would be better served living with Reine's parents and sister while attending school in France until things improved in England. They could then bring them back home. These years in France had been far superior, in quality and education, to what she could have had in England. The two children lived in France seven long years – years in which both Roy and Violette became French children, living a French way of life with the settled French bourgeois family of grand-mama Blanche Leroy, grandpapa Eugène Leroy and with Tante Marguerite, housekeeper to the Chorlet household, then married to M. Victor Hoëz. The French extended family lived in Pas-de-Calais, Picardy and Nord, close to the Belgian border. The local accent was that of Picardy and the border towns – quite different to a Parisian accent.

These seven long, character-forming years in France were bliss to the two Bushell children; they became indistinguishable from their French cousins and friends in the sleepy villages of Quevauvillers, Pont Rémy and Englefontaine. Reine visited them only rarely, when she had saved for the fare and a little extra so as not to seem impoverished by contrast with the French Leroy family.

Vi, as she was called in England, received a good education in France, at Noyelles-sur-Mer, near Étaples and at a Catholic boarding school in Abbeville. This was roughly interrupted at the age of twelve, when her father Charlie recalled her and her brother, Roy, to England to join the rest of the family. He did not want them to become foreigners, strangers to their own growing family.

He wanted his family to be English – as he was – and to speak the bloody language as well. Violette and Roy now had brothers in England: John and Noël

---

3 Reine = queen. It is pronounced like the little bird, 'wren' with a French or trilled 'r'.

(known as George), followed by Harry, a sweet child who died aged five of diphtheria, and, in 1934, the youngest, Dickie. The death of Harry saddened Reine very much. Many years later, in Australia, she still spoke of the pain of losing that child. She had feared that maybe Dickie would be the next. She missed her two children in France and needed them beside her now.

Charlie and Reine were looking forward to their family growing together. However, a third of the way through the Great Depression, by 1932, Reine had a shrewd idea of what Roy and Violette would be giving up by returning to the relative poverty of living in London in Talbot Road, Bayswater; with the added difficulty that now they could barely speak English. Lessons in England were difficult for Roy and Violette, not only due to language but also because of the dissimilar manner in which subjects were taught and, naturally, with different national emphasis.

Although hot-tempered, often quite the martinet insisting on his own brand of discipline, Charlie was something of a spendthrift in his generosity to friends or those he thought of as friends. He loved his children and was proud of the burgeoning family he and Reine had created, and of his pretty, discreet and accomplished French wife, who stubbornly announced that if she must cook English fare then she would do it better than the English. She also taught herself to speak and write excellent English but never lost her delightful French accent. Charlie had always loved Reine, his independent French wife, passionately; their love continued into old age. Even after his children had grown up, Charlie Bushell still wrote love poems to his wife, Reine, his queen.

✝

Although Charlie was enterprising with a strong streak of independence, he just did not have a good head for sustained business. Starting them up, yes – the original idea always found a niche in some market or other – but painstaking planning and persistence simply did not come easily to him. He refused to do anything illegal, but it was a thin line at times. One of Charlie's sisters, Florrie Lucas, used to say jokingly that one day he would surely be in trouble with the police.

He was happy to receive poached[4] rabbit and game. He was always 'into something' and ready to make a go of it which led to his having been cashiered by the army in the First World War over 'supplies', he redeemed himself and was promoted from sergeant to lieutenant in the Royal Horse Transport. 'Bucking the system is not a crime,' he would tell his friends, ending with 'but breaking the law is.' His resolve to be an honest and upright citizen was bolstered by the horrors he had witnessed as an ambulance horse and lorry driver on the front line

---

4 Poche = pocket in French – hence 'poached eggs' (in a watery pocket) and 'pocketed' literally as in 'poached rabbit'.

in the First World War. He had been lucky to come through in 1918 alive and outwardly unscathed.

‡

The new war had hardened into ferocious fighting by 1940. The search was on for potential agents to slip surreptitiously into France and other European countries to help nascent resistant movements by setting up SOE circuits in those countries; initially to establish and supply sabotage networks, to organise reception committees and the training of Résistants, to find suitable terrain for supply drops and later to gain and pass on intelligence arising from these activities.

While the first agents were creating their first networks and exploring how France was functioning, Violette was talent spotted by George Clement[5] just before he went into the field as Édouard, a wireless operator for the *Parsons* circuit set up around Rennes in Brittany. Violette was security cleared by 1 July 1943.

George also acted as SOE adviser under the name E. Alexander, who mentioned to Captain Jepson he had met a possible recruit, suggesting she be telephoned on her Bayswater 6188 number before she was snapped up permanently by the Belgian section where she had been active in some way and impatient to 'do something useful'. Violette's northern French accent was perfect for working both sides of the Franco-Belgian border, and she knew some Dutch and Flemish. She had been familiar with the area as a child and teenager travelling to Liège with Tante Marguerite and the Chorlets, briefly working for them in their factory offices when war broke out.

George Clement, four years older than Violette, was born in Petrograd. He had gone to school in England, then studied at Brasenose College, Oxford[6] before joining the army and then SOE. He had met Violette on various occasions at 'swanky' London clubs. Through these chance meetings, he felt she might be good material for the Service. She had mentioned her wish to continue doing something in the north of France, where her aunts and French grandparents lived. Unbeknownst to her, Violette had already been thoroughly checked out by SOE and put through various tests; she was then invited by Captain Jepson to join the French Section (or F Section) of SOE.

After working in the Land Army in 1940, and just before joining SOE, she spent much of 1941 on the predictors along with her friend Elsie Gundry under Colonel Naylor of the 481 (mixed) Heavy AA Battery. Then in 1943 at various SOE special training schools (STSs) (the first was the induction school STS 7 at Winterfold in

---

5 George Clement was trapped and caught transmitting on 28 November 1943.
6 A Royal Charter established the body of principal and fellows on 15 January 1511/12. It founded a College to be called 'The King's Hall and College of Brasenose' (in this sense Brasenose Hall still exists) for the study of sophistry, logic, philosophy and, above all, theology.

Cranleigh, Surrey), she submitted herself to rigorous training regimes, where she found herself living, no longer just mixing, with an eclectic mix of people, from the downright criminal to the cultured and sophisticated of British and European society.

Another comment on Violette in the report with an illegible signature is:

```
Although I am absolutely sure that she has not the faintest
idea of what is going on the other side, she does not seem
to bother to find out in the least, which in my opinion is a
very bad sign.
```

The reason is clear to me. She knew probably better than the writer of that report just what was going on in France at that time. It is my thinking that Violette was wholly intent on being trained for whatever might be in the offing. She would have had a good idea – she was not unintelligent and by living in France had already been involved albeit on the periphery of clandestine work. It was not her place to be inquisitive regarding future plans. She was to hold her own counsel which she obviously did. Many trainee agents failed in this respect and were found employment in less sensitive areas.

This was a life she had embarked on with enthusiasm, optimism and a certain seriousness. Her training, physical and mental, was tough and exhausting but here she was living in manor houses with beautiful grounds, learning about the few artefacts that still graced them and their surrounding cottages. It was a gateway to knowledge of the arts and, through the lively conversations, the cultural and intellectual life in England and Europe. She had desperately missed the bourgeois life in the north of France and dressing up for special occasions. Now she was seeking to reach upwards and outwards, not realising this would be reaching for the sky in ways she had not imagined.

‡

As well as the bourgeois social scene of Paris, Violette had encountered the London social scene at the Savoy Hotel in the Strand where her older brother, Roy, worked as a hall porter, having been promoted at seventeen from pageboy. He asked Violette to partner him to the Savoy Staff Ball in the autumn of 1937 as a gift for her sixteenth birthday. She was delighted.

Roy had discussed the ball with his mother beforehand addressing his parents' concern that Violette could be steered in the right direction by attending with him her first ball thus giving her a first taste of society. He could not have spoken better. It was both parents' fear that Violette was too headstrong.

Reine could not have agreed more, saying she would make her a lovely dress and thanking him for thinking of her. Roy described the evening planned by the

Savoy to his mother saying there would be a big Glen Miller band, a superb meal by French chefs and some very nice people. He went on to say that the staff rankings, usually so stiff, would be relaxed a little, while everyone chatted and danced. He thought Violette was not half pretty and that with her slight Frenchiness and fluent French she would be a wow even with all the staff wearing the finest evening wear they could afford or ill-afford.

Reine decided to make her a fine satin gown like the dresses she had made for young women presented to King George VI, but not in debutante white, rather a soft oyster cream. Violette must attend the Savoy in a ball gown that would be something special, marked by Reine's experience as a dressmaker in Paris. Her mother made the dress to be slinky in oyster satin but not outrageously so, reminiscent of the 'roaring twenties' – a simple low square neckline edged in a darker satin and inch-wide straps. Around her neck Violette wore a borrowed gold art deco snake chain. Reine also bought her a pair of size-four golden slippers. Then she made her a small satin purse with material left over from the gown's straps.

Violette was over the moon. It was an interminable wait from summer to autumn as she watched her mother design, cut and sew the dress by hand in her spare time. She was very excited and determined to look beautiful, speak beautifully and dance beautifully. She knew she was good-looking but perhaps did not realise how stunning she could be. She followed the twenties theme her mother had started and wore very red lipstick, to the grumpy tut-tuts of her father, enough eye make-up to highlight her large sparkling eyes,[7] a light face-cream, and powder to stop the shine.

She did not need to be heavy with makeup or flashy with clothes and followed her mother's simple, classic and wise guidelines. Violette decided on a mass of kiss curls on her forehead and a tight chignon at the back of her neck, topped with a multi-coloured festive tiara.

She met many interesting people that night, even spoke French with a few and danced the night away, impressing everyone with her glowing beauty and knowledge of France, the French and French writers and artists. At sweetest sixteen, she was, in turn, impressed and absolutely loved being in the grand institution that was the Savoy Hotel, mixing with the directors, high-ranking staff and their partners. Roy was somewhat miffed when the Savoy's manager asked Violette to dance and he was left to whirl the manager's wife around the dance floor. Roy's friends and colleagues commented on her soft English, her vaguely foreign ways and her gaiety and easy laughter. And how well she danced!

'It's all just top notch, isn't it, Gig? Oh thank you for such a swell evening.'

---

7 Her irises were edged with violet, like the young Elizabeth Taylor's; hence her French name Violette.

'Come on then, let's have another dance. I'll even admit to being quite proud of you, and you do dance like a dream.'

'For the moment, you're my favourite brother!'

‡

2

At the Farm

Wednesday 5 to Thursday 6 April 1944,
during the week before Easter Sunday

Grey outlines, faint in the night's gleam, were silently moving towards her. Fear prickled again so she felt relief as she recognised Philippe – with a man and a woman from the reception committee dressed in farming clothes. Philippe Liewer, *Clément Beauchamp*, had divested himself of his parachute kit. He strode along in a well-worn and somewhat crumpled French suit, shoes now muddied from the field. He had no firearm and refused to carry one, until after D-Day in June. Philippe also refused Violette permission to carry a firearm. He considered it more dangerous in this heavily patrolled area than not carrying.

In French, he asked Violette: 'You okay?'

'*Très bien,*' she answered.

He continued: 'We're hopping on a couple of bikes and following these two to a nearby farmhouse where we'll eat and sleep. Tomorrow, at dawn, will be soon enough to start that long haul on their crazy bikes to the station. That's where we'll get the afternoon train to Paris.'

'*D'accord,*' said Violette. 'Hope there's some good *pinard d'un bon pinot*[8] to soothe our dreams.' She laughed quietly at her own pun.

Monsieur Chantelle, whose farm they had landed on, extended his hand in warm greeting. '*Tu n'es pas blessée, petite? Tu pourras te réchauffer et manger chez nous à la ferme. Ma femme a prepare une belle omelette.*'

'No, not injured, *merci.*' Violette smiled shyly in the dark. 'How nice to get warm again and have a bite to eat. *Merci beaucoup, monsieur.*'

---

8 While *Pinot* is an old and distinguished grape or vine, *un pinard* is a wine to set your teeth on edge and you on fire. But it is, even today, quite acceptable to remark appreciatively that the wine being consumed is '*un très bon pinard*' without necessarily giving offence, a bit like saying 'a pretty good bottle of plonk'. Where the UK has 'Poppy Day' arising from the terrible slaughter of the First World War, the French, after victory in 1918, were encouraged to drink '*le pinard des poilus*' – the fighting man's grog – '*poilus*' being the nickname given to them since they were unshaven and thus 'hairy'. In fact, *pinard* was bought at quite a price after the war to help support the orphans and widows of France. Now the French have the blue flower of remembrance.

A warm welcome awaited Philippe and Violette at the farm. Monsieur Octave Chantelle was not only a rich farmer but also the mayor of a tiny commune. He introduced his wife, Madeleine, and then brought from the cellar an ancient bottle of very special white wine in true French hospitality. The local red *pinard* was young but a perfect accompaniment to the farmhouse feast laid on by Madame Chantelle – a huge *plat de charcuterie*, an equally large *omelette espagnole*, made from leftover potato slices, fried onions and peas, accompanied by hot French bread straight out of the kitchen oven, made from their own wheat.

As they tucked in hungrily, two members of the reception committee gave them the latest information. They were reminded that they had arrived in the Easter season with people moving about around the country to visit family and friends, making it considerably easier for Violette and Philippe to blend in.

This was not the first time the small farming commune had put its members in direct danger of capture, being beaten, perhaps tortured and even killed. Many were Communist to the core, hating the Nazis and totally bent on ridding their '*belle Marianne*', *la belle France*, of the *sales Boches* or, the *sacrés Fritzs* – the 'damned krauts or Jerries', as the British called them. Octave Chantelle was not a Communist but fervent in his disgust at the '*attentistes*' – the wait-and-see brigade – and Pétain, once his hero, he now considered nothing but an old and diminished puppet, dancing to the German tune.

While munching contentedly, the group quietly discussed the activities of the local Résistance fighters plus plans and training to be implemented by *Paco*, i.e. Bob Maloubier.

The Résistants explained to Philippe they were short of everything – especially coffee and clothes for those living rough as members of the growing Maquis, and, of course, ammunition and explosives. They all discussed the help urgently needed from England: hard cash, armaments and training.

Gaston Dubras, from the area around Valençay and leader of many reception committees, grumbled that it was necessary to put an end to those bastards by destroying their lines of communications to which Philippe agreed wholeheartedly letting them know that they would 'continue to give it to them in spades!'

Philippe then asked Violette to outline a few of the instructions from London for blowing up German lines of communication, without jeopardising them by giving too much information at this stage. It was, after all, not their immediate area. Violette and Philippe were going much further to the north. Gaston confirmed that the train service, although reduced, still ran, but not necessarily on time.

'*Vous savez*,' Madame Chantelle explained, 'The trains are about the only good thing. At least they run fairly regularly – simply because the Germans need them to get from place to place. Things are going to get infinitely worse. Those filthy Jerries are incessantly piling requisition on requisition and our poor mayor is – like others all over the country – absolutely worn out by the daily battles against their demands for more, more, more. Damn them all, I say. We need our food, our equipment and all the rest.'

'But the Maquis showed up just last month in Beynat[9] and made the transporters unload six cows and calves destined for the abattoirs and then Germany,' the farmer stated with pride. 'Twelve armed men got them off Monsieur Bugeat's lorry and then the Maquis leader said the purchase commissioners could take delivery but only on their solemn promise that the cattle would not go to the Germans. "We're for the people," he said, "and we won't let the lousy *Boches* step all over them".' Octave gave a satisfied laugh.

Everyone clinked glasses and drank to victory.

The two guests from London were astounded on being told that on 11 March 1944 various commercial organisations must have caught a whiff of victory – of the promised Allied invasion – and they chuckled when they were shown the local occupation newspaper asking the French to take four empty champagne bottles 'in good condition to their usual supplier' and they could 'have delivered as an absolute priority as soon as transport facilities will allow and certainly before 31 December 1944 one bottle of their favourite champagne'.

The farmer remarked that the factories and retailers were putting subscription lists together nine months in advance. He felt strongly that, now, they must have a whiff of something.

In containers dropped with them, Violette and Philippe had brought for these Résistants provisions of real coffee, cigarettes, clothes, small arms, various explosives, ammunition and money as due recognition of the danger in which the reception committee and local people had put themselves. Warm thanks were passed to Philippe and Violette for all the British were doing, but these men of the Résistance were understandably impatient for more and concerned after the debacle of Dunkirk.

'Bet the bloody British scarper and leave us high and dry,' said one angry young French fighter, part of the reception committee – still untrained, untried.

'Wait and see,' said Philippe, somewhat tersely. 'It'll be interesting to see how you stand up under the London instructor's training regime, young whippersnapper, never mind the real thing!'

'*D'accord, d'accord, ne t'en fous pas!*'

Although Philippe was coldly calm, his tone had made the young chap lower his defiant eyes. The general fear was still that the British would fade away and leave the French in the grip of the Vichy puppet government and the Nazi organisations.

Philippe grinned then, handing them a bulging packet. Dubras' second-in-command gasped, '*Mon dieu! Ça fera l'affaire pendant un bon moment.*'

---

9 A group of communes in Beynat canton, in heart of lower Corrèze, near Tulle and Brive (Limousin), south of Limoges.

'Damn well ought to last!' Philippe said, adding to himself somewhat sourly, 'Bloody hope so, anyway.'

‡

'You know, Vi,' Philippe had said, just before they left England for France, 'It's time for you to learn exactly what I've been up to in *la zone interdite*. But first you tell me what you know about this forbidden area.' He was staying with her at her parent's place, 18 Burnley Road, in Stockwell, south London. It was in a pretty terrace of small Georgian houses with a small garden at the back. Reine and Charles Bushell rented two floors from the owner to house their now rather large family.

'Okay. As far as I understand it, the zone where my Tante Marguerite lives is the area the Germans are administering from German-occupied Brussels. That's more or less Picardy and Nord. Then you've got the *zone interdite* that stretches from Calais through Amiens and Pont-Rémy, where Mum married Dad after courting for three years during the last war.'

'Is that right?' asked Philippe. 'So when did they actually get married?'

'At the end of the war. It was just a small ceremony in 1918 in Pont-Rémy's Town Hall. They didn't get married in church because Dad wouldn't become a Catholic. He was darned handsome, you know, and very dashing in his best uniform. He was a champion welterweight boxer in the army. He couldn't be a soldier or a pilot because early in his military service he'd been in an explosion that permanently caused him some deafness – not that he would accept that – so he became a driver on the front line – supply vehicles and ambulances, frequently horse-drawn, often bringing the wounded and the dead back from the front. He still won't talk about it. Anyway, that's where Mum and Dad fell in love and got married. Their romance was as sweet as roses to him, just a short distance away from the muck and blood of the trenches.

'*Alors mon chef*, back to the present! This first forbidden zone stretches down south-east to Laon. It was extended in November 1943, all along the French coast off the Channel from Calais past Le Havre and Rouen on to Cherbourg and St Malo. I suppose it includes the occupied Channel Islands off the French coast. Then as far as Brest on the western tip of Brittany and all down the Atlantic coast as far as Bayonne and the borders with the French Basque and Spain. Is that about it?'

'Yep. It was extended just as I was leaving the area. Seems the Germans were getting twitchy. Many arrests then. Which is why it's going to be even more dangerous for you than it was for me.'

'Why did you return then? Because you knew the zone was to be extended?'

'I had very carefully and slowly set up an extremely good network, you know the one, the *Salesman* circuit. That was my mission – to set up and organise a secure network of men and women and to train the men in sabotage up to and after the invasion. This I did from April last year. I stayed with the Francheterre family the entire time in a small flat in a large *cité ouvrière*[10] block of ninety-six. I couldn't have found a better safe house. The people were extremely brave and generous. We had some great evenings with the whole family cramped in their tiny flat. Friends would drop by for *un petit Ricard*.[11] I had spent over a month going backwards and forwards from Paris to Rouen when eventually Madame Micheline – I met her through my wife's Tante Evelyn – said she had a branch of her fashion shop in Rouen run by a Monsieur Sueur. He's a Gaullist – about forty-five or fifty – a bit old for all this stuff but he was overjoyed to be a *boîte à lettres* as well as a contact point. He proved a good dead-letter drop and store. It's through him I met the Francheterres. I insisted they knew the danger they were running. They didn't care. Longed to do something against the invader.

'It's odd, you know, in Le Havre they say the people of Rouen don't have a lot of courage. They're certainly different from *les Havrais*, that's for sure. *Dieudonné* (one of Bob Maloubier's *noms de guerre*) and I were the only two I could find safe houses for, but those couple of hundred or more who did help couldn't have been braver. We owe them!'

'Philippe, tell me what happened in Le Havre again. It's good to go through it like this; I can remember it all so much better. You eventually met a chap there called Roger Mayer, a chemistry prof in a high school, I think you said.'

They were in John's tiny bedroom, which Reine had made warm and comfortable for Philippe to stay in while John, one of Violette's three younger brothers, was in REME.[12] Another brother, George (Noël), was away in the navy and Roy had joined the army. Violette and Philippe were left in peace in the tiny bedroom to spend the necessary time going over and over the situation that Philippe had left in France and what Violette might expect when she eventually got there. Rick – Dickie as he was known then – was with his mother, Reine, running around, getting under her feet, and they were both laughing.

Violette sat in the armchair, resting her feet on the end of the bed while Philippe lounged on it, hands tucked behind his head. Both wore jumpers and slacks but still had their slippers on. They spoke almost entirely in French for Violette's benefit. The operation ahead took up all their waking moments.

'At this time in Normandy and Seine-Maritime,' continued Philippe, 'I found the area brimming with German troops. However, not many Vichy police were in evidence, as it seems the area is considered a safe zone of pro-German loyalties. Nevertheless, there is a head of the Milice who's got a nasty reputation. The only other organisation I came across was the National Front, but it's damned

---

10 *Cité ouvrière* is a workers' housing development, almost equivalent to council housing in the UK.
11 Ricard is an aniseed-based alcoholic drink.
12 REME = Royal Electrical and Mechanical Engineers, British Army.

badly organised. That's the French commies. Each time they got a hundred or so together, they were caught.'

'They're mostly pro-Communist, y'know,' confirmed Violette. 'I'm sure there're many other groups. And I bet that each group is probably fighting for its own political survival as well as building up a strong Résistance entity, particularly as there's something big in the air – an Allied invasion.'

'True, Vi, true. Those that I had gathered had already been involved in obstructing the Germans and had had some pretty good successes – blowing up electricity plants – and I trained up some 200 men with Bob Maloubier's help.'

'He's quite a character. Came to my flat in Pembridge Villas and met little Tania. Great fun to spend time with, dining and dancing, but his eyes are only for roaming.'

'True,' laughed Philippe. 'But he's a bloody good sabotage trainer and landing-committee organiser. Comes on a bit too strong, though, which has proved to be awkward in the field. On arrival he was shot, spent the night in a near-frozen stream, stumbled out and was holed up in a house, where the visiting doctor, Dr Delbos, pronounced the need to get a coffin ready as this fellow was sure to be dead by the morning. Blow me, if he didn't defy the doctor to recover and carry on. He trained many men in sabotage techniques for before and after our invasion, to put obstacles in the path of the German military, to receive armaments from parachute drops, hiding them at secret dumpsites until just before we invade, and to sabotage railways, electrical plants and viaducts.

'It certainly took courage to get through that injury and the conditions to survive after lone gunfights with the enemy,' mused Vi. 'I just hope he also has the courage to save or protect others in a similar tight spot.'

'After I returned to England, at least one chap in Rouen had talked, and one way or another pretty well the whole network has been compromised, if not utterly destroyed. It took me twelve bloody months to set it up – with the utmost care and attention to detail. And now men and women that I persuaded to do this dangerous work have been arrested, some tortured and some shot. I'll tell you, *ma petite*, it's hard to bear. All because my lieutenant in Rouen wouldn't act quickly enough and wanted to wait for me to return! A brilliant lieutenant but incapable of independent thought. All those bloody people …'

Violette understood his agony. 'I'm so sorry, Philippe. When my husband was killed, I didn't think I wanted to live. I'd walk down to my flat – our flat – in Pembridge Villas with tears completely unbidden streaming down my face, knowing I'd never see Étienne's face light up with pleasure,[13] his gentle teasing and we'd

---

13 Adjutant-chef (13e DBLE) Étienne Szabó was awarded many honours, some posthumously, including the military Légion d'Honneur, Médaille Militaire, Croix de Guerre with Star and Palm, plus his Colonial Medal. He was killed at El Alamein on 24 October 1942 below the plateau of Qaret El Himeimat. In their hall of fame, Étienne is one of the Legion's heroes.

never dance again. He was so quiet, yet so tough. I loved him and longed to live life with him in the south of France, having brothers or sisters for Tania.

'One of his closest friends and his commanding officer in the Legion was the Georgian Prince, Lieutenant Colonel Dmitri Amilakhvari. I met him and their general, Koenig, in Liverpool where Étienne and I spent five wonderful days, plus a few in London, on a sort of second honeymoon two years ago. Étienne and Amilakhvari were both killed at El Alamein – eighteen months ago. It was lucky I had Tania. She was what kept bringing me back to reality. I had a child to protect and bring up. Mum will *enjoy* helping out, and meanwhile I've put Tania with a friend, Vera Maidment, in Mill Hill. I pay her enough to at least make sure Tania eats well and has whatever she needs. She seems happy enough there whenever I've visited. I miss her but I know she's safe.'

'On to money matters. *Now* – that is, last year, 1943 and this year, 1944 – the pay of a *sergent* in the French army is 2,000 francs per month. Under my code-name of *Beauchamp* while in Rouen late last summer, I paid the wireless operator's bodyguard, a Pole, 2,000 per month, about 10 quid – same as a British sergeant, I think. I raised it to 5,000 in November, and for my lieutenants in Rouen and Le Havre I paid 5,000 francs, raised to 10,000 in November. They did not always want the money but I insisted, and so some used the money to support underground newspapers, families of arrested Résistants in difficulties, general expenses and in other useful ways. It's important for you to know this, Violette, when you discuss money matters for or with any of the surviving *Salesman* network.'

Philippe insisted on paying his men and women at what could be termed decent rates to ensure they did not have the extra burden of monetary worries and their families were properly provided for. He also ensured that money was made available from London to help families whose members had been taken by the enemy, possibly tortured, then shot or, at the very least, sent to Compiègne for deportation to Germany as forced labour in the German war machine.

'*En effet*, my lieutenant in Le Havre, poor old Mayer, did not want a penny for himself and accepted it for the clandestine newspaper he'd been running prior to my arrival. As you said, he was prof of physics and chemistry at the Lycée, about thirty-two – my age – and very savvy and cautious. I told them all, paid or not, if ever they needed help, they could always come to me.'

'Listen, Philippe, Maman's calling us down for one of her "abominable" English meals doubtless cooked to perfection. You can lead me through the whole setup later.'

‡

Now, in this early April of 1944, in war-torn France they were enjoying a very comfortable evening, everyone friendly and helpful. The packet Philippe had handed to the group's leader, Gaston Dubras, contained the substantial sum of 20,000 francs (equivalent to £115 at that time – a lot when a penny or two could still buy a meal!), and he promised them more parachute drops of urgently needed ammunition and other provisions. This largesse brought smiles all round. Philippe still had about a million francs. Violette had a further 250,000 in case they had to separate before reaching Paris and his wife's aunt's flat.

He had instructed her that she should have a large sum on her at all times: the larger part of it well-concealed in her worn-looking leather shoulder-bag with a cleverly disguised double lining and base, perhaps some in her jacket, more in her money-belt. Once she was on her own, which could be at any moment, she might need the extra cash for travelling and living expenses, for bribes, buying various clothes and accessories for disguises, getting and paying for forged ration cards or new forged identity cards, maybe even buying a car, truck or bike – with or without motor. Everything had to be considered.

Finally, Philippe impressed upon her that, although SOE boys and girls liked to joke that the weather was a greater hindrance to entering and operating in France than were any German activities, it was definitely not so in the area Violette was about to enter – the heavily defended *zone interdite* which was about twenty-five kilometres deep from the Channel coast. In spite of their jokes, the staff in London did take this very seriously and in the spring of 1944 the organisation of Allied 'counter-scorch' parties to keep French port facilities intact was being discouraged because 'it is extremely difficult to infiltrate agents into the maritime areas as the Germans keep a very strict and careful watch on all the inhabitants.' However, Violette, along with other agents, saw the *zone interdite*, with its special passes and regulations, as simply another set of hazards to overcome. One of the skills Violette had learned in training at Arisaig in Scotland was the technique of silently getting in and out of dinghies and skiffs. Peter Harratt[14] noted in his interrogation[15] on 15 December 1944 that, generally speaking, the best landing points were near a German pill-box, as their garrisons did not expect the British to be such fools as to attempt it. His best beach, which he used six times, was within 40 metres of an occupied pill-box. Ben Cowburn noted in his book *No Cloak No Dagger* that dinghies were 'absurd little things … about as seaworthy as an inverted umbrella'.

‡

14 Peter Harratt, DSO, MC, the DF's sea landings organiser and a leading expert at Arisaig, had been a hussar officer; his cavalry training was no hindrance to his maritime ability. DF or D/F was SOE's escape section, 'most DF operators lived in hourly peril of their lives. Their task: to provide communications to and from western Europe by sea & land; mainly to run escape lines across France into the Iberian and Breton peninsulas', M.R.D. Foot, *SOE in France*, new edition p.21.

15 The word 'interrogation' during the war in the forces was used innocently as a by-word for 'debriefing'. It is only after the war when it was realised the extent of the Nazi atrocities committed during their interrogations that the word itself often became synonymous with terror and torture.

Violette's gaiety put a smile on every face. They all noted that even during those first few evening hours her French had improved in leaps and bounds. How good it was to be back in France, and soon to be in pretty much the same region as Tante Marguerite, even if I can't have any contact with her, she mused. She was surprised she was starting to think in French again. Speaking to the others, she concentrated on every word, every syllable, every nuance.

Philippe was amazed at the transformation of south London girl to young French woman, totally in control of herself. He could see the care Violette took, not only with respect to her accent, but also to build the best relations, not talking too much or too loosely and giving only essential information in clear, unambiguous words. He was feeling much more optimistic in his choice of courier. I think she'll do just fine – and what a sweet demeanour she has, hiding the steeliness that I've glimpsed on more than one occasion, he thought to himself.

Retiring early to their bedrooms, they quickly washed from the jug of still-steaming water provided by their bustling hostess who continued to fuss over their clothes, ensuring they would be clean and dry and that they would be well provisioned on their journey to Paris with a little something left over on arrival. She knew, without being told, that it might be useful for them to have some little *cadeaux* in the way of *friandises* and good plain *saucissons* for distribution as special treats.

They rose with the dawn chorus and after a cold lick-and-promise from their refilled water jugs and a hearty breakfast, the pair set out on bicycles for the station, and the train that would take them to Paris.

They packed the generous lunch provided by Madame Chantelle and a bottle of the local wine plus a thermos of hot black coffee made sweet with black-market sugar. Knowing how hard rationing and food generally was in Paris, Madeleine felt they should take a gift for their loyal friends there, in addition to the little presents already deep in the basket. Very carefully she packed a dozen eggs, a large Berrichon pâté, goat's cheese and a cured ham in an old cloth bag. Before securing their lunches, they first strapped onto the rear of the bikes their small French leather suitcases, battered and scarred, containing a change of clothes and other essentials. The extra gifts of food went into the commodious basket at the front of Violette's bike.

After hugs and kisses on both cheeks, a hurried *allez hop, au revoir* and *adieu*, they pedalled off into the distance along the poplar-lined byways of middle France.

‡

3

Train Journey to Paris

6 April 1944 – Maundy Thursday

It was a cold clear morning, and the wind coming from the south made progress a little easier.

'Glad I brought that jumper,' shouted Violette to Philippe as they cycled. 'Mind you, we'll be warm enough in a short while, with the miles we've got to cover and those damned hills.'

'*Bon, ben!*' puffed Philippe, not enjoying the trip. First had been the parachute drop – which simply petrified him, but it had to be done – and now this, a long hike on gearless, rickety old bikes. '*Eh, mademoiselle*, not another word in English, or no share of the jolly lolly when you get back to Paris! *Piges? Pas de pognon!*'[16]

'*Oh, monsieur, pardonnez-moi, je vous prie!*' retorted Violette, grinning from ear to ear in mock apology, loving each moment of this journey. She was used to cycling for miles with cousins and brothers. A real athlete, she could outlast and overtake them all, but she was careful not to outstrip her boss by too much or too often. Philippe huffed and puffed, grumbling away in *la langue verte* – 'green' French.[17] Violette noted Philippe used this gentle swearing almost as an indication of equality. She found it easy to chat away in a friendly unaffected fashion; Philippe did not overwhelm her. They had worked and relaxed together in the UK and had formed a solid friendship. Violette respected Philippe as an extremely careful planner committed to any task passed to him.

The long stretches of Roman roads in this part of unoccupied France were peaceful. At eleven, they decided to turn off into a sheltered wooded area for rest and refreshments. As they chatted, Violette's attention instantly sharpened when Philippe moved onto the business of their mission, plans and messages, the task ahead for Violette in the forbidden zone, her lone journey into the unknown and the dangers she would surely have to face. But right now the trip felt a bit like a springtime *randonnée à vélo* – a relaxed and informal bicycle ride.

---

16 *Piges?* = Get it? Do you understand? *Pas de pognon!* = No dosh!
17 *La langue verte*, or 'green language', is known as 'blue language' in English. It can be compared to *film vert*, or blue film. The French are much more down to earth!

However, at no time did their watchfulness diminish. From time to time, German soldiers in military trucks, weapons visible, flew past, followed more slowly by lorryloads of provisions and a noisy tank or two. A solitary armoured German jeep sped along in the opposite direction, the driver, an overcoated general and another high-ranking German soldier staring impassively ahead. A number of armed motorbike messengers roared by, as did motorbikes carrying a senior German soldier in the sidecar. Each time they heard motorised traffic approaching, Violette and Philippe slipped hurriedly into the roadside fields or thickets. When such traffic came upon them too unexpectedly they slowed their speed and kept to the edge of the road, heads down – just another French couple going about their business. At such moments, a tremor of fear would send blood thumping into Violette's head, until she mastered it and calmed her thoughts.

They had to cycle about sixty kilometres to Valençay, up and down hill, occasionally taking circuitous routes to avoid military vehicles and personnel. From there, they would take a train to Paris, which would be slow and liable to hold-ups. There was a real danger that they would be asked to show their false identity papers, perhaps be searched and certainly questioned on where they were going and why. If the German officer, guard, Vichy police or Milicien did not like the response, being taken to Gestapo or Vichy police headquarters was the most likely outcome.

Violette, they had agreed, should remain as quiet as possible, letting Philippe handle any such eventuality. He was much better acclimatised to wartime France than she could possibly hope to be on this, her first visit since the *drôle de guerre* – that seven-month period of phoney war from September 1939 to 9 April 1940. At that time, it had been incumbent upon her to stop work and return home to England, leaving her beloved Tante Marguerite. She had been informally active with her aunt in the Nord and over the border into Belgium in their nascent resistance movement, helping in some small measure to hide downed Allied pilots and agents on the run, moving them along newly established escape routes. Belgian escape routes extended as far as Spain and often through to neutral Portugal, finally to a plane or boat back to England. Sometimes the route was along the coast into Brittany and Normandy, where small fishing boats or submarines picked up such fugitives in the choppy Channel waters. Doing this, Violette and her aunt gathered significant information to report to the Belgian Section in London.

Her return to England as the phoney war ended turned out to be on the last boat. All the vessels were full to overflowing – no more passengers allowed – but Tante Marguerite had raised her voice: '*Alors, vous ne voyez pas ce petit enfant de quatre ans? Sa sœur doit le rendre à ses parents. Qu'est-ce que vous allez faire – laissez-le aux Boches?*'[18]

So determined was she that Violette accompany her four-year-old brother back to his parents in England, the *douaniers* and French police finally let Violette and

---

18 'So, can't you see this little four-year old child? His sister must get him back to his parents. What are you going to do – leave him to the Krauts?'

Dickie through. The siblings adored each other and Violette knew that, no matter how much she wanted to stay and help her aunt, she was duty bound to get Dickie back home to their mother in London, who would be anxiously waiting for them at 18 Burnley Road.

‡

The two cyclists finally arrived in Valençay, a pretty town between Issoudun and Blois, notable for its beautiful château. There were two direct rail links from here to Paris: one from Toulouse and one from Lyon. As they had plenty of time before the train left for Gare d'Austerlitz in Paris, Philippe suggested they walk their bikes around the château. Over this Easter period, it would not hurt to act like happy holidaymakers awed by fine architecture. It was just a few minutes from the station and dominated the tiny town.

'The station looks just like a mini château!' exclaimed Violette.

'*Sûrement*,' replied Philippe. 'It wouldn't do to have a dump of a station serving this astounding Renaissance château, now, would it, *ma chère*? It was Talleyrand's!'

'You really know your stuff, don't you, *cher maître*?' mocked his willing listener.

It felt good to be with this thirty-two-year-old Frenchman – Violette soaked up his French view of the world, the war, his educated French accent and their common heritage as he made comments while they ambled along.

She was feeling safe, enjoying every smell and sight. German soldiers strolled past, courteous to the population, absorbing the experience of French Lent and Easter, occasionally politely checking papers of passers-by. There was no sign of Gestapo or Milice on duty. Shops were preparing for Easter; even though they were impoverished and no longer really free, they continued their preparations for the festivities, especially for the children. It would provide some relief from the tedium of restricted movement, ration cards and shortages. There had often not been enough fuel for fires or heating during the winter; electricity was intermittent, petrol commandeered by the Vichy French for the Germans.

'You realise', said Philippe, 'this whole region is just one extended, very flat plain, rich in agricultural produce and ideal for landing clandestine planes by the light of the moon. Like that superb goat's cheese we ate.'

Violette's face was a picture of suppressed laughter.

'*Non!* I don't mean goat's cheese flies! I mean agricultural produce.'

This produced further gales of laughter. 'So now agricultural produce flies, does it?'

'*Oh, en effet*, Vee, be serious! I am trying to give you important details of French life that one day just might get you out of a jam! Parisians who have family here don't go so hungry under the damn Germans.'

'Is that why so many *réseaux* are concentrated around here?' Violette asked.

'Yes, partly,' Philippe replied, 'and not because of the cheese! It's because the terrain's high and flat. There's a veritable tapestry of networks scattered all over this Berry region – like a huge series of spiders' webs where each one only knows his neighbours and friends.'

'It must be a very fragile web.'

'Yes, it is. In fact, it's constantly being attacked and dislocated, even infiltrated, by Vichy police and their informers. The Germans aren't so stupid, either. They know how to set up their own networks and infiltrate ours. Quite frequently arrogance gets the better of them and they're spotted and dealt with, but they're dangerous. When circuits are *brûlés* they are just rewoven by new arrivals from SOE and even by agents leaving.'

'Yes, I suppose so,' said Violette thoughtfully. She could not quite grasp how those leaving could reweave blown networks, but presumed he meant they went on to other circuits, or even created new ones within the same area. She could not resist saying, 'Flying cheeses and spidery agents weaving endless webs as they flee.'

They both collapsed into giggles as passers-by turned to stare. Some smiled.

‡

The train arrived on time. The carriages were crowded with people travelling to see relatives and friends in other parts of the country and to take part in restricted religious services to celebrate Easter.

Violette and Philippe had bought first-class one-way tickets to Paris and quietly sought out a first-class carriage. Once on the train, they settled into the stylish compartment. Appearing quite well to do in good-quality but worn clothes, they smiled briefly at other passengers looking their way and chatted inconsequentially to one another. The journey to Paris took nearly five hours instead of the usual two.

At one point a Wehrmacht soldier came to inspect tickets and identities, making a random search of shopping and luggage. Philippe said to Violette: 'Watch this: I've used this manoeuvre a few times now and, so far, it has always had the desired result.'

'*Monsieur, vos tickets et cartes d'identité, s'il vous plaît,*' asked the soldier firmly but politely in Teutonic French.

'Here you are, but I don't understand why we should be searched when we're doing all we can to help the Germans. It's very frustrating and rather insulting, don't you think, *chérie?*' grumbled Philippe, turning to Violette.

'*C'est affreux,*' replied Violette, looking quite furious at the poor soldier, who hurriedly handed back their tickets and identity cards and refrained from any further search. He apologised as he uncomfortably made his way further down the carriage.

'You see,' Philippe said, turning to Violette with a look warning her not to laugh.

'I'll certainly remember that ploy,' grinned Violette.

About an hour later, after a scheduled stop, Violette had the opportunity to practise the charade. There was the usual inspection, spot-check, an eviction of two people from the train. Keeping his head down, Philippe was amazed to hear Violette angrily grumble about '*terroristes*' disrupting everyone's lives, ensuring that the inspector hardly looked twice at two such obviously confirmed Vichyists!

Apart from those two incidents, which could have been fatal had one of the inspectors searched and found the huge amount of money they each carried; the journey to Paris was easy and enjoyable. There were two further checks but not in their carriage, and one unscheduled stop. Two men and one woman were dragged away at gunpoint. Despite this harsh interruption, the chugging of the locomotive had a calming effect on everyone. The weather remained bright and sunny and Violette was happy to watch the French countryside drift by.

‡

Part II

Part II

4

Arrival in Paris

Evening of Thursday 6 April to Sunday 9 April 1944

'*La barbarie allemande en effet ne se révéla pas …*'
'German barbarity in fact did not reveal itself …'

The train drew into the Gare d'Austerlitz at seven in the evening on that Thursday, billowing steam and smoke over the platform, passengers and luggage. Violette and Philippe quietly mingled with the bustling crowds busy seeking train times, transit platforms, friends and families. German soldiers gathered in small groups – arriving for, or departing after, their special leave in Paris. Worn leather suitcases and the farm's bags of supplies in their hands, Violette and Philippe walked out of the station and saw eager women selling *bons-bons* – with pure sugar!

The seller said that these were officially reserved for the Wehrmacht soldiers' rations in France and the J3.[19]

Angry and astounded, Violette replied that it was always the *zazous*, and the damned Jerries, surprising the seller with her vehemence. Violette had suddenly thought of Tania, her young daughter, and a burst of irritability was the best defence to cover her confusion.

To buy ration books they needed points. Philippe politely asked the seller how to get these when they had no coupons left and none for children. The seller, looking daggers at Violette, explained that it was easy. They just needed to go to one of the métro exits even during the day and they were bound to find as many *cartes de rationnement* that they could need. Violette was amused and not a little surprised to find black-market ration cards at the station, especially when SOE had gone to such great pains to forge perfectly the ones they carried. Certainly buying ration cards at the metro station meant they did not immediately need to use theirs, thus lessening the risk while increasing the possibility of purchasing further daily provisions.

---

19 J for *jeunes* = young people aged thirteen to twenty-one: from 1943 they could be issued with ration cards to receive more substantial rations than adults.

Violette and Philippe headed for rue Saints-Pères, Paris 6, where Tante Evelyn lived. It was about a two-mile walk from Austerlitz, but it was a mild evening with a light breeze sashaying down the left bank streets. Turning to Philippe, she remarked pleasantly, using his present identity: 'You know, *Charles*, I love travelling by train. Going first class, too, that's quite something. But now I'm a posh Parisian, aren't I?'

'Well, I'm not too sure, the way you spoke to that seller just now! Poor woman.'

Their luggage was not overly cumbersome and the walk would give Violette an opportunity to observe the Parisians and the enemy. From Gare d'Austerlitz they followed the river Seine on the left bank north on quai Saint-Bernard and turned into Saint-Germain-des-Prés.[20] As Octave, the farmer, had pointed out, there were many people on the streets, carrying all manner of bags because of Easter, so again they blended in easily. It felt very strange, and eerie, too, with grey-uniformed soldiers mingling with the grey crowds in the grey twilight.

Violette was struck by the sadness, anxiety and nervousness in the Parisians' faces. The pinched look of hunger showed too frequently in the working-class people they passed in the streets. In trains, streets and pavement cafés the unfortunate French, once the darlings of the world, would avoid one another's gaze, or stare with distrust.

'You know, Charles, I'm certainly increasing my vocabulary of good French insults. For example, how about "*Va donc, eh! vitaminé!*"[21] or I heard a woman shout: "*Espèce de sans-carte!*"[22] How awful it must be for them, worse even than for us in London – at least at home we're free from occupation!'

There were also still smart areas in Paris, as is always the case in occupied cities; places where wealth mingles with occupier, where people shop in glittering boutiques and dine in sparkling, haute cuisine restaurants.

‡

The time was approaching when Violette would travel to the *zone interdite* where Philippe had, over eight months from the previous April, set up the highly successful *réseau, Salesman*. He and Bob Maloubier[23] had trained the men who had carried out sabotage at Déville-lès-Rouen on 10 October 1943, at the factory of the Société Française ès Métaux (the French Metal Company) and, on the 31st, the destruction of Dieppedalle's electric substation. Reprisals became more frequent and harsher.

---

20 *Pré*, plural *prés* = meadow, plural meadows. *Près* = near or close.
21 'Get along, vitamin bag!'
22 'You're a cardless sod!' on the black market.
23 Bob was also known as *Robert Mortier* and *Paco*. He was a Frenchman who had been trained by SOE and often met Violette socially in London.

In Le Havre, besides the activities of the different movements represented at the Comité de Libération,[24] the two local groups – *Heure H* and *Vagabond Bien-Aimé* – continued their activities. Philippe had close connections with these through his *Hamlet* sub-circuit. Raymont Guenot, one of his best men, was arrested in July as one of the main leaders of *Heure H*, a mainly communist group, and shot in Rouen during the first days of November 1943. Philippe, with some anguish, recounted to Violette how Guenot had died without knowing that his '*deux vœux*', his 'two wishes', had come to fruition. First, they had set up efficient contact with the Résistance outside the country, notably with London; contact had been made shortly after his arrest, by his friend Paul Desjardins. Then, in September 1943, under Roger Mayer's leadership, *Heure H* had received its first parachute supply drop.

‡

The two travellers finally arrived, tired and dusty, at Philippe's aunt's apartment. Philippe introduced Violette as *Corinne*, which was her undercover name for this mission. Tante Evelyn warmly hugged and kissed Violette on both cheeks in welcome. After being shown their rooms, bathing and changing, they came down to a warm celebratory dinner.

'You know, Philippe,' Violette noted that first evening, 'your aunt is so courageous, putting her life at risk for us and the Allied cause. I wonder how she can do it.'

'Because she loves me! Why else?' riposted Philippe, with a laugh.

'I'm old but not deaf, my dear nephew,' came from the kitchen. 'Apart from the fact that I might have some residual affection for you, I look around me each day in this city that I dearly love and watch it trampled underfoot by the enemy – an enemy we've fought many times before. I've watched bright, happy faces turn grey with apprehension, lack of nourishment and all manner of restrictions. I will not stand idly by; I am not an *attentiste*[25] and I will do what I can to rid this city of such vermin.'

'*Corinne*, you must make this your home while you're in France. I'll give you a key. This way, you come and go as you please. However, *never* bring anyone here. Meet them out walking in a park or one of the main squares nearby.' Philippe's aunt did not live very far from the Pont du Carrousel, the Tuileries and the Louvre.

---

24 The Comité départemental de libération (departmental liberation committee) was part of the French Résistance. In 1944, there was a civil resistance structure (the Comité) and a military one (the French Forces of the Interior). The Comités developed out of the desire of the MUR (Mouvements Unis de la Résistance) and the Free French Forces in London under De Gaulle to give political representation to the Résistance forces in France. In each commune, a Comité local de libération (local liberation committee) represented the Comité départemental de libération.

25 *Attentiste* = a wait-and-see type of person.

To avoid endangering Violette and his aunt, Philippe would not stay longer than one night. He wanted to liaise with several circuits regarding the planned Allied invasion, to encourage them to carry out carefully timed sabotage, to get kit and equipment ready, continue training and check their vehicles. He later informed London of the sabotage groups' requirements for munitions, money and other supplies during debriefing.

Philippe had a strict policy of shunning clandestine meetings in cafés and restaurants: it was too easy to be overheard or to appear conspiratorial – particularly true in Paris from late 1943 to early 1944. There had been hundreds of arrests and around a hundred Résistants shot. Parisians continued to resist, many continued to be caught, tortured and disposed of, leaving behind networks, friends and families to press on in imminent danger.

None of this prevented Violette living with Tante Evelyn in rue Saints-Pères. Her papers were expertly forged in the name of *Corinne Leroy*. She looked exactly like the young French woman she was, seemingly walking to work or to the shops in Paris' wartime streets. Tante Evelyn became Violette's base for this mission, her *boîte à lettres* (that is, her dead-letter drop, meeting place or message relay), as well as the safe-house she could race to if necessary. The old apartment, in a *grande maison* of Paris, had some ideal places for concealing people or objects.

‡

The morning of 7 April, Vendredi Saint or Good Friday, Philippe left early and he knew the two women should spend as much time together as possible so Violette could immerse herself in all things French. He knew there was no faster or better way than for her to pass a couple of days with his aunt, allowing her to become accustomed to the occupying enemy and daily life for the French.

France does not close down on Good Friday and the shops were mostly open. It was the right weather for a long walk, and the two women strolled arm-in-arm, with Violette soaking up the distinct ambience of both banks of the Seine. She felt the enemy presence and saw it in action in the streets. If stopped and questioned, her story was that she was visiting her aunt for Easter.

Tante Evelyn had an idea to give Violette a treat before her hazardous journey. She suggested having lunch in Le Grand Café.

As Violette did not know it she asked what is was like. Even with the hateful Germans, Tante Evelyn explained that it was still a fabulous place. One of the most fashionable places of Parisian society – amazing art nouveau furnishings and décor, big, glamorous, and great fun. She felt sure that Violette would love it.

As they entered, Violette glanced around; it was certainly glamorous. Tante Evelyn was greeted by the genuinely smiling maître d', whom she knew well, and he guided them across the thick carpets to a well-positioned discreet corner banquette, secluded enough for their own privacy but from where they could see the other diners. The menu was wonderfully varied, especially compared to war-torn London, and they accompanied their meal with house wine, a carafe of water and not-so-ersatz coffee. They chatted the whole time. Violette asked question after question about the fashions – so stylish and so different from London – about the politics of the day, about comportment in the streets and how to respond when stopped for papers. Tante Evelyn, happy to educate this lovely girl, thought Violette utterly charming. It amazed and frightened her that someone so innocent of the ways of the world and unused to present-day France should be embarking on a dangerous mission, so she told her everything she could, with many small but vitally important details about France generally and Rouen and Paris in particular.

Violette absorbed everything that, in the comparatively sterile atmosphere of the SOE training schools, would otherwise have taken her time to digest, understand and remember. But here, it was not only her mind that was learning but her eyes, ears, nose – in fact every fibre of her being.

The dining room resonated with laughter and the clink of cut-glass goblets. In the far corner, a tuxedoed pianist softly played the melodies of the day. The ornate stained-glass ceiling reflected shimmering light. Two steps from l'Opéra, the Grand Café's richly lit windows glowed. War or no war, it continued serving the best and freshest seafood platters day and night.

The food was perfect. Violette handed Tante Evelyn her ration cards and sufficient francs to pay for the entire meal. Including wine, the bill came to the equivalent in today's money of about £100 each, plus the mandatory 15 per cent tip. Violette was amazed by the opulence, never having paid more than a couple of pounds for her and friends at the local eating houses and pubs. It felt special and exciting: an antidote to bombed-out buildings and rubble-strewn streets.

They left the restaurant at about three in the afternoon, rosy cheeked and happy, yet careful about what they said within earshot of other people – Parisians and Germans alike. Tanks, guns pointing forward, moved slowly along the boulevard and some of the smaller streets, reminding the occupied city just who were the masters.

Violette had been introduced to the most cosmopolitan wartime Parisian restaurant. Near the *grands magasins de luxe* and the *haute couturiers*, it was the meeting place for business people, for friendly gatherings, and where Germans would take their wives or French mistresses. At times, German military and civilian parties took over upper halls for more private repasts – often with a bevy of beauties hired from a madame who rented the top floor of a building from a local villain and consummate Résister, François Véler.[26] She therefore often provided him with good intelligence learned from the enemy in pillow talk.

The Paris streets stirred up distant memories of Violette's young childhood when Charlie Bushell ran his private taxi service, driving wealthy US and British travellers from Paris to Switzerland and Italy. Charlie had been constantly at odds with the 'blinking language' and only rarely took on Parisian clients, but Violette's mother, Reine, had adored being back in Paris, making beautiful couture clothes for the same group of wealthy ex-pats and Americans. Charlie, my grandfather, recalled driving his limousine, speeding around dangerously narrow hairpin bends high in the Alps, terrifying his rich clients. After her parents had left Paris, Violette, from 1928 to 1934 (age seven to thirteen) had also made a few special day-trips with Tante Marguerite to the capital.

‡

Violette's emotions were torn between excitement and apprehension. She was doing precisely what she wanted to do, had volunteered to do, had trained so hard to do. At last she was going to be of real help in the effort to defeat the Nazis. She would be contributing, even on a small scale, to get the Germans out of her aunt's life; to avenge her Legionnaire lover and husband, Étienne; she was fighting for her daughter, and the rest of her family. For all these reasons she intended to do her level best to help win the war. Violette knew that in SOE, run by Colin Gubbins,[27] and in SOE's French Section under Maurice Buckmaster and Vera Atkins,[28] many were of the opinion she was not quite the right material. She intended to prove them wrong on her first mission into an occupied country and so she did – solo.

‡

---

26 François Véler, otherwise known as 'Frank', was the brother of Paul E.F. Holley's mother. Both were involved in clandestine activities – Frank as a small-time racketeer and his sister as a wealthy self-made business woman. Their courage and spirit shone and they both survived the war. Paul, born in Jersey, was on the last boat out of Jersey when it was occupied and became an intelligence officer in the UK.

27 Major General Sir Colin McVean Gubbins, KCMG, DSO, MC, had a razor-sharp brain, great insight and tenacity. Diplomatic and experienced in intelligence activities, he was considered the linchpin of SOE. He was also a rare supporter of Charles de Gaulle, since most of the Allies were concerned about an unknown quantity taking over the government of France on liberation.

28 Vera Atkins was Maurice Buckmaster's assistant in the French section of SOE. Sarah Helm's biography of her – *A Life in Secrets* – is erudite, well researched and truly interesting.

On Easter Saturday, 8 April, Violette went out once again with Philippe's aunt. All apprehension had disappeared and she thought what a bonus it was to be in Paris prior to the difficult and dangerous task she would be facing alone in the next weeks.

'I would love to stop for a snack in the *brasserie*,[29] I forget its name, at the bottom of the Champs-Elysées to watch the passing people. Could we?'

'Oh, *Corinne*, I think that's an excellent idea. As we sip awful coffee and maybe have an equally awful omelette, we can bone up on your French with some useful idiomatic expressions *of the ladylike kind* while we watch the enemy stomp past.' She laughed.

'*Merci beaucoup, Tante Evelyn*,' Violette laughed in her turn. Obviously, Philippe had been telling tales out of school.

Tante Evelyn continued on a more serious note that while they were in the Champs-Elysées, they should contact André Malraux,[30] the writer, as Philippe had instructed. Claude Malraux, Andrés half-brother was Philippe's second-in-command of the *Salesman* circuit in Rouen. Violette said that she would do her best and report back on her findings as she understood how desperate he must be for solid news about Claude.

Overnight fog had almost cleared by nine o'clock and, after chatting for a while, the two women slipped out of the apartment to stroll over the river to the Champs-Elysées. They mingled with the people of Paris, the less affluent looking terribly tired and wan, the result of strict rationing. To keep out the chilly air, Tante Evelyn loaned Violette one of her own fur coats: a dark brown three-quarter-length astrakhan coat made by one of the best furriers in Paris. Tante Evelyn wore her favourite fox coat. Coats thrown over shoulders in Gallic fashion, they would not feel the chill in the air as they sat on the terrace of the Brasserie d'Alsace. Violette felt like a million dollars – and looked it.

The sky was grey, matching the mood engendered by the grey/green-uniformed German military going about their wartime duties. There were many German civilians too: industrialists, government officials, wealthy Germans, all luxuriating in the safety of their conquered city. Their own cities were bombed night and day by the RAF and the US Air Force. Germans took short breaks in a Paris that still had much to offer in refinement, luxury goods, fine restaurants and thrilling cabarets. Paris, eternal seductress, eased many millions of Deutschmarks from German pockets, smiling politely while sneering behind their departing backs at their often coarse behaviour and arrogant ways.

---

29 In France a brasserie is a restaurant serving beer and other alcoholic and non-alcoholic refreshments with the food.

30 André Malraux, well-known French novelist, author of *La condition humaine*, a member of de Gaulle's Résistance movement commanded directly from London. After the war he was rewarded by de Gaulle who appointed him Ministre de la Culture.

In London, Philippe had remarked to Violette that she must be very careful of her accent. An English accent had already been the downfall of several agents. It was imperative for an agent to have an authentic French accent for missions in France. It was not so important with regard to communicating with the Gestapo but essential when talking to someone who might be an informer or when questioned by the Vichy police or Milice. Violette's accent was hardly English but the regional accent of Pas-de-Calais. Still, she took Philippe's digs about her accent to heart. Better he should notice it, than some French collaborator or informer. She had not realised she had a Nord accent at first and so was unable to challenge the error of those at SOE's special training schools who insisted she had an English accent. Nevertheless, it ensured she paid direct and strict attention to what she said and how she said it.

‡

They finally met André Malraux after midnight, when they were attending the Easter vigil in the Sacré Coeur. The interior of the church shimmered with soft lights and hundreds of candles. The rejoicing of the choir filled the dome and filled hearts with hope and momentary joy.

André Malraux approached Violette and Evelyn on the steps outside, inviting them to the café in the square that was used frequently by the Résistance. He was often seen in Parisian café society, flitting easily from one café to another. He was a member of *Combat* (the Parisian group) along with Albert Camus, author of *La Peste* and *L'Etranger*. Unlike the very careful and circumspect Philippe, André was unconcerned, flamboyant even, in holding clandestine meetings in Parisian cafés and was delighted to entertain two such charming ladies. He quickly broached his request: he was greatly concerned for his half-brother, Claude Malraux, code-named *Cicero/Serge*, and would appreciate her reporting to him directly on her return to Paris. Violette, a little taken aback by his rather arrogant assumption that she would do his bidding, replied that she would do her best and let him know through *Charles* (Philippe) anything that was pertinent to his brother. After that, they chatted about many things, including a little about his involvement and his remit directly from de Gaulle to bring the disparate groups of resistance into one fold. Dawn had broken when they parted, André assuming he had recruited a fine new courier, as he later claimed in his book, *La corde et la souris*.

Tante Evelyn had watched discreetly while Violette had André describe various events and, seemingly spellbound, listened as he talked about his pre-war travels and writings. Violette promised herself she would read one of his books one day. Even though she did not take to him particularly, she knew he was an accomplished author and had travelled to French Indochina where Étienne had served from 1937 to 1940. André Malraux was now involved at a high level in de Gaulle's Résistance movement, and after the war he became Ministre de la Culture.

The two women walked slowly back to the apartment and Violette went to pack for her journey into the unknown.

‡

The strong defensive Atlantic Wall constructed by the Germans along the coast of Europe would soon become offensive under Hitler's plan to invade and conquer the British Isles. Occupation of the Channel Islands was merely his first step. He ordered the use of forced labour from Russian, Polish and Spanish prisoners to excavate warrens of concreted tunnels to house not only hospitals and command posts but also weapons like the V rockets in the war tunnels of Jersey, for example. These Hitlerian plans were to be indefinitely postponed.

Churchill required SOE to co-ordinate sabotage along the Atlantic Wall and then to provide him with intelligence while contributing to the build-up to *Operation Overlord*, the planned Allied landings in France on D-Day. The War Cabinet agreed that Colonel Buckmaster, head of SOE's French Section, should set up at least one circuit to cover Le Havre and Rouen, where the Germans had built depots for refitting U-boats. It was also rumoured that some technologically advanced secret weapon was being assembled in Normandy and, although SOE had some forty to fifty circuits dotted all over France, those most in danger were therefore those formed in Brittany and Normandy. By the end of 1941, twenty-nine agents had been sent by de Gaulle's *Colonel Passy*,[31] creating a constant trail of sabotage from Morlaix in western Brittany to Calais and beyond.

Violette knew that tomorrow she must take a train to Rouen. She felt that time was passing too quickly – it was already 9 April and she was still in Paris!

‡

---

31 *Colonel Passy* was in fact André Dewavrin, head of the Bureau Central de Renseignements et d'Action [militaire], (BCRA[M]).His codename was taken from the Paris Métro station of the same name.

5

Train to the Unknown

10 April 1944, Easter Monday

After the midnight high mass at the Sacré Cœur and meeting with André Malraux, a good sleep till mid-morning was in order. Then it was time to prepare for her journey the next morning and gather together the few things – some useful and some rather nice that Violette had bought in Paris to further establish her cover stories. Monday morning was windy, and somewhat chilly. Violette decided to take the train to Rouen from Gare Saint-Lazare, walking there so she could steep herself just one more time in the atmosphere of wartime Paris.

Silk scarf tied tightly over her ears and knotted under her chin to keep the chill at bay, Violette slipped on a light brown coat over her French long-jacketed navy-blue suit, slung her bag over her shoulder, and picked up a canvas bag – a gift from Tante Evelyn – in her left hand and her battered suitcase in her right. She looked like a thousand other young French women returning home at the end of the Easter holidays.

She had decided that she would walk along the *quais* of the Left Bank, ignoring the many uniformed and civilian Germans who were swarming through the streets of the Rive Gauche. Alone now, she felt distinctly uncomfortable. She saw only enemy faces and suddenly realised just what a dangerous position she was in. In the relative safety of the farm, then with Philippe and finally with Tante Evelyn to cushion her first days in France, imminent danger did not seem to raise its ugly head. Even the incidents in the train journey from Valençay to Paris had caused her to laugh rather than to fear.

Now the enormity of what she was embarking upon struck Violette like a sledgehammer. What had possessed her? What on earth did she think she could possibly do that would be of any consequence? And what if she caused danger and death to others through her mismanagement of awkward situations that would surely arise? Fear of failure now gripped her whole being and she felt truly faint. But she walked gamely on, shooing away such thoughts and gathering her courage with each step; she smiled sweetly at the passers-by while checking each scene for signs of danger. There seemed to be none.

Arriving early at the station, as she had intended, she went to buy her first-class ticket to Rouen. She whiled away the time in the station café, contemplating the scurrying masses before her, ordering an ersatz coffee and croissant at an exorbitant price with her forged ration card. It was a pause to gather her wits and stifle the fear in the base of her stomach. Doing these ordinary things here, where danger seemed a little more distant, was practice that might make it very slightly easier in the *zone interdite*.

‡

While drinking her coffee, she went over her plans. Once in Rouen, her main task would be to discover what had happened to the *Salesman* network so assiduously set up and run by Philippe from April until November 1943, when he was recalled to London, leaving the network in the hands of his Rouen lieutenant, Claude Malraux. She wanted to discover as much as possible about Claude, not only for her London masters, but now also for André Malraux, his half-brother.

Violette also had other work to do. One task was to persuade the remaining resistance in and around Rouen and Le Havre to sabotage the Barentin viaduct. There were other tasks too: to find out about preparations in Normandy for launching what we now know were the V1 and V2 flying bombs aimed directly at the heart of London. Before leaving his aunt's apartment on Good Friday, Philippe had once again gone over everything with her.

'You know, *Corinne*,' he had said, using her cover name, 'that I brought back extremely disturbing information about runways being constructed all along the Channel coast in northern France, opposite the English coast. And also about the new weapon the Germans are constructing – some kind of rocket, and possibly a second, more powerful one.

'The launch bases are concrete. To mix the concrete, lorry loads of sand and cement are required. Luckily for us, there are many, some from my own *Salesman* circuit, who are only too happy to sabotage them. Simple but effective sabotage, very hard to trace. For example, when he can safely do so, the man bringing the sand sabotages the runway by mixing iron filings with it. Often, too, prisoners making the base throw shovelfuls of iron objects into the cement.

'It seems the rocket or torpedo, or whatever the damned thing is, is equipped with a compass so the Germans can aim it towards its target, but as the compasses are sensitive to metal, particularly iron, the rockets are easily sabotaged by disorientating them magnetically so they go off course and explode well off target.'

'Two sources, unknown to one another, both talked about catapulting. My source on the runway talked about it being of the right dimensions to take a contraption to catapult some machine into the air. And then another of my sources, who had worked on the launch system, mentioned a torpedo with wings that could be catapulted – their words – from runways and sent over England to wreak havoc on civilian populations. Now then, *Corinne*, and this is important: most of the information came from the Préfecture de la Seine Inférieure, from which I've only ever had absolutely reliable information. The French workers were all dismissed once the runway was completed and have not been allowed near it since December. This line of runways, each about ten kilometres apart, is pretty well parallel to the coastline, extending at the very least from just north of Rouen south-west to Cherbourg, including Auffay and Tôtes.'

'I remember now, *Charles*. You told me that three of the French workers described exactly the same construction: a concrete runway about ten metres long, exiting from the ground with a 7 per cent slope upwards. But we don't really know what the walls or sides of the runway were like. Concrete, I expect.'

'Yes, but don't forget that, at the rear, descending deep into the ground, was a ten-metre square chamber. There seems to be some sort of cavity to hold something on three of the sides – the fourth being the opening leading to the start of the runway – entirely lined with concrete. All a bit vague, I'm afraid, although I visited the Tôtes one at the beginning of November and estimated the runway to be about three to four metres wide, emerging from the ground into an open field. This is on the Normandy plain. A flat plain with a few wooded clusters – not uncommon in the area, but I guess the copses could conceal runways as they're being built. Easy to dig, as it's fairly dry chalk terrain. The riverbeds are about thirty metres lower than the plain. There're no odd buildings or abnormal activities in the vicinity. What I found strange was that there was no steel construction on top of the concrete and nothing suggestive of anything like an underground airfield. So, if you can shed any light on these and their exact positions or persuade any Rouen or Le Havre network groups to do a little sabotage on them, you'd really be doing something.

'I first heard talk of *fusées* – rockets – not *torpilles* or torpedoes. You can see the danger to the southern and eastern coasts of England and London itself. Perhaps, if you can dig up sufficient information, it'll be enough to go in and bomb the bunkers to smithereens.'

'Well, you know I'll do my damndest. Didn't you say that, although you couldn't take any precise compass bearings because there were Germans around, you thought the runway was facing north – which it must be anyway, logically, to attack England?'

'Right! But last August I didn't see any runway being constructed in Auffay. Still, the Germans work damn fast when they need to. I also don't know whether any rocket parts have arrived in northern France, but if they have they're probably about ten metres long and one and a half wide. It seems the rocket is in three sections. The first is the projectile, weighing around ten tons. The two motor parts are, I've been informed, being built in France by French workers while the runways have been constructed by forced labour.

'In early 1943, the Nazi Todt Organisation[32] looked for somewhere with a good electricity supply for oxygen compressors, and these two areas certainly had that. It seems the motor parts are in cast iron and the rear part falls to earth roughly fifty kilometres after the rocket's been fired. Certainly, the actual contents of the projectile are made only in Germany. It also seems that it's directed by some sort of magnetic or radio device with about a twenty-kilometre margin of error – so, if it's aimed at London it could fall somewhere even ten kilometres from the outer edges of London.

'So you see, *Corinne*, again, it is imperative that you try and shed any light on these and their exact positions, or persuade Rouen or Le Havre groups to sabotage them in some way.'

'For sure, *Charles*!' Violette's eyes hardened into angry pinpricks as her face took on a stubbornness that family and friends had always had the good sense to steer clear of, as she thought of the danger to them – never mind the devastation that would be wrought on the population and infrastructure of London. After all, London and England were as much her home as any town in France. She would not have it! Such damage wrought on her beloved England from sites in her beloved France.

'I'll damn well start something in Rouen if it kills me. There must still be Résistants as angry as me; in Le Havre, too. If I'm still free, and have the time, I'll find out what Tante Marguerite, the Chorlets and her friend, maybe husband by now, Victor Hoëz, are up to. I'm pretty sure they've continued to be involved in some kind of resistance – probably across the Belgian border.'

Carefully Philippe and Violette went over all the contact details three more times to ensure Violette knew perfectly everything possible about the people, streets, environment and problems she would come across – and how very wary she must be walking into a nest of intrigue and informants.

Again Philippe reminded her, 'When I went there for the first time to start the Résistance group, I was sure of one contact. I had Claude Malraux – known either as *Serge* or *Cicero*. But you'll have no contacts at all and not even a wireless transmitter to keep you in touch with London. I've prepared this list of people who used to be in the group – but we have no idea if they are still there or, if they are there, still with us. You'll have to memorise all this and destroy it. You can't take it with you. All that you can be sure of is that you're going into great danger. You'll hardly be able to move without being watched and followed. It's a pity you have to go alone. But if I came along, it would only increase the danger.'

---

32 Todt Organisation was formed in 1933 by Fritz Todt as a Third Reich civil and military engineering group. In the early years it relied heavily on compulsory labour from within Germany, but increasingly used forced labour from Germans rejected for military service, concentration camp prisoners and a large number of POWs and compulsory labourers from occupied countries.

'I know, I know. I've memorised it all a dozen times with nothing on paper. I'm not daft and I did learn a little at "finishing school", you know!' retorted Violette somewhat heatedly.

How *brûlé was* the *Salesman* network? Who remained, and amongst those, who could be trusted and then relied upon to push forward any possible action before and in concert with the Allied offensive? Finding out was Violette's main task.

‡

Violette was both delighted and terrified to be here, waiting for her train to Rouen. Young, brave and beautiful, still only twenty-two, on her own, with an important job to do in France. She enjoyed the bad coffee and minuscule croissant, knowing she looked the picture of youthful, innocent womanhood, pretty and neatly dressed, legs crossed demurely with her leather suitcase at her feet and bags on the chair beside her. Yet she felt a shard of icy fear in her abdomen, thinking what her suitcase and bag held: forged documents and coupons, counterfeit French francs and a few marks. And in her head, vital plans to impart to Résistants to assist the invasion to come.

Smoke poured from trains along the platforms into the main area, up into the rafters. Whistles blew, doors slammed, steam hissed and people milled around. Organised pandemonium reigned. Violette moved unnoticed – except for some admiring glances – through the crowds to her platform and train.

The distance to Rouen was some seventy-five miles but would take roughly two to three hours by what would be a *lanterne*[33] train even if there were not too many unscheduled stops along the way. Her first-class ticket ensured her a seat but the platform was very crowded. She knew that some of the first-, second- and third-class compartments were reserved for German military personnel and Gestapo.

As she passed one of the first-class compartments, she was stopped by a German officer who, bowing politely, uttered in very guttural, slightly imperfect French: '*Mademoiselle, je vous prie d'y entrer. Vous trouvez aucun autre place dans ce train, je vous assure.*'

Surprised and not a little confounded, she noticed his braiding with two gold pips; she had learned in training under Paul Emile that this was the rank of Oberst, a colonel. Violette wondered if she was about to be searched or questioned. Shocked, she kept from revealing the stab of fear and politely thanked him, as she followed the colonel's direction and took the proffered seat.

All the other carriages were already packed. The corridors of the second- and third-class carriages were overflowing with luggage and soldiers' war-stained green duffle bags. The stale smell of old food, old beer, sweat and cigarette smoke

---

33 A *lanterne* is a very slow train stopping at every station en route where lamps signal them to stop.

permeated every corridor and every carriage. German military were moving about the corridors, peering through dirty windows, smoking and shouting in German at one another or dozing wherever they could.

Civilian passengers were mostly French labourers returning with their special passes to jobs in the forbidden zone – jobs to keep German communications in good repair and operating as smoothly as possible. The train shunted and rumbled out of Paris, slowly building up speed, its smoke trailing behind, its whistle imperious in warning of departure.

This particular first-class carriage was full of Wehrmacht[34] officers returning to Rouen and Le Havre after leave in Paris. They were in markedly jovial spirits and much enjoyed the presence of this lovely young woman. Having all jumped up to offer her their seat and vying to place her luggage in the rack above her head, they made room for her to settle in the window seat, her shoulder bag firmly tucked in beside her. If it, or her luggage now out of reach, were searched, it would be *very* interesting.

'*Vous fumez, mademoiselle?*'

As beautifully hand-hammered gold, silver and fine kid leather cigarette cases were quickly offered, she picked a cigarette from an old silver case covered in embossed trailing flowers, reminiscent of one her father had, and replied: '*Oui, merci bien, monsieur.*'

Then out came the cigarette lighters. She took a light from the nearest one, belonging to an *Oberstleutnant der Abwehr*, a lieutenant colonel in the Abwehr, the German military intelligence organisation.

Violette nodded her thanks to the *Oberstleutnant*. She could not help smiling at the sheer absurdity of the situation and what her family and friends in London would say if they knew. But for all the amusement she experienced at the German officers dancing attendance upon her, she reined in her impulsiveness, keeping a sharp hold on her tongue. Fear simmered not far below the surface but her face transformed it to the natural reticence of a young woman among so many men. She spoke little, answering in monosyllables whenever possible to the inquisitive questions thrown at her. She adroitly turned the conversation around to themselves and their families. Out came the photos of wives and sweethearts, children, parents and a few massive dogs.

As the suburbs and small townships gave way to open country, the train clattered ever on, mile after mile. A church with two spires caught her attention as the train sped by. The Seine appeared alongside the railway line at regular intervals with willow trees bending at the water's edge. The river was an opaque green dappled by the shadows falling across it. The occasional house and farmstead lay along the line or further out towards the distant hills. Some distance away, dark green and

---

34 Wehrmacht = Defence Force and was the German armed forces, especially the army, from 1921 to 1945 disbanded at the end of the Second World War.

brown hills kept the landscape snug within their contours while poplars stood at attention in long green lines, hinting at roadways.

At one point, a Gestapo officer entered to check identities. On seeing two full-blown Wehrmacht colonels, he eased himself out after a cursory glance and perfunctory '*In Ordnung.*' It jolted Violette to remember the danger inherent in finding herself casually chatting with the enemy. Her uneasiness evaporated once the officer had saluted and left the carriage. The journey was passing more quickly and pleasantly than she could have imagined. And then Colonel Niederholen, who had first approached her and seemed to take a proprietarial interest in her, tried to strike up a conversation. Prickles of fear stabbed behind her eyes.

'And, what is your name, *mademoiselle?*'

'I'm *Corinne Leroy.*' Worried, but smiling. A trickle of sweat rolled down her back. Fear or the heat of the carriage?

'Do you live in Rouen?'

'No, actually, I don't. I live in Le Havre, but I've been in Paris for Easter and now I'm spending a few days in Rouen before returning home.'

'I see. You must have family there, then.'

'No, not really. A distant uncle is missing from his family and I was asked to see if he is in Rouen. He'd gone on business there as a supplier and there has been so much bombing by the British that we are concerned for his safety.'

'*Mademoiselle,*' Niederholen said, 'Here is a card for my hotel in Rouen; I stay there for a few days. Please do not hesitate to contact me if I can be of assistance to you in this worrying matter.'

'Thank you very much,' replied Violette, as coolly as she could. Her stomach had contracted with anxiety under the gentle questioning, but she kept her voice level and smiled politely.

She hoped her mentioning the bombing by the British would be taken to show her loyalties did not lie with the Allies. As the train rumbled on towards Rouen, her nerves gradually settled down again. Desultory conversation in the carriage was muffled by the chugging locomotive. Violette joined in whenever a remark was directed at her.

She was surprised that she was not filled with overwhelming hatred towards these enemy officers. Her cold, implacable hatred was for the horrendous Nazi regime that had so easily taken sway in Germany and Austria and overrun so many countries with great cruelty. Most of these military men were not of that ilk, of that she was sure. Yet Violette knew these were the same fighting men who had killed her husband, Étienne. Were they really the same species who flew over her London, trying to bomb it out of existence and causing so much distress, death and destruction? The same human beings who were collecting those they considered undesirables, then sending them to death camps? Well, she thought, it's quite possible this colonel could have been in the desert in 1942, commanding his men to attack the legionnaires south of El Alamein. There were no SS or Gestapo in the carriage.

She was determined to help the Allied cause in any way she could, including being a friendly young thing in an enemy-laden carriage, if this could in any way help destroy that wretched Nazi regime, so any of these soldiers had better watch their step! She turned to watch the Normandy countryside glide past; it was looking a little the worse for wear but showing all the early promise of spring growth.

The weather was holding. It seemed to her very much colder than it had been a few days ago. It had been quite a long journey from the warmer mid-France to Paris and then the colder north – now the weather was more like that of England or Wales.

The train slowly entered Rouen Saint-Sever station. As it did so, Violette saw how much damage had been inflicted on the industrial south-west of the town. On the right bank the steeple of the Gothic cathedral gleamed in sad welcome above a haze of dust that seemed to hang low over both banks of the river.

Once the train came to a standstill, soldiers scrambled off, to be brought to strict attention on the platform, luggage neatly before them. The officers in Violette's carriage stood up, gathered their things and helped her with the utmost courtesy to take down her luggage from the rack. With punctilious salutes and clicking of heels, they took their leave and bade her farewell.

It was with real relief that she descended the train to make her way into the town. Just as Violette was about to walk across the bridge to the right bank of the river, Colonel Niederholen approached her and suggested she ride with him. She accepted.

‡

Part III

6

Friendly Lodgings in Rouen

10 April 1944 – Easter Monday

Trains from Paris arrived into Rouen at Gare Saint-Sever on the left bank of the Seine or Gare Rive Droite[35] on the right bank. The Allies bombed the lovely old station of Gare Saint-Sever on the left bank even while Violette was in Rouen, to keep the German military from using it for transporting troops to and from Paris and elsewhere, especially as D-Day was just a few weeks away.

Once he was deposited at the *Hôtel de Ville*, Colonel Niederholen ordered the driver of his armoured car to take Violette where she wished. As she had not reserved a place to stay, she decided she would put her luggage in the *consigne* at the Gare Rive Droite while she got her bearings. The colonel suggested a couple of hotels, including his own but, Violette explained, they were somewhat out of her price range as she must conserve her funds. He was not, as yet, suspicious.

Stepping out of the armoured vehicle at the stylish art-deco station, Violette brushed down her skirt and coat, smoothed her hair and, with luggage in hand, walked with quiet assurance to the station entrance. She now needed to re-assemble her thoughts and plan her movements for the day after her intensely stressful journey.

High-ranking German officers had entertained her, enemies of her country and herself. She had been slightly anxious and somewhat aloof, as was only to be expected of a respectable young French woman. Still, she had managed to laugh at their bad French, bad jokes and bear with the bad smells of unwashed, sweaty bodies. She had captivated them; a small but significant battle won. Most of these military men were not card-holding Nazis, but soldiers loyal to their country which had been dragged into fanaticism by a fierce minority exercising a mesmeric hold over the people of Germany.

It was coming up to lunchtime and, her luggage safely in the station *consigne*, Violette decided to stroll around before looking for a café-bar or brasserie within a short distance of the station. She wanted to review the information buzzing in her head and the strange experience of mixing with the enemy. The hostile civil and

---

35 Also called Gare de Rouen, Gare Rue Verte.

military landscape she had travelled into needed to be assessed. Groups of soldiers, fully armed, were parading through the quaint streets of Rouen, stopping people and checking their papers, sometimes arresting them on the spot. Civilians were hurrying about their everyday business. Fashionable women, suited and hatted businessmen and self-important civil servants mingled with tired-looking, shabbily dressed, unshaven men; a sprinkling of women and ragged children were queuing where there were rumours that goods had suddenly become available. To Violette's tired eyes and stressed mind it was on the whole a mournful scene, full of menace.

She did not need to remind herself that this was the dangerous *zone interdite*, the forbidden zone, which she must penetrate to discover what had happened to the *Salesman* circuit and whether there were Résistants enough to keep the network going, or whether it was possible to set up a new group to gather information, receive parachute drops and carry out acts of well-planned sabotage – especially with a view to facilitating the imminent Allied invasion. It made no difference whether the invasion took place here or further along the Atlantic Wall. Only a handful of people around Winston Churchill knew the exact spot, which would depend to some small extent on the weather. For everyone else the job was to get on with allocated preparatory work to start the liberation of Europe.

Philippe's words came back to her, 'When I went to Rouen for the first time to start the circuit, I was sure of one or two contacts. I had Claude Malraux and Jean Sueur. But you have no contacts at all. You don't even have a wireless transmitter to keep in touch with London. You will be entirely alone. You have nothing except the list of people who used to be in the group.'

'That's fine, I'll manage. You can bet your last farthing I'll be careful – a dead agent's no good for anything.' Violette smiled.

'True,' agreed Philippe as he had continued, 'I'll give you the best descriptions I can of certain people, too. All you can be quite sure of, *Corinne*, is that you're going into great danger. You'll hardly be able to move without being watched and even followed.'

'Well, providing I'm not too much of a dope I should be all right. After all, I speak French; I've been there every year since being dragged back to England when I was twelve. Damn it, I *am* French. I know how they think – including you, I wouldn't wonder – well, at least a little,' turning bright pink, she suddenly remembered he was her commanding officer and that due respect should be shown.

In an uncanny way, Philippe's being in France – somewhere – engendered a feeling of his presence even if he could not be contacted until she returned to Paris at the end of April. Before her lay twenty days of searching, noting and constant vigilance. Fear was now her only and constant companion – to be contained by her will.

‡

Violette could see the devastation Rouen had suffered. From aerial photographs and intelligence she had studied back in London, she knew that the right bank directly facing the *quais* and the Seine, plus part of the left bank, had been destroyed in 1940 by the French to prevent the advancing German army making use of fuel and other materiel.

The French had also blown up certain strategic points to the west, on both banks, that would have been useful for the enemy. Since then, she knew from reports and all Philippe had told her, there had been continuing sporadic damage to the town.

As Violette walked along she noticed that most of the bridges spanning the Seine had been bombed, including Pont Corneille. Much of the area between the cathedral and the *quais* had been reduced to rubble. Across the way, the Germans had constructed temporary link bridges in place of those damaged beyond repair. From time to time, these were bombed too, only to be rebuilt by the Germans before being bombed again by the Allies. She watched for a while as pedestrians and cyclists crossed the bridge. Some cyclists hung on to the military and civilian trucks to save pedal power, even though it was *verboten*. Few cars other than military vehicles were in evidence.

Strolling across the town centre via rue Grand Pont, Violette checked to see if she was being followed. She did not believe she was, but it was best to put her training into practice. She must not leave anything to chance. After all, it was not just her life in the balance. It had been a longish walk but pleasant enough and very instructive. The scenes she had witnessed did nothing to improve her confidence; she felt quite anxious and the stress and strain were tiring. She now wanted nothing more than to find a room, to bathe in a warm, bubbly bath, crawl into a warm bed and feel a little bit safe.

Violette sat under the large awning of a café-bar in rue Louis Ricard, which led down to the cathedral, not far from Gare Rive Droite. She quietly observed the armed soldiers patrolling the streets, a few Gestapo and Miliciens strutting around, pulling people off the streets, sometimes at gunpoint, sometimes shouting harshly, pushing them into the backs of trucks and hauling them off to one of the interrogation centres. She was used to the bombsites of London but this really frightened her. It was infinitely more savage than Paris. She began to understand just how dangerous would be her work. And how solitary.

An old waiter approached her: '*Bonjour Mademoiselle, vous voulez?*' he asked without ceremony, indicating the *plats du jour* – a choice of two meals chalked on an *ardoise*, a slate board. She ordered her lunch of *omelette aux tomates* (made from powdered egg and not very appetising) and *salade verte* along with a carafe of water. She was decidedly hungry and thirsty after her journey and enjoyed the small meal. As she ate, Violette felt the stress and apprehension of the train journey begin to fade.

She noted she was not far from the *Frontsammelstelle*, the German regrouping point for newly arrived German recruits. It was interesting that a lot of them were either very young or rather old for recruits. Many could be no older than fifteen or sixteen and the older ones well into their fifties. Violette mentally squirreled away this information on German morale and military might for later debriefings by her superiors in London. As she left the café, the scene that met her eyes was charming and quaint. The cathedral stood out as a splendid landmark, and the river flowed calmly towards Le Havre and the English Channel.

The Germans defended the river and Channel very strenuously – these arteries were important links for operations and supplies. At Le Havre, they operated a base where ships and subs were repaired and renewed. The port, also harbouring German installations for communications and energy, was heavily guarded at all times.

The pall of German occupation hung over the hustle and bustle of Rouen. And yet life went on; Violette watched a group of children skirmishing at a corner, laughing and crying out in great glee over some favourite game. Many of the Rouennais in the streets were business people going about their affairs, while straggling Easter holidaymakers returned to their homes with prizes of food lying in wicker baskets or tied in scraps of brown paper tucked securely underarm. Soldiers, in happy or sombre mood going on or returning from leave, wended their way to and from the main station, knapsacks thrown carelessly over shoulders. She also saw eyes darting from girl to girl, whistles and shy stares, the beginnings and endings of affairs. Some girls stood sadly by, deprived of their German soldier-protector, afraid now of repercussions and being dubbed *collabos horizontales*, or Jerry-bags.

Violette observed German *Sicherheitsdienst* (SD)[36] soldiers checking identities alongside the Gestapo, while German motorised vehicles bullied their way through the lanes. She saw a few remaining Jews wearing the yellow star on their clothes hurrying through the narrow streets. They were not sent to extermination camps since their work could not be continued by others.

The plight of the Jews saddened and angered her. Many of her friends were Jewish, and a few years before she had met Étienne, she and a young Jewish man, Manny Isbey, had fallen in love.

His sister, Polly, told me how they had delighted in Violette's sweet personality and spent many pleasant fun-filled afternoons in the Isbey household. But Manny's parents forbade the couple to marry and wanted Manny to marry a Jewish girl. Violette and Manny had been truly in love, deliriously happy, but it was not to be. He immigrated to New Zealand with his family and had a fulfilled and successful life. In 1978, he was elected as Labour MP for Papatoetoe; a great labour rebel in politics who stood up for the indigenous people at all times. He always kept Violette's photo close, with her words of love to him on the reverse. His sister said

---

36 *Sicherheit* = Security; *Dienst* = service, duty; *sicher* = sure, certain, secure.

that he always regretted his decision to follow the advice of his family, although he had a fine marriage and family of his own and very much loved his wife.

‡

The recent history of northern France and Belgium was something Violette knew quite well from living as a French girl and hearing tales of war and politics from her French extended family. A successful escape line from Belgium had been established to help crashed Allied airmen avoid capture by the Germans. This line extended from the northern end of France, through Picardy and Pas-de-Calais to Rouen and the surrounding areas of the Seine-Maritime (Seine-Inférieure at the time), all the way down to the south, over the Pyrenees into Spain and across to neutral Portugal, and then by boat or plane on to England and safety. It was a hazardous journey of over 4,000 miles. Safe-houses were found and kept ready, guides instructed and food and clothes supplied in greatest secrecy. Violette had already been helpful in this during her times in France in 1939 and 1940, working alongside Tante Marguerite so intelligence could be passed to the Belgian Section in London.

By April 1944, the war had been going for over four years. It was to be expected that the people of Rouen, like everyone in England and the rest of Europe, were, by now, weary of war and winter. Depots and strategic installations as well as the Rouen quays on the Seine were bombed time and again by the Allies. The Allies were kept informed through the various networks, including Philippe's *Salesman* and *Hamlet* circuits,[37] of repairs completed so the new installations could be damaged again. Kept under strict curfew and travelling restrictions by the Germans, citizens in the *zone interdite* were checked and rechecked by Gestapo and Milice. They went short of food, often living in homes that were barely more than rubble. The Germans were getting more vicious by the day. It was not good.

‡

Violette carefully went over in her mind what Colonel Maurice Buckmaster, head of the French Section of SOE, had told her about the reports – some of which came from Philippe and others from other agents and the French Résistance itself – on the effects of war to date on Rouen and Le Havre. As she gazed about her, Violette recalled a conversation she had had with Buckmaster telling her that she would be entering very much the most dangerous place in France and that she needed to remember that when the Germans entered Rouen on 9 June 1940, the destruction of that lovely old town was started by a major fire lasting four days. And then the centre of Yvetot had also been set on fire and Le Havre was occupied on 13 June.

---

37 *Hamlet* was one of Philippe's cover names and his sub-circuit in Le Havre. *Salesman* operated in Rouen and surrounds.

Violette knew much about that, as she explained, from her Belgian friends and that as many details as possible would be useful, as she should be able to participate in any conversation just like a girl who had lived there all her life.

Buckmaster, not particularly liking the reference to the Belgian Section to which he had almost lost Violette, was well into the swing of his recitation, saying that Rommel had managed a 250-kilometre trek without firing a shot but, on 10 June, Cherbourg fell and, one month later in the French parliament on 10 July, twenty-one of the thirty-two Normandy deputies voted to give full powers to Pétain and Vichy. 'Two-thirds of the blighters! Bloody stupid and they should've known better,' Buckmaster grumbled. But between May and December 1940, the British had bombed Le Havre twenty-three times and a further twenty-seven times the year after in an attempt to stop the Germans embarking from there. It was a well-equipped port and well defended by the Germans making it extremely dangerous for the Allies.

Violette had then jumped in, wanting Buckmaster to realise she had some background knowledge too, saying that in late February 1942, they had sent a commando team to the Bruneval radar station, north-east of Le Havre, which they very successfully raided. But with the successes came defeats. In mid-August an Allied raid had turned into a disaster, with close on 1,200 dead and 2,000 taken prisoner of the 6,000 Canadians and British who were put ashore at Dieppe. Later, in November, Violette could not help but add – clearly relishing this nugget of information – that Monsieur Duchez, a painter from Caen, had succeeded in stealing the German plans for the entire Atlantic Wall from their office. She was sure that stuck in enemy's throat!

Buckmaster nodded, with a taut smile of approval. He did think she was one of the most stunning young women he had ever come across. To himself, he added, 'What on earth were the instructors thinking in their rather damning reports? Particularly on her intelligence. Fools! Bloody fools the lot of 'em! She's perfect for the part. Let's hope she damn well survives!'

‡

'Buckmaster's a cold fish, isn't he?' Violette had remarked to one of her fellow agents, Harry Peulevé, one evening a few days after that meeting, as they chatted and danced at the Studio Club in Kensington. The club was the favoured haunt for pilots and officers of all ranks and nationalities serving in the Allied forces.

'He certainly gives that impression,' said Harry, 'but you know, I don't believe it for a minute. I've seen him in relaxed mood. Then, he shows another side. And he's not the best organised of men – that's why Vera Atkins is always close by. She's a bit of a stickler for detail and follows up every single loose end that Buckmaster leaves trailing, making sure it's tied fast. Marvellous, she is, really. Just like you.

You're just too adorable for words and I love you, I really do. After this is all over, we'll sit down and talk, won't we, Vi?'

'Yes, for sure, Harry. Anyhow, we shouldn't be talking about these things here. Keep mum – haven't you seen the signs?'

Harry was smitten with Violette. She was very fond of him too and always greatly enjoyed spending time with him. He was tall and handsome and had something of the eternal child about him. She was still too angry and sad over the life with Étienne that had been snatched from her to make any commitment. It was strange it was war that had brought them together in the first place for their hauntingly sweet and short-lived love affair. Her imagination had sparkled and soared at the dreams of a life shared with her gallant legionnaire, full of vitality and laughter. They would have had an active and adventurous life in the south of France after the years of war, with her travelling to exotic destinations as a legionnaire's wife for a few years and then he would have retired as a French officer and with French nationality merited, as they said, through blood shed for his adopted country. Violette had looked forward so much to the life they would build together. But it was not to be; he was gone.

She still got on with life, and she and Harry had been out together many times, dancing in the popular dance halls, to the local pubs and the cinema. Life went on, but the sadness remained deep in her glorious eyes.

Violette and Harry had both been trained by SOE. Harry had already been sent to France, where he'd broken his leg; he had come back and, after further training, asked to be sent again so he could achieve something. Violette was just about to be sent. When they had first met in 1943 at one of the clubs like the Studio Club, he was under the impression that she knew nothing about his clandestine work. He did not realise how savvy she was. She knew he was 'up to tricks' in France in the same way she had learned to spot other men who were agents. She reflected once that it was infinitely more difficult to spot the women, even after spending some time in their company. She thought that women attracted to this sort of work revelled in the fact that they were involved in something secret and confidential. She did and her mother along with Tante Marguerite typified the woman who could hold her own counsel at all times and did.

‡

Violette finally left the café-bar and wandered the quieter lanes and streets, where sometimes there was not a German in sight. She found the peace of these small cobbled alleyways and streets helpful in sorting out what to do first. She decided to collect her luggage immediately and find a small private hotel choosing one in a small street, rue Saint-Romain, a short walk from the station in the north and the destroyed Pont Corneille to the south.

As she entered the hotel, she remarked to the *patronne*, '*C'est beaucoup de dégâts, non?*' gesturing towards the damage in the town.

'*Epouvantable, épouvantable*,'[38] wailed the owner, Madame Thivier, a woman in her late fifties who looked closer to seventy, as she glanced out at the dreadful damage across the small square. Madame Thivier explained how lucky they were not to have been hit as so many had been killed by the Allies and it really made you wonder whose side to be on when such damage was done by friends.

Violette nodded and asked if there was a room for a few nights to which Madame Thivier offered one right next to the bathroom and asked if that would suit. Violette thought that perfect and revelled in the idea of a bath after her long and stressful journey. The *patronne* agreed, warning that each bath would cost a little extra but if Violette did not mind that she would be entitled to one bath a day, perhaps not with hot water but that she did her best regardless of Boche restrictions.

Violette thanked her hostess adding after noting the comment about the Boches that it must have been dreadful having all those enemy soldiers marching by each day in those lovely old lanes. She asked if many came there to stay while she was trying to decide whether this seemingly elderly, tired-looking woman was a *collabo* or not.

Madame Thivier replied adamantly in the negative. She said that they were either in their barracks or officers who stayed in luxury hotels or requisitioned houses as it pleased them. She went on that they did do a lot of stamping about, though, marching here and marching there, checking people's papers every few seconds. She felt it was degrading, utterly degrading and then her eyes narrowed as she hoped her new guest was not some busybody informer. She was suddenly afraid and suspicious, knowing she did not know how to hold her own tongue.

'No, just passing through,' Violette reassured her with a warm smile, explaining that she was just passing through having been in Paris for Easter. She explained that in a few days she would have to go home to Le Havre and was afraid of what she might find there. Carefully checking for Madame Thivier's reaction she continued that it was a terrible war and the sooner peace was declared the better. She had carefully controlled her accent, watching surreptitiously for the woman's reaction. None. Now that was a relief!

As Madame Thivier took Violette up to her room at her request, she explained that she had the prettiest room overlooking the courtyard and that breakfast was served downstairs from seven in the morning until eight thirty. Chatting casually, Violette asked where she might go that evening for dinner.

Madame Thivier eagerly suggested a little café-bar two streets away that would do nicely – cheap, clean, good local food and decent folk. Not many Germans went there as it was out of the way. She offered Violette an umbrella if she needed it.

---

38 *Epouvantable* = dreadful.

Violette thanked her politely feeling more comfortable with her hostess as they descended the stairs. She accepted the room and offered her papers as the *fiche* was filled in. She went up to her room and unpacked.

She luxuriated in a hot bath, ridding herself of the dust of travel and the smell of sweat from her fellow travellers. For the next few hours Violette stayed in her room, which was basic but comfortable. A blue flowered china jug of water stood in its matching basin. She had already hung up her few clothes, putting her underwear in a drawer. It was a nice room and she felt reasonably secure. She hoped the woman was who she seemed, and not a canny informant. She lay down on the bed, relaxed and thought what she ought to do the next day.

Looking out of the window on to the courtyard, she saw that there were chickens in a run and a few rabbits in hutches. Vines and other plants grew in tubs and buckets: a veritable pantry of fresh fare. There was a gate into the yard that seemed to open out on to an alleyway.

It did rain, and hard. When it stopped, Violette ventured out to the *estaminet* recommended by the *patronne*, Madame Thivier, taking the offered umbrella with her against further showers. As she was feeling a little drained from the excitement of the day, she felt she would eat quickly and return to rest. She found a table in a corner and, after quietly ordering her meal, watched who came and went and who spoke to whom, wondering if there would be a friendly face. Each person cast a glance in her direction but to her relief made no move to strike up conversation. She ate a simple meal followed by chicory-laced coffee and returned to the hotel early for a good night's sleep.

‡

7

Finding and Meeting Madame Desvaux

Tuesday 11 April 1944

Next morning, Madame Thivier provided a breakfast of steaming chicory-rich coffee, bread and jam. The coffee available in the shops was what was termed *café national* and it was better to be unaware of what its infamous mix might be. The bread was freshly baked but with ersatz flour that made the bread dark and lumpy. It was unceremoniously known as *pain caca* or 'poo bread',[39] but the taste was disguised by the *patronne*'s plentiful homemade *confiture aux groseilles*, jam made from the gooseberries grown in the hotel courtyard.

As Violette walked out onto the street, doubt hit her, mixed with fear of the unknown. She was in an unknown town looking for unknown people under the watchful eye of unknown enemies. That nice French woman with her son walking beside her – was she enemy or friend? Keeping her nerve, she forced her panic back down. Wise to be careful, she told herself, make sure you're not followed, but otherwise get on with your plan for the day.

In London, she had studied Rouen in detail on Buckmaster's acquired maps, brought back by people already doing dangerous work in this area, and aerial maps taken from bombers and spy planes. In fact, she remembered that a certain Albert Pognant had sent across a bulky pack of up-to-date route and topographical maps, current identity and ration cards. New sets of cards had been cleverly forged from dozens of originals and given to people like her, in her case four for her own use and a few sets to pass on to others.

Violette had memorised the list of people with whom Philippe had worked. She also knew from Philippe how untrained and partially trained French men and women had already been of great service to the Allied effort and their own country, stealing coupons and identity cards, performing sabotage, garnering

---

39 During his proofreading, Leslie Jackson, friend and financier, informed me that in England the flour was grey in colour and white flour a rarity. 'I know this,' he wrote, 'because on my ship we did have *white* flour and when going ashore to see Peggy, my fiancée, a 1b-bag of white flour was greeted with delighted surprise.' During the war in France there were some 55,000 bakeries – one for about every 800 people.

information on troop movements and passing it on to the Allies through Philippe and other agents.

She just had to take her time, Violette told herself, and be very, very careful. She must continue to look like a happy young woman going about her daily affairs while remaining ever watchful. She had learned well at Beaulieu in England how to check whether she was being followed and how to lose any such tails. As trainees, she and Cyril Watney, a wireless operator, were never caught. On the other hand, they caught all the trainees they tailed, except one, their friend Jacques Poirier, a Frenchman, who would take over Harry Peulevé's *Author* circuit in the Corrèze after Harry's arrest. The best thing was to think of all this as a training exercise and, in that way, keep fear and anxiety locked away.

As Paul Emile, a friend as well as an intelligence officer who had been her class instructor on the German military and security services, once told her: 'Do the thing you most fear to do and that is the almost certain death of fear.' Each decision she would take over the next few weeks would, indeed, be the thing she most feared to do. His phrase would come back to encourage her many times over the following months and would help her each step of her perilous way.

‡

Violette's tenseness began to evaporate as she put her thinking processes into gear. She needed a bicycle and knew that most of the garages renting bikes were on the *rive gauche* so she would need to cross one of the bridges guarded by the military. That should not be too much of a problem as her papers were excellent forgeries. It also gave her an excuse for walking around the city and also past where Madame Desvaux lived, whom she thought perhaps she should visit first, and walking thus get a feel for the area. It would probably take more than one foray to find one of the two garages used as a storage dump for weapons and ancillary materials. These supplies had been parachuted into the region by London for Philippe, Bob Maloubier or the reception committees to collect and hide until the Allies invaded, or to be deployed in various sabotage exercises to weaken German defences and plans. Georges Philippon, known as *Jo*, had hidden away a substantial cache of weapons over the last year for Philippe and for the very secret network of which *Jo* was an external member. Violette would soon discover this group was called *Les Diables Noirs* – the Black Devils – established not too far from Ry, some thirty kilometres north-east of Rouen. One of the most secretive groups in the operation, the *Diables Noirs* had been set up not long after the beginning of the Occupation, formed to receive the first parachute drops of material and to gather intelligence, and later expanded to train young *réfractaires*[40] as fighting units in the Maquis. Still today, few

---

40 *Réfractaires* = draft dodgers, but in the Second World War *les réfractaires au STO* were French civilians who refused to work in Germany or on German installations in France and thus constituted the foundation of the Maquis.

in France – and certainly not elsewhere – know of its existence and the great work its members did, and continued to do even after they were very nearly destroyed.

Deep in thought, Violette was suddenly halted by a German soldier: '*Ausweis, bitte!*'

She was shocked to the core by the bark of the order. She managed to utter, '*Tenez, voilà*,' as she moved away from the kerb and handed over her forged identity papers in the name of *Corinne Leroy*.

'*In Ordnung!* And where exactly are you going?'

'I-I'm looking for a bike to hire,' she replied with a frown of worry and anger. She instinctively acted like a young French women properly incensed at being questioned in the street.

'Ah, and why might that be, *mademoiselle*?' asked the German, eyeing her up and down appreciatively. Asking questions to keep a pretty thing close for a few minutes was not an uncommon activity to relieve the daily tedium.

'So that I can try and find a relative who might still be here or might have been killed in one of the raids by the damned British.' Said with evident annoyance.

'Oh? Where does he come from, *mademoiselle*?'

'From Lille, and hasn't been heard of for three months and his family, knowing I live in Le Havre and had permission to visit Rouen, asked me if I would look for him. Of course I said yes, especially as I was coming through Rouen after my visit to an aunt in Paris for Easter,' she replied somewhat sharply.

'Very well, be careful not to buy anything on the black market. The punishments are grave.'

'Yes, sir. Of course not. *Merci et bonjour*.' She hurried on, heart thumping, nerves jangling. Yet, a small, contained feeling of satisfaction coursed through her that she had fooled another Jerry soldier. She had learned at SOE school to keep everything as close to the truth (cover story truth, at least) as possible to help avoid mistakes.

It was quite possible, Violette thought to herself as she walked on, that she would be stopped and questioned again. After all, Rouen was quite a small town.

‡

Violette walked slowly down to the quay, recalling maps, photos and aerial photos she had painstakingly memorised, and comparing them with this damaged city; bomb craters all around, dust and rubble covering thousands of square metres of this ancient town. Most was from a raid carried out in 1940 by the Germans before they marched from the north down Route de Neufchâtel into rue de la République. In response, the French had launched resistance from the *rive gauche* after setting fire to the town's vital supplies of oil, destroying bridges and scuttling boats and barges. The German military soon vanquished the French and took over a town of rubble and pain. They had refrained from bombing the beautiful Gothic cathedral under what was rumoured to be a direct order from Hitler. The enemy generally behaved themselves over the first two years: they were professional soldiers of the Wehrmacht, proud of their soldiering discipline and fighting capacity; theirs would be a benevolent and disciplined occupation of territories conquered. These were not the vicious SS Panzer divisions that had massacred their way through Poland, Czechoslovakia and Russia.

From the promenade, Violette crossed over to walk along rue Jeanne d'Arc. Sections of this area were relatively intact but she found more devastation. However it was less damaged than the formless, vague terrain strewn with rubble sloping down towards the Seine that she had just left. She had seen that the Halle aux Toiles – within view of her hotel and just a few lanes to the north – was in ruins, but had not realised the devastation beyond, towards the west and the city centre. She would cross one of the temporary pontoons, vital arteries across the Seine, not merely for workers, including forced labour, but for German supplies, tanks, guns, soldiers and civilians.

First, she decided before venturing over the bridge to find a bike and thus confirm her cover story, she would check out the fate of Madame Desvaux. She had discussed it with Philippe and they had decided this could well be her first step. It seemed only logical to try and find Madame Desvaux's house. This woman had been an independent dressmaker. From July 1943 until February 1944 she had sheltered the wireless operator, Captain Isidore Newman, known here in Rouen, as *Pierre Jacques Nerrault*. As Philippe's trusted wireless operator he had remained in the Seine area of Normandy after Philippe's recall to London about two months before Violette's arrival.

When the *Salesman* circuit was blown, Isidore was captured and interrogated. His radio was with Broni,[41] his 'bodyguard' as Philippe referred to the Pole, who needed it to transmit for the *Diables Noirs*. Isidore decided there was no point in not giving all his radio keys to the interrogators as they would be of no further use to London or anyone else since he was certain Broni would warn London immediately. So now the Germans would not be able to use Isidore's specific codes and checks; even Broni could not use them for his own transmissions. As a result there was no point in torturing Isidore, but he was imprisoned about a month before Violette arrived in Rouen. Violette thought that she just might get to talk to Madame Desvaux and gambled that the woman would not hand her over to the enemy. It was said that she was very pro-Allies. Violette hoped, too, that with her

---

41 Bronislaw Pionteck, a skilled wireless operator. He had been born in Poland but was naturalised French in 1934, and joined the French Air Signals corps. He and his brother Felix were attached to the *Hamlet/Salesman* circuits and probably also to the *Libé-Nord* and the *Diables Noirs*. He was mentioned in Philippe Liewer's debriefings as *Bruni*. He and *Pierre* worked closely together and Broni was probably *Pierre*'s instructor in French as *Pierre* was not entirely bilingual, and in this way acted as his bodyguard by doing most of the talking. Broni was awarded the Légion d'Honneur, Médaille Militaire with Palm, Croix de Guerre and Médaille de la Résistance.

Morse code training, she would be able to use the wireless set with her own keys to London, if she could find out where Broni might be hiding out.

Although accustomed to the bombing raids over London, Violette was shocked to the core by the desolation of the area. Most of the houses in rue Jeanne d'Arc were still standing, but would number 12 be there? It had stood at the Quai Corneille end of the street where intensive fighting had taken place in 1940 and where bombs had fallen in the years since. As she turned into the street, she saw she was in luck – or rather, Madame Desvaux had been. At this southern end, on the right, stood the block where Madame Denise Desvaux had lived.

The block of apartments containing number 12 was still standing amid the rubble of one or two surrounding buildings, its walls bearing the scars of war. There were large cracks and nearly all the glass in the windows was missing or had slivers edging the window frames. Glass had been replaced by blackout paper, boards or thick curtains drawn across. The pervasive but dying stench of old fires and rubble was strong as Violette walked along slowly, noting these details.

She was feeling extremely uneasy and tense in this terrible expanse of destruction, surrounded by a fully armed and tetchy enemy and by those who collaborated. She walked towards where an old man was sitting on a crooked pile of bricks and rubble, picking through some strewn bits and pieces of what must have been his home; tears had made rivulets down his dust-covered cheeks. On getting closer, Violette saw that he was not an old man, probably not more than forty. His grubby and shredded clothes, shoulders hunched forward, spare bony body and the deep weariness and desolate sadness of his eyes made him appear years older.

A woman, head covered in a shawl, scurried past with a child of about seven at her side. She looked at Violette suspiciously as she hurried past, making Violette aware that she must make her own clothes look more worn and tired looking. She let her shoes scuff along for a few steps in the dust as the first step in creating a look more in keeping with her new surroundings. Then she bent as if to pull something from the rubble, let her hands drift in the dust and stood back up brushing her clothes down with those now dusty hands, as if straightening them. This left a few patches of dust smearing her light coat. Then she rubbed them down to clean off the excess, thus leaving the inevitable dust stains that appeared on the clothing of most of the people in the streets of Rouen.

‡

Finally, Violette warily stepped into the concierge's office in the apartment building. It was empty but she found Madame Desvaux's name on a pigeonhole, walked up the two floors and knocked. A woman of forty-something came out quickly and asked: 'What do you want?'

'I'm looking for a friend of mine; he's living with his aunt, a Madame Desvaux. I wonder if you would be his aunt, as this is the number of the flat he gave me, or would you know where I could find them? I understand *she* makes beautiful clothes and does extremely professional repair work.'

'*Mademoiselle*, that may well be true. But he's not here and I'm very busy,' the woman replied, wondering why this girl was asking about her nephew. It's been two months since Pierre was arrested, she thought to herself, and this morning I heard he was being deported via Compiègne. When this was his safe-house the cover story was that he was my nephew, helping me in my business. Could she possibly mean him?

'Actually,' said Violette, hesitating a little, while she gathered her thoughts. 'He said I might ask if you *repair knitted garments.*'

She involuntarily shivered; the wide hall was cold and dark and her light summer coat was not heavy enough to keep out the chill of this old but elegant *maison*. Private dwellings were forbidden to use any form of central heating. Even electricity and gas for lighting and cooking were severely rationed, sometimes limited to as little as one hour a day.

'Oh,' sighed the woman, clearly scared. 'I don't know if I can help, but do come inside – you look chilled to the bone.' She looked anxiously up and down the corridor. 'Yes, I can do *most repairs on knitwear*; it just depends on what you want done. I'd need to see the garment. Come on – come in!'

This last seemed to be said to satisfy the curiosity of a woman walking up the stairs at the end of the corridor. She nodded amiably enough in greeting to the two women and continued her climb to the next floor.

Within this brief conversation of introduction, Violette and Madame Desvaux had also exchanged a coded signal of recognition. The mention of the knitted garment was intended to establish Violette's *bona fides*.

Once inside, Madame Desvaux walked towards the kitchen. 'You could do with some coffee, I should think. You're doing something very dangerous, you know. You could get yourself, and me, into serious difficulty and probably worse.'

'Yes, I know, *madame*. Could you please confirm your name?' Violette stayed just inside the door for the moment; she had learned in her training the usefulness of some basic questioning techniques, such as the unexpected stance she now took.

'*Mais oui, je suis certainement Madame Denise Desvaux.*,' the woman replied, a little taken aback.

'Thank you, Madame Desvaux. I'm *Corinne Leroy*. I had to ask, you see, as I've been sent by *Charles* to discover what has happened to his network. Is *Pierre*, to whom you so bravely gave shelter, still living here? *Charles* and our people are extremely worried about what has happened to his circuit and to *Pierre*. We received a very strange message and my masters have sent me to discover the extent of the damage to *Charles*'s circuit. We'd heard *Pierre* had probably been arrested.'

'Oh, my goodness. You don't know the half of it. It was utterly terrifying and my poor *Pierre*, I don't know what will happen to him. I was arrested and interrogated over a whole week. After that, I went to see him, *Cicero*[42] and Jean and Florentine Sueur once a week. When I was told it was for the last time I thought they were going to shoot them. But no, they're to be sent to Germany tomorrow. *Pierre* is such a lovely man. We became very close over the nine months he was with me. I pray every day that he'll survive.' She took out a handkerchief and wiped her weeping eyes. 'You know, you're lucky I got back early. I go to Madame Sueur's shop with the clothes I've finished after I've visited *Pierre*, *Cicero*, Jean and Florentine – they're in the same cell, you know. Not Jean, but *Cicero* and *Pierre*. But today, after hearing they're to be deported, I was just too upset to go anywhere.'

'Could you tell me what happened?' asked Violette in a diffident manner. She did not wish to seem to interrogate Denise. The woman was upset and frightened. She was attractive, slim and well dressed, although her clothes were old.

Violette was alarmed by what she had just heard. Not only Isidore, but also Philippe's *boîte aux lettres*, Jean[43] and Philippe's lieutenant, Claude Malraux, had been seized. This confirmed the message radioed to London in March, but the blow was no less terrible: Philippe had necessarily informed Claude Malraux of all he knew and plans for the *Salesman* circuit so that Claude could take full charge after Philippe had been recalled to London in February.

'*Asseyez-vous, Mademoiselle, je vous prie!*' Madame Desvaux gestured towards a chair at the kitchen table while she made coffee. As she sat down, Violette felt strangely at home, strongly reminded of her last visit to Tante Marguerite. She looked at all the familiar objects and fleetingly felt happy; nevertheless she remained extremely tense. The news was disastrous, and poor Madame Desvaux did not seem at all pleased to see her. And who could wonder at that? It was very dangerous.

'You could have been followed, you know, *mademoiselle*.'

'No, *madame*, I have been extremely careful and made a number of detours as I made my way here. Definitely, I was not followed.' She continued softly, 'I wonder if you would be willing to help me in any way at all? I realise how dangerous it is for you, but we are getting so close to winning this war and bringing all the destruction, privations and fear to an end. The people here have been superb, what with all the sabotage they've carried out over the last four years, and information they've passed to London. My mission is to discover what has happened to everyone and see what London or I can do to help, and to see if we can resuscitate the network. I'm here to help in any way I can and have certain instructions to pass on. I can give financial help to the families left without an adequate breadwinner. There must have been some treachery somewhere, mustn't there?' commented

---

42 *Cicero* – code name for Claude Malraux.
43 *Serge* was the code name for Jean Sueur, and also a code name for Claude Malraux. *Néné* was another of Jean Sueur's aliases; he was an important contact to Philippe and manager of the Rouen branch of Madame Micheline's women's fashion shop. He was also an external member of the *Diables Noirs*.

Violette briefly, and then continued quickly without waiting for a reply. '*Charles* has sent me, and given me carte blanche to do whatever might be required and to assist wherever possible.'

Charles Beauchamp was the name Philippe used in certain parts of Rouen and for which he held identity papers, and *Clément Beauchamp* in others. He, as did Violette, held the all-important German-stamped passes for the *zone interdite*. Anyone anywhere in this zone without a pass bearing German stamps would be arrested and questioned.

'Well,' said Madame Desvaux, softening a little, 'I'm afraid the news is not at all encouraging. So many have been taken in for questioning, arrested, tortured, deported and, in too many cases, shot. Including the two who held the weapons dumps – that's *Jo* and Chevallier. It has been a dreadful time. Our whole network, it seems, has been destroyed. There are only a handful of people left and they're now perhaps too afraid to do anything. Not just afraid for themselves, but also for their families and friends.' Tears welled up again but were contained. She went on to describe some of the events and prevailing sentiments: 'And then, to top it all, the Allies bombed us, so we're all feeling pretty dispirited. Thank God the bombs have mainly fallen on specific targets: the gas works and the like, but as you can see in my own street, we've been pretty badly hit, all the same.'

'Yes, I know,' said Violette, quickly thinking how she might gain the other woman's confidence. 'It's been just like that in London, but at least we know it's only from the enemy. For you people of France it's even worse. You have to suffer bombing, too, not only from the enemy but also from your allies; plus you are living under the guns and interrogations of hostile invaders. It must all make everything particularly difficult and confusing, too.'

'Yes.' She smiled at Violette's sympathetic gaze. 'Have some more coffee – it's almost real coffee. I add just a little chicory to make it go further as I don't know when I'll be able to get any more.[44] And the sugar's black market; *Pierre* got me a huge brown paper bag full!' She stifled a sob at the thought of his being deported today to Germany to God only knew what fate.

'Thank you very much.' Violette added: 'I shall replace the coffee for you as I have a packet hidden in my suitcase at the little hotel where I'm staying.'

'Are you sure your hotel is safe? The Abwehr, the Gestapo, the Milice, especially that *salaud*[45] Chief Inspector Alie, and even the ordinary police sometimes, all make a particular effort to check the register of hotels and guest houses and the identity papers and zone passes of the guests. When they find anyone suspected of being involved in clandestine activities, they're particularly brutal.' She looked carefully at Violette and asked: 'Can't you find a safe-house to stay in? Haven't you

---

44 Leslie also informs me that another additive was ground figs; this was called *feigen Kaffee* and still drunk after the war, particularly in Austria. It should probably be written *Feigenkaffee*.
45 *Salaud* = bastard.

seen the notice in the hotel hall ordering everyone to have identity cards, *permis de séjour* or other permissions for just about everything?'

'Well, I can't be absolutely sure of the hotel. It's in rue Saint-Romain. The *patronne*, Madame Thivier, has been very kind so far and seems to dislike the Germans. It's the small private hotel just north of the bombed Halle aux Toiles and two steps from the cathedral.'

'Ah, if it's the one I think it is, I know her just a little. A friend of mine said how angry she had been a few months ago at the Germans bullying their way around and asking all kinds of impertinent questions about her guests. She gave them a hard time, it seems. And still does. I think you're safe there, at least for the moment.'

Violette decided that this woman was brave to have put her life in danger by housing *Pierre*, and she was being very hospitable. But still, this visit could prove disastrous, even fatal to her if Madame Desvaux were not what she seemed and decided to report her to the enemy authorities.

Madame Desvaux poured the coffee and carefully assessed her visitor. She was taking to this discreet young woman who had come knocking so unexpectedly at her door. She must have had a dangerous journey from England. She knew she had to tell Violette everything that had happened on 9 March, just one month ago, and her own unfortunate reaction.

Madame Desvaux explained how Isidore (*Pierre*) had used fifty-four different locations with at times as much as forty miles distance between them for sending clandestine messages to and receiving them from London. She described how he had lived with her since mid-July 1943 and they had become lovers, in spite of his younger age, and held one another in genuine affection. Therefore, she knew more, perhaps, than she ought. Colin Gubbins, head of SOE, later wrote in the citation for Isidore's MBE that he worked untiringly in an area thick with enemy troops and Gestapo, making possible the delivery of arms to his circuit on a large scale. On this mission, Isidore had sent fifty-four messages to London.[46] How on earth had he done it and survived for so long? Violette knew it was careful security procedures and tenacious courage that had made it possible. She had been told in London that he always took elaborate precautions and followed every security rule available to him. She remembered he had been the wireless operator for Odette and Captain Peter Churchill[47] but left, refusing to send over-long and unnecessary messages to London for one of Peter's men. Isidore considered such behaviour a huge and unnecessary security risk. At the beginning of March 1944, Isidore had stopped sending messages after nearly eight months of steady contact. Had his radio been detected by a German listening van?

---

46 Notes from Martin Sugarman in his paper for *Jewish Historical Studies*, vol. 41, 2007.
47 Odette (Hallows/Churchill) Sansom GC (see biography and film entitled *Odette*) said of Violette, 'She was the bravest of us all'.

When Philippe slipped out of Rouen in November 1943, coming back once or twice before his return to England had been arranged by Lysander in early February 1944, he had put Claude Malraux, his second-in-command, or his lieutenant, as he preferred to refer to those he had placed in such positions, firmly in charge – divulging to him all the important details of the *Salesman* circuit, including weapons dumps and letter drops – those people trusted to receive clandestine visitors and verbal, even occasionally written, messages; people like Georges Philippon (*Jo*) and Jean Sueur, the staunch Gaullist and respected external member of the very secretive group Violette hoped to contact.

Madame Desvaux went on to say that she knew that Claude had been a worried man who clearly did not know quite what to do. Claude and his partner[48] met Madame Desvaux and Isidore socially from time to time, usually in a restaurant or sometimes in one of their homes. She said that Claude seemed preoccupied, as if he knew something was afoot but was powerless to take action.

Claude had told *Pierre* that the main arms and explosives dump at Philippon's garage had been raided by the Gestapo. He had gone on to explain that the Gestapo had seized the five-ton truck that Philippe had used to transport arms; information which Violette knew *Pierre* had transmitted to London.

Violette asked when *Cicero* had told all this to *Pierre*. Madame Desvaux said that on 7 March, two days before they were all arrested that they decided to have dinner at her place on 9 March, a Thursday, so that they could discuss what they should do. She reiterated that *Cicero* seemed listless and incapable of making decisions or taking action.

At the memory tears welled up again but were held back.

Denise really did not know what to think as both *Pierre* and herself did not know if it was through sheer lack of nerve or because *Cicero* was expecting *Charles* to return that he took no action.

Violette thought that it was probably a bit of both: but privately that Claude waiting for Philippe's imminent return was pure procrastination. She thought if she or Philippe had been there, they would have immediately sent Georges Philippon, his wife, Jean and Florentine Sueur, plus Philippon's close friend Chevallier with his wife, into hiding for the duration of the war. This may have meant sacrificing any further contributions those people could have made, but it might have saved half the organisation. She surmised correctly that the usefulness of this group of people had probably reached an end and so they should have been protected at once. It was clear that instead the violent loss of these people was a crippling blow, especially to the internal arrangements of the rest of the organisation and the ongoing preparations for the Allied landings.

---

48 There is some question whether the woman in Claude's life was his wife, fiancée or lover. As far as I can ascertain her name was Anne.

Madame Desvaux broke into Violette's thoughts with the news that Georges Philippon and Chevallier were shot on 12 March, three days after the Gestapo came for them all. The thought that it was because of the rest of them that they were arrested and shot was simply too awful to contemplate. Denise could not recall any of them mentioning their names. She said she certainly had not but then it was impossible for her to believe that *Pierre* had, either there or in prison, and surely *Cicero* had not given anything away. However, under interrogation and Denise thought especially fears for one's family, one just never knew. At least *Pierre* did not have that problem.

Madame Desvaux told Violette that *Pierre* had gone out very early on 8 March to meet his bodyguard and wireless operator, Broni, so they could transmit together as Broni had messages to send to London from his own groups. He had asked Denise to meet Broni a little earlier and take him to their agreed meeting place. *Pierre* would go there by a separate route. *Pierre* and Broni had been good friends, going everywhere together. They were certainly not an uncommon sight and it was generally believed, encouraged by the two men, that they were involved in the black market. So, Violette concluded as Denise continued her narrative, *Pierre* must have had some serious concerns otherwise he would not have suggested such a devious plan for their meeting. Violette hoped he had told Broni to find himself a safe-house and keep out of sight for a while. *Pierre* had returned in the late afternoon, continued Denise. He did not seem unduly stressed, or particularly concerned. Denise asked him if he had put his wireless set and crystals in their hiding place, but he told her that Broni needed them as he had many messages to send for his group. He'd get them back tomorrow or the day after, he said, when they next met.

Poor Broni did not have the slightest chance to escape. Later, on 11 March, he was cornered by the Gestapo in his own home with his brother Felix who, having grabbed his pistol, was shot dead. It was absolutely typical of Felix to resist arrest. However, Broni was captured and taken away. After being badly tortured, he was sent first to Auschwitz, then Buchenwald, and finally Bora but miraculously survived.[49]

Denise recounted the events of the planned dinner party on Thursday 9 March. It had been arranged that Claude and his partner Anne would arrive at half past seven in the evening. By nine he had still not appeared, although Anne had arrived at the agreed time. Already anxious, Anne decided to hurry home to see what had happened.

The concierge was at the door of her block of apartments. She asked him quickly if he had seen Monsieur *Serge*.

---

49 Broni was finally liberated and lived to the ripe old age of ninety-three, having married and had three children. Among his activities, he had participated in the sabotage of a German minesweeper in the port of Rouen as part of *Salesman/Hamlet*.

The concierge replied in the negative, explaining that Monsieur *Serge* had gone out at about four o'clock this afternoon, looking worried and in a bit of a rush, and he hadn't him since, saying he hoped he was not in any trouble.

Anne muttered a quick *merci* and rushed back to Denise, only to discover that he had not yet arrived there either.

Pierre was now seriously concerned that disaster had struck. He admitted at dinner to the two women that Claude had said how worried he was, 'as things were getting hot'. *Pierre* went on to say that it was time for him to disappear. If he stayed, he was sure, it was not only his own life that was in danger, but also that of Denise, Broni and several others – and all those safe-houses he and Broni used for transmissions, too.

Even though the women thought that it was too late to go that day, *Pierre* felt that there was still just under two hours until curfew, it was a beautiful moonlit night – easy to cycle without a lamp – and even if he could not get very far, he could sleep in a field and continue to a safe-house the following day.

Denise was enormously sad at the prospect; it was dangerous and she was afraid. Anne announced that she would go home. Claude might be on some assignment or other, or he might have received urgent information to disseminate to other members of the organisation. She thought it would be better to wait until tomorrow and then meet again, probably with Claude in tow, when they could all decide their next steps together.

Denise enthusiastically agreed, saying they should come the following day at one o'clock when they could discuss everything calmly and make new plans for their safety and that of the other group members. Reluctantly, *Pierre* agreed. An extra night would surely not hurt.

Violette was aghast at the reasoning and could not help wondering about it. Was Denise telling the truth? The idea that Claude could be out performing some task was not altogether out of the question. It was a weak argument for lack of action perhaps, but still, on the other hand, it could have been the case. Nevertheless, it was extremely dangerous to wait and turned out to be fatal.

‡

8

The Confession

Tuesday 11 April 1944

Denise continued, saying that the next day, Friday 10 March, Denise, *Pierre* and Anne had met again as arranged for lunch in Denise's flat, continued Denise. But still no Claude. He had not been seen or heard of and had left no message.

While they were eating, the Vichy police had arrived, accompanied by two Gestapo and a few German soldiers, who remained on guard with the vehicles. Their officer banged heavily on the door and demanded to speak to the 'lodger'. It was Vichy Chief Inspector Alie, a French North African Vichy police officer enlisted by the Gestapo for his particular penchant for cruelty in interrogating suspects. With him was Inspector Jean Déterville, who was in fact playing an extremely dangerous game in clandestine communication with the Résistance. Denise replied that she had no lodger, as the French were supposed to declare all lodgers to the authorities, but said she had a friend living with her. Chief Inspector Alie barked out that they knew he was a *réfractaire* – and that he refused compulsory work service.[50] By April 1940, some 200,000 workers were on the run. The Pétain government had recently been encouraged to send more young Frenchmen to Germany to work in factories and weapons industries, where they laboured under gruelling conditions; workers dropped like flies and the German war machine needed constant replacements.

'It was terrible, *Corinne*, there was a lot of shouting from the Milice and Chief Inspector Alie led them in. I was beside myself with fear. They just knew so much about us all. I was so upset that I shouted out, "You can't do that to a British captain." I knew that, as *Pierre* was a soldier, he could become a prisoner of war, not be sent to slave labour in Germany.'

Aghast at what Denise had said, Violette blurted: 'But, don't you realise a military man in occupied territory *not* wearing his country's uniform can be summarily shot as a spy?'

---

50 Compulsory work service – *Service de travail obligatoire* (STO) was initiated by the Pétainist government by law on 26 February 1943. It had the effect of making those young men and their families and friends the enemies of the government. The men went into hiding and the Maquis was born; their families and friends became the nascent Résistance.

'Oh no! That can't be! I was trying to protect him.' Tears streamed anew down her face at the horrendous mistake she had made. 'It can't be true!' She had had no idea, fully believing that British officers went straight to POW camps.

'I'm afraid it is true.' Violette's voice was serious. 'Please, Denise, tell me the rest so I have a chance to assess the situation a little better. I know how painful this is for you, but we must go over every aspect of what happened to them and to you, so that we can plan better for the days ahead.'

Wiping her eyes and blowing her nose, Denise explained that the police knew exactly what they were talking about, in detail too. They had never set eyes on her before but they obviously knew who she was before they started to question her. They found a photo of a man in her bag which, Denise thought, may have told them who she was. Violette was not able to establish from Denise that the woman's name was really Anne but Denise thought it was; nor could she ascertain that it was Claude's photograph the Milice found, although it was fairly safe to assume it was. Philippe had not mentioned this woman's name in his later debriefing reports either, although he must have known it from working closely with Claude Malraux. Denise surmised that the police knew she was Claude's partner, or at least that she had some close connection to him since it transpired that they had arrested him only the previous evening. Violette was unsure of the logic of this but could get no clearer explanation from Denise.

If *Pierre*, Denise and Anne were the only ones who knew of the planned lunchtime meeting, was one of them the traitor? And where was this Anne? On being asked, Denise did not respond, but instead said that she and *Pierre* had a prearranged story that exonerated her from any knowledge of his activities.

Going over the deeply disturbing events again and again, Denise told Violette that Anne had been saying she thought Claude was on his way to tell another group that the weapons and other material at Philippon's garage had not yet been found by the Gestapo and they needed to hide them elsewhere. Anne believed he had been told, or realised when he went there, that there remained a well-concealed cache of weapons as yet undiscovered by the enemy.

Denise then reluctantly explained to Violette that it seemed *Pierre* had broken down almost immediately, as the very next day, Saturday 11 March, the six families who had allowed him to use their homes for transmitting and receiving were arrested, every one of them. This came to a total of about twenty people. Who else would have known about all these families? Violette replied that it was quite possible that he and his bodyguard had been followed for the last few weeks, maybe even months, by Vichy police, Gestapo, Milice or informers. It was, in Violette's opinion, highly unlikely to have been *Pierre* who gave the information as he had proved to be such a robust operator; it was much more likely to have been a betrayal within the networks. Perhaps security had been getting lax; the fact that Denise herself came into the equation remained unspoken.

The Gestapo had taken everything that *Pierre* possessed in Denise's apartment, including a hoard of 50,000 francs that Philippe had left with him rather than Claude before returning to London; money to be used to fund various resistance activities.

Whatever the reason for those arrests, it was devastating, thought Violette. She insisted to Denise that she must contact those left behind; at the very least she could help them financially. Would they even be prepared to talk to her if they even remotely thought one of her own group had seemingly sold them down the river? Did they realise the persistence of the enemy to infiltrate and harm? It was very demoralising for the remnants of the circuit. Or was Denise placing the blame elsewhere in order to protect herself?

From all Violette had heard of *Pierre* it was inconceivable that he would break so completely and immediately. Was Denise telling her the truth as she saw it? Did she even know? Had they *all* been followed and not realised? This seemed to Violette to be much more likely. She did on the whole feel that Denise was being sincere and honest.

Violette spoke quietly, thinking aloud, explaining that maybe this raid had been timed to coincide with a number of others. It was likely that there existed at least one infiltrator or collaborator, or perhaps a careless high- or low-ranking member in one of the clandestine groups, who over a period of weeks, maybe even months, had led to the destruction of *Charles's Salesman* circuit and other networks. It was something she and Philippe thought quite possible.

Denise certainly agreed saying that some of these homes where *Pierre* transmitted from, were thirty to forty-five kilometres from Rouen. The Gestapo arrested everybody in each home. She felt that it could only have been *Pierre*, Claude or, just possibly, Anne who had given away the whereabouts of these people after the Germans gave their word that nobody would be shot.

Violette still had doubts about this. It was likely that the raids had been planned and orchestrated over months. The Germans were not fools and more than capable of letting networks continue to train, receive armaments and supplies and so forth, only to arrest the members after they had been trained and grab the delivered weapons – textbook tactics.

On the other hand, Denise's relationship with Isidore was so close that Isidore had asked her to go to Broni that morning. What else did she know? Violette desperately wanted to keep on questioning Denise but it was vital that she remain sympathetic so that Denise would help her to reach other circuit members or other groups. Softly, softly, she reminded herself.

‡

After Denise had made yet more fresh coffee, Violette came back to the serious business of her mission, asking if Denise would mind telling her again what happened next to *Pierre* and Claude. Reluctantly she did although she was not proud of her actions. Violette was gentle in her thanks.

Then, in an extraordinary confession, Denise told Violette that, in the hope that the treatment of *Pierre* would be lenient, she had promised the Gestapo that she would tell them if she saw *Charles* – Philippe – again. Hands shaking, Denise burst into uncontrollable sobs of shame and embarrassment.

'I–I was so scared, *Corinne*, I didn't want anything dreadful to happen to *Pierre* and so I promised. I still don't know to this day whether I would have kept such a promise. I don't think I would. I was so terrified for *Pierre*, I just blurted it out. I did know I wasn't in a position to give *Charles* away as he had disappeared, apparently to England. But I shouldn't have done it. I've visited *Pierre* as often as they'll let me, taking him food and clean clothes, and I've seen that he hasn't been badly treated at all. Nor, for that matter, have Claude, Jean or Florence.' *Pierre* had confirmed to her that he had not been tortured, or even beaten up. The leniency even went further: *Pierre* had been allowed to share a cell with Claude in the Palais de Justice in Rouen. This perk was, no doubt, given to see if the enemy could elicit useful information from listening in on their talk; most cells were bugged.

Violette was shocked by the story. She sympathised with the woman but felt let down. And very scared. She kept her voice as calm as possible and tried not to show just how distressed she was. Denise was weeping quietly.

'Shush, now, don't worry, Denise,' calmly soothed Violette. 'What you've told me is so useful. I know it's difficult but I need to know everything so that we can make the right assessment and decisions about we can do in the weeks ahead. We all do things we wish we hadn't but we do them for what seem to us the best reasons at the time. Sometimes, as with what happened to you, there aren't even seconds to decide what to do.'

Violette, this time, made another small cafetière of coffee. She went to rinse the tiny cups in the sink. Busying herself gave her pause to ease the tension building inside her and to try to think a little more coherently. What if, after such a confession, Denise felt so diminished that she decided to report *her* to the Milice or the Gestapo? It had happened before with other people who, mortified by their weakness, blustered into betrayal. Or what if all she had heard was just a story to lure her into something worse? What if the Gestapo were keeping a careful watch on the house at this very moment? She was very, very scared.

‡

After a while, they began to talk more generally again about Rouen, the war and where it was leading. Denise described again how she was able to visit Isidore three times a week and bring anything she liked to him, Claude, Jean and Florence – cigarettes, food and so on. Violette then realised that it was not the Gestapo nor the French Milice who had imprisoned them, but the Vichy police, as they were imprisoned in the cellars of their headquarters in the Palais de Justice. It seems possible that Isidore and Claude had somehow been protected from torture by the clandestine Résister, Inspector Déterville, or one of his undercover people that Violette did not yet know about. Violette asked Denise if she was sure it was Louis Alie, the head of the French Milice, with his men, who came to arrest them all that day.

Denise thought so but did admit that one despicable Milice officer looks pretty much like another to her. She was sure there were Gestapo there as well. There were four or five altogether, she thought, with a couple of black cars out the front carefully guarded by Miliciens and German soldiers. She explained that the Vichy police on the whole preferred to keep to civil criminal matters and nothing more. But Alie was specially recruited, along with his chosen men, commonly thought of as a shower of Vichy louts and fanatic Nazi supporters, just like the Milice, which was generally known as the French Gestapo. Then there was the SD – the Nazi Party police force – the Gestapo and the French GMR, the reserve mobile groups, Vichy's mobile police forces. This reinforced all Violette had learned at SOE school and briefings in Orchard Court, Baker Street and with Philippe.

Denise explained there had been just as many Résistants who continued working – much more carefully, to be sure – for the Allied cause, and just as many who gave nothing away under the most horrible interrogations imaginable. The Gestapo, she said, were nothing but vermin that should be destroyed but it must be said that, overall, the Wehrmacht, the regular army, was not so bad. The Abwehr, the military police, were harsh – but the Gestapo was a vicious secret police agency, directly answerable to Himmler and Hitler – cruel and merciless from top to bottom. The harm they had done was terrible indeed.

‡

The morning had slipped by, but Violette thought that spending this time with her first contact was worth every minute. Even so, she should leave soon; the questions she so much wanted to ask would probably upset Denise too much. Biding her time would reward her more. They spent a little longer discussing happier moments and Denise described how, although they were lovers, she felt like a second mother to her *Pierre*; and how he had taken her to Paris, where they would chat about their plans after the war's end. She repeated many times how happy *Pierre* was to return to her place and that he felt so secure and comfortable there. Violette listened carefully to all this and felt unaccountably sadder. There was something … too effusive, too scared … eyes which were not always direct … Yet she did feel Denise would strive for her people now, try to eradicate her growing feeling of self-loathing.

Violette was convinced this talk would somehow lead to a new contact. With luck, Denise would be anxious, now that she had got the worst off her chest, to prove her renewed strength and desire to help. Violette was equally anxious; she was still disinclined to believe that *Pierre*, or even Claude, had given away anything of use to the enemy.

She hoped that describing England, London and the suffering of its citizens, and talking about the man in her life, killed before they could live even a few months of their life together, would bring her and Denise closer together by showing her sincere compassion and understanding, and thus help reinforce Denise's resolve. She did not mention that he had been a legionnaire and an early member of the Free French Forces under de Gaulle in London, or that she had a daughter.

For her part, Denise's desire to help *Corinne Leroy* and undo any wrong she might have perpetrated was growing. As they talked, Denise remarked that *Corinne* did not have an English accent. She thought *Corinne* may have come from the Pas-de-Calais or even perhaps Belgium, saying *Pierre* had a marked English accent.

Violette, laughing, was relieved to hear this. It was a laugh that chimed right to the heart of Denise and made her smile through her drying tears. Violette told her she had worked like the very devil to get rid of any accent. At first she didn't realise her accent was from the Pas-de-Calais. Perhaps she should have known, as she had spent a large part of her childhood in the area, and many holidays since.

In the streets below were the afternoon sounds of people talking, sometimes laughing, sometimes yelling in argument. Every now and then, the women could hear, through the general daytime murmur, individual shouts and the screech of tyres as military vehicles hurtled up and down. There were very few private cars and most of those were old jalopies running on God-knew-what, known as *gazogènes*.[51] The sounds mingled in a steady background buzz as the two women began to strike up what could become a lasting friendship, if trust could be firmly established.

Although the age difference was a good decade, it seemed not to matter. Violette, mature and self-contained for her years, could make Denise laugh a little. Her lively nature bubbled under the surface and, on this, her first vital visit, broke through just often enough to soothe and beguile her older companion. Violette recognised that Madame Desvaux had a wealth of experience to pass on to her and that she was an intelligent if not exceptionally strong-willed woman.

'Let me suggest something to you, *Corinne*,' Madame Desvaux proposed. 'I think it would be much safer if you came to stay with me. We can easily explain, if we have to, that I'm an old friend of the family and bumped into you in the street. You could tell the *patronne* of the guesthouse, Madame Thivier, that you've met up with a family friend who invited you to stay. Try not to give her the name or address so that your whereabouts in Rouen remains unknown or at least elusive.'

'But you would be putting yourself in great danger again, *madame*,' protested Violette. Also, it could be a trap, although she did not think so.

---

51 *Gazogènes* were vehicles produced in France fuelled by burning wood and other vegetable-based materials. They enabled the French with or without vehicular and travelling permits to still run trucks, cars and motorbikes.

'I'm used to that now and, anyway, a bomb could come and do the job anytime. And I would be delighted to have a little company for a while. Please do accept. I will sleep easier, knowing that you are relatively safe under my roof.'

The apartment had three or four good sized bedrooms along the wide halls. Although looking somewhat the worse for wear, it was a well-furnished apartment, comfortable, with lots of space. All of which could give a false sense of security, an extremely dangerous state of mind. Violette would feel very safe here if she were just a little surer of the loyalty of the lady of the house, or if she knew that the house and its occupant were not under constant or partial surveillance. Would she really be safe here?

'I don't know how to thank you for such a kind and brave offer. But I think I should stay in the guesthouse as I'm established there. If I check out now before leaving town, I would draw unnecessary attention to myself. That's not good, is it? And I would not like to put you in unnecessary danger. It is so very kind of you, though. But maybe you can help in another way. My job is to meet as many of *Charles*'s circuit members as I can to see who has escaped the clutches of the Germans and what, if anything, can be resurrected or planned. Can you help me in this?'

She hoped that mentioning Philippe and his circuit again remind Denise of her reason for being in Rouen, and that time was of the essence.

'You're very wise, *Corinne*, for such a young person.' said Madame Desvaux. 'On reflection, I think you're quite right. However, you will join me for lunch here tomorrow, won't you? I'd like to think about how I might be able to help. It will indeed be difficult. Terrible things have happened in the last months, and I will tell you more about them tomorrow. I won't suggest dinner because of curfew. Lunch tomorrow. Around one o'clock, would that suit you?' There was no hesitation in Violette's response although her heart contracted a little at the thought of the possible danger of coming back here to a waiting Gestapo ambush.

'Perfect. I'd better leave now to have a bit of a look around and familiarise myself with the town generally. If anything crops up, you could leave a vague message at the guesthouse. If you mention a piece of orange clothing or a scarf, not red, it will mean "danger" and blue, not green, will mean "be careful but no obvious danger".'

'Good thinking. And be prudent, child, as you walk the streets. Put your scarf back on your head. You are very beautiful and the scarf makes you less noticeable. *Au revoir* until tomorrow, then, *petite*.'

'Thank you, *à bientôt*!' Violette pulled her scarf tightly round her head and tied it under her chin. As Madame Desvaux closed the door behind her, she walked along the corridor and down the stairs, relieved not to have bumped into anyone, and reached the entrance. Taking a deep breath, she stepped outside.

‡

9

Dubito Ergo Sum

Tuesday 11 April 1944

Dubito, ergo sum
I doubt, therefore I survive
  The motto of many of SOE F section's best men and women, *d'après* René Descartes

Violette was not keen to step outside into danger again, but it was her job. So she walked resolutely back to the relative safety of her hotel. Her jangled nerves were beginning to settle after her encounter with Madame Desvaux, but her feet were beginning to object to being made to walk over cobbles and more cobbles, no matter how well laid and smooth they were.

She would drop into a café-bar where she could put her thoughts in order while meditating over a late lunch. A strange feeling of unreality invaded her. Except for those with bomb damage, most of the streets at first glance looked the same as streets in any French town. She had walked along the quays, passing a parade of German troops, and turned into rue Grand-Pont. At the crossroad with the small rue du Petit Salut she noticed ahead that pedestrians were being halted and taken aside to be checked by a group of young Doriotistes, who were effectively a bunch of French Nazi thugs, liking nothing more than to bully and put fear into their compatriots. It was from this group of fanatical right-wingers that the Milice had emerged the year before, but the Milice had the huge advantage of real and overwhelming political clout, and they used it on a whim to inflict hurt and terror.

Heart suddenly thumping, Violette quickly turned left into a small lane and walked hurriedly into rue du Bac. As she came onto rue de la Pie she saw long queues of people waiting to get hold of a few clothes from the tailor's shop and food from the grocer's shop next door. Everyone there looked scruffy, worn out and resigned. The tailor's shop window was blown, the feeble protection of hanging brown paper was torn, leaving a gaping black hole. An iron guardrail had been added across the shop fronts to a height of about two metres, to prevent looting and help control unruly queues.

A little way along, Violette noticed a printer's shop by the name of Wolf and made a mental note of it. She recalled that she had heard the name before, probably at one of the planning meetings for her mission. There were unsightly notices of German *Ordnungen* posted on windows, doors or hanging from makeshift posts: orders designed to control the population, to insist on compliance, sometimes on pain of death by firing squad.

The *Hôtel de Ville* had huge red, black and white banner swastikas hanging from roof level. As she walked along the opposite side of the large square, Violette saw the shops reduced to scruffy exteriors with empty shelves that had previously been piled with essential or luxury goods. Windows were cracked, empty or covered in cardboard announcements stuck on at odd angles. Many shops, all over the town, looked shut or abandoned. There were queues for bread and other essentials. She watched a number of disputes burst out about who was next, or just how many ration points were needed. She passed five street checks in as many minutes.

The clouds skittered above her in the stiff breeze. Violette felt utterly alone; she was alert and very tense at the thought that an officer might demand to check her papers again. Had Madame Desvaux walked round to the Milice or police and reported her? She repeatedly checked covertly to see if she was being followed and felt just a little paranoid. She decided to treat her movements about town exactly like her exercises under SOE training – like a game.

Violette felt that the visit to Madame Desvaux had been worthwhile as a starting point, even if it had scared her. After those first uneasy fifteen minutes or so, they had warmed to one another, at least superficially. By the exchange of what was relatively inconsequential but emotionally charged information (mostly already known to Violette), they had begun, it seemed, to establish a certain level of trust. If not, she would soon be disabused of that idea. Denise held all the cards and Violette felt uncomfortable at the thought of being entirely in her hands.

She felt safe enough in the guesthouse for the time being, but maybe it would be prudent to have a bolthole. After all, she could create the cover of staying with a friend while looking for her fictitious uncle, or persuade someone to act as her lover and supply her with lodgings for a while. She could, at a pinch, contact 'her' Wehrmacht colonel, Colonel Niederholen.

Even if Madame Desvaux turned out to be as determined as she seemed to help the Allied cause, Violette surmised that staying at her apartment would be entirely inappropriate as the woman had already had a 'nephew' staying on to help her. Violette was sure it would be unusual and therefore remarked upon by neighbours if Denise should have another relative or friend to stay just a few short weeks after the first had left.

A small café-bar beckoned in a tiny side street on the way to her hotel. The *plat du jour* was a simple but tasty dish of beans and small chunks of bacon. Beans were in good supply most of the time but meat was rare; there was just sufficient bacon to give a little taste to the beans. There was also bread of the 'national' kind.

While Violette ate, she pondered again the danger of staying too long at the hotel. It might be possible, she thought, to find another safe-house. She would mention that tomorrow at lunch with Madame Desvaux.

‡

While she was eating, two German soldiers came in, sat at a neighbouring table and smiled broadly in her direction, trying to catch her eye and engage her in conversation. She ignored them, forcing herself to continue eating even though her stomach clenched tight. Trying not to hurry, she finished her meal and settled her bill using her forged ration cards. She opened the door and walked out, heart thumping, trusting they would not follow her as they were only halfway through their meal. She remembered Denise's advice and quickly pulled the scarf tight round her head and retied the knot under her chin. She walked rapidly and with purpose towards the protection of her hotel room.

What a relief to see her guesthouse at the end of the next street. She would ensconce herself in her room for the evening. She had already stopped at a little *tabac*, bought a magazine, a newspaper and a French historical romance; these fitted her cover as a young commercial secretary and would also help to refresh her idiomatic French. She had also purchased food to eat later that night in her room while reading. She would ask the *patronne* if she could have some fresh coffee brought up during the evening.

As she entered the hotel, she heard herself being called urgently over to the reception desk where Madame Thivier handed over a package that had been delivered for Violette. She surreptiously whispered to Violette to be very careful with all that she was doing and the people she was visiting.

Violette thanked her for her concern assuring her that she was being very careful. Then, as she felt a little drained, she asked for some coffee or hot chocolate to be brought up to her room a little later to which the *patronne* said it would be her pleasure in about half an hour, smiling anxiously as she watched Violette climb the stairs to her room

Violette read the note as she walked along, noticed the word blue and remembered she had asked Denise to use that colour if everything was reasonably safe. That was certainly a good start. She opened the package to find a cardigan with instructions to take it first thing in the morning to the boutique managed by the Monsieur and Madame Sueur. Violette had looked forward to meeting Florentine Sueur who was imprisoned and now it would be her assistant, Lise Valois, whom she saw. Things were slowly moving forward – at last. With luck, the pace could pick up in the next day or so, if she gained the confidence of these two women.

‡

Violette had a hot bath and afterwards stretched out on the bed as the last rays of the setting sun streamed through the window. Madame Thivier brought in a tray of steaming dark chocolate and cake. Violette thanked her, and after the door closed started to read the newspapers, especially the advertisements showing her where and what various businesses there were – boutiques, florists, grocers, garages, cinemas, *cafés-théâtres*, cafés and the plethora of small businesses that towns of any size contain. There were many German and Vichy advertisements and notices warning people about official orders, new regulations and certain goods that would be restricted. She could not help but giggle aloud when she read a German notice ordering the population to use the pavements correctly, that they must walk on the left and pass on the right! Never push past a German – soldier or civilian – but always show deference – under threat of a fine.

For a while, Violette read her historical romance then, concentrating, went over her plans. It was hard to know where to begin. She went over the list of names and activities that she had memorised in London, and the reports and debriefings that she had read and reread. As she considered her meeting with Madame Desvaux she realised she had made a few significant discoveries helpful to piecing together the disintegration of this successful circuit. From Madame Desvaux's account, Isidore had been arrested at her residence. She and Isidore had had an ongoing sentimental and physical relationship up to the time of his arrest. The shock of the arrest had been great and Denise was a very frightened woman. Her actions manifestly showed that she should no longer be trusted. And yet … and yet … Tomorrow would shed more light on Madame Desvaux and the arrest of Isidore. Denise's trustworthiness worried Violette greatly but for now she needed to push it to the back of her mind.

She returned to going over the background information she had received in London. Philippe had been in Rouen since April last year. Philippe and Isidore had over the months met quite openly and frequently, mostly at the Brasserie Marigold in place des Emmurées on the left bank. Since December, Philippe and Bob Maloubier had been on the run from the enemy, along with four other agents from other circuits, putting Henri Déricourt's safe-houses in danger through overuse during the terrible winter weather of 1943. Philippe had been ordered to withdraw; this was probably due to the increasing number of round-ups perpetrated by the Gestapo now that the Germans' attention had been galvanised by the stream of sabotage carried out by his *Salesman* circuit from June 1943. She wondered whether this could be evidence of a much wider net being cast by the Gestapo, not only over SOE circuits but also over de Gaulle's movements and circuits, and those of British SIS (MI6) and others. She would try to discover whether there could be any basis in fact to her conjectures.

Philippe had reported on his return to London that the Germans had made just one attempt to penetrate his circuit but Violette believed it was more likely that they had not only penetrated circuits, including *Salesman*, but also had informers inside the circuits. It would not be possible, Philippe had told her in London, to rely on his contacts in the Rouen police for much longer, although they had been efficient in the past in warning him of arrests in the offing.

She had studied very carefully the garbled message received in London from the *Author* circuit, situated far south of Rouen in the Corrèze, ran by Harry Peulevé, Violette's close friend, under the alias of *Jean*. André Malraux and his FTP[52] group had been in touch with Harry and, although up to this time Malraux had not been too involved in the war, after the death of his half-brother, Roland, an important member of Harry's circuit, he put aside most of his writing and involved himself in what seemed to some French historians as somewhat bizarre ways – for example, in calling himself *Colonel Berger*, when he had no military standing whatsoever. This taking on or bestowing of temporary military titles was not unusual among the many factions, groups and sub-groups of the Maquis and semi-military Résistance in France and, of course, SOE. Philippe was a French journalist and yet held the British temporary rank of major,[53] *Major Charles Staunton*, and Violette was a lieutenant in FANY (ATS). André Malraux was attached to de Gaulle's networks, not SOE's, entrusted with uniting the various factions, of which there were many, under one umbrella – an unenviable task yet essential to prevent the country falling into chaos after liberation. Violette mused that the cells were not all self-contained and contact between them was not perhaps as secure as one would wish.

Over 250 kilometres south of Rouen, the message sent to London from Harry Peulevé's radio set in the Corrèze read, word for word, error for error:

```
TOR 1028     12TH MARCH 1944
BLUFF CHECK OMITTED                 TRUE CHECK OMITTED


73 SEVEN THREE STOP
FOLLOWING NEWS FROM ROUEN STOP XLAUDE MALRAUX DISAPPEARED
BELGIVED ARRESTED BY GESTAPO STOP RADIO OPERATOR PIERRE
ARRESTES STOP IF CLETENT STILL WITH YOU DO NOT SEND HEM STOP
DOFTOR ARRESTES STOP EIGHTEEN TONS ARMS REMOVED BS POLIFE
STOP BELIEVE THIS DUE ARRESTATION OF A SEFTION FHEIF WHO
GAVE ASRESSES ADIEU
```

From this garbled text, Violette, Philippe, Vera Atkins, Maurice Buckmaster, Gerry Morel – Director of Operations from the end of March 1942 to July 1944 – and

---

52 FTP[F] = Francs-Tireurs et Partisans [française] = [French] Partisans and Sharpshooters, the armed section of the French Communist Party. Frequently the final 'F' is excluded, as it is obvious they are French. A partisan is different and not so all-inclusive as a patriot. The first belongs loyally to a specific group while the latter belongs loyally to a specific country.
53 Temporary rank meant usually for the duration of the war.

all those in Baker Street party to the puzzling missive agreed the '73' probably referred to the number of people arrested. Violette would discover that in fact the total was at least ninety-six members of *Salesman*, *Hamlet* and associated Maquis and Résistants. It struck Violette that the message was unmistakably clear in that the doctor they used in the Résistance in that area had also been arrested, and that eighteen tons of weaponry had been removed by the police.

Violette surmised that the 'section chief' could be an important key. Could this refer to Claude Malraux, deputising for Philippe while Philippe was in England, or to Philippe himself? Either way, Violette felt that this just did not feel right. Firstly, Claude was not a 'chief' but a second-in-command; secondly, Philippe had not been questioned and therefore could not have given away any addresses. Thirdly, 'section' meant something different to 'circuit'. There could be several circuits in a section.

Could it refer to a section chief in London, like Bonnington, Buckmaster's second, or 'Buck' himself, heaven forbid? Or perhaps one of de Gaulle's clandestine section chiefs or one of the home grown French organisations? She must remember to add this to her list of things to discover more about. The message went on to insist that *Clément*, one of the Rouen aliases for Philippe, stay away from the area. It did not say why. Why would they want him to stay away? She mulled this over. Either because of danger to himself especially with the 'wanted' posters all over town and those around him or because they feared he may have been careless and therefore in some way had betrayed them, which was highly unlikely.

Violette, knowing a little more about Broni, thought it possible that he relayed Néné this message minutes before being captured. If arrest was seconds away, it would account for inaccurate sending and transmission without due security checks. Baker Street had received this message on 12 March, the day of the arrest and capture of Broni. But the distance …?

It was that message that had inspired the choice of Violette for a solo mission to Rouen and to delay Philippe's return to France until April, travelling with her just as far as Paris. As it was imperative that Philippe not go to Rouen, after considerable discussion, Philippe was adamant Violette be sent instead; untried as she might be, he had complete confidence in her. She would meet and report back to him in Paris at the end of April, having had about three weeks to make discreet inquiries and to deal with other tasks entrusted to her, such as finding out about the launch sites for the German rocket weaponry targeted at England. It would be up to Violette to discover all she could and persuade those left to continue the struggle, dispirited though they might be.

‡

The people she knew she could try to contact were Denise (which she had done), Jean Sueur and his wife Florence. Jean, the manager of Madame Micheline's ladies' boutique, had been Philippe's first contact in Rouen. He had set up a place for Philippe to live and also helped him establish his whole network. Violette would later learn that under the alias *Nénesse*, Jean was an important external member of the *Diables Noirs*. She knew he spent a considerable amount of time liaising with Résistance groups all over the Seine-Maritime. Florence Sueur, his wife and business partner, ran the day-to-day business of the boutique and of the *boîte à lettres* and drop-in-point for members and external members of those groups as well as liaising with British agents.

There was also Hugues Paccaud, saboteur; Georges Philippon (*Jo*), garage owner, main weapons dump for *Salesman* and reception committee leader, and his wife. *Jo*'s friend, Chevallier, ran the secondary dump at his garage. Violette knew there was a very scared insurance man who had insisted that Philippe did not give his name to anyone. Was he the weak link? He had a friend in a local *Mairie*[54] who provided ration cards. A Monsieur Quenot provided information on train movements – where they passed, their speed at any given place and time, etc. Quenot promised full support for railway sabotage before and after D-Day. Now, what was the doctor's name? *Docteur Debos, Deboucq ...?* Before she could remember his name exactly, Violette had fallen into a deep and dreamless sleep.

‡

---

54 *Mairie* = mayor's office; *Hôtel de Ville* = town hall.

10

Madame Desvaux, Lise Valois, the Blue Cardigan

Tuesday 11 April 1944

Madame Denise Desvaux was worried. Violette, whom she knew as *Corinne Leroy*, had left, but that did not lessen the danger to either of them. She was terrified that the young woman had been followed and there would be a knock on the door from the Gestapo[55] or the Milice.

Denise had been shocked when Violette knocked and spoke the coded message that she, trembling, completed. She did not want more trouble; she had already suffered enough. She had lost her husband, her children were cut off from her – safe, she hoped. She had spent a week under arrest and harsh interrogation and today *Pierre* was being deported. Denise tried to help him, even promising to betray *Charles* to the police, should he reappear. She had heard those arresting her mention *Charles* over and over, so she had offered to report him. Had she meant it? She still did not know. But she was struck by Violette's calm courage and took heart from that.

Strengthening her resolve, the first thing to do, she decided, was to have a chat with Lise Valois, the manager of the shop. Since they worked together in the fashion trade, it would seem odd not to go to the boutique and do business with Lise in Florence's absence. Although Jean Sueur ran the business, looking after the financial and sales aspects for the owner, Jeanne Micheline, Florence Sueur, his wife, had always run the shop itself, helping clients with their fashion requirements while he visited Madame Micheline in her Paris shop. Now, of course, since the Sueurs' arrest, Lise Valois had to do everything to keep the business going as best she could. She was an elegant, small woman in her late forties, slim with high cheekbones, and wore her light auburn hair fashionably short.

---

55 SOE's F Section second-in-command, the Scottish accountant, Lieutenant Colonel R.A. Bourne-Patterson, recorded, 'The Gestapo were encouraged to believe that we were unaware of the extent of the penetration, and deliveries of stores were continued to circuits known to be Gestapo-operated, in order to give time for new circuits to establish themselves.' This raises interesting questions the answers to which may have burnt in the 1945 SOE fire.

For all the strictures placed on commerce by the alien occupation and Vichy government, the Sueurs' business was doing very well. Its links to Paris ensured garments would be *le dernier cri* for younger and wealthier women including German women and collaborators. Many of the clothes were designed and often tailored for the Sueurs' boutique by people like Denise Desvaux, who produced garments from the best materials or altered ready-made items. The Sueurs' visits to Paris also proved useful in the clandestine work of the Résistance for contacting other groups and planning combined operations – but it was risky. The Sueurs' contacts were a select group; among them were Tante Evelyn and a friend of hers, Colonel Gentil. The colonel was arrested and died in Dora concentration camp along with his nephew Paul and other friends.

‡

Thoughts and plans scurrying through her mind, Denise collected the two dresses she had completed and folded them carefully over her left arm. She picked up her travelling sewing box and clip purse then slipped quietly out of her apartment, locking the door behind her.

It was a mere ten-minute walk to the fashionable cobbled streets of Rouen *centre-ville*. There were not too many soldiers around, but a number of military vehicles rumbled past, guns pointing ahead. She was used to this and not the least concerned. Denise came to the boutique on rue des Carmes. Entering it, she caught Lise Valois' attention. She told her she had brought along the dresses to be tried on by the clients a little early but wished to have a chat first.

Lise smilingly welcomed her in, wondering what might be up. She told her to go through to the workshop and that she would be with her in a few minutes.'

Denise walked into the workshop and watched the woman and girls working on alterations or restyling garments. About ten minutes later Lise Valois came in, cool and elegant. 'Come into my office, Denise,' she said.

They went in, Lise moving a rose lamé jacket from the visitor's armchair and indicating Denise sit there while she went behind her cluttered desk.

Denise enquired urgently whether they could be overheard. Lise replied not at all but that she, Denise, looked as if the devil were chasing her. Giving her account of the morning Denise described the sudden visit of a young lady from London on behalf of *Charles*.

She said the young woman, under the name of *Corinne Leroy*, wanted to know what had happened, the state of the *Salesman* circuit and what she could do to help the families that were now suffering financial hardship. She also, it seemed to Denise, had instructions from London to pass on to any Résistance group who would listen. Denise was not sure there were any left who wanted or were even capable of listening, never mind helping. She wondered what Lise thought.

Lise, astounded, asked abruptly if Denise believed her to be who she said she was. Denise described how they had spent a few hours together in her apartment and talked of many things and that the young woman had the right password on woollens to start with. The shock was still visible in Denise's face – she had been so frightened. She wanted to know if Lise would help her decide who *Corinne* could talk to who might be able to help.

Lise immediately said she should be the one to meet her after checking that she had had the correct password. She asked Denise to get her to bring in something for repair, thus keeping up the cover of a knitted garment.

Denise had a cardigan that could do with some new buttons. It was blue and fitted the code she and Violette had decided on before she left. Denise explained that Violette had said that any messages should contain blue – not green – if everything seemed safe and orange not red for danger. Denise thought it very clever as did Lise.

After some discussion, it was agreed that Denise would take the blue cardigan straight round to the hotel where Violette was staying and leave a written message that everyone could read if they had a mind to, or she could speak to her openly at reception if Violette was already back at the hotel.

‡

A short while after, Denise returned home to pack the cardigan to leave for Violette. She walked to Violette's hotel, mindful that she could be followed and taking a few basic precautions. At the hotel she greeted the woman at the desk. It was the *patronne*. Good, thought Denise.

She addressed Madame Thivier, asking her to pass on the package for *Mademoiselle Corinne Leroy*, requesting that *Corinne* be given the package before retiring that night. Madame Thivier gave her word, mentioning what a lovely young woman *Corinne* was and enquiring if they were friends.

Madame Desvaux said they were only acquaintances but agreed she seemed nice. She explained that as the young woman wanted a cardigan, she brought one that was in need of some repair work before wearing. A pretty one that and went well with her colouring.

As Denise left, Madame Thivier looked at the note and read it. That *seemed* innocuous enough, she thought to herself. As soon as *la petite* comes in, I'll give it to her. Now, if I'm not mistaken, that woman was arrested by the Gestapo recently and her lodger was imprisoned and then deported to Germany. My young guest must be very careful indeed.

‡

11

En Route to the Boutique, Lise at Le Bristol, Lunch at Chez Denise

Wednesday 12 April 1944

The following morning, Wednesday 12 April, turned out warm and sunny. Violette dressed fairly casually in jumper and skirt, a light and very pale blue blouse underneath, with the collar folded neatly over the jumper. The collar, rimmed with slightly frayed Morlaix lace, had been expertly aged by the tricks of SOE's forgers, working alongside French seamstresses in London – including my grandmother. Tante Marguerite had knitted the beige jumper one year ago as a birthday gift for her sister, Reine who, having put on a little weight, had passed it on to Violette who had thought the colour far too insipid and unfashionable to wear in London but now it truly came into its own as it would certainly not attract attention. The brown A-line skirt came about two inches below her knees. Violette wore white socks and a pair of brown shoes. Around her neck she had tied an inexpensive but pretty cotton scarf, ready to be pulled up over her hair should she feel the need. She wore no makeup except a light touch of lipstick, and her short dark hair was swept back off her face. She looked like the smart but relaxed commercial secretary she was portraying.

Violette had wanted to become a film star, and felt that perhaps she still could fulfil that desire after the war. She had had some fantastic portfolio shots professionally taken that she left with her family in London after giving two signed ones to a friend and an aunt. She had already been an 'extra' in a few movies. The best drama tutors had been co-opted by Baker Street to help SOE's fledgling agents to learn and live undercover personae; Violette had enjoyed every moment of their coaching. Now she saw in the mirror that her face was taking on a wary and slightly drawn quality, not unlike that of other women living and working under enemy occupation. She had also lost a little weight from the frugal meals, cycling and walking since parachuting into the country, and of course the tension of knowing she was now a solitary agent in a dangerous land. She had never expected to be so happy and relieved to look just ordinary and a little tired.

Violette slung her bag over her shoulder. Carefully concealed inside its double linings and false bottom was a fortune in large denomination wartime French francs and her false papers. In her purse she carried a large sum in smaller denomination notes: some forged, some genuine. Although the amount in her purse would be extremely difficult to account for, she had decided to explain it away as money from her Le Havre boss for purchases to be made in Paris that she had not been able to make and now must return the money to him, with, perhaps, a little joke about what she could have done with all that money in Paris. The rest would remain hidden. Or so she hoped.

‡

Breakfast was being served in the dining room as she entered, holding her brown paper package with the cardigan and the note still clearly attached. Sitting at a table by the window was another guest, a commercial traveller selling *vin ordinaire* who was a regular of Madame Thivier. Violette sat at a table near the window facing the door.

Madame Thivier came in to serve breakfast and chattered on about ration difficulties, the latest gossip on arrests and the weather. The food was filling and tasted marvellous. Studiously avoiding glancing at Violette, she commented on a front-page article in the *Journal de Rouen* in which the enemy announced another great coup in capturing many *'terroristes'* in planned simultaneous raids and today they would deport those still alive to forced labour in German factories and munitions plants.

'*Terroristes, mon oeil!*' she muttered, seething. 'They'd done no damage to nor hurt any member of the civilian population, unlike the dirty Boches, the real terrorists!'

The commercial traveller looked down at his plate, nodding half-heartedly. Violette asked for more coffee. A nod and no further dangerous talk rewarded her. Instead, she managed to chat with the guests and *patronne*, gleaning some interesting information. The travelling salesman, discussing the war in general after Madame Thivier's outburst, commented that he was sure the war would be over within twelve months or so, repeating 'whoever wins', thus protecting himself, his family and his firm from unwanted attention.

Violette saw that his remarks reflected the opinion of many in France and further afield. A glimmer of optimism was slipping in, a fillip to those wishing to see the Allies win. She expected that there would now be growing numbers joining the Résistance and the Maquis groups throughout France for the final push to end the tyranny. This she would pass on to London on her return. After chatting on more innocuous subjects; she wished everyone *une très bonne journée* and made her way into the street.

She walked to the Sueurs' shop, taking a circuitous route to make very sure that no one was following her. If she were stopped and asked why she was wandering around, she could say she was just window-shopping before the shops opened so that she would not spend any money. Adding a smile or a tickle of humour nearly always disarms the antagonist. Violette had discovered this long before SOE training school in the ordinary run of life when her strict father was up in arms over some, possibly imagined, wrong doing by his sweet but stubborn daughter.

‡

The exterior of the fashion boutique was immaculate, as were the neighbouring shops. Violette was glad she looked neat and well-dressed even though her clothes were relatively inexpensive. Nothing was war-torn or shabby about these businesses.

This smart and fashionable shop was one of the most successful dead letter drops in France. Jean and Florence Sueur, professional, well known and well liked, were in a position to welcome any person into their environment. A wealthy or not-so-wealthy Résister or giver of valuable information came in under the guise of buying some expensive item. Salesmen and women came with materials for the shop to sell and to do their clandestine business in the back office. Deliverymen drove their vans up to the side door and entered with any number of cartons and boxes containing the usual materials and occasionally other, more clandestine goods. Designers and workers came to the workshop; boyfriends and girlfriends came to meet their partners for lunch or after work. Repairmen and the local press all visited at one time or another. It was an ideal cover for anyone on a secret mission. Violette later discovered that Florence as well as Jean was an external member of the *Diables Noirs*.

She walked into the store and breathed in the expensive air. A bell jangled as she opened the door. A woman looked up and came towards Violette introducing herself as Lise Valois and asking if she was *Corinne Leroy*. Surprised, Violette said that she was while shaking hands and then it occurred to her that it was the package from Madame Desvaux that gave her away. She said softly that she was delighted to meet Lise and, sticking to her cover story, that the package contained a lovely blue cardigan in need of some care and attention.

Lise showed Violette through to the workshop. Violette saw the grey of tiredness in Lise's face, carefully disguised as it was by makeup, but nothing could mask the sadness deep within her eyes. As she directed Violette to her office in the workshop, Lise discreetly observed Violette's unhurried demeanour. A good start, she thought to herself. A young woman of humour and discretion. And wasn't she lovely? She was not tall; they must be about the same height. She was slim without being in the least skinny. She looked slightly athletic and in the best of health, moving easily and lightly. She certainly did not look like an Englishwoman in Lise's eyes.

Lise asked her assistant, Marie, to bring some coffee and biscuits. Marie went off to do her bidding ensuring privacy for the two women. Turning to Violette she asked how she could be of service so Violette went through her cover that Denise Desvaux had delivered the cardigan yesterday evening with a message to pop into the shop first thing in the morning. Denise had pointed out that the buttonholes could be repaired, the torn silk lining changed and new buttons added. Violette was dying to wear it and hoped it could be done soon. Lise replied it could all be done, probably by Friday, before if it were possible.

Violette thought to herself that would be almost halfway through the month. Only sixteen days before she had to rendezvous with Philippe in Luxembourg Gardens in Paris.

Marie came in with a tray of coffee and set it on the table, whispering in Lise's ear as she did so something Violette could not catch about a visitor. It seemed urgent and the girl was clearly agitated. Lise instructed Marie to take the visitor to the back of the workshop. She would speak to him when she finished and when she had checked that Marie had completed her chores for the day, her beau could then spirit her off with her blessing.

Violette, warming to the kind but business-like approach of the woman, immediately got down to the real reason for her visit in that she needed help to discover as much as possible about the events in February and March, what led up to them, and the present situation for the *Salesman* network. She also needed to pass on some instructions that could be further passed to the right people about the Allied invasion, even though she could not tell them exactly where or when the invasion would take place. Violette lastly offered funds to help any of the families who had been caught up in the dreadful nightmare. Her message was brief and to the point.

Lise poured coffee and sat down. To give herself thinking time, she leafed through a few of the papers strewn across her desk, putting them into rough order and then pushing them aside. She was convinced of this girl's integrity and would certainly help. *Corinne* had nothing duplicitous about her; she was controlled and knew what she was about. What would Jean and Florence think? Her employers had been through hell, she knew from her visits to them since their arrest. She had been questioned, too, quite brusquely, but had been unharmed. It was some time since she had last been permitted to visit and she was concerned for them.

At that moment, a young man came bursting in: '*Madame*, I really must speak with you. It is of the utmost urgency.'

'Well, *Corinne*, this is unexpected, but maybe it will go a long way to helping you with all you've told me. Let me introduce you: *Corinne*, this is Lucien, who is a civil servant in the Palais de Justice in Rouen. He and Marie are considering a future together – should this beastly war ever end. But please, tell me, Lucien, what is it? You can speak plainly before *Corinne*. She has been checked out and is bona fide.'

'*Bien, madame*. Isn't it dreadful, *Nénesse* and his wife – I mean, Monsieur and Madame Sueur – are being shipped from Compiègne today to Germany.'

'*Oh, merde, merde, merde!*' The news brought bitter tears to Lise's eyes. 'And I suspect the rest of your news is just as terrible, eh?' Lise tried hard to contain her fear for her employers, but theirs was a friendship that had enlivened twenty years of business. Their imprisonment had been bad enough; their deportation was horrifying.

'Yes, *madame*, I'm afraid so. All the men arrested in February and March are being deported from Compiègne to Germany. Except, of course, for those who have died at the hands of the Gestapo or been shot. I think Broni is still being held. He apparently managed to send a rushed last message to London. Ninety-six people are on the transport, Madame Sueur included, with a number of other women. I'm so sorry, *madame*.'

'Thank you for letting me know so promptly. At least they're still alive. I shall pass this on, as will *Corinne* to London. Now, can you help her further? I think she should meet a group leader at the earliest opportunity, Lucien. You know who I mean. In the first instance, a meeting can take place at Le Tabac near the *Gros Horloge*[56] or at the Gare de Rouen – the sooner the better – and maybe with one of his lieutenants. Meanwhile, *Corinne* and I shall go for a walk while I fill her in on what I know, and see how she can help some of the families of these men. It is part of her mission here to do exactly that and she has the immediate means to do so. That's so, isn't it *Corinne*?'

'Absolutely! Except I'm supposed to have lunch with Denise – in her apartment – at one o'clock,' replied Violette with a brief smile and nod.

'It's just after quarter past ten. We have time to stop for a Viennese coffee in an establishment frequented by German officers and their gals. It'll help for you to be seen with me. After all, I dress most of their womenfolk. Lucien, you come to Madame Desvaux if you get news with regard to meetings.'

He nodded his assent.

'Perfect!' exclaimed Violette. 'By the way, my "reason" for being in Rouen is that I've just arrived and am on my way home to Le Havre after spending Easter in Paris. I've been asked by family to find – or find out what has happened to – an uncle missing in Rouen. So, I really need a bicycle. That's the story I gave to a soldier who inspected my identity papers, so they'll expect that, and that I meet people. A bike would be ideal – can you help me with that, Lucien?'

'Oh, of course! It's difficult to find one that's at least in halfway decent working order these days, but I shall make sure you have one for tomorrow. Where shall we deliver it to?'

'I'm staying at a little hotel, in rue Saint-Romain. Madame Thivier is the *patronne*. She'll be happy to take delivery for me.'

'Perfect. She's a good woman and can be trusted, even though she's not attached to any group. We're thinking of using her as a cutout.[57] I must be off – my office will wonder where I am. I'll mention a little problem with my young lady and that'll keep them quiet!' He laughed as he gestured towards Marie, who turned pink. '*Au revoir à tous!*'

'*Au revoir*,' chorused all in the office and workshop as he strode out into the street.

‡

---

56 *Gros Horloge* is the Rouennais for referring to their town clock. In French it would normally be *grosse horloge*, in the feminine.

57 A cutout is someone who acts temporarily as a courier or delivers messages or other items.

Lise and Violette were left in the office to finish their coffee. It turned out that Lise had, over the years, spent many hours working with and liked Denise Desvaux. While they were chatting, they discussed whether lunch was wise, and Lise felt that the blue cardigan was a perfectly good reason to discuss business over lunch with Denise.

And so it was decided.

‡

It was with a feeling of relief that, for a while, Violette would not have to walk alone in the streets of Rouen. Now about eleven in the morning, Lise and Violette decided to have a coffee in the ground floor café-bar of Le Bristol, which is still on the corner of rue aux Juifs in this quaint and busy area today. Comfortably dim inside, here clandestine meetings took place on a regular basis in the restaurant and in private rooms on the first floor. It was not difficult to find a corner table, where they ordered two *grands crèmes*. Lise felt safer not discussing their clandestine work in the more fashionable cafés which the Germans tended to patronise. They chatted about inconsequential things and then Lise described what had happened around her, saying that they had been having a pretty grim time since Inspector Alie was recruited by Vichy. He had completed a wide ranging roundup from Le Havre to Rouen and surrounding areas. He personally had maltreated a number of men; some died in excruciating pain under torture and, often enough, were summarily shot on his orders. Alie had been most assiduous in his chosen task, particularly two weeks from the end of February to early March. Violette listened, horrified. Jean and Florentine had got wind of what was going on and had tried to persuade Claude Malraux to get away while he could. He refused. Lise, however, had tried to insist that Jean and Florentine disappear but it was already too late. They had been arrested, along with Claude Malraux and Isidore. Roger Mayer, who had led the Le Havre group, had been arrested and beaten to a pulp. He had planned and participated in the derailing of a German troop train. His saboteurs had also blown sky-high the entry gates to a factory that produced U-boat components, thus gaining access for other saboteurs.

The women, including Lise, had also been arrested and spent several nights in prison, been interrogated but not tortured. Florentine had been questioned three times but she gave the impression she was strongly against all Résistance activity because of reprisals. She did not care a whit what they thought she knew; she would not tell them a thing of the very great deal she did know or could surmise, or about the activities she had been involved in.

Lise had helped the Sueurs in all things. Under his cover name of *Nénesse*, Jean Sueur was an essential liaison between the *Diables Noirs* and Claude, in contact with Philippe's *Salesman* circuit. Lise had now taken their place as best she could. Violette understood her sentiments and felt Lise's passion and strength mirrored her own feeling.

She understood from Lise just how people had broken under the strain of arrest and fear. Among those left, many were far too frightened to continue resisting except passively but that there were still quite a few, even in Rouen, who continued the work building up to an invasion by the Allies – more than Philippe might have thought after the disaster of his blown circuit. It was essential to be so very careful to whom one spoke. Lucien from the Palais de Justice was a good man, Lise reported. He had helped them enormously in procuring papers and stamps, having them carefully copied and returning the originals so that nobody was the wiser. As an external member of *Libé-Nord* and *Diables Noirs*, Lucien had a hand in many nefarious activities, causing much damage to the enemy. He had intimated to Lise in an aside earlier on, she had told Violette, that he would willingly act as messenger or guide, if she needed it, to deliver information, instructions or plans and to attend the financial needs of stricken families, or receive intelligence for delivery to London. He was entirely trustworthy, Lise added, after having undergone a number of trials.

Violette asked when she could meet other Maquis members and Résistants and also wanted to know if she could get to Le Havre. She had her full set of perfectly produced false papers for the region stating she was born in that zone and lived in the town as a commercial secretary. Le Havre was one of the most difficult areas to enter as it was in the red zone of the restricted area. German military and naval personnel had flooded into the town. And, of course, the Gestapo, SD and French Milice were constantly on the lookout for those involved in sabotage, clandestine printing and intelligence activities for the Allies.

Violette was happy to have some company at last. She felt the tension easing in pleasant, unhurried surroundings. She carefully studied the barman, the waiter and customers while they surreptitiously looked her over. They knew Lise well, and she chatted to them and introduced Violette as one of her new clients. This coded message told them that Violette was to be trusted and helped, so one or two smiled at her in greeting. The fact the coffee was real was equally a silent welcome, part of the unspoken code of recognition. Violette felt she could turn to the staff if she so needed, but knew too that she had to prove her worth in the first place.

An hour later, after a few *à tout à l'heures*,[58] the two women strolled to rue Jeanne d'Arc with a few detours to shake off anyone who might be interested in their destination.

'You know, *Corinne*, in spite of the privations, women here remain remarkably well-dressed and even elegant.'

'A lot more so than English women, I can assure you!' lamented Violette.

Lise continued, 'My nineteen-year-old niece, Édith, raided the attic and found piles of old clothes. From them, she has made an entire wardrobe, even her own bras (with a little help from me). She makes her own shoes, as do quite a few

---

58 *À tout à l'heure* = 'see you soon'. The phrase was picked up by soldiers, including my grandfather, Violette's father, in the First World War trenches, to be corrupted by many to 'toodleloo'.

women. They buy the wooden soles ready-made and shaped, join them onto uppers made of material, old leather and other leftovers and now wear them as the most fashionable article around! They do look good, too.'

'We put make-up or dye on our legs and then run a pencil line up the back of the calf to look like real silk or nylon stockings,' commented Violette.

'Oh, yes, we do that here too. And the son of a friend of mine found an abandoned pair of British soldier's boots. He repaired them with bits of canvas and leather. He's still wearing them. Amazing really! How quickly we become scavengers. And yet scavenging with style, I'd say!'

They both laughed, enjoying one another's tales. It helped Lise to put aside for a while the dreadful plight of her employers. She did not want to talk about them for she was sure she would burst into tears, and she wanted to keep her composure in front of this brave British agent.

They picked their way through an area of ruin and rubble, stopping to watch a teenager digging furiously with his hands in the debris. Finally, he triumphantly held high a box of tools to show his two pals, then went back to scrabbling, hoping to find more treasure. Suddenly Lise nearly fell and grabbed Violette's proffered arm. Looking to see what had tripped her, they saw an arm bone, almost fleshless, its stiff fingers pointing along the ground. The lad must have dislodged it while digging. He studiously ignored it, and them. They both grimaced and walked on.

In the next square, a girl was bent over her upturned bicycle next to a German marine, replacing the chain. Violette thought how strange it was to see a peaceful co-operative scene of occupier and occupied while just around the corner some black outfitted officer was pushing and shouting at someone.

‡

They arrived at Denise's apartment building and climbed the stairs. Lise knocked, and immediately Denise opened the door and ushered them in with a smile of surprise to see Lise accompanying Violette.

'I see you've brought my dear friend to join us, *Corinne*. Thank goodness I managed to get an extra baguette. After our conversation yesterday, I went to Micheline's and we made the plan with the cardigan. It seems that I made the right decision for once. You couldn't find a better person than Lise to help you.'

'Glad to help in any way,' smiled Lise, pleasant and charming. She took a large pot of pâté from her handbag and presented to Denise who thanked her. Lise looked exactly what she was: the manager of a ladies' fashion store; elegant and worldly wise. As she walked in, she put her gloves and purse on the hall table. 'We shall have a good discussion, the three of us, *Corinne*, on how we can assist you.'

'You have already been so kind, Lise, and you too Denise when I knocked on your door so unexpectedly,' replied Violette quietly. 'I'm truly delighted to have met you both. I had heard so much of the help that you've given to my friends over the last year. *Clément*, or as you may know him, *Charles*, asked me to tell you that I will do anything I can to help you. He is particularly concerned about the families: should any of them find themselves in difficulty – financial or otherwise – I am in a position, and very much wish, to help.'

Lise updated Denise with what Lucien had told her of the Sueurs. Before Denise could comment, she insisted they move into the kitchen, where they could discuss things while Denise put the final touches to the meal. The two women clearly had a good relationship – socially and commercially.

Since their beloved Normandy had been occupied by the enemy, through the Sueurs' Micheline fashion store, Lise and Denise, along with Jean and Florentine, had been serving the German military male and female staff, wives, fiancées and mistresses at highly inflated prices while serving the Allied cause through their clandestine activities. The occupiers' edict was that German marks must be accepted, which was not popular with French businesses, but it was very easy to inflate the prices by two or three times when the enemy wanted nothing more than to impress the woman beside him.

'I'm sure you would like to share a bottle of a very special wine I've been keeping for the right occasion. I can't think of a better moment, can you?' Receiving affirmative smiles, Denise asked Lise if she would open it. 'We should be eating in the dining room. I don't know what the world's coming too,' she laughed as she took the bottle and poured deep red burgundy into lead-crystal glasses.

'*Charles* proved to be an exceptionally careful man and set up excellent networks before the terrible events of November of last year. He's had great success but now all that has changed – very much for the worse, I'm afraid. Of the hundred or so members in the Rouen group alone, only a handful remain,' explained Lise.

Violette said, 'I do hope Lucien can provide me with a bicycle as I need to get around much more quickly to meet your Résistants.' Laughingly, she explained: 'I'm already suffering from blisters from all the walking I've done in the last few days over cobblestones. I don't want to use the tramways too much nor taxis, of course, but walking everywhere on foot is so slow and I think I'd be much less noticeable with a bike, don't you?'

The two women nodded.

Violette continued, 'It's important I meet a few people in this zone, discover more precisely what's happened and who's been arrested, who's still free and willing to continue. And there was a *garagiste* …'

'That cannot be so easily arranged,' remarked Lise drily. 'You see, he has been shot, as has his friend, our other garage owner, Chevallier.'

'Yes, I *do* know that,' interjected Violette. 'But the remaining stores and plans …?'

'Perhaps it would be useful if you accompany me to the garage that Georges Philippon owned in rue des Abattoirs. It's unbelievable that he's been executed.' Tears welled unbidden. Lise blew her nose and continued, 'It's also a huge blow, as *Jo* was not only the main dump for weapons in Rouen but also the leader of one of the principal reception committees.'

Lise and Denise went on to explain what they understood to have happened. They were a little unsure here and there of exact names or field names, but generally they went back over the ground Violette had already covered over the last two days and gave her as much detail as she could possibly absorb in one sitting. She was now forming a much clearer picture of the events over the last six months.

'So there must have been a serious betrayal, don't you think?' interrupted Violette. The two women looked at one another, embarrassed. But Violette continued, 'I believe this is linked to other groups that have been blown in the south and further to the north. My feeling is that it started much further up the chain of command. But I can't imagine where. What do you think?'

'It's certainly possible,' remarked Denise, relieved that she wasn't being targeted.

'Well, you've undoubtedly understood the situation quickly. I've heard some things, but first we'll fill you in on our specific network, *Charles's Salesman* circuit,' cut in Lise. She gave a quick review of the situation, with Denise filling in where she was able.

It turned out that Georges Philippon (*Jo*) had been another external and much valued member of the very successful Maquis group that had worked so hard behind the scenes for Philippe. For security reasons, Philippe did not wish to know personally too many of the Maquisards who undertook some of the activities he had planned with Bob Maloubier (*Robert Mortier*). Bob was involved in training members of the Maquis, some of whom passed the training on to other members and groups.

Without the work of these two SOE agents, the *Diables Noirs*, a highly effective Maquis group, and affiliated groups would not have received nearly as much material or medical supplies. The Maquis were now hidden in a huge manmade cave and many of them would have died of starvation and illness – especially when there had been a deadly outbreak of diphtheria in the huge underground cave. So, in return for the help and very quietly, through intermediaries and cutouts, they had helped carry out most of Philippe's sabotage activities in Rouen and Le Havre as well as collecting much military intelligence and items such as coupons, identity papers and *zone interdite* passes. Without the work of the *Diables Noirs* and affiliated groups, SOE and Philippe would not have had the success they had.

'I was pretty sure,' interjected Violette, although no direct mention had been made of the *Diables Noirs*, 'there were more involved than those within the confines of *Charles's Salesman* circuit. Monsieur Philippon had a large cache of arms, mostly dropped from American and British aircraft over the last few months, but I do realise some members of the Maquis are complaining that they've had no supplies for some considerable—'

'Quite,' cut in Lise sharply. 'The problem is keeping the weapons out of the hands of young chaps who start running amok, thinking they're winning the war all by themselves. Georges kept a tight hold on his depot of weapons and other supplies. He had been waiting for directions from London via agents like you.'

'It will be vital,' Violette explained, 'to find two more secure dumps because, as the invasion is imminent, the British are impatient to send over much larger supplies of weapons so the Résistance movement is well armed and can prepare the ground by disrupting the enemy in every possible way. There're viaducts, railway lines, telegraph and telephone lines to be destroyed as well as enemy fuel dumps, food supplies – all possible lines of communication.'

'Let's eat!' declared Denise, amazed that things might start moving fast indeed and trying to lighten the mood a little. As they settled down to the meal, she told them with rare gaiety that as the meat ration was so small, everyone said it could easily be wrapped in a Métro ticket! However, from the farms around Ry she had found some black market sausage and put some sliced *saucisses* into the pie to give it more flavour. She explained to Violette that Ry is about thirty kilometres from Rouen, on the way to Amiens.

Lise thought the meal was superb and did not know how Denise could manage so well on the rations saying that she must be one of the best *débrouillardes* around. She said she had heard that the greatest victory the Germans had achieved so far is getting the French to eat swede. But they were a good substitute for potatoes if needs must. Denise smilingly exclaimed that, awful as they were, they might even get a taste for them as they all laughed.

They chatted more generally over lunch. Denise shared some of the tips women used to create meals in these hard times of short rations. Although farming country with plentiful produce, Normandy had most of its output requisitioned by the Germans to feed the local troops or to send by rail and truck to Germany. *Bien entendu*, the best went to Hitler, Himmler and the rest of the Nazi Party elite.

Violette half-listened while considering all she had heard: places, names and activities. She could write down some of what she was hearing on rice paper to be sewn into one of her garments. She did not want to make notes in front of these two women as it would affect her own competence in their eyes. She needed to remember it all as accurately as possible, perhaps just write down a few words using her own code to refresh her memory. In debriefings in London they could extract significant yet small and forgotten details by having agents recounting their activities ad nauseam, writing it all down, going over it again and gently – or sometimes not quite so gently – teasing out little details that could have large import.

‡

As the afternoon drew on, Violette produced her promised gift to Denise of a bag of coffee beans. The aroma as Denise used the coffee grinder brought sighs and smiles.

Lise groaned at the wonderful aroma and asked where on earth did it come from to which Violette quipped, laughing lightly at their evident pleasure, that it was not exactly the back of a lorry, but a hole in something a little higher in the air. She added she had a bag for Lise, too.

They all enjoyed the coffee while they relaxed and chatted about the general state of affairs, their views on the Allies, and the occupation itself.

As it approached four o'clock, Violette decided to take her leave first. The conversations over lunch and coffee – although not always directly connected to her mission – had given her much on which to reflect. She now had confirmation of the arrest of a few others, but still no names of those at liberty. Did they distrust her? Or, more probably, they were preventing her betraying anyone if she was caught. A sobering thought.

Violette thanked Denise for the lovely meal and afternoon which had been informative and relaxing. She turned to Lise saying she was looking forward to the visit to the garage asking when and where they should meet and if there was anything specific that she should do.

Lise replied that she would meet Violette at the station, Gare de Saint-Sever, the next morning at eleven o'clock. She wanted to drop into the store first thing to make sure everything was fine and complete a design for an evening dress. She mentioned that there would be an arrival of a train full of *permissionnaires*, soldiers returning from leave in Paris. Even if the train were late the platform would be crowded. There would be other soldiers on leave or secondment for Le Havre as well as the usual business and commercial travellers. A relatively safe place to meet. To which Violette agreed.

Turning to Denise and then to Lise, Violette said with great formality and a broad smile thanking them both most sincerely for everything that they were doing and that their courage was an inspiration to her. Denise smiled back saying it was a pleasure and that Violette should not hesitate to visit here if she needed anything at all. She smiled kindly and opened the door, quickly glancing along the hall to check everything was safe for Violette to leave.

‡

Violette left and Lise turned to Denise expressing how impressed she was by *Corinne*. She was well informed, modest and intent on ensuring the orders she had been entrusted with were passed on and acted upon. She was also fun to be with.

Denise was of the same opinion saying that she had courage, too, and *sang froid* in abundance judging from what she had told her so far. Level headed, cautious and able to think through a problem and make good suggestions, added Denise who then said how she had refused her offer to stay at her house and that her reasoning was faultless, which was that Denise had already had *Pierre* with her who had now been arrested and deported. Denise said that Violette considered that if she, Denise, had another person staying so soon afterwards it would be looked upon with considerable curiosity. Denise was delighted by her but also afraid for her.

‡

12

Back to the Hotel, Arrest, Palais de Justice

Around four o'clock, Wednesday 12 April 1944

Violette had some time to spare before the curfew at sunset. She needed to be off the streets and back in the hotel no later than seven thirty at night. Back in London, Buckmaster had handed her maps of Rouen and Le Havre, saying that bomb damage might make recognition of the streets difficult. Now, as she walked down to the quay, she could lay her mental image of the maps over the destroyed areas she saw before her. Some of the medieval winding streets had disappeared. She had also memorised geographical and topographical features in Normandy, Rouen to Le Havre and from Paris to the Belgian border, recalling her annual journeys to and from Tante Marguerite, criss-crossing Pas-de-Calais, Picardy and Nord, as well as her school days at Noyelles-sur-Mer.

She strolled down to the Quai de Corneille to examine the temporary bridges spanning the river and the various boats and barges moored along the banks. She counted the German patrol boats, barges carrying all manner of industrial equipment and how many bargemen she could see. Violette also tried to assess the weaponry on the patrol boats and other vessels commandeered by the enemy. Her SOE training in Paul Emile's classes included recognition of German uniforms, stripes, insignia, medals and weaponry. Among the activity on the river, she attempted to differentiate military from civilian.

As she ambled along, she noticed a group of German soldiers on bicycle patrol lounging about along the wall of the *quai*, their bikes lying against it or propped at the kerb with packs strapped on the back, helmets slung from the handlebars. The soldiers wore peaked cloth caps and satchels. Peaceful, thought Violette, mostly young and enjoying a break in the late afternoon sunshine. Civilians passed by, ignoring the soldiers. One or two greeted them, then she saw a couple of young urchins running by, spitting in the soldiers' direction, shouting obscenities, laughing wildly at the Germans and quickly skipping across the road to disappear into the labyrinth of lanes; an indication to Violette that the people of Rouen were fiercely resentful of the enemy occupier.

The rural people had all along been vehemently opposed to the occupation of their territory. Townspeople are always more inscrutable, but as Violette had been discovering, the people of Rouen bitterly hated the restrictions on their freedoms, the hunger and other privations, the bombings and the resultant loss of life, dreadful injuries, loss of home and possessions. The STO added to this resentment. She should pass on to London the citizens' present mood as well as her other intelligence. She would try to get a message back to London within the next twenty-four hours. If that proved impossible, it would have to wait until her return to England, but that was not for another couple of weeks. She still had so much to do.

Violette decided not to tempt fate by walking past the patrol. She crossed the avenue to go towards the cathedral instead. On reaching Place de la Cathédrale, she was blocked from crossing the square by a soldier. He was not interested in her papers or herself. His task was to stop people entering the square. She wondered why but did not mind the forced pause. It gave her a chance to rest her aching feet and quietly look around on the pretext of admiring the cathedral. As she looked up at the spire, she heard, then saw, singing German soldiers marching onto the square from the rue des Carmes on the other side. Though these soldiers were the enemy, the richness of their singing was moving.

As they reached the square, and on a single note, the soldiers stopped their chant, halted. Their officer saluted the cathedral. The soldiers marched on. As the last soldier marched from the square, their song soared through the streets once again. How curious – moving, yet comical. Violette heard a giggle from a second-floor window of the corner house. She saw a bemused child burst into laughter over the serious antics of the cathedral-saluting officer and his singing soldiers.

She walked on, a smile lingering. There were German signs, sometimes all haphazardly collected on a single post. As she passed, intent on working out their meaning, a French Milicien tapped her on the shoulder and asked to see her papers.

‡

Rigid with surprise, she handed over her fake identity papers. The Milicien slowly looked them over. Although forged, the papers had come straight from the Le Havre printers who printed local Le Havre and Rouen identity papers, ration cards (*cartes d'alimentation*) and accompanying coloured stamps (*tickets*[59]), passes (*Ausweise*, or in French, *laissez passer*) that were strictly allocated by the German authorities. She knew they were perfect. Résistance or Maquis groups would regularly steal wads of them from various printers scattered along the French Atlantic Wall. That's where she remembered the name Wolf from! Wolf Printers had supplied many of the documents. A large batch had been secreted out by Lysander in early March. They had been stolen by a Le Havrais friend of one of the local Résistants in the *Diables Noirs*. They were therefore up to date, including minor modifications in

---

59 Typically, the French here are using the English word, *tickets*; while in England the French word *coupons* was used.

German and French and also bore current stamps. These small differences were implemented by the Germans to ensure rigorous security. In England, *zone interdite* identity cards and passes were filled in by hand with the agents' cover names by French or German-speaking people from Alsace with distinctive French or German handwriting.

Papers had to be carried at all times. An inquisitive Milicien gendarme or civil servant (*fonctionnaire*) could demand their production on the spot.

‡

The Milice, always extreme right, and the Maquis, often extreme left, were closely entwined in the fight for France in a series of harsh encounters that continued up to and well after D-Day. The Milice, cruel, collaborating and uncompromising, envied the local support the Maquis had. Furthermore, the Milice were poorly equipped even to the point of being ordered by the German authorities to stuff their pistol holsters with paper; this applied even to inner-circle salaried Miliciens due to a German natural reluctance to arm *any* Frenchman.

The Maquis also had to exist from 1941 to early 1944 with little or no armaments and poor or limited training. But this changed from March 1944 through to the end of the war when the Allies began supplying the Résistance, and thus the Maquis, in earnest. This included huge quantities of weaponry, money and other supplies as well as agents, wireless operators and liaison officers like Violette and Isidore Newman, in addition to sabotage, reception committee and weaponry instructors like Bob Maloubier.

‡

'*Venez avec moi!*' barked the Milicien.

'*Mais pourquoi, monsieur?*' No reply, so she followed the Milicien, wondering how she should react. Heart beating uncontrollably, she quickened her pace to come alongside him. '*Monsieur*, I find your insistence somewhat troubling, not knowing why you wish me to follow you,' she said evenly.

'There are questions concerning you that require answering, *mademoiselle*, as you are not in possession of a *permis de séjour*,' he replied as they walked to the Palais de Justice.

At least he isn't taking me to the Donjon or Gestapo headquarters, Violette thought to herself, as she hurried painfully beside him. Her feet were killing her. Not that the Palais de Justice would be much better. Milice and Gestapo have administrative bureaux there and neither are soft interrogators. I hope he doesn't take me down to the basement. I'd be in trouble. Probably taken out and shot at the Stand aux Fusillés.

As she walked beside the Milicien Violette thought: How will I hold up if they take me to the basement in the Palais? I already know far too much, including names and addresses. I should have kept my 'L' pill.[60] I understand now why many accept it. But after my training I've got an idea how determined I can be to keep silent if need be. Like Joan of Arc, I'll keep reminding myself, 'We'll get them!' Her knees felt like rubber and the palms of her hands were clammy.

At the Palais de Justice, the Milicien ordered her to sit on a hard-backed wooden chair in the main hall while he went to his superior's office. The floor was wood, the wall panelling stretching down both sides was wood and the chairs were wood – all honey-brown and highly polished. She waited two hours. Functionaries hurried back and forth, heads bent forward – clearly on serious business. Doors opened and closed quietly or occasionally slammed. All was subdued but intense activity. Violette watched, sitting quietly on her wooden chair against a wooden wall. At least her feet weren't hurting. She used the time to review her story and felt it was watertight. There were a number of directions she could take it, depending on their questions. She was trained to expect the long wait, knew it was part of the softening-up process. She was beginning to feel weary, bored and sick in the stomach at the thought of what might lie ahead.

Violette suddenly realised this was where Lucien worked. And now she understood Philippe's report that referred to a helper of great importance in the Palais de Justice. There was no sign of him, though. The huge building had a plethora of offices, hallways, staircases, lifts. She hoped he would not appear. He could do nothing to help her and she was fairly confident she was in a good position to be released soon. Fingers crossed.

Finally, a young, very erect, smartly uniformed woman ushered Violette into the captain's office. There were two low-ranking Miliciens present, plus the one who had arrested her. The young military woman sat primly to take notes.

Holding herself modestly erect, seemingly serene, Violette waited for the captain behind the large ornate desk to look up and speak. A framed photo-portrait of Pétain and Hitler hung on the wall. She clasped her fingers in front of her, thinking it unwise to appear too calm. In truth, she was feeling anything but calm. She was a simple secretary, her papers said, and she must act that part. Not difficult; she felt small and minor in the opulence of the office. She took a deep breath to steady herself – it helped. She was not entirely play-acting. Fear dried her mouth.

The captain had her papers arranged in front of him.

'Your name, *mademoiselle*?'

'*Corinne Leroy.*'

'Address?'

---

60 The 'L' pill was the lethal cyanide pill that all agents were offered so, if they were caught and tortured, they could end the horror and prevent themselves from talking by cracking it in their mouth. Death was but a few seconds away.

'7, rue Thiers, Le Havre.'

'What are you doing here in Rouen?'

'I've been asked to look for a relative who might be here, whilst on my way back from visiting family in Paris for Easter.'

'My officer has noted that you do not have the requisite *permis de séjour*, but you do not live here.'

'Yes, that's true.'

'*Pourquoi?*'

'I have not been to register, having just arrived. I haven't visited here for years, since I was a teenager, in fact, and it's a lovely old town. But what a lot of damage! I am happy to register now.'

'Wise,' was the gruff response. 'But it doesn't account for what you have been doing, *mademoiselle*.'

'That's true, *monsieur*. I am appalled by the devastation. The British have really caused havoc here, haven't they? It's such a pity. I'm trying to find where I might hire a bicycle. And I wanted a cardigan repaired, a lovely pale blue cardigan, and the dress shop is going to do that for me.'

'Why have you been asked to look for a relative here in Rouen?'

'Because his family is worried about him. He hasn't been heard of since coming here a few months ago. They're afraid he may have died or been injured in a bombing raid. Maybe you could help me?'

'Go to the Town Hall. That's where the lost or missing persons' office is. For the moment I have no further questions, *mademoiselle*. You may go. Before you leave, register your address in Rouen to the young lady here, along with the name of your relative. She will stamp your *permis de séjour*. Should we hear any news regarding him, we can contact you.'

'*Merci, monsieur*,' She went over to the secretary, gave her the name of the hotel and the name of her invented uncle. She turned to go.

The captain raised his head. '*Un instant*, you've forgotten your ID. Go quickly now, so you can be off the streets before curfew.' He handed the papers over. She noticed how soft his hand was. Her own hand was trembling as she held it out to take the documents.

As the door closed behind her the captain looked at the others and said that he thought the Milicien had perhaps been a little overzealous in bringing that young woman in. She was clearly afraid, and there was no deviousness in her manner. She seemed just a little naive. However, he ordered her name and addresses to be kept on file.

‡

The relief nearly overwhelmed Violette as she walked back down the hall to the entrance. The door seemed a mile away at the end of her sudden tunnel vision.

She felt faint, her knees weak. Sweat trickled down her neck. All she wanted was to get out of there as fast as her trembling legs could carry her. But she must not rush; take time, head held high but no show of arrogance. She hoped her fear was not too patently obvious.

At last she reached the open air, took a deep breath and walked in the direction of her hotel. It was going on for seven o'clock and light was fading fast. Along the way, in a little patisserie, she bought herself a *crêpe* and a small *tarte aux pommes* and asked for them to be wrapped so she could take them to her room.

Violette felt exhausted. It was getting too close to curfew for comfort. There was barely any traffic and, as dusk drew in, the streets took on a sinister air. She desperately wanted the safety of her room and a cup of hot chocolate; she hoped Madame Thivier would make one for her.

Arriving at reception, she rang the bell. When Madame Thivier appeared, Violette asked if she would be kind enough to make her a cup of hot chocolate. Madame Thivier looked at the young women, noticing the deep lines of anxiety on her sweet face, damp hair and the residue of sweat on her upper lip. Her heart went out to her. Making no comment, she told Violette she would bring it to her room in about half an hour, giving Violette time to freshen up and relax.

Luxuriating in yet another bath, Violette went over the arrest and brief interrogation. She reviewed her day with the two women, deciding it had been successful. She mulled over the details she had been told and those half-whispered between the two women just after she had arrived regarding her bona fides and the news confirmed by Lucien.

Feeling cleansed and relaxed, fear having vanished in the warmth and afterglow of the hot bath, she dried off and went to her room, where she found a jug of steaming hot chocolate and a plate of chocolate-coated biscuits. What a luxury and how very kind of Madame Thivier.

Making coded notes on her rice paper, Violette ate her *patisseries*, slowly drinking the delicious chocolate. She saved the buttery French chocolate biscuits for another time.

Violette got into bed feeling much better and, to stop herself having a sleepless night of reliving the frightening episode with the Milice, she settled down to read until she fell asleep.

‡

13

Teenager, Philippe, Lise, Marcel, Lucien, Posters

Thursday 13 April 1944

The next morning, Violette felt fully restored after a good night's sleep. It's Thursday 13 April, she thought as she ate her breakfast; I've already spent nearly three days here in Rouen. There's so much I have to do and I've hardly made a dent. I've talked socially with German officers on the train, been questioned by Germans in the street, dragged off to the Palais de Justice by the French Milice for questioning, passed the time of day with ordinary German soldiers and French people, probably including some *collabos*. At least I've met Denise Desvaux, Lucien and Lise Valois, who will take me to meet someone who was close to Georges Philippon. He might be someone I can do something more concrete with than just meeting and talking. Although, I must admit, meeting Denise, Lise and Lucien has led directly to this, and I've learned a damned lot that should stand me in good stead, I should probably only stay in this hotel for a few days more.

She pondered over what to do with the money she held. Violette knew that it would raise serious questions if large numbers of high denomination franc notes were found in her possession. On the other hand, they were well hidden in the linings of her jacket and bag, as well as in her belt. Both had easy-to-split double linings that could be quickly resewn so she could transfer the notes from the bag into the jacket lining. Once she handed them out, whoever received them could take these counterfeit notes to a friendly bank manager to break down into manageable, smaller denominations of real money.

‡

A neatly dressed boy of about thirteen came running and panting into the hotel reception. The *patronne*'s grey eyes twinkled as she asked him what he was doing in here. The lad politely asked if he could talk to *Mademoiselle Leroy*.

Madame Thivier directed him to the dining room, wondering what it could be about and knowing somehow that it was not conducive to good relations with the enemy. The girl, *Corinne Leroy* as she called herself, was certainly mixed up in something. It might rebound on her and her hotel, but Madame Thivier didn't care a rap. She would try to protect the girl as far as she could.

The boy approached Violette as she sat near the window, looking at the people walking by.

'*Mademoiselle Leroy*?' he asked her.

'*Oui?*' she affirmed, puzzled. What could this teenager want? Perhaps he came on behalf of Denise or Lise. 'Have a seat. *Comment t'appelles-tu?*'

'Martin.' He replied seriously. '*Charles* asked me to tell you he's waiting for you at Le Tabac under the *Gros Horloge*. He's there now and he'll stay there today till you arrive. He told me to say you don't need to give me anything 'cos he's already done it.'

'Well, thank you very much. Off you go now. Shouldn't you be going to school?'

'I'm going now. I hate the dirty Boches, so when I can do something I do. At the start of the year they confiscated me bike. Me an' me friend were just about to go over the bridge to the *rive droite*, to rue Louis Ricard. The Germans stopped us and pinched our bikes. We 'ad to walk to school. That really got up our noses and when we're a bit older if they're still 'ere, we're joining the Résistance properly so we can sabotage their transport. Till then, we both do little things like passing on messages. You see we look very innocent, don't we?' All this he said in a quiet quick voice so the other people breakfasting did not hear what he was saying. They simply saw a happy, well-behaved lad of about thirteen talking to a pretty woman.

'Yes, you do look very innocent. It's really very brave of you. You will make a fine Résister one day. But if you get caught, you and your parents would be in dreadful trouble. So be very, very careful. And thank you.'

'Me dad's already involved. Me eldest brother was taken to Germany as forced labour. Me dad works on the rocket construction. Well, that's what we all think it is. He often puts stuff in the concrete to mess it up. Usually bits of iron. *Au revoir*.' And off he went with the happy grin of a job well done.

Violette finished her breakfast as fast as she could, trying not to look rushed, thinking she must persuade Philippe not to stay in Rouen. Stupid fool. It was so bloody dangerous for him. There were posters with a price on his head – she had seen two yesterday – and the Germans were getting nastier by the day. She wondered what brought him here. Didn't he trust her to do the job properly or had some emergency cropped up?

She collected her coat, scarf and bag, and she waved a cheerful goodbye to the *patronne* as she headed for the door.

As she was leaving, Madame Thivier informed her that a bicycle had been delivered for her by a young woman. Violette thanked her eagerly and wished her *bonne journée*.

‡

She found the bike in the yard and started pedalling slowly towards the cathedral rue du Gros Horloge. Violette praised the group's attention to detail in delivering the bike. A girl pushing a girl's bike would not be noticed at all. A man doing so just might be hauled in for questioning or, at least, noted.

Even over the cobbles it felt a damned sight more comfortable to cycle than walk – and so much faster than on two blistered feet. She had noticed the little café-cum-tobacco shop Le Tabac when she had wandered down here before. Approaching it as if she had known it all her life, Violette parked her bike down the alley on the left where she could just see the edge of the rear wheel. Philippe was sitting outside at a tiny table just near the door, sipping a demitasse of coffee. He smiled and waved to her.

'*Bonjour Corinne, comment ça va, ma chère?*'

'*Très bien, Charles, et toi?*'

'*Pas trop mal,*' he smiled wanly and pulled out the other chair for her. He looked tired and drawn and was clearly on tenterhooks. In turn he saw a few tense lines of worry around her eyes and mouth that weren't there in Paris. She had lost some weight too, which wasn't at all unusual in their line of work, he reflected. 'Had a bit of a hard time, have you, *Corinne?*'

'Not really, *Charles*, but I have been hauled before a captain of the Milice at the Palais de Justice. Didn't like that very much, I must say. Apart from that it's not been too bad, really. I've met Madame Desvaux, Lise Valois, Lucien, and later this morning I might be meeting a friend of his and, as you can see, they've found me a bike.'

Violette gave him a full report of her meetings and observations while setting out her plans for the next day or so. She added that she'd seen posters of him around the town, joking that she would not need to find a wireless operator, nor pigeon, because she had Philippe as her stool pigeon. He looked just like one of them. He grunted, then laughed. She felt a bit guilty but the thought tickled her. She also described the increasingly severe and vengeful German mood, as well as the increase in Gestapo and Milicien men stomping around the streets of the town, enquiring into everything and everyone. Violette explained that people here were really frightened after so many had been taken, as well as everything she had seen on the river. She told him everything she knew about the fate of members of the *Salesman* circuit, and the ideas she was forming about betrayal coming initially from a higher source, perhaps from the Organisation civile et militaire (OCM).[61] She asked him to tell her the names of as many as he knew and their structure, which he did.

'*Charles*, it's far too dangerous for you to stay here, even if the posters hardly look like you, and even though I'm pretty sure Denise Desvaux would not inform them

---

61 The Organisation civile et militaire (Civil and Military Organisation) had the remit to bring together under one central authority all the disparate Résistance, Maquis and military groups.

that you're here if she knew. I'm getting on with the task quite well, as you can see. I still have another ten days or so. I know the news is very bad, with so many having been captured and either shot or deported, but I also know that there are a good number who will fight with all their being and, with perseverance, we'll jolly well get them to prepare the ground for the invasion.'

As they talked, she watched the Rouennais bustling past. This area of the town had been quite untouched. It was good to see Philippe laugh outright to see a young boy stick his tongue out at a passing Gestapo officer in his black uniform. Violette smiled too, but continued soberly, 'We need to get more weapons to them and I'll check out the drop-zones today or tomorrow. Although many are too scared now, there're still a lot of people in various Résistance groups willing to have a go. I think the fact that I'm female, and not too bad looking, and that I've come over the Channel helps because the men feel obliged – at least in part. And that I've got family here too, although of course I don't mention who and where. I'm sure being French helps you a lot in France.'

'You're right there. Okay, *Corinne*. You've done remarkably well so far. I have complete trust in you. And I'll leave, as I'll only be a danger to you and all our contacts here. I've got a few things to do today and we'll meet this evening at six o'clock in Place des Emmurées at the Brasserie Marigold. Unless you've already planned something else? How does that sound? As you know, I don't like meeting and planning in cafés. An evening off, if you will.'

'That sounds great. See you at six. Look after yourself, *mon chef.*' She got up, smiled and pulled her scarf back on.

'You too, *mademoiselle,*' smiled Philippe. He was absolutely amazed at what she had achieved in just a few days.

‡

It was only just after ten o'clock and her appointment at the station wasn't until half past eleven that morning, so Violette cycled slowly along rue Grand Pont where German shelling and Allied bombing had damaged or destroyed most of the street. Most of the bombing had taken place in 1940 and 1941 and since then the town had been somewhat tidied up. Men and women of the Défense Passive, the equivalent of the air raid wardens in London, were still clearing up and helping people find a few meagre possessions among their damaged houses. They were also responsible for setting up air raid shelters in the cellars of hotels, large houses, official buildings and some restaurants.

As Violette cycled along she saw a young man of perhaps eighteen. His mate shouted '*Michel, regarde-là, les Chleus!*',[62] at which Michel turned to look insolently at a pair of German officers. He pushed past them, hustling one of the Germans off

---

62 *Chleus* = pejorative for a German during the Second World War.

the pavement. The other officer came straight back and gave him a terrific punch in the face and, fortunately for the lad, they both walked on. Shocked at the violence, a shudder coursed through Violette's body. It further hardened her resolve to be very, very careful. Michel's friend rushed over, helped him stem the flow of blood, then put his arm under his friend's armpit, yanking him to his feet as they stumbled off to find some first aid.

Violette had been checking if she were being followed. So far, it seemed not. She got off her bike to check in the reflection in the window of a shoe shop while she looked at the shoes on display. Two Milice walking towards her. Fearful of another encounter, she studied all the shoes then walked into the shop. After enquiring about one of the pairs in the window, trying and rejecting them, she left the shop and got back on her bike. She turned left and left again, back to where she had come from, when she rode straight into a German patrol. These soldiers were bullying and pushing pedestrians to walk on the right side of the pavements, gesticulating towards a large unsightly notice that ordered pedestrians to walk on the right in the manner of motorised traffic being driven on the right. Violette rode along carefully to avoid attracting attention. It was decidedly difficult to keep a straight face at this comic Teutonic display of orderliness and procedure.

She was heading towards Quai Corneille, over the bridge and to her meeting with Lise Valois. In rue de la République, another squad of soldiers was checking that pedestrians crossed the road only at the junctions. Violette made a sensible detour while smiling broadly at the enemy's antics.

‡

She finally arrived at the station at twenty-five past eleven. Leaving her bike in the designated area and tightening her scarf under her chin, she walked over to the station entrance. Crowds of people arriving and departing were milling around. She queued to have her papers checked by the Gestapo. The one who checked her identity card and zone pass gave her a cursory glance then allowed her through. This is all part of the aftermath of the round-up and deportations, thought Violette. I bet they're on the lookout for Philippe, and others.

Violette joined the throng, making her way to wait on a bench under the large clock on the wall. Two railway workers – *cheminots* – were taking a few moments' break to roll a cigarette. The *cheminots* had been instrumental in many hundreds of train delays and accidents and were beginning to co-ordinate much more serious damage all over the country as D-Day approached.

She sat there quietly, carefully noting how many German soldiers, officers, Gestapo and Milice were present. As she watched, one elderly man on a bench and a young couple near the newspaper stall were hauled off into the office that the Milice used whenever they wanted to question someone.

'*Mademoiselle, bonjour,*' murmured a soft but firm feminine voice. She looked up and saw Lise Valois with Lucien. She greeted them with pleasure. Lucien was of medium height and about thirty years old, with the quiet dignity and confidence that overcoming moments of fear gives.

Next to Lucien was another man. More imposing. He was around thirty-five years of age, also of medium height, but powerfully built. His dark hair was curly and unruly. '*Corinne,* I would like you to meet Marcel. He arranged delivery of the bike,' Lucien announced proudly.

'*Enchantée, monsieur.* And thank you so much for the bike. I can't tell you what a difference it has made just this morning.'

'*Enchanté, mademoiselle,*' said Marcel with a deep warm smile. 'It is truly my pleasure. And a friend tells me you were at Le Tabac having a quiet coffee with a mutual friend!'

She was too slow in disguising the shock and said, 'Well, you lot really are good! I didn't notice a tail – friendly or unfriendly. I'm usually good at losing those who follow me.'

'I know that. We've tried twice and failed both times. But no, you wouldn't have noticed a *friendly* tail this time because there was none. The waiter who served you is one of ours!'

'Ah!' Violette smiled. She now knew why Philippe felt comfortable waiting there all day. Marcel was a carpenter by trade. Violette could see he concealed a sharp intellect behind an apparently open demeanour. He wore shabby clothes and heavy boots that had been repaired many times. His accent was that of a Normand of the deep country, perhaps slightly modified by mixing with Frenchmen from all regions and social strata through his craft.

Violette was delighted at last to meet a man who could clearly open up a real course of action for her to take. She felt sure, although she had not been told anything about him, that he was a leader, perhaps of a Maquis group.

'Let's go to the Brasserie de la Gare,' intercepted Lise. 'We can get a corner banquette and have a quiet chat over an aperitif.'

The four of them walked through the throng of people. Turning to Violette, Marcel said, '*Corinne,* you will notice we are using our correct names for this meeting. That is because, as Lise has told me, you already know some, and as you have legitimately been looking to hire a bicycle to get around on, and for a lost relative, there is no reason not to use our legitimate names, *n'est-ce pas?*'

'*Oui, d'accord,*' replied Violette, just a little thoughtfully. She felt reassured that they were, in fact, using her mission name of *Corinne Leroy* as if it truly were her own. 'Maybe we can talk a little later about various matters and assign the work that's to be done, including helping out families who're in financial need.'

'You can come back with me to my workshop and we'll sort out any problems with the bike and the other things there. *Ça vous convient, mademoiselle?*'

'*Parfaitement*. It would be very useful to have a large basket on the front, at least, and perhaps a tyre repair kit and pump if such wonders still exist,' she grinned somewhat cheekily. 'But I can cope quite easily if not comfortably with solid tyres. I'll probably be spending time here on the left bank and possibly cycling further north. Le Havre might be necessary too.'

Surprised, Marcel asked, 'But you know that Le Havre is a long way, along heavily patrolled roadways? It would be better by train or in one of our trucks. Le Havre is a very dangerous place.'

'Yes, but I must spend at least twenty-four hours there.'

They made their way to the station brasserie, where Marcel ordered *cafés-cals*, coffees laced with Calvados, for the four of them. The barman was another friend. They chatted about bikes, riding around and the general state of the town. Marcel, Lise and Lucien were quite astonished at Violette's knowledge of the town and recent events and the surrounding area that she hadn't even seen yet. At no time during this meeting did any one of them mention the real purpose of their meeting. Violette had lost all trace of any accent and was steadily building her own slightly northern rhythm and colloquialisms particular to the area. She constantly listened to the language and sounds around her. She loved it!

Four people, intent on freeing their country from tyranny, spent a pleasant forty-five minutes chatting innocuously. Violette felt, briefly again, safe and secure in the company of these folk.

‡

As they left the bar, something caught Violette's eye on a wall in the ticket hall: two posters of wanted men affixed by German order with such awful images that the two men were hardly recognisable:

X ... dit Clément, Charles Staunton
and X ... dit Mollier R.

It was the first time she had seen the posters close up. The first was of Philippe Liewer, with his cover names of *Clément* in Rouen as well as *Charles Beauchamp* and *Charles Staunton*; the second was of Bob Maloubier, printed on the poster as *Robert Mollier/Mortier*. The Germans had the right field names but seemed not to know exactly who they were. The fact that they had the name of *Staunton* disturbed her greatly as it was Philippe's UK alias. How and from whom did they get that? The pictures luckily bore little resemblance to the two men. The one of Philippe accentuated and deepened the long lines from his nostrils to mouth and showed the early growth of a dark beard. This all aged and helped disguise him. He looked every bit his cover of the little overworked accountant from Lyon on secondment to Rouen, renting a small room from the Francheterre family in Place des

Emmurées, or as Violette had commented earlier, a somewhat suspicious type. Bob looked uncharacteristically subdued, properly suited and without his trademark moustache. She preferred him as she knew him: dashing, exciting, good looking with an indomitable stare and moustache – and always good fun.

This time the 'Wanted' notices were prominently displayed and Violette decided she would return to rip them off that wall or some other wall. She would wait until she was about to leave for England as it would be dangerously foolhardy to have them in her possession while staying anywhere in Normandy. She nudged Lise and surreptitiously indicated the notices. 'I'll come back and tear off one or two when the way is clear,' she muttered softly. 'Are there many around the town?'

'Oh, yes. All over the place. But be very careful when you take and hide them,' advised Lucien, who had overheard. That jolted Violette, who thought she had spoken very quietly to Lise.

'Of course I'll be damned careful,' retorted Violette, angry with herself. 'But I want a couple to take back across the water. Just before my return to Paris will do nicely. School taught me how to thieve and cat burgle and all manner of wicked things. And I'm very good at them!'

'*Bon, ben ma p'tite*, don't get your knickers in a twist,' teased Marcel. 'We've watched you over the last couple of days and are quite impressed by your demeanour. We saw you dragged along to the Palais de Justice, too, and noted how you behaved in the captain's office.'

'What! And you didn't give me a bloody bit of help!' stormed Violette, but her volatile temper quickly subsided. 'No, no, I'm sorry. Quite impossible under the circumstances! And thanks for the compliment.' She smiled apologetically, and then grinned. 'How about another of those fantastic drinks on me – coffee and Calvados – unknown in my hometown!' They all laughed and accepted her hospitality as she walked across to the bar. 'By the way, Lucien, I was so relieved you didn't appear in the Palais,' she whispered in his ear.

Astonished, he blurted, 'How do you know that's where I work?'

'Ah, I know you're a senior *fonctionnaire*, serving civilly, all the while scuppering German orders in naughty ways. But, if I told you how I knew, that would be telling, now wouldn't it?'

‡

The group gradually split up, with Violette and Marcel going to his workshop a few doors from Georges Philippon's arms dump in rue des Abattoirs. Violette and Lise arranged to meet at the dress shop the following day, Friday, to see if Lise or Marcel had anything to report to Violette, or even later that day if Violette needed to see her. If Lise wished to contact Violette, she would do so through Madame Thivier at the hotel. They agreed on innocuous coded words to express danger, times, places and such. The repaired cardigan was a fine motive for their meeting up.

Violette informed everyone that Madame Thivier was trustworthy, adding that the woman would make a fine cutout for groups and couriers or leaders from the area or further afield. She recounted the kindness shown her and the woman's obvious concern when she arrived back a little fraught from her unpleasant episodes. It had been fortuitous for Violette to find the little hotel.

‡

Marcel and Violette headed off to collect their bikes so they could get to the workshop and chat more discreetly.

'I'll pedal ahead of you and you follow behind. You know the rules, no doubt, about not pedalling side by side,' said Marcel. 'Take about five minutes to get there.'

'Thanks, Marcel. I'll be right behind you all the way.'

It was well after midday when Violette and Marcel set off to his carpenter's workshop, about a mile to the west of the railway station. The streets were grim and desolate and this side of the Seine reeked of poverty. Feeling watched, Violette turned to see a man in a dark overcoat observe them, making a note on a notepad. 'Monsieur Marcel, do you know that man? He made a note and was looking quite hard in our direction.'

'It's the Gestapo, *en pékin*,'[63] growled Marcel, a frown darkening his face. 'It doesn't augur too well. We'd better be damned careful. We'll see if we can change that bike of yours for a better one and look for a suitable basket, have a quick chat and then I'm afraid you'll really have to leave my workshop and garage. We'll use your cover story. Maybe I can suggest somebody who knows somebody who might be able to help you search for your relation.'

'Right, that's good. The Wehrmacht colonel on the train knows, and it's recorded at Milice HQ through the check I underwent that I'm looking for a bike to hire and searching for an uncle who might've got caught in the bombing raids,' Violette filled in for Marcel. 'So it shouldn't prove a problem that I'm seen in your garage looking for a better bike and a basket.'

'Yes, and it gives me an excuse to consider the matter overnight, time to contact friends and then it's appropriate for you to return tomorrow or for us to meet up somewhere. If we find another bike, that'll be good too – an extra reason for meeting here. So, I can keep this one to fix and then you can return for it later on. That way, I've got good answers, should someone come snooping. You too, if you're stopped again. It keeps your story credible while giving me time to sleep on what we discuss.'

---

63 *En pékin* = in mufti, in plain clothes.

They dismounted from their bikes to climb a steepish hill on foot, walking side by side, pushing their bikes on their outer side giving them privacy to chat. As they walked along, seemingly unaware of danger and enjoying the walk, the Gestapo man followed behind awhile. Then they heard the clack of his boots as he caught up. Addressing himself to Marcel, he said: '*Ausweise, bitte!*' As the officer examined their papers, Marcel grumbled, 'It's just damned awkward, you know. Everybody's looking for bikes and I've hardly got anything left. Can't the authorities let us have more? People do have to get to work and kids to school.'

'When they're available. Now, explain to me what you're doing, where you're going.'

'Young lady's looking for another bike, and a basket! Every day I have someone looking for some kind of transport. I've enough work in my workshop, never mind keeping an eye on that damned garage and its apprentice boy. Don't know if he'll be able to find one for her. We're riding there now. We might be in luck.' He grumbled on, 'I ought to put my regular customers first. Those bloody British bomb us; you lot keep us under lock and key, so to speak – I'm fed up with it all.'

'Your papers are in order. Be thankful I'm not arresting you.'

And he walked off. He was fed up with the whining French and their stupid demands.

'Phew,' breathed Violette. 'That was a fine moan. Got right up his nose.'

'Yep. Just cross the road and we're there,' replied Marcel. 'Garage first, I think.'

‡

It was a typical garage, with old rusting machinery shoved into corners, bits of tyres and springs and all manner of dusty, creaking things. This was fun. The tenseness dissipated as Marcel showed her around, even pointing out where *Jo* had hidden the dump. It had been so well hidden, he explained, that only half had been found by the Germans, the rest had been secreted away by Claude Malraux.

He ushered her through a side-door into another garage where all manner of bikes and spare parts were lying around or being cleaned up by Philippon's workers, including Mich, his very bright and dedicated apprentice.

'Okay,' Mich said to Marcel. 'I think this one should do the trick. Old enough but we can clean up the chain, add a couple of hidden gears and make the tyres look like hard ones although they won't be. Easier to ride but not appearing so.' There were hardly any tyres available and gears were unlikely on a simple bike in occupied France. Dangerous, therefore, to have them.

'That's marvellous. And a good point. Let me pay for the bike and any work you do. My friends can afford it,' smiled Violette. She could see Mich's grin mixed with relief in the semi-gloom.

'Thank you, *Corinne*,' Marcel replied. 'We can do with all the money we can get. Even counterfeit – better still really. It all gets spread around. Helps get intelligence from our informers at the occupier's offices and departments of one kind or an-other.' He looked around. 'Hey Mich, can you lend a hand here, please? I need a couple of old baskets for the bikes.'

'*D'ac*,' shouted Michel as he walked towards the other workroom. 'I'll have to pop to the farm. Have a feeling there's something okay down there.' He went off at a trot, happy to help Marcel all he could. Mich had a pretty good idea what Marcel was up to much of the time – just like his boss, Georges, had been – but they never talked about it, until now.

'When he's back, I'll make them a little more worn. The handlebars are covered in leather with a light – new battery – but don't use it unless you must. The brakes'll be checked and renewed if needed. Then we'll exchange bikes. Now, where are you going next, *Corinne*? Can I help in any way?' asked Marcel.

'Well, I'd like to ask your help in a few things. For example, there's an important viaduct, the Barentin viaduct, on the Rouen–Le Havre rail route to be blown up before our lot invade. The railway line to Dieppe must be cut to prevent enemy troops being transported. The main road arteries from the north to Rouen need to be made impassable if at all possible—'

'Hey, hey, wait a minute. Let's get to my workshop, where we definitely won't be interrupted. No reason why I can't ask a pretty girl in there, now is there?'

'Absolutely not! And thanks for the compliment. I think!' retorted Violette, grinning. She liked him.

They walked the short distance to Marcel's workshop. Violette waited while he pulled at the door. No lock was in evidence, just like the garage. They went in.

‡

Violette and Marcel were soon ensconced in his comfortable but shabby office. At least Georges Philippon's garage and Marcel's workshops had survived the bomb-ings, if a little the worse for wear. Violette shivered slightly in the chill but said nothing. No fire was lit and she presumed Marcel was, of necessity, careful about how much paraffin he used. The wind quickly dragged clouds across the sky, leav-ing only the occasional glimmer of sunlight. A frosty wind was gusting in from the northeast, rattling through the shell-tattered building.

'The group that *Charles* had most contact with has now been all but destroyed,' commented Marcel as he went about attempting to provide a little heat from a bat-tered paraffin stove, much to Violette's relief. 'His group, along with my own and *Commandant Fantoma*'s group, carried out some pretty successful sabotage, acquired all manner of coupons, identity documents for the forbidden and red zones and disrupted telecommunications and many rail links especially from Rouen to Le Havre, Abbeville and Amiens,' explained Marcel, his pride edged with sadness and anger. 'Some of the coupons and documents were sent over to London so that they can print up fakes, but we keep most of them as they are "*de vrais faux papiers*".'

The chaps who get hold of these "real fake papers" are a secretive lot. Tragically, their leaders, *Commandant Fantoma* and his brother, *Capitaine Cartouche*, have been arrested and deported to Germany. Lucky they weren't just shot out of hand. They were both very badly tortured but gave absolutely nothing away. Bloody brave buggers. I hope to introduce you to others in their group, *Corinne. Charles*, by the way, knew *Fantoma* as *Lieutenant Marceau*.'

'Your two men showed unbelievable courage, I must say! In London we've produced many forged papers, including the most up-to-date German language passes that are required in this *zone interdite. Charles* also told us of an insurance agent who did not want his name mentioned, even in London, who provided him with a contact in the Town Hall and then supplied him with ration cards. I don't think that contact is Lucien. I've got quite a few sets of papers and cards on me. A few sets are for my own personal use, so that I can change identity if and when necessary. There's a cover story for each identity.'

'*Parfait.*' Marcel was fishing about among some papers strewn across his desk.

'I understand that it was a pretty substantial cache of arms that *Jo* kept hidden.'

'Yes, it was. And not just from the bloody Germans but from those young livewires he keeps on a short leash. They'd soon be out putting firecrackers under every German car, causing innumerable civilian reprisals. They're under constant training now and complain in lively fashion that they've got nothing to fight with!' He laughed grimly at the thought while Violette nodded. She concentrated and became utterly businesslike. She explained that, before the Allied invasion, actions needed to be undertaken to hinder the German military calling up reinforcements from any direction, adding that it would be good if he could help her find out whether any new installations were being prepared for launching some sort of rocket. British intelligence suggested that they would be able to reach London, so anything that could be discovered and passed on to London would be of the greatest importance. Violette expressed her desire to visit one of the sites to form her own picture.

Marcel thought that quite a tall order and said he would think it over that night. He described how scared everyone was since the *Salesman* circuit had been blown noting that many of his people had withdrawn and refused to do anything further. He considered Claude Malraux an incompetent and weak if not downright traitorous – not a good leader. He promised Violette that he would have a chat with a couple of people and see what he could come up with by the time Violette got back tomorrow. Marcel looked at the packet that Violette offered him for the bike: a large wad of franc notes to replenish his dwindling funds and sighed, calling it manna from heaven. She had already proven her good will by the fact of her coming from her safe home to this dangerous place. But the money was very gratefully accepted.

Violette retorted that it was not such a safe home and damned dangerous these days, what with the German bombers raiding London, thousands killed and maimed and dreadful fires.

Marcel concurred saying he did not know where they had found her but that she would do just nicely. He continued his report with his suspicion that most of *Salesman* and many of their people in the *Diables Noirs* and others in Normandy were shopped by an OCM courier. The OCM should never really have been allowed to have such wide-ranging knowledge of so many groups all over the country, including Russian and Polish communists, Gaullist and SOE circuits, as well as many home grown Résistance networks.[64] I'll get some coffee on the go and then you can be on your way.'

'Great!' exclaimed Violette, settling back in her chair.

She was intrigued by Marcel's comment about the OCM as this coincided with her own thoughts that betrayal had begun much higher up than at individual group level or by local informers, although obviously there were those who assisted the Vichy police and the German security services.[65] In fact, the Vichy police and Darnand's Milice were the most dangerous. They were French and could all the more easily infiltrate any Résistance movement or catch an SOE agent whose French let him or her down.

'Marcel, can you tell me a little about the OCM, the Organisation civile et militaire? I don't fully understand its *raison d'être* nor its members.'

As Marcel made some aromatic fresh coffee and rustled up a few *amandier de Bouziques* and *biscuits zézettes*[66] he explained to Violette that the OCM was a civil and a military organisation that recruited high-ranking and junior French officers into its service along with French professionals in the teaching sector, law and various industries. Many of the officers were right wing but not of the Nazi mind-set. This was where its weakness lay.

Violette never suspected that the French would embrace fascism. But in her walks around the town she had seen it in the faces of passers-by, including some *fonctionnaires*. There were many who wanted nothing more than the return to an ordered, disciplined life, who continued to be very concerned by the eruption of communism since the early 1930s; maybe some had already been involved in

---

64 As M.R.D. Foot leads us to believe, 'it was certainly never any part of F section's intention to send them straight to their death; nor indeed were their deaths intended by anybody else on the Allied side. They were unfortunates who happened to be caught on the exposed flank while it was exposed.' Here, he is referring to the spring of 1944, around the time of Violette's April mission, where several agents were dropped along with provisions to the *Phone* and *Butler* circuits that had been operated by the Gestapo over the previous four or five months.

65 'It was the networks in the areas we have been studying most closely, Paris and the highly civilised Loire valley and the industrialised north, that were most heavily hit [by German infiltration and the capture of agents]. There was not much here that survived from the early days to greet D-Day', Jean Overton Fuller, *German Penetration of SOE*, p.147.

66 *Amandier de Bouziques* – an almond biscuit from Bouziques that melts in your mouth, even today made by hand with the same natural products. The *zézette de Sète* is another delicious small biscuit with *vin rosé* manufactured in the picturesque Mediterranean town of Sète. Both are excellent Languedoc-Roussillon biscuits to accompany coffee or aperitifs.

suppressing communist groups. This did not make them Nazis but they were thus vulnerable to Nazi tendencies and to being manipulated by Nazis to betray their friends, family and country.

'Roland Farjon was a young leading officer from a wealthy family, a graduate of the Saumur military academy. He's even a distant relative of Charles de Gaulle. He was leader of the Nord A Region before he was arrested in October in 1943 by the Gestapo,' explained Marcel. 'It's pretty well agreed he delivered several hundred of his men and women to the Germans. Firstly through his unbelievably arrogant carelessness, then allegedly by handing over friends and comrades under interrogation. Couldn't hack the claustrophobic cells and harsh questioning, I imagine. Pity he hadn't remained an officer soldier pure and simple. That's his kind of courage, his kind of leadership. He would have been a fine leader, cool and courageous in the face of the enemy at the front line. In the Résistance you need a different kind of courage. Met him once, a bit high-handed, certainly overconfident. Nevertheless, a charming, handsome man, amusing to be with in normal circumstances, fine soldiering character, a good organisational brain – but not a clue as to security.'

'Does Region A include Rouen and surrounding area?' asked Violette, troubled by the devastating news and unintentional betrayal. 'Is that how we lost about a hundred of our best Frenchmen and women in *Charles*'s *Salesman* circuit?'

'Yes, in part. The Germans – SD and Gestapo, in fact, ably assisted by the Milice – have been observing then arresting members of the Résistance gleaned from the lists of names and addresses that Farjon had stupidly written down in clear. He hadn't bothered to put them into code! Then they had group members or exterior helpers followed and observed over a period of weeks, possibly a couple of months or so and, in that way, found out who their contacts were or arrested them (or both) and got as much information as possible from them through interrogation, beatings and, frequently, torture. Then they would often shoot the poor bastards. *Excusez-moi, mademoiselle.* Another OCM leader in the south called André Grandclément also caused innumerable arrests.[67] His was betrayal of the worst kind, and he even declared that he did so to protect the Maquis there. He took the German, who had befriended him and so easily turned him, to the various dumps, handing over weaponry and equipment, food stores and clothing dropped by London.'

'Ah, yes, I know something about Grandclément. He worked with a pal of mine who's still down there, but I won't go into that.'

---

67 André Grandclément, the chief of OCM Bordeaux, French double agent, and his wife were court-martialled, sentenced to death and executed by a French Forces of the Interior (Forces Françaises de l'Intérieur – FFI or 'Fifi' as it was nicknamed) tribunal at Belin, 28 July 1944 (*Set Europe Ablaze*, by Edward Henry Cookridge (pp.206–8). See David Thompson, *A Biographical Dictionary of War Crimes Proceedings, Collaboration Trials and Similar Proceedings Involving France in World War II*, 1999–2002.

'Right, *Corinne*, nor should you,' exclaimed Marcel. 'You're pretty canny for your age.'

'Good training and common sense, that's all,' replied Violette modestly. She sipped some coffee.

Marcel went on to explain that reception organisers and wireless operators (unlike circuit organisers who probably knew within twenty-four hours either through the police or their own men if there had been arrests) could not easily know if, for example, a safe-house had been blown in a district they had not visited lately. Such a difficulty was aggravated by rumours of Allied night-time air attacks, which raised doubts in many heads about which side to be on. There were also the usual *collabos* in each town and village; such rogue elements could even be found in families committed to the Résistance, sometimes through indoctrinated ideology but more frequently for revenge, spite and pecuniary reward. But it was rare that a *collabo horizontale* betrayed anyone in the Résistance. These women, a few men too, were often prostitutes or simply succumbing to the need for money and sustenance to keep themselves and their children alive. Some enjoyed it for the fun and danger it presented. They liked being on a German officer's arm, being entertained and receiving gifts, but they would never betray their friends. They often displayed surprising bravery in helping the Allies by passing on intelligence they picked up in such company. A dropped comment between enemy officers or soldiers in a dance hall about supplies or transport from one place to another could lead to sabotage activities being directed at a certain railway or road convoy a few hundred miles away.

Violette felt it was essential that the Farjon case be passed on to her superiors in London. They might have been aware of it but perhaps had not realised the devastating effect of such far away but far-reaching betrayal. Violette pressed Marcel for any details he could give her.

Continuing, Marcel described the Résistance as not just one single organisation but an all-too-often changing unstructured series of disparate groups and groupings. The Free French powers in London and France hoped that the OCM and the organisations directly linked to de Gaulle in London could bring them all under one umbrella group. André Malraux was instrumental in this but not succeeding too well from all accounts – especially with the communists and those groups who trust no one but their own chosen people. In fact, some were wondering what this author was up to, and said he should stick to writing. And, naturally, leaders and their groups felt threatened by the fact that they could lose their autonomy and security by coming under some distant, centralised organisation. He joked that Paris might have always been partial to centralised government, but the provinces were not! They both laughed over that Gallic characteristic and drank their coffee in companionable silence for a while.

Violette commented that Marcel seemed to know an awful lot about the higher strata of the Résistance in the area asking how that was possible. She felt she could not have met a better person to pass on some of my instructions and ask how she could give financial aid or who could connect her to the next person.

The BCRA(M)[68] had given Marcel a certain mission leading up to the time the Allies arrived. Part of that mission was to liaise between about twenty small groups from Senlis to Pas-de-Calais, Abbeville and Amiens as far north as Lille and west to Caen. That was why Violette was directed to talk to him rather than anyone else at this point. Violette rejoined that their jobs meshed perfectly.

They talked on, discussing the situation in Rouen and further afield until Marcel suggested Violette join him for lunch at the Gare Rive Droite on the other side of the river. He had convinced himself of her bona fides and character during their chat and was now keen to introduce her to a couple of other undercover people – without her realising it. They had spent more than enough time here. That snooping Gestapo agent could have followed them and might come back at any moment.

First Marcel wanted to find a basket to go on the front of Violette's bike. She chimed quickly that he should not forget one for the back as well, if possible. He said he would do his best, raising his eyebrow at her sassy boldness and saying he would be just be a couple of minutes.

While he was gone, Violette pulled out a piece of rice paper from a hidden recess in her bag and made some coded notes on their discussions. She did not want to forget anything.

‡

---

68 BCRA(M), Bureau central de Renseignement et d'Action (Militaire) = Central Bureau of Action and Information (Military). This was run by Dewavrin, in Duke Street in London. See also the RF sections in Foot's *Official History of SOE*.

14

Back across the River to Gare rue Verte and Dinner with Philippe at the Brasserie Marigold

Thursday 13 April 1944

Marcel returned with two worn but solid baskets that Mich had found. He fixed them to her bicycle, and then he and Violette pedalled off, back over the bridge towards Gare Rive Droite. As they rode down the ramp from the bridge, they were stopped by a Wehrmacht soldier whose duty it was to check cyclists in pairs between their twenties and forties. He did not know what he was looking for, but would do his duty carefully. He asked politely enough for their papers, identities and zone passes and checked them agonisingly slowly. He asked a few questions. Marcel, somewhat aloof, answered him in monosyllables while Violette gave the impression to the young German soldier that he was being a complete ass. But she did answer all his questions in a dutiful manner. His eyes travelled from her laughing eyes, lingering down her body to her feet, trying to regain his authority, but to no avail. In the end, he angrily waved them on. He saw nothing malicious in the laughing eyes – just teasing, which had made him blush.

'Poor bugger,' Marcel laughed that she had left him pink as a lobster and warned her not to overdo it.

They rode on, careful to obey traffic regulations on hand-signals and crossings, finally parking their bikes to the left of the station. Most of the vehicles, Violette was unsurprised to note, were German military, many crammed with weapons. Transporters carried all sorts of appropriated merchandise, most hauled to Germany or used by the occupying forces in France. Rouen was, and is today, an important communications link between the south and the north; it was strongly defended by the enemy and actively sabotaged by the Résistance.

They walked into the wide station hall and entered the brasserie. A waiter approached and with a wink directed them to a bench table in a corner behind the semi-circular zinc counter. Once seated, Marcel excused himself saying he wished to make a telephone call to a friend.

While Violette sat there, discreetly observing everything around her, Marcel made a call on an internal, seemingly secure, phone to a room above. He asked to speak to Jacques, the maître d' of the brasserie whose brother was the stationmaster. Both worked for the Résistance. Marcel told Jacques that he had the most beautiful girl in town downstairs looking for an uncle who had gone missing in Rouen. Could he help? Although the line seemed secure, he never spoke about Résistance matters on it, using code or cover stories. They had already spoken about *la fille anglaise* who had parachuted into France. Jacques said he would come down in a few minutes to see this vision of loveliness. If the line were bugged, or if someone nearby had overheard Marcel, then the conversation that had taken place sounded quite innocent and supported Violette's cover story.

Meanwhile, a Wehrmacht colonel had approached Violette. '*Bonjour, mademoiselle.* Do you remember me from the Paris–Rouen train? You most charmingly shared our carriage.'

'Ah, yes,' replied Violette, aghast at being recognised, but smiling nonetheless.

'So, what are you doing here? Waiting for a boyfriend?' Colonel Niederholen asked with a paternal smile.

'Oh no, an acquaintance. He's gone to make a call.'

'I see. Is he helping you?'

'Well, I hope he'll be able to, sir. About my uncle, missing in Rouen. This gentleman has a friend in the Préfecture who might be able to throw some light on those missing or those who've died here. That's what I'm hoping, anyway.' She smiled sadly at the colonel.

'Permit me, *Fräulein*, to give you again my card, and if you have not luck, please I shall be entirely at your disposal to help further. Why not come to lunch with me tomorrow and we can talk about it. Say midday at that fine place in rue Grand Pont?'

At that moment, Marcel returned. Violette introduced him to Colonel Niederholen as Marcel, apologising for not remembering his surname and explaining to Marcel she had met the colonel on the train and he had kindly offered to help find her relative.

Marcel had overheard the colonel's invitation and having thought very fast, said to Violette, 'That's very kind of the colonel, *Corinne*. And some more good news: my friend *Paul Beaupuits* wants us to look at some records tomorrow around midday to see if they help – you said your uncle was helping the authorities with something, isn't that right?'

'Oh, right. And thank you both so much. It is so kind. Colonel, thank you for your card. I shall certainly keep it close by – and for the invitation to lunch tomorrow. Unfortunately, I cannot miss the opportunity of meeting *Monsieur Belpoil* tomorrow,' she went on sweetly, purposely getting the false surname wrong to confuse the colonel's memory.

'Of course not, *Fräulein*. May I extend during this time to you my sympathies for your distress? And my offer is open to you at any moment, if I can be of service, *Fräulein. Auf wiederschauen.*'[69]

'*Merci, mon Colonel, et au revoir,*' said Violette with great politeness and respect.

The colonel walked away thoughtfully. What an appealing young woman. She seemed genuine, but who knew these days with so many pesky troublemakers about? He would do a little discreet checking. He did not want the German security services or Milice getting involved. Nasty thuggish bunch of good-for-nothings, he thought, as he rejoined his table.

‡

'Phew,' breathed Marcel with relief. 'You handled that admirably. I especially liked what I presume was your deliberate confusion over *Paul Beaupuits* and *Belpoil*. Anyway, it's not *Paul*'s real name but it'll do for the moment. I want you to meet him and his wife, *Marielle* – not her real name either.'

Violette voiced her concern that the colonel would take the matter further. They talked until the waiter, Yves, came over to take their order of *cassoulet à la Normandie*[70] and half a carafe of watered-down red wine. There were even a few slices of baguette to accompany the meal. Nothing like a good dollop of fear and adrenaline coursing through the body to build a healthy appetite.

A small wiry man came to the table as they were finishing their meal and drinking the last of the wine. '*Bonjour tous les deux,*' he said amiably.

'*Bonjour,*' chimed Violette and Marcel.

After introductions, *Paul Beaupuits* joined them for coffee and they talked inconsequentially, giving *Paul* and Violette a chance to size one another up while Marcel surveyed the brasserie customers with care. The colonel had returned to his table and was laughing and joking with his compatriots. He glanced toward their table a few times in friendly fashion. He seemed a decent sort. If he took the matter any further, he would do so through his own channels, not those of German security forces, thought Marcel.

As they broached the reason for Violette's presence, *Paul* conducted them upstairs to the clandestine meeting rooms, where they could talk without being overlooked or overheard. Violette reiterated her wish to access those in financial need and her instructions to gain more intelligence on the new weapons and launch sites.

---

69 *Auf wiederschauen*, local dialect of southern Germany, Bavaria and Austria, equivalent of '*auf wiedersehen*' = 'goodbye'; exact equivalent of *au revoir* and *arriverderci*.

70 *Cassoulet à la Normandie* = a fine bean stew made with sliced *saucisse de Toulouse* (a lively red-coloured succulent sausage) and ordinary sausage plus loin of pork as the three main ingredients, but includes sliced carrot, onion, tomato, cream, garlic (*naturellement*), goose fat (or butter and olive oil), wine, bouquet garni, pepper and salt.

Philippe and other agents had informed London, she told them, that it seemed there were four different types, probably rocket launchers. She also wished to impart the instructions she had brought over to make preparations for the Allied invasion, wherever and whenever it might take place, and to discuss what effective sabotage could be done to the German secret weapons on French soil.

Violette also passed on to Marcel and *Paul* an important message to be murmured in the first place to a trusted few – a rumour with no discernible source but spread quietly about. Since January, the aerial bombardment of Rouen and its suburbs had increased. Many strategic points were hit, among them railway and road bridges, as well as several communes where constructions were under German military control. Fortunately, houses in the old parts of Rouen had domed cellars which the Défense Passive designated '*caves-abris*' – basement shelters. The rumour to spread was that the Germans had indiscriminately bombed parts of Rouen while putting the blame squarely on the Allies. The two men found this a comical and very effective way to sabotage German propaganda. It also happened to be true. Violette wanted to reiterate in the strongest terms the warning that the Allies would soon shell Rouen so people would flee the town until it was over. They were aware that, although the bombing would be strategic, there was no way of ensuring its accuracy. Navigators could and did get it wrong, targeting could be hit and miss and the weather unhelpful. She concluded that citizens should keep listening for BBC messages to that effect.

The meeting ended and Marcel decided to take Violette to visit the Vincent family. Just for a chat. The opportunity was there for Violette to meet some involved in the Résistance, while giving her an hour or so to relax. They left their bikes at the station and walked.

The Vincents were having a party for their eldest son's twenty-first birthday; family, cousins and distant cousins, friends and fiancés were all there. Violette was warmly welcomed and immediately felt at home. The children were all over her, bewitched by her carefree smile and quiet poise. She asked lots of questions on how they were all coping, and talk of cellars arose again.

Jean, a lad of sixteen who was intermittently helpful to the Résistance explained that people did not like entering the shelters as people are reluctant to go into *caves* whenever there was bombing. They were always afraid of being smothered or crushed so they also had trench shelters. There was one in place Saint-Gervais, which was where Jean went whenever he could.

All schoolchildren, Violette learned, were advised to take a small satchel with a sponge in it in case there was a gas leak. But it seems no one knew what to do with it in such an event. A little girl of ten, Alice, told Violette as they sat around the table that she would probably wet the sponge and put it over her nose. Violette smiled at her intelligent remark.

Alice's friend Claude, a girl from the other side of Rouen, explained that everyone was very organised, going into the shelter when there was an alert, but her father insisted she, her mother and brother get under a big solid oak table in the café where they lived. If bombs were not falling on Rouen, then Claude and her brother would get up on the flat roof of the small building that housed their café and home. There they sat watching planes pass overhead. The DCA[71] or anti-aircraft guns would shoot up into the sky to bring down the bombers, they explained to Violette, having no clue she had been a trained and experienced predictor operator in London.

Violette was aware that worse was still to come. In fact, Allied bombing raids would last until June as a prelude to the Allied invasion. Not knowing exactly when it was to happen, she had been instructed by London to warn people to get out of town for their own protection. She asked Marcel to pass this on to the party in the Vincents' house. He explained that many had already left and were, indeed, expecting more bombing raids. He continued that, from the gardens at the rear of the building, it was possible to access shelters in various basements of the *Hôtel de Ville*. People made their way to bomb shelters there and to the northern heights where more shelters existed under high hills overlooking the town. Violette was relieved to hear it.

A couple of hours later, Violette and Marcel moved on to a small hotel where the proprietor was a Résister. Violette was now meeting a good number of people seriously committed to liberating their country. All seemed casual and relaxed but she understood how worried they were by the danger of betrayal. She had some serious thinking to do and was looking forward to getting back to the seclusion of her room. She needed to make a report, turn it into code for transmitting to London, but first she needed to make her rendezvous with Philippe.

Lucien, just arrived, had gained access to a local French wireless operator and said that Violette could use it to send her report the next day. Marcel also arranged contact with some women involved in one of the Maquis groups in a small village some distance from Rouen. She could cycle there independently and was actually looking forward to getting out of Rouen and onto the open road. Good progress so far, thought Violette.

‡

All in all, things had gone well, and a while later Violette walked back to the station and collected her bike to cross back over the river to meet Philippe. She cycled to Saint-Sever station, where she picked up intelligence from new timetables of trains and destinations. From notices and talking to ticket sellers and railway workers, she discovered what trains would be transporting goods and which ones would have troops, when one company of troops would leave and another would replace them and who their commanding officers were. This was done so casually that not one

---

71 DCA, *défense contre avions* = defence against aircraft, i.e. ack-ack batteries.

person she talked to realised they were giving her invaluable intelligence regarding enemy movements. She acted the worried young lady needing to find out how she could get to Le Havre, or possibly where else to seek her uncle. She even found out a little detail on 'her' colonel and felt he could perhaps be useful at some time.

As it was getting late, Violette made for place des Emmurées and her meeting with Philippe.

‡

At the appointed time, Violette parked her bike by the corner pillar of the market in Place Emmurées and waved to Philippe, who was already sitting at a window inside Brasserie Marigold. Pulling off her scarf and pushing her fingers through her hair, Violette entered and joined Philippe at his table. '*Bonsoir Charles, ça va?*'

'*Oui*, everything's fine, *Corinne*. What will you have?'

'Their magnificent omelette as you suggested, *Charles*. Ham, if they have it. And a *salade verte* to start with.'

'Okay. Gui, *deux omelettes au jambon et deux salades vertes*. Any wine?'

'Yes,' the waiter replied, 'some table white just came in. It's not too bad. Bit watered down, but better than nothing. Carafe of water, too?'

'Please.' Philippe turned to Violette. 'I've got some pretty bad news, I'm afraid. In one sense it's good, I suppose. You won't get into Le Havre, after all.'

'Why not?' asked Violette concerned. 'I'm quite prepared to go. On the other hand, it'll give me more time to get things moving from here. But tell me, *Charles*, what's happening?'

'In Paris I met René Charles. He told me the situation in Le Havre. The members of Le Havre *Hamlet* sub-circuit, my offshoot of *Salesman*, are dead, imprisoned or scattered to the four winds. It's just so dangerous there now. His family live just outside Le Havre and he went to visit them for family business, saying he'd be back in Paris in three or four days. So I thought it'd be a good idea to ask him to check out Le Havre. Four days later we met again in Paris. He reported there have been seventy-four arrests, including Roger Mayer, my lieutenant, which we already knew. A complete disaster. It must've been through *collabos* or infiltration, or an unknown mistake by any one of them, including Roger himself.'

'You know, *Charles*, I get the distinct feeling this whole disaster from Rouen to Le Havre is linked with a much larger disaster. I don't think the treachery, if that's what it is, is local, in the first instance, at least. I think it goes higher up the hierarchy. It seems one of the culprit organisations is the OCM. I'm going to be asking some discreet questions. Bet I find out something, too.'

'Right. But don't get too cocky – otherwise you'll get too dead! René reckons that there was nothing and no one left worthwhile for any work to be done.'

'Well, *Charles*, I'll still try to get there through some of my contacts here. At least I could give some financial assistance to those stranded by arrests or where the breadwinners have fled to the Maquis. They'll be in desperate straits right now and it's the least we can do. You must agree.'

'Well, I'm not so sure, *Corinne*. Perhaps you're right. But be damned careful and don't spend too much time there. I'm rather pleased to know you still have some of the dosh.'

'Nope! Spent most of it in Madame Sueur's shop right here in Rouen!' she smiled provocatively, then continued, 'Don't worry, I know just how important this cash is – London has sure given me enough – I'm going to make jolly sure it goes to the right places.'

The waiter came laden with their meal, real bread and wine. 'Your omelettes, *messieurs-dames*.'

'*Merci*.' Philippe waited until the waiter had moved away and then continued, 'I'm back in Paris tomorrow to link up with a couple of circuit leaders east and south-east to sort out where to set up a new circuit that'll be of maximum impact. I've plenty of contacts there and wider afield, especially the south. My wife's safe, I hope, way down in Antibes and not averse to giving a helping hand every now and then.'

'So, no network to resuscitate in Le Havre. Just like here. That gives me an easier time in one sense as it's a new start, with different people. With this bike, I can travel fair distances to see people. Should leave me time to get to Le Havre, if not Calais.'

'You did well to get that bike, girl. Looks perfect for what you need.'

'Yep, no more blisters, either! I can get anywhere I need, but perhaps I will go to Le Havre by train and then on foot and use tramways there. The only contact you gave me was the professor, Roger Mayer. As he's been arrested, I'll need to meet up with his wife, start from scratch, building a small group of two or three.'

'Right. Good thinking, as always, *Corinne*,' was Philippe's satisfied comment. 'So, what are you going to do now?'

She told him she was going to have a message sent next day to London, about the 'wanted' posters of him and Bob plastered all around town. 'Before I leave Rouen for Paris – obviously not a moment sooner – I shall take a couple of them and bring them back to London. You really look funny with what looks like a beard drifting round your face. You look like some petty criminal, maybe a crooked accountant.'

'Well, at least it's not a giveaway of me, don't you think?'

'Yes, I suppose so. But you really do look funny.' And her eyes sparkled in wicked merriment, laughter tinkling over the table. Philippe found it impossible not to join in.

'*Charles*, I think you should leave early tomorrow morning. It's too late tonight to get to Paris. Curfew and all that. But I know there's a train around half past eight in the morning taking workers to various stations on the Rouen–Paris line from Saint-Sever.'

'*Du café, messieurs-dames?*' interrupted the waiter.

'*Oui, deux grands, s'il vous plaît,*' ordered Philippe. 'You're pretty busy tonight, Gui.'

'*Oui, monsieur.* We're doing quite well.'

At that moment, two German officers walked in, passing from one table to the next, inspecting each person's identity cards.

Violette's merriment evaporated. She felt sick to the pit of her stomach. Not again. She pulled out her papers and rather sullenly pushed them at the officer when he came over telling him she was fed up with always showing her papers, complaining it was the fourth time that day Then she smiled at the officer, and he, smitten, could only nod that everything was *in Ordnung* and that she enjoy the evening. After having cursorily checked Philippe's papers in the name of *Charles Beauchamp*, with the fictitious profession of accountant on secondment from a firm in Lyon, the officer collected his colleague. They both smiled at Violette and then they were gone.

Violette and Philippe sighed a great sigh of relief. He was a wanted 'criminal' with a price on his head, but under the names of *Clément* and *Charles Staunton*, and they were relieved that the name of *Charles Beauchamp* had not appeared on the posters. Violette presumed that was why he was able to come into this particular district and feel secure. Nobody here had informed on him. Tonight, he was clean-shaven and looked every inch the neat professional accountant on important business, enjoying a pleasant evening in delectable female company, as fitted his cover. Nevertheless, they were taking a risk.

'I don't know how you do it. He was ready to take you to task for being sullen, then you smiled and he melted on tick. You certainly turned his attention away from me.'

'Of course, dear chap,' replied Violette, mock-haughtily. 'By the way, how on earth do the Germans know your cover name in England, that of *Charles Staunton*? Do you think there's a leak in London?'

‡

'It certainly is of concern and noted by a number of agents in the field, too. But that's for another day.'

They drank their coffees and Violette said she must leave to get back to her hotel on the other side of the river before curfew.

'Now, you will take care of yourself, won't you, my girl?' muttered Philippe, clearly concerned about the safety of his liaison officer. His pride in her endeavours was clear to see. She had given him a great deal of vital intelligence that he, too, would radio back to England.

'Don't you worry, *mon chef*, I value my life and limb very highly. I have every intention of getting the teams of Résistants working to harry the Boches at every turn, so you can rest assured I shall be very, very careful. There's a lot of planning to be done, people to be helped and current intelligence to be gathered throughout the region. That's my job and that's what I'm going to do.'

'Your turn to calm down, old girl!' he said, laughing out loud at such an outburst. Her eyes were sparking, her cheeks gathering colour, mouth set in determined single-mindedness. 'Off you go, then, and I'm off to my bed across the road to rest up for whatever tomorrow may bring.'

'*Bonne nuit*, and you take great care, too,' was Violette's earnest farewell. A kiss on the cheek and she was gone, fleet as the breeze.

She grabbed her bike and rode furiously over the bridge to her hotel.

‡

15

Le Havre

Friday 14 to Monday 17 April 1944

Violette needed to reach Le Havre and discover what was happening in the port town and try to get as far as Calais. It was now Friday 14 April. She had to meet Philippe in Paris in eleven days, on the 25th. Since the beginning of April, a number of trains had been sabotaged in their Dieppe depot by a Rouen team with Robert Legoux (*Bottes*) from the *Libé-Nord* group. Two more had been destroyed in Auffay, not far from the Auffay rocket site.

Just the previous day, the 13th, the railway in Préaux had been sabotaged by *Lieutenant Pelletier* and his team.[72] Violette was to pass on instructions that these teams and dozens more should continue their activities and sabotage the same lines again and again as soon as they were repaired. Her additional tasks were to get intelligence on Le Havre and, if possible and if London instructed, Amiens and Calais. Amiens was pretty much out of the question considering the time she had available before returning to Paris.

Calais, far to the north, was a closed city. The German military administered the entire Pas-de-Calais and Flanders region from the city. Most of the inhabitants, except those essentially employed, had been evicted from the city since it became the main repository for secret weapons and the town was now populated mostly by German nationals. Gestapo and Wehrmacht troops were on full alert and vigilantly guarded the weapons sites. These were principally the VI flying bombs, stored in well-constructed underground silos from which they could be launched, aimed directly at London and the south of England. South-east England had already been shelled by the Germans from their railway and coastal guns in France. Hitler and his generals remained duped into believing that the Calais coastline would be the site of the Allied offensive, so they had heavily defended the area against Allied amphibious assault. In Calais, German security forces and military pulled people over to verify not only their identity cards but also who their friends and family were, and exactly what they were doing that day.

---

72 The team consisted of Messrs Masset, Masson, Messon, Gohé and Le Fortier.

It seemed a well-nigh impossible assignment for any SOE agent to infiltrate Calais unless they posed as an essential worker. An agent disguised as a German clerk or labourer was in constant danger. Perfect German and an intimate knowledge of the regions, cultures and everyday German life was indispensable. Such agents would be constrained to minimal operational activity. Violette clearly did not qualify for this; her German and Dutch were minimal. She could have passed as one of the few essential French national workers, *petite fonctionnaire* or even a *collabo horizontale*.

She decided to concentrate on her first task – to discover whether Résistance groups in Le Havre, Rouen and Dieppe were ready to receive arms and follow instructions from London, to be co-ordinated from London and Algiers[73] in the run-up to D-Day. She would wait for further instructions from London if the promised use of the wireless were possible.

SOE were misled in believing that Hitler would take his forces out of France and other European countries to concentrate on the Eastern Front against the Russians. They did not heed or properly grasp that Hitler would not countenance any withdrawal. Where SOE had got things right was to seize the moment, knowing French civilians were increasingly prepared to take up the fight to oust the Nazis.

The Germans had seized scores of arms dumps comprising countless tons of Allied supplies; two such raids being in the Rouen area and during the Grandclément disaster in the south. It was now imperative for the Maquis and Résistance groups to do battle during April and May, so SOE with the Tempsford-based RAF Lysanders and Hudsons, as well as the Harrington-based American OSS[74] modified B-24 Liberator bombers, started in earnest to parachute in thousands of tons of weaponry and supplies all over France. It was part of Violette's mission to find relatively secure drop zones and security-minded groups to organise reception committees, while also gathering intelligence on links, organisations and activities – co-operative or individual – of groups in upper Normandy.

The Gestapo were particularly active in this forbidden red zone, especially in the militarised river and seaports of Rouen, Le Havre and Calais. At every point of exit and entry into, and at many points in the streets of the two Channel port towns black-uniformed Gestapo stood guard or their patrols goose-stepped in unison, revolvers loaded and rifles at the ready. They were on high alert throughout Normandy and the Pas-de-Calais.

---

73 The Allies secured Algeria, and its capital Algiers, in November 1942. The AMF, the organisation under de Guélis, mostly Giraudists, was the duplicate of SOE's F Section. Taken over by Brooks Richards in October 1943, it took on the mantle of the RF, de Gaulle's French Section within SOE, gradually fusing distinctions, becoming out-and-out Gaullist in tandem with SOE. From here, instructions were sent to Résistance groups, with an eye to D-Day and beyond. Being so much closer to the south of France than England, Algeria had many agents going to and coming from that region.

74 OSS – the American counterpart to SOE. After the war it would evolve into the CIA.

Roger Mayer had taken over Guénot's[75] *l'Heure H* group, only to be arrested and tortured before deportation on 11 March when the Gestapo, assisted by the Vichy Police and the Milice, cast a systematic dragnet from Calais all the way to Morlaix at the western tip of Brittany.

To carry out her instructions in Le Havre, Violette needed to discover what remained of groups like *l'Heure H* and who was left to continue the battle. She was beginning to understand that there were far more Résistants than London was aware of. It seemed to her that they were seriously underestimating the potential and actual strength of the Résistance and the Maquis. Among the untrained braves were Frenchmen and women with considerable strategic planning skills implementing security measures by setting up cells of Résistants and Maquisards where only the leader of each cell knew the leader of one or two other cells. London supplied every type of explosive material and ancillary equipment – but, to the constant irritation of the cells, not very much in the way of weaponry.

This had been the express design of the War Office and related services, like SOE. They now deemed it the right time to drop weapons, as the Allied offensive was fast approaching. The moment to fight the German military, not just obstruct it, had come. Violette was instructed to find appropriate sites for huge parachute drops of arms, agents and paratroopers. She had heard of ideal terrain near Buchy, north of Ry and east of Rouen.

Another two groups that Violette was meeting were *Vagabond Bien-Aimé*, named after a little dog, and the FTP, strongly Communist. In the two previous years these groups had sabotaged, demonstrated in the streets, used grenades in street battles against Reich soldiers and thrown bombs into cafés frequented nearly exclusively by the Germans. The reprisals they suffered consisted of arrests, deportations, torture and death.

A third group was *Libé-Nord*, whose leading member was Raoul Leprettre, editor of the *Journal de Rouen* newspaper, who in February was instructed from Algiers to bring the Rouen groups under the newly formed Comité départemental de Libération nationale (CDLN) to co-ordinate sabotage and intelligence gathering within the Seine-Inférieure (today the Seine-Maritime). Now there were links between groups; it was that very linkage between cells that weakened the security of each person in that group.

---

75 It was in Amiens that Léon Gonier, a Freemason, became one of the founders of the Résistance group *Libé-Nord* (nickname of the *Libération-Nord* group) in 1941. When Philippe started his *Hamlet* sub-circuit, Raymond Guénot liaised with *Libé-Nord* through his *l'Heure H* group (specialising in producing false papers) and with *Hamlet* and thus, through Philippe, with London. In November 1943, aged twenty-nine, Guénot was shot in Rouen, crying out, '*Vive la France!*'

Although Violette was not aware of individuals' names, she understood that from the north down to Rouen and further afield, the groups continued to replace those who had been captured or injured with new and equally determined Résistants.[76]

French communists had made it difficult, sometimes impossible, for London or de Gaulle to monitor, influence and work with them, but from early 1944 the French Communist Party (PCF) and its armed section, the Francs-Tireurs et Partisans (FTP), were starting to welcome SOE and OSS help against their common enemy. Violette was thus able to accumulate intelligence on their whereabouts and activities to pass on to London.

‡

Violette understood that should the Gestapo discover her presence, whether she remained in this area or ventured further north, it could only help in the deception of where exactly the Allied landings would take place. She had heard some strange stories about agents being inexplicably caught even as they landed; some said it was betrayal pure and simple, others that it was a diabolical plot of leading lambs to slaughter designed to throw the Germans off the track. She had no intention of being captured, revealing what she knew or being dead. And she was definitely no lamb.

Life and personal freedom were what mattered to Violette. They gave her the opportunity to fight the enemy with everything she had. She hated their destructive regime and that they had killed Étienne. Although she had lost him, she had her daughter safe in England and her families in England and France to live and fight for.

Having received no directives with regard to Amiens and Calais, Violette continued making plans to get to Le Havre and discover the state of the French Résistance groups there, the damage done to Philippe's *Salesman* and *Hamlet* circuits in that town; and to rebuild them.

‡

---

76 Then there were Maurice Vast and Leon Tellier, socialist mayor and deputy mayor, who exercised great influence on the entire *Libé-Nord* group that proved very active and highly successful. This group, stretching into Rouen territory, acted or passed on a series of relayed instructions from agents like Violette from Algiers or London. These were delivered during March, April, May and June to co-ordinate efforts in the lead up to D-Day, directed and implemented hundreds of sabotage activities, including the capture of weapons in Montivilliers and freeing detained political prisoners on 14 June 1944. It was on 6 April, a few days before Violette arrived in Rouen, that the weapons were transported from Cléon to Saint-Pierre-des-Fleurs and on the 9th, from Poix to Aumale, by Renée Lefebvre, a woman.

That Friday morning, Violette met Marcel in the station café. 'Marcel, I still need to get to Le Havre and pass on my instructions. Can you help? I'd like to do that before going to see other groups in this area. That way I can co-ordinate plans with yours when I get back.'

'It's damned dangerous there. You say you have papers, but even if they'll do here, in Rouen, they may not work, not there. I'll see if one of the chaps with a truck can take you. Perhaps even bring you back. How long do you want to be there?'

'Only a couple of days. I don't have many contacts, sadly, and I'm pretty sure the circuit is irretrievable. Just hoping I can persuade others to take on the work that needs to be done. Or perhaps they're already expecting instructions. And London needs to know.'

'I've one or two contacts. I'll see what I can do,' smiled Marcel, who knew far more than he would let on. He was fully aware of how much the presence of this young woman would affect anyone she met. She was willing, and he would use that willingness to give fresh impetus to the Havrais people.

That afternoon he met Violette again in his workshop. After ushering her into his office, he said, 'Well, there's a young lady who will lend you her German pass and identity card. You're about the same height, dark-haired and similar features. She'll need it in three days though, so make sure you're back by then. You will first meet Madame Mayer, Roger's wife. She will introduce you to the leaders of *l'Heure H* and *Vagabond Bien-Aimé* groups.'

'That's great, but I don't really need it as my papers say I live in Le Havre, but please thank her. London has asked me to ensure that the Barentin viaduct, central to Dieppe, Rouen and Le Havre, is blown. It seems that a combined operation might be the best. Or a shadow one to ensure that it's done. Would you like me to discuss this while I'm there with the two I meet, and bring you back their response?'

'Yes. I'll give you my thoughts to pass on. It's extremely powerfully built and well-guarded night and day. Built by an Englishman, it collapsed from weak concrete so he rebuilt it at his own expense and set the norm for a strongly reinforced structure. But if we can at least weaken its supports on each riverbank then perhaps the Allies can do the rest in a bombing raid.'

'It's a prime rail link from Calais and the north to Rouen, Le Havre, Paris and Brittany. Will I be able to leave tomorrow morning?'

'Yes, *Corinne*. Crack of dawn. You'll meet a supplier, *Jean Marais*, with a truck-load of produce for Le Havre, at place Cauchoise, where the route for Le Havre can be accessed. Your code will consist of *hail and harsh wind* while his reply will include *won't see much more of that, let's hope*. You should be at Madame Mayer's no later than midday. You will stay at her friend's place – a five-minute walk – and you will meet the two leaders. I then suggest you come back on Monday morning, again at dawn. Coming back, *Jean* will be waiting for you in rue Thiers, under the trees – he will wait one hour, from six to seven. You'll have Saturday afternoon and all of Sunday in Le Havre.'

‡

The next morning, Saturday, having retained her room, Violette put a few essentials in the canvas hold-all and cycled to the agreed pick-up point. The thought of new meetings and travelling to Le Havre excited her, tempered by the certain knowledge of entering the most dangerous zone in France, apart from Calais. She crossed the square to a beat-up old lorry idling under a tree and greeted the driver.

'*Bonjour, monsieur,*' Violette said with a slight smile. 'Got caught the other day in that *hail and harsh wind.* Today looks better.'

'Yup,' said *Jean Marais*. '*Won't see much more of that. Let's hope so anyway,*' he mumbled, opening the cab door for her. He hoisted her bike into the back, then climbed in behind the wheel and they were off – direction Le Havre on the D982.

Violette settled in the seat as the truck rumbled along. She was very satisfied with all she had learned and was finally on her way to Le Havre. She asked the farmer to take a route close to the viaduct carrying troop and provision trains between Rouen and Le Havre. She needed some idea of its construction and the lay of the surrounding land so that if Allied bombers were to strike they could keep civilian casualties to a minimum.

The viaduct was huge; her recommendation would be for an air strike as well. She believed that sabotage could only be incomplete but the Maquis would put together one of their specialist teams to do their best to at least weaken the structure ready for an air strike, she hoped.

She and *Jean* chatted aimlessly all the way to Le Havre. At three intersections they were stopped and their papers checked. The truck and her canvas bag were searched on each occasion. As they arrived at one of the main arteries leading into the town, they were stopped yet again. This time, after their papers were checked and the truck thoroughly searched, they were asked by the officer, 'Where are you going?'

'Home,' replied Violette.

'I gave the young lass a lift from Rouen,' interjected *Jean*, looking bored. 'Look, got to move off and deliver this stuff to your headquarters.'

'In a minute,' ordered the officer. 'First, what were you doing in Rouen, *mademoiselle.*'

'Oh, my whole Easter was spoilt. Had to look for a distant uncle. Think he got caught in one of the British bombing raids. I'll tell you, they're bastards. I'm sure my uncle's dead. Couldn't find any trace and spent days looking for him.'

'So, you haven't been to work, young lady?'

'Will do tomorrow, unfortunately. I'm a secretary in a department store.'

'Very well. You can leave. Be careful how you go.'

Sweating, they both said thank you to the officer, climbed back in the truck and *Jean* drove on in the direction of the town centre. She's cool, he thought.

'You did well, lass. I'll drop you on the corner of rue Thiers after passing by Madame Mayer so you know where she is. Not far, then you can cycle back. Looks as if I've driven you home. Okay?' Rue Thiers was Violette's fictitious address in Le Havre.

'Thanks very much. And I'll see you on Monday, at the end of rue Thiers. Is that correct?'

'Absolutely. Now you be very careful. Don't take any stupid risks. Not worth it. Not for you. Not for us.'

'I will. I really appreciate your help. Bye.'

As they arrived, she jumped down, *Jean* got out and helped her pull the bike from the back and she pedalled off as he had directed.

‡

She found the apartment building easily. Madame Mayer, still deeply traumatised by the horrendous treatment meted out to her husband, welcomed her quietly and led her into the salon.

Madame Mayer presented Violette to an air force lieutenant, Alain Phillipeau of the FFI – Forces Françaises de l'Intérieur – which had recently taken the *Deux Léopards* group under its command. They exchanged pleasantries and then Violette got down to the business of what they could all do to help after the awful decimation of the *Salesman* circuit and the arrests.

They sat and talked all afternoon, made plans around London's directives and then chatted informally for a short while until dinnertime. Lieutenant Phillipeau left, happy with the clearly explained requirements and having told Violette that they would do their best, but the viaduct would be difficult. No promises, but he would talk to his comrades, including Marcel, and try to implement a plan. He reiterated how important it was they receive more explosives from England as the Barentin viaduct would take most of their stock. Violette was hopeful but would have liked further reassurance. Still, she was sure the lieutenant would make the attempt.

When the two women were left alone, Madame Mayer asked Violette to stay with her as it would be safer, and she was desirous of company. Violette accepted immediately with her heartfelt thanks. Madame Mayer had prepared a light dinner, which Violette helped her carry to the dining room. Tomorrow, Madame Mayer would take Violette to a friend's house, a few blocks away, where Violette could meet the group leaders of *L'heure H* and *Vagabond Bien-Aimé*.

As promised, the following morning they went to Madame Mayer's friend. The visit was highly successful. Violette told them of her meeting with Lieutenant

Phillipeau, who would offer any help to co-ordinate the attack on the Barentin viaduct and other sabotage projects as per London's instructions. Both leaders were happy with the plan so far and London's instructions. They then thanked Violette for coming over from London on such a dangerous mission. She thanked them for being willing to continue the work considering the dreadful and sad events leading to the deaths of so many of their friends. Having slept on cushions and mattresses dragged into the living room, the following morning, Sunday, after much laughter and boisterous hilarity over a long lazy breakfast, they got back down to business.

Later on, returning to Madame Mayer's apartment, Violette handed a considerable amount of money for her to pass on to families in need. She slept well and was up early to meet *Jean* for the trip back to Rouen. It was now 17 April.

‡

16

Back to Rouen

Monday 17 April to Thursday 20 April 1944

'Rise up!
No truce, no rest, no sleep;
Despotism is attacking liberty.'
Victor Hugo (while living on the island of Jersey), author's trans.

Violette saw that resurrecting the *Salesman* circuit would be best forgotten. Its members had been shattered and scattered too far to come together again as a forceful unit. That *Salesman* in the Seine-Inférieure had had its day would be Violette's observation/report when she returned to London. Its very success had ensured its destruction. The circuit had caused so much damage and dislocation to the Germans that they needed to eliminate it. Nevertheless, it seemed that there were hundreds of men and women still active in Résistance operations and begging for weaponry and other supplies for the impending Allied invasion. Violette also discovered that, as SOE was now working in tandem with de Gaulle out of Algeria as well as London, the French were very much happier to accept their recommendations.

Another factor that helped create a more optimistic climate was the weather. Spring was here at last and parachute drops were being made again. She had transmitted to London details of areas ideal for the job. Supplies dropped from the skies never failed to bring a smile to the lips of the reception committees and Résistants.

‡

With her bike thrown on the back of the farmer's truck, she was satisfied with all she had learned and passed on in Le Havre. *Jean* had also given her good intelligence from his criss-crossing of Normandy and supplying the Germans.

After being dropped off, Violette cycled back to her hotel, where she was pleased to see Lucien and Marcel talking with Madame Thivier. The men had plans for Violette to meet with several people. During their discussions, she discovered that the Rouen *Combat* circuit had been destroyed after Claude Malraux (known as *Serge* in the *Combat* circuit and *Cicero* in the *Salesman* circuit) had been arrested at five o'clock on 8 March from information received from Dieppe by the Feldgendarmerie, and by four the next morning Dr Delbos and his wife, for whom Philippe had arranged the drops of medical supplies, but had difficulty working with, were arrested and interrogated. This led to the remaining members of the group being arrested, shot or deported, including the Sueur's, Louis Corroie and Felix Pionteck, a Pole and Broni's brother, Schlaich, from Alsace, and all their friends, along with Isidore Newman (*Pierre*), the SOE wireless operator living with Denise.

Three of the people she had met in her travels, Violette distrusted on sight and would have nothing more to do with them. Two more distrusted her and would not work with her. But there were several others, as well as Marcel, Lucien, Lise and Denise, who, during the rest of April and May, were instrumental in liaising with other groups to perform operations at her behest, which ensured the success of her mission.

She handed a small but ample sum to a family devastated by the recent raids. The father had been tortured before being shot, leaving his wife and three children quite penniless, their home gutted by the Gestapo as a warning to others. Marcel had introduced Violette to them during the afternoon, and the mother told them that the only place they could seek refuge was in Brittany, where her family lived. They needed enough to cover fares, food and accommodation for about two weeks.

Violette handed over the cash to the family and wished them all the very best of luck. The mother grasped her hands and kissed them in gratitude, tears running down her cheeks. She told Violette that her husband had died silent and honourably for France. She repeated that they must not stop, they must fight on, otherwise her husband's death would be in vain. Violette told her that her own husband had been killed by the enemy, so the woman felt reassured by their common ground and of Violette's avowal that they would, indeed, win this war and regain their freedom.

The next morning she noticed she was still losing weight, but not too much, and her eyes showed the tension she was under. Madame Thivier was there on Violette's return each day. Knowing what *la petite* was up to and to counteract the strain she was under, she ensured she had hot water, warm towels and plenty of hot chocolate and tasty black market snacks. The situation felt surreal to Violette: she, an SOE agent bent on sabotaging the enemy's efforts; the German armed services swarming the town, weapons at the ready; Madame Thivier clucking around her, cosseting her in the little hotel. What contrasts. Violette made her coded notes again and retired early that night.

‡

It was Tuesday 18 April and Violette still had much to do. She told Lucien, whom she met near a small café, that she was riding out as decided previously, to meet up with Denise and Lise at Marianne's home in the northwest corner of Rouen. She got there at about half past six and Lise introduced her to *Marianne*, a long-term external leader of the *Diables Noirs*. Her real name was Suzanne Dupuis.

Marianne had prepared them a light simple supper, finished off with Violette's contribution of another packet of coffee beans. *Marianne* had been asked by the Boulanger women to cast an eye over this girl from London, about whom word was slowly spreading. *Marianne* found herself beguiled by Violette, and saw the depth of her commitment and her understanding of the situation in Rouen.

The group were in excellent spirits and once the business of checking through the activities that Violette would be involved in over the next few days was completed, laughter rang out. On 18 March, all radios had been ordered to be taken to the Kommandatur at the *Hôtel de Ville*, but *Marianne* proudly brought out a hidden radio to place it on a sideboard. They half-listened to the BBC while chatting late into the evening until it was too late return home – well after curfew. *Marianne* offered them the spare bedroom and divan in the living room and all gratefully accepted.

At thirteen minutes past midnight, while they slept, a squadron of Allied bombers roared low overhead, dropping flares attached to parachutes. As they spiralled down through the night sky the town was illuminated in dazzling white light. This alerted the people who had not fled as they had been warned to do the week before to take immediate shelter.

So Wednesday 19 April 1944 started as a day of terror and courage for the Rouennais. Sirens screamed and people scrambled. Allied bombers swept over like rolling thunder, dropping hundreds of tons of every imaginable kind of bomb over specific targets on the outskirts to the east and west of town, then onto military targets on the right and left banks.

Violette and the three women ran out into the garden of *Marianne*'s house to watch in horror. Fifty minutes of terror, noise, screams, huge explosions, fires and falling buildings. People were crushed, buried alive in shelters whose exits were blocked by falling debris. Fires raged that would continue to burn on for another ten days while firemen were called in from the suburbs as well as from further away: Elbeuf, Dieppe, Louviers and Evreux. Paris was under similar attack.

As the suburbs and the town itself contained German command centres, fuel depots, Gestapo headquarters, the German army and naval headquarters, sites for stocking the new rockets and wharfs holding German matériel, they were all targeted: Rouen, Sotteville, Saint-Étienne-du-Rouvray, Petit-Quevilly and Grand-Quevilly,[77] as well as Bois-Guillaume, Amfreville-la-Mivoie, Blosseville-Bonsecours and Belbeuf. There was no way the civilian population could be avoided. Many died or were horrendously injured during that dreadful night.

---

77 The neighbouring village of Quevauvillers has a street here named after Violette Szabó because the family lived there awhile.

Leaving *Marianne* at home to comfort her children, Violette, Denise and Lise rushed to the centre of town to gauge the extent of the damage. Denise on her bike and Violette with Lise on the back of hers pedalled furiously until they could get no further. Rubble and fallen buildings covered the streets of the centre, and they struggled to push their bikes through the debris and around burning fires, hearing the screams of those trapped and dying or badly wounded, pushing past people fleeing and wardens frantically trying to save lives and fire engines rushing to spray river water over the burning ruins.

The Germans had taken shelter and none except the dead remained on the streets. Several soldiers were killed by shrapnel and bomb blast. There was not a lot the three women could do. Denise's apartment house had been destroyed; she was now homeless. They found that the Micheline boutique managed by the Sueurs and Lise Valois had been all but wrecked, as was the other chic boutique that Denise worked for, the Monique-Couture. They struggled to Violette's hotel and found it still standing. Madame Thivier was cheering on the bombers from an upstairs window – not caring whether or not her hotel was destroyed and she along with it.

On their headlong rush into the town, straight into the pandemonium of destruction, they had seen crowds of people desperately trying to find family members and neighbours or fleeing in fear from collapsing buildings and raging fires. After a quick greeting to Madame Thivier, they decided to go back out to see what they could do. Violette also wanted to make a cursory inventory to report to London.

The three women left the bikes in the hotel yard, now full of rubble, clambering awkwardly through piles of bricks and mortar, upturned jagged paving stones and cobbles blown into sharp fragments, on through the scorching wind. Seeing two very young children sitting on the pavement crying, they stopped to help them find their mother, who was bruised and in pain, half-buried under her porch where she had been standing watching the flares falling from the sky. After extricating her and checking she was not seriously injured, they reunited her with her children, her bruised face smiling in relief and thanks. One hundred and eighty-five targets had been bombed, most on the left bank, but fifteen at Bois-Guillaume in the north-west of the town. In the main town on the right bank, sixty streets and squares were hit, with a similar toll on the left bank. Even the beautiful cathedral was hit. Le Bristol, where Violette had had coffee with Lise, was hit. An outside wall was gone. In all, 600 buildings were badly damaged and 512 were razed to the ground. Corpses and body parts were everywhere. The smell of blood and scorched flesh was overpowering. At least 900 people died, but a final figure was never possible to establish. It was as bad as anything Violette and her family had survived in London. There were 500 wounded, 370 of them were hospitalised.

The Palais de Justice was badly damaged. Violette was not overly saddened by that, as it was the Milice headquarters. But she hoped they would one day be able to restore its Gothic beauty, and the cathedral and half-timbered houses. And so it was. After the war ended, an immediate start was made to rebuild and repair old

Rouen and the left bank. Le Havre had been hit just as hard; the centre destroyed beyond repair. On liberation, architects and builders began to design and construct new, modern centres.

‡

With their hair and even eyebrows scorched from the hot winds surging from the fires, the three women wearily returned to the hotel and ran inside, calling for Madame Thivier to come down. She appeared before them, a spectre from the night, making them all laugh. Dust covered her from head to foot. They were all filthy, scratched and covered in bruises. Looking at one another, they burst into laughter; even Denise managed a wan smile. Lise and Violette made hot chocolate for them all.

Denise was shaking and in shock but gradually regained her composure. Madame Thivier offered her a room in the hotel for as long as she wanted; Denise said she had relatives she could go to as her home had been flattened in her shop, but in the meantime would help Lise and Monique sort out the debris of their stores. Lise was very grateful and they agreed to first go round to Denise's the next morning and retrieve anything recoverable – especially anything salvageable that would help her continue to work, plus objects of sentimental value. Then they would look for Monique and go to both shops to see what could be recovered and repaired. No doubt some of their girls would return too; they would be sent home unless they wished to stay and help in the clear-up. They would be paid what Lise – and later, when they found her, Monique – hoped would be their full wages. It later turned out that Monique was safe in her home and Lise's home was untouched. Both were on the outskirts of the town.

It was agreed that Violette's planned trip to Ry and further north should definitely take place in the morning. She had much to do and time was passing. She could not linger in Rouen to help her friends.

‡

The next morning, Thursday 20 April, the four women were at breakfast, discussing the terrible bombardment when Lucien and Marcel walked in.

'*Bonjour, tout le monde,*' they greeted everyone as they shook the dust off their torn clothes, eyes red and weary but animated. 'What a terrible night and a terrible day. Allies, you know. Bloody awful, but they have to do it. What a mess, so many dead, so many injured, so much destruction. Thank God, many people heeded the warnings and had already left. I've spent all night out there. I don't know – war is such shit, *merde, merde, merde* – excuse me, ladies.'

'*Ah, mon pauvre Lucien, mon pauvre Marcel entrez, entrez donc!*' cried Madame Thivier. 'You look all in. Let me take your jackets, come, and sit over here. I'll get fresh coffee on the go.'

'Thank you, *madame*,' came their exhausted reply.

Marcel took Violette to one side. '*Corinne*, the Bois-Guillaume has been hit, but I don't think the neighbouring Château in Mont-Saint-Aignan has been. That's in the north of town where the German naval headquarters are. While you're here, you might wish to have a quick look at the area. The same applies to Canteleu-Dieppedalle in the south-east on this side of the river. It seems pretty well intact. That's where some sort of secret storage or construction is going on. Probably for those new damnable weapons.'

'Yes, I definitely will have a look-see before leaving for Paris. But, more importantly right now, how are you?' queried Violette with a worried frown. She wondered about his family, about his friends. She was also anxious about Denise. 'You know, Marcel, I think poor Denise is in a very bad way. This war has been very cruel to her. Her husband dead, her lover deported, she was interrogated, and now her home destroyed. Her children are far away. She not robust and needs help. I can certainly give her some money, which I shall do before I leave for Ry shortly. But she needs more; she needs company and help.'

'Yes, I'll see to that, *Corinne*. I'll talk to a Norwegian family of farmers not far from where you're going, and see what they can do. I know they're desperately wanting to do something more as one of their sons, Biscuit, a sailor, might have been instrumental in some of ours being arrested. I'm not so sure, but I certainly understand their sentiments and fears.'

'Would you like me to see them?'

'It wouldn't hurt. But one part of the family is in Bezancourt and the other in La Feuillie. Why not mention it to the Boulanger women? They'll know how to handle it.'

'Okay, that sounds perfect.' Violette turned back to the group and heard Lucien say, 'I'm okay. So's my family. Got them out, just in time. Marie is staying with me in a safe-house but, Lise, she'll be at the shop tomorrow to help in any way she can.'

'Marie is a brave girl, Lucien. By the way, how did you know we were here?' asked Lise.

'Ah, I was told at the Préfecture this morning by a known informer. Informs both ways. Reluctantly to the Germans – family threatened – and less reluctantly to us,' explained Lucien, with a sardonic smile. 'However, this is the main reason for my visit. *Corinne*, you must be very careful. Denise and Lise too – I know you two are associates, and therefore can be seen doing business together, but both your people have been deported and you've both been interrogated too, so, no doubt you're under surveillance, which could easily affect you, *Corinne*. And you too, Madame Thivier – you're a very gutsy lady, but this same informer said you were observed last night, shouting encouragement to the British planes. Please take care, all of you.'

'*Bof!* I'll go on as I always do. Some little informer isn't going to frighten me at my time of life!' Madame Thivier stalked off to make more fresh coffee.

Violette smiled and said to nobody in particular, 'She seems to have an unlimited supply of "real" coffee, cocoa and other grand foods she couldn't possibly produce in the hotel yard.' There were nods of agreement all round.

‡

Violette then prepared to leave, explaining she would be back in a few days. After piling her canvas bag and a parcel of goodies packed by Madame Thivier into the baskets on the bike, she hugged and kissed her friends and co-conspirators and pushed the bike through the rubble until she found a clear roadway out of Rouen.

‡

17

Les Diables Noirs, the Boulanger Women, V Rockets

Thursday 20 April to Friday 21 April 1944

Having arrived in Ry, Violette was about to meet members of the Boulanger clan. Some of the men and women were still at liberty, hiding in the Boulanger caves, still training. They only exited for sabotage, reception committees and sorties to premises holding stocks of ration cards, coupons, tobacco and other essentials for survival. It was only over the last few days that Violette had heard the name of the group, the *Diables Noirs*, mentioned openly. She already knew something of the Boulanger brothers, Henri (*Commandant Fantomas*) and Raoul (*Capitaine Cartouche*); their courage could not be exaggerated.

The brothers had been captured and had kept silent under appalling torture in their own farmhouse, then later at Gestapo headquarters. Raoul's shinbone had been broken and exposed through the flesh, his head a mass of contusions, cuts and blood. After all this, the brothers were sent to Compiègne to be transported to a concentration camp. Only one would survive. The *Diables Noirs* members had been told to disperse until called for. A few stayed; some simply remained in their homes nearby, doing their normal work; some disappeared to Paris and elsewhere. A highly trusted few remained active. Violette felt sure that this group would continue to act and would co-operate with other groups. She was going to meet a group of women, including members of the Boulanger family. As the Boulanger brothers kept security extremely tight, it was decided that Violette would not meet them at their farm where the extraordinary underground hideout had been built (accessed through an innocuous, narrow kitchen cupboard), but in Ry.

Before leaving Rouen, Violette had gone over the map and directions with Marcel and Lucien, who knew the area well, at least dozen times so that she would not have to ask her way or go to the wrong house. All this seemed to Violette like a test, an initiation for meeting women involved in the Résistance. She had not been the least embarrassed to go over it time and again while asking a thousand and one questions, many of them repeated. She did not want to make a mistake and did not care if they thought she was slow-witted. The two men were very patient and went through it as many times as she wanted. Violette asked about the village, what was in it, where the main buildings were and what they were used for; needing to know these things in case she was stopped and questioned. There were, at most, 200 inhabitants in the tiny hamlet. Marcel admired her insistence on knowing as much as she could about the geographic and commercial layout of the route and the village of Ry.

‡

It was almost midday by the time she arrived, wet and cold. En route, Violette had hidden in undergrowth whenever she heard traffic approaching. She found her way directly to the house, let her bike fall against the inside wall of the yard, grabbed her basket and rushed into the house as if she had known it all her life. Anyone watching would only see a bedraggled girl, soaked from the recent downpour, hurrying into a house where she obviously belonged.

Madame Pascaline Boulanger (*Calourette*)[78] took care of her, towelled her hair, took her wet jacket and shoes and ordered another woman to prepare a hot tisane. Pascaline looked at the apparition before her, lovely even in her drenched state, eyes shining with the excitement of it all and talking quickly about the ride and the hail while she checked over the people in the large warm kitchen. 'My dear,' exclaimed the older woman, 'You'll catch your death of cold.'

'*Madame, je suis Corinne Leroy*. I've come from Marcel in Rouen. I wish I could believe that *the spring blossoms were still lovely this year* after what I've just ridden through,' she laughed gaily.

'*Bon, ben, mademoiselle, moi, j'suis Calourette*. And I agree, especially *with the poor blossoms* – the wind and hail has really buffeted them about.'

The coded exchange made, they all sat round the table smiling at the dishevelled Violette, now in petticoat and bare legs with a child's blanket pulled tightly round her shoulders. She felt at home among this group of farming women – earthy matrons so fiercely protective of their people.

There had not been much traffic on the roads, she told them. There had been a convoy carrying some kind of long machinery or weaponry on a number of armed lorries. She asked what that might be. They, in turn, wondered how she had made the awful journey on the rusty old bike outside, among enemy convoys and without having ever been to this house, hamlet or countryside before. Violette explained she had been given excellent directions, the rust was camouflage on what was really a fine bike and cycling was her hobby in peacetime. They liked her modesty and were mesmerised by her.

Pascaline looked anxious when Violette talked about the convoy. Violette realised that it could be a delivery of the rockets that she had been sent to find more about. It had been heading from the north, southwards, and another woman,

---

78 Mother of Raoul and Henri, leader of the *Diables Noirs* now that her sons had been taken.

known as *Marianne*,[79] explained the rumours about a construction site somewhere at the lower point of a triangle from Rouen to Ry and south towards Paris. She thought it was at the quarries of Saint-Leu-d'Esserent, about thirty miles from Ry, but was not sure. Although it was mostly German labourers working there, STO men had been brought in to increase the workforce doing twelve-hour shifts, keeping the work going around the clock, seven days a week. Stories were heard of incredible flying bombs being assembled for transport to launch sites on which Philippe had already reported. He had not, as far as Violette knew, reported on a storage and transport facility. The Germans were clearly in a hurry. It seemed that the site was a concrete bunker for the storage of large quantities of some newly invented weapon, fuel or parts.

Violette asked if it would be possible for her find a way to visit the site – perhaps with some cleaners or cooks working there. The women were aghast at the risk, but Violette was adamant that it was essential her superiors knew as much as possible about these sites and weapons. She was keen to journey to Saint-Leu-d'Esserent and perhaps on to Dieppedalle on the western outskirts of Rouen where there were rumours of heightened activity and security.

‡

Night had fallen. The women kept telling Violette that what she wanted to do was not possible. She retorted she had her bike – all they needed was give her reliable directions to the village of Saint-Leu-d'Esserent so she could pedal down to see what she could find out. The women were troubled, but as she insisted they agreed to organise one of the men to take her and her bike down on a truck. Once there, she would be on her own. Violette agreed, calming down now that she had her way. She thanked them for helping her as she knew how dangerous it was for everyone. However, she felt that she must get the information back to London by the end of April, if not before. As she needed to get back to Rouen, she explained that she would not return through Ry again.

'Here's *Gaston*, he'll take you with him. Won't you *Gaston?*' demanded *Calourette*, then introduced him to Violette.

'*Bien sûr*, anything you say, *patronne*! Where exactly do you want me to go? I have an important load of produce to take down to Chantilly. I'm setting off at first light. It'll take a couple of hours especially if there's any holdup on the roads. And there's bloody bound to be, I'll wager. If it keeps raining a couple of the bridges might be flooded.'

---

79 This *Marianne* is an alias of a leader of another group of which Georges Philippon's friend Chevallier had been a member.

'*Monsieur*, that's where I want to go. As I understand it, Chantilly is not too far from Saint-Leu and I can ride my bike from Chantilly in an hour or so. What do you think?'

'*Ouais*. But you can't go in them fancy clothes. *Marianne* or *Hirondelle*, haven't one of you got some farm clothes for *Corinne*?'

'Sure,' answered *Hirondelle*, a friend of the brothers. 'I'll pop back home and get an old skirt and blouse to put under your long jacket – mismatched, but you'll blend in better.'

'I am very grateful to you all. Let's bloody well win this war and celebrate together afterwards,' laughed Violette, a determined look about her.

‡

Violette retired to a bedroom in the rafters. Although a little apprehensive, she was actually tingling with excitement to be going into a dangerous area to seek out further intelligence useful to her government.

It seemed to her that the tide of war was turning – a certain will to fight on to victory no matter the cost was gaining ground. Among the *Diables Noirs* and the external members of this group, she felt the fighting spirit was alive and well, albeit battered and sore. Violette felt honoured to have met the Boulanger women. Good, strong-minded women of the Norman agricultural community. Fiercely independent like herself.

Her plans for the morrow felt right; she had transport as far as Chantilly and had only a few short miles to pedal from there. She would be wearing appropriate clothing, the remaining money well hidden in her belt lining. Violette hoped only for a mild day, a nice breeze and no stops to check identities. That's unlikely, she thought. Bloody Boches can't leave it alone. And they're as jumpy as hell, feeling the end is approaching. The Germans had gone too far, been unspeakably cruel and now the people were getting ready to strike back. All the Résistance needed was good organisation and decent weapons to do maximum damage. She would do everything in her power to help this happen.

‡

Next morning, Friday 21 April, Violette was called down to breakfast in the steaming kitchen just before dawn. Bowls of steaming coffee were being placed on the table, with baskets of rough-hewn bread, a jar of home-made plum jam, a bowl of hard-boiled eggs and some of last autumn's apples that had been stored in the grange roof. Before leaving on her task, Violette handed to the Boulanger women sufficient cash to help the bereaved families in their Maquis group, *Diables Noirs*, decimated at the same time as Philippe's *Salesman* circuit, and enquired into the activities of the remaining members.

Then they all trooped out into the farmyard, where *Gaston* tucked Violette's bike into the back of the truck, which was otherwise crammed with fresh produce, including a crate of hens clucking away. Violette, in her farming clothes and faded scarf tied under her chin, got in beside *Gaston* and off they went with a pop, rattle and shake of the wood-fired gazogène engine.

A couple of hours later, they uneventfully arrived in Chantilly where *Gaston* warned Violette to be careful and not to do anything rash. She nodded, smiled and thanked him warmly. The bumpy ride in the truck beside an impassive, monosyllabic but kind *Gaston*, the passing convoys of troops and weapons and one search of the truck had brought her firmly down to earth. *Gaston* unloaded her bike and she cycled off.

On the winding roads, it was about an eight-mile ride. Violette stopped after about fifteen minutes when she reached the D44 before turning left to Saint-Leu. At that moment, three German jeeps shot through with high-ranking officers in deep discussion on the back seat of each vehicle. They were going in her direction and were clearly in a great hurry. Interesting. She had dived into an overgrown thicket as soon as she had heard the sound of the motors and just had time to settle with her bike well hidden before they were upon her. Following a short review of her plans and a quick overview of her mental map of Saint-Leu, she moved off at a decent pace.

Around midday, she arrived in the town centre, which was swarming with soldiers. There were a couple of bakeries, one grocery shop, three garages, hairdressers and several cafés and restaurants; it did not hurt the little town financially to have the Germans here but there was a strong Résistance movement headed by the communist Raymonde Carbon, who became the town's mayor after the war.

Gaston had given Violette the names of Madeleine Blincourt at one of the café-bars and Joseph Le Cauvin, a garage owner. She was hungry and decided to go the café-bar for a snack and to see if Madeleine could help her. As she entered, she found herself in the midst of German soldiers drinking and singing, with a French female singer leading the sing-along. The soldiers had clearly been drinking for some time and whistled as Violette hurried over to the bar and asked for Madeleine. Violette ignored the whistles and turned her back on the room. 'Hello Madeleine,' she said to the young woman who introduced herself. 'Glad to see you. *I'd like a tisane if you have any, as I am feeling a little under the weather. Gaston dropped me in* Chantilly and I've ridden from there. Chilly.'

'Of course, dear girl,' answered Madeleine. '*You must be careful not to catch a chill in this weather. Gaston should have brought you here.* Come with me, I've a friend I'd like you to meet.' They had exchanged the coded greeting.

Violette followed Madeleine to the backroom, where they sat near the kitchen stove. Violette explained what she wanted to do, and would appreciate a bed for the night. She would ride back to Rouen the next morning unless Joseph Le Cauvin could arrange a lift part of the way.

Madeleine suggested setting out immediately and that they should ride ahead to the turning into Chemin des Carrières. She told Violette that it was about two miles north and not far from Saint-Maximin, where she explained there was a German transport depot hidden in the same woods. They would not be able to get much further as there were too many sentries all along the quarries and the forest area at the rear. She went on to explain that Henri Bonaventure worked there and he would be able to give Violette some information later that evening, as he came to the café for his evening meal every day. They laughed as they talked, to disguise the undercover nature of their jaunt. Just a couple of women chatting away; one young and decidedly pretty, the other a little older, but still attractive in a blousy kind of way.

‡

As they rode out of the village Violette made mental notes of everything and everyone she saw around her, including the mood of the villagers and the German military, which seemed in both cases calm and purposeful. The quarries were huge and hidden in the forest about half a mile from the river Oise.

Two Gestapo stepped into the middle of the road leading to the quarries and demanded their papers. Studying Violette's papers, one of them asked why she was so far from Le Havre, which her documents stated was her hometown. She replied that she had been asked to look for her uncle in Chantilly and as Madeleine was her friend, she came to stay on her way there. She did not say that she had come from Chantilly, but rather that it was her destination. Then, if the Gestapo decided they were interested in her, they would not think she would be heading for Rouen and Dieppedalle. 'Perhaps you could tell me if Colonel Niederholen has arrived yet from Rouen? He's such a kind man and I'd love to meet him again if he is here,' smiled Violette sweetly with a coy sideways look at the Gestapo officer.

'Not that I know of. If he is here, I will pass on your message. Where are you staying?'

'At the café-bar in rue de la République.'

'Proceed. Do not enter the areas beyond the signs. Those areas are *verboten*.'

'No, sir, thank you,' replied Violette.

Poor Madeleine was pale as a sheet and trembling. 'How on earth did you manage to get away with all that?'

'Because I do know Colonel Niederholen; met him twice now. I do believe he would much enjoy my company if the occasion arose. If he were here, I would be happy to spend a little time with him. He's a decent bloke for a bloody German and would not take undue advantage. But I damn well would!'

'Well, I'll be …' gasped Madeleine. 'You've got a cheek, that's for sure.'

They rode some distance further and decided to push their bikes into the undergrowth and take a closer look. Violette was amazed at what she saw. Great caverns had been dug deep into the quarries. She observed that the Germans could assemble and stock a huge amount of weaponry there. And peeping out of one corner, ready for transportation, was a long weapon that looked very much like a torpedo but with small wings towards its rear. Violette had struck gold. Her intelligence would be invaluable back home.

After about twenty minutes, with Violette moving from one position to another, Madeleine was getting decidedly jumpy.

Violette whispered to her to stay hidden where she was and not to move. She would be back in about fifteen minutes. She moved quietly from bush to bush, tree to tree to get a closer look. She heard a whistle blow and almost fainted. It was the lunch break for the German labourers. Violette decided she had seen about as much as she safely could, returned and gestured to Madeleine that they recover their bikes to head back to the Café de la République.

As they rode back, they laughed over Violette's shock over the whistle. 'What about me,' exclaimed Madeleine. 'I almost wet my pants. Didn't know where you'd got to, either.'

Madeleine explained that Joseph had seen some similar objects around the area of Saint-Maximin, just a few miles north-east on the other side of the river Oise, again near the woods. More for London.

Once back at the café-bar, Madeleine introduced Violette as *Corinne* to Joseph, who promised to take her about three-quarters of the way to Rouen the next morning. The three of them chatted away while Madeleine's aunt brought in a hearty meal of bread, beans, chicken and salad. A carafe of light rosé wine accompanied the meal. Joseph told Violette everything he knew about the Saint-Maximin weapon sites and much else besides. He described the site in the Bois de Clairefeuille, only four kilometres west of Buchy. Just then, Henri Bonaventure arrived. He ate his meal hungrily, while telling Violette that secret arms were ordered by Hitler to be stocked in the underground bunkers on both sites. He went on to give her details of stocks, site dimensions and more. They went over the details again for clarification and then spent a brief time chatting.

Finally, they bid one another good night and Violette had retired to her tiny room at the back of the building. She pulled out some rice paper and quickly noted down in code all that she had seen, surmised and been told. She was so pleased that she had come here.

‡

From late 1942, London had started to hear rumours about German long-range 'secret weapons'. Then the details had trickled in. In April 1943, Duncan Sandys in the British War Cabinet undertook a full study of the reports, resulting in the advice that a threat from German 'secret weapons' should be taken seriously. Philippe reported in his February 1944 debriefing that he had seen the sites that he thought were launch pads not far from Rouen along the Normandy coastline, and this was where his and later Violette's intelligence gathering proved so useful on their return from their respective missions in 1943 and 1944.

British intelligence estimated that the damage inflicted by the bombing raid on the installation at Watten in August 1943 would require as much as three months to repair, but continued reconnaissance of the French coast revealed new constructions of a similar type, all in the Pas-de-Calais region. These sites were huge and the larger sites, like Mimoyecques, with their connecting tunnels and underground chambers, had been estimated to have housed at least 200,000 rockets in just one site.

Millions of aerial pictures had been taken, guided by intelligence reports as they came in from agents on the ground like Violette, along with ground photographs of sites taken at great risk to the photographers. These were all studied by hundreds of aerial photographic interpreters like Paul Emile and interpreters of accompanying data to provide more technical information and targeting for bombers.

From continental areas all along the Atlantic Coast, including the English Channel, sites had been constructed to bombard England and especially London with German pilotless aircraft. The first such bombing did not take place until 13 June 1944, seven days after the Allied invasion of Normandy. The V1 flying bombs[80] flamed across the dark skies from Pas-de-Calais and one exploded on a railway bridge in the centre of London. By the spring of 1945, when Germany finally collapsed, more than 30,000 V rockets (approximately 16,000 V1s and 14,000 V2s) had targeted England and advancing Allied armies on the continent.

The Saint-Leu-d'Esserent site near Creil, not far from Chantilly, had been designed to house batteries of long-range guns and rockets. The quarries had been turned into a factory for assembling and stockpiling V1 flying bombs. From these underground installations, they were transported by train to various launch sites along the Atlantic coastline of France, particularly Normandy. Through Violette's information, confirmed and built upon by other sources from late spring 1944, the Allies intensified their strikes on the Saint-Leu-d'Esserent quarries, destroying everything by the end of September.

‡

---

80 'V' designation originally meant *Versuchmuster* (experimental type); interpretation of the 'V' as representing *Vergeltungswaffe* (vengeance weapons) was a later addition by German propaganda agencies.

18

To Dieppedalle, Arrest and Déterville

Saturday 22 April 1944

Waking early, Violette hurriedly dressed in her own clothes, folding the farm clothes borrowed from *Hirondelle* in Ry and putting them neatly on the bed. She went down to breakfast with Madeleine's family in the large kitchen. Joseph was already there, a thin, reedy cigarette stuck between his lips and a smile of welcome for a game lass who wasn't half pretty.

Before Violette had appeared, Madeleine had done nothing but talk about *Corinne*, about this extraordinary girl and what she had done on their trip to the quarries yesterday. When Violette came in, Madeleine smiled at her warmly, 'You slept well I hope, *Corinne*. I was scared yesterday but you were so calm. You smiled so sweetly at the *Chleu*. I could have taken you for a very willing *collabo horizontale*.'

'That was the general idea,' affirmed Violette, 'And I think it worked. I hope the Allies bomb the *salauds* into the ground.'

Everyone looked up with surprise at the sweet-looking girl swearing so ferociously. They all laughed, understanding the depth of her pure hatred for this destructive, tyrannical force. After a hurried breakfast they went over the route Violette would follow. She thanked them all for their kindness and courage in fighting the enemy. Most of them were communists and she had to admit she admired their commitment if not their claims and aims.

Madeleine took Violette in a great hug, wishing her luck and saying she would miss her.

By the time they were ready to leave, it was pelting down. Violette was relieved she would be sheltered in the cab of Joseph's truck. Her bike was shoved under torn tarpaulin next to two crates of pigs being taken to the Kommandatur in Gournay-en-Bray. Joseph suggested that they might have time for a snack in Gournay-en-Bray before parting company.

The journey was uneventful except for the constant squealing of the pigs. The storm passed, but it drizzled for an hour. Joseph chatted about all he had seen within the very wide area of his travels from Belgium to Paris and Senlis to Rouen. He acted as a liaison officer between many different Résistance groups and only met those he knew he could trust and were leaders of their respective *réseaux*. He never used a telephone, never travelled any other way but in his truck, which was well known to the military authorities and the Milice as well as the French police. He held all the necessary German papers as well as his normal identity papers, as he worked legitimately on their behalf, delivering produce for their hungry soldiers and administrative staff. He gave a few perks to a few useful sentries so they would turn a blind eye when he was caught out in some suspicious activity.

Joseph needed no encouragement to talk about everything he knew, as he was adamant that she report all the crucial intelligence he had gathered over the last few weeks to London as soon as possible, by pigeon if no other secure method was open to her, before she returned herself. He knew someone in Rouen who had some English pigeons that would fly to the Isle of Wight if that would prove useful. She assured him she would report to her superiors everything that he told her.

Joseph supplied the locations of the German army's headquarters and barracks over the entire area, describing all that he knew of the strange bunkers and launch sites. He told her what kind of sabotage was possible by those working on each military installation and on the uneven development, as he saw it, of a central agency to bring all the Résistance groups under one central military and civil organisation directly linked to de Gaulle in London. His information was invaluable and urgent and Violette did her best to remember it all, making mental pictures of each place and situation to help recall it all later.

As they rattled and squealed into the heart of the Pays de Bray, and on into the large market town of Gournay-en-Bray on the edge of the Forêt de Lyons, well south of the ancient villages of Ry and Saint-Denis-le-Thibault, the rain finally stopped and the sun poked through the thinning clouds.

Gournay-en-Bray is about a hundred miles north of Paris, thirty miles east of Rouen and sixty miles south of Dieppe, an important commercial, agricultural and market garden centre. It had been a pretty country town whose heart had been almost destroyed on 7 June 1940 by the armies of the Third Reich. They sacked the town and stayed over four years. The Kommandatur had garrisoned in the lovely old town hall, hanging a huge red and black swastika flag over its main entrance. Once again, destruction and desolation were everywhere.

The mood of the town was decidedly unfriendly. It swarmed with enemy soldiers, grey-green Wehrmacht, black Gestapo and the ever-present Milice. Weary people looked around furtively as they scurried on their way. There remained, however, many whose fighting spirit received a boost from the rumours of the Allied invasion to come. The strong communist element, carefully hidden, quietly – and sometimes not so quietly – continued their Résistance work in the town and in the small surrounding villages.

Joseph parked the truck, checked the pigs were settled and safe in their crates and led Violette to a brasserie for lunch. The windows had been blown out and covered with blackout paper making the light dim and a fug of cigarette smoke hung in the air. They were left undisturbed as they ate in a corner; the waiter, a passive

Résister and friend who occasionally acted as a cutout, came and chatted a while, quietly remarking on the increasing activity of the Germany military and passing on other useful intelligence to Violette to take back to London. After an hour or so they parted company.

‡

Violette rode off into the early Saturday afternoon sunshine, glad to be on her own so she could ponder all she had learned. She stopped a while on route to make further coded notes and considered trying to find the pigeon fancier Joseph had told her about, to fly her intelligence to the Isle of Wight, but it might be better to use the radio, as she had already done. She remained ever vigilant for odd sounds, patrolling sentries and, as before, whenever she heard motorised transport she moved off the road and hid in thickets or lay low in the fields. She saw more military traffic with long lorries, carrying what must have been heavy weapons towards Rouen or further afield. To be stopped, searched and questioned would be disastrous at this stage.

Towards late afternoon, Violette arrived back in Rouen. Joseph had told her to find and talk to a young man called Pierre Legros in the Vieux Marché. He gave her the introductory coded message to use to him, or others who might help her to find him, and the reply to expect from Pierre or other comrade whom she could then trust.

In April 1944, le Vieux Marché truly was the Old Market of Rouen, although business was slack. Violette felt an uncomfortable presentiment but dismissed it and wandered nonchalantly through the market. She approached a knick-knack stall and asked the female stallholder if she knew Pierre Legros. She said that Joseph Le Cauvin had said that he might help her find some long-lost friends. The woman looked at her with great suspicion and angrily shouted at her to '*fichez le camp!*'[81] as she was a busy woman and knew no one of that name. Under lowered eyebrows the woman watched Violette walk away, turned angrily to her neighbour, and gesticulated in the direction of Violette. A French policeman noticed the exchange and made a note on his pad.

Wandering around the market as if she were looking for something to buy, picking up one thing after another, occasionally asking the price of some article or about Pierre then moving on when the price was too high or the answer negative, she came to a vegetable stall where a young man of about twenty was yelling to anyone who would listen that his produce was the best. Violette repeated that Joseph had said Pierre could help her find some friends she once knew. This time the young chap grinned widely and said he sure did know him.

---

81 *Fichez le camp* = Scram!, Bugger off!

'In fact,' he went on, 'there he is just over there. Hey, Pierre, come on over here. Joseph wants me to introduce this young lady.'

The young man came over. '*Salut*, how can I help you?' he asked Violette politely.

'Joseph asked me to tell you that *he's taken the pigs to Gournay-en-Bray at long last,*' replied Violette with her part of the code.

'Ah yes, about time. *By now, they should be well and truly fattened and ready for the slaughterhouse.*' And they both laughed. Two-sided code established.

'I'm *Corinne Leroy* and I'm hoping to gain some information,' she continued.

Pierre was a young man about Violette's age and belonged to the Serquigny group from the little town of the same name, although he did not tell Violette this. Philippe had already had some contact with this group and, although they had lost some of their people, they were trustworthy and competent. She explained she wanted to see two places: the quarries at Canteleu-Dieppedalle and the launch sites on the heights of Bois-Guillaume on Mont-Saint-Aignan. He said he would be happy to help, having already heard about her.

Pierre suggested they should pretend to be a young couple getting to know one another and acting a bit silly so they could ride their bikes around the area, racing one another from time to time and generally looking like a couple of youngsters full of the joys of spring.

Violette agreed and so they cycled slowly, and sometime furiously, along Route D93 towards Canteleu-Dieppedalle, while Pierre told her what he knew. The Germans had imported Todt and Russian slave-labour to build two factories in the quarries and also deep within the caves to produce liquid oxygen. He felt sure this had something to do with the huge concrete caverns with launch sites rising from under the ground near Calais, here in Rouen, Tôtes and Auffray, and a number of other sites along the entire coast as far west as the Cherbourg peninsula. It seemed to him that the Germans had invented some kind of rocket contraption that they could sling out across the Channel like a catapult.

As he was talking, he smiled happily and from time to time they gazed into one another's eyes while riding abreast – forbidden by the German authorities, but they judged that they would probably get away with a severe ticking-off if they were stopped. They laughed as they discussed serious matters to disguise further their real intentions. Once they dismounted, seemingly to study the daffodils that had sprung up along the road, but in fact they were looking directly up at, and carefully examining, the quarries with their terraces. They cycled in the direction of La Bouille until they came to the railway line that disappeared into the far end of the quarry. Violette had a general idea of the size of the site, leading away to the north from the right bank of the Seine.

She noted much of the area was disguised by small thickets and copses dotted all along the river front, but the railway was just visible and had a branch entering the quarry, as Joseph had described to her. They could not get close enough to see it properly but there was also an embarkation area for boats plying up and down from Paris to Le Havre.

Violette considered Pierre was probably correct that the Saint-Leu stockpile of rockets could be transported to this area, not only by road along the D93 hugging the riverbank, but by rail and also by barge along the Oise then the Seine to Canteleu-Dieppedalle, or onto Le Havre. Rail or road would be necessary to take such weapons on to Tôtes, Auffray or Watton. However they travelled, the weapons could collect their fuel of liquid oxygen here.

The Germans used the deep caves of these quarries to build installations that would function within a network of solid vaulted galleries. The rock extended to anything between 150 and 240 metres above the caverns' floors. These ancient caves were now heavily fortified and guarded day and night to produce and store oxygen. This oxygen was then transported to launch sites to fire the V1 and V2 rockets.

They walked down to the water's edge as budding lovers do, parked their bikes and looked across the Seine. They had deliberately turned their backs on what most interested them to deter suspicion from nosey passers-by. After a few minutes, they turned back. There was nothing further to discover in Canteleu-Dieppedalle from the outside and it was dangerous to hang around any longer. As the afternoon was advancing, they also needed to reach the north of town soon.

High above in the forested hills was the Château de la Moissonnière in Canteleu, explained Pierre. This beautiful château had been occupied by the Germans and had become one of the command posts for troops stationed in the Seine-Inférieur who were attached to the defence of the Atlantic Wall. The area was more heavily guarded than any area Violette had so far seen. Also, as troops were stationed in the château, it meant there was a supply of troops ready for twenty-four-hour close surveillance.

‡

Laughing and chatting, the two seemingly innocent young people rode all the way back into town, stopped for a coffee in a bar on the Quai de la Bourse and then continued north-east and on to the other side of the town, to Bois-Guillaume and Mont-Saint-Aignan. Here they had a quick recce of the German naval headquarters in the Château Jean-Pierre. Their frivolity was not all false front; they were two young good-looking people enjoying their task together. This cover was used for all it was worth but neither let down their guard for one moment. There were far too many checkpoints and soldiers, police and Milice about. From the vantage point of the high northern plateau, Violette was shocked anew by how much of Rouen had been flattened in the 19 April Allied bombing raid.

Château Jean-Pierre of Mont-Saint-Aignan and the manor house, Tamareau, had been requisitioned by the German navy. Violette could see no connection to the main energy supplies in Rouen and asked Pierre about this. He explained that they must have installed their own stocks of oil and coal in deep bunkers and that they had their own generators. There were also a number of concrete structures for housing officers and ordinary seamen.

Pierre, who had a good command of German, had overheard a German officer talking to an admiral that the German code name for the underground factories was 'Granit 1308'. As they left he also told her a story from Ginette, the eight-year-old daughter of his father's neighbour. 'It seems there's a launch site for some flying torpedo in the forest not far from Saint-Saëns. Ginette's father was required last year to work near Buchy. One day, the Germans came looking for people and, at their insistence, he left between four Germans, which was not very reassuring. It was explained to him that he and some others were going to work for these Germans. They took him to the station in Sotteville in the morning and they embarked for Buchy. Ginette heard her father say to a mate before leaving, "We've got contacts with the Résistance and we have the order to do whatever we can so that this runway will never work." They committed small acts of unnoticeable sabotage so that it would not operate properly. Production must have been near to zero. Her father was responsible for transporting sacks of cement to make the runways and Ginette heard her father admit, "There were days when, for the whole day, I took the same sack back and forth in my wheelbarrow." In the end, that runway, the one in Buchy, never worked.'

Pierre then went on to tell Violette exactly where this runway or launch ramp was, being under the Bois de Clairefeuille, in the commune of Monterolier-Buchy and about two to three miles west of Buchy. It was a network of underground galleries dug deep into the '*marne*'[82] for protection from bombing and to stock Hitler's secret weapons. In their obsession, German planners ordered the extracted chalk dumped in adjoining fields to be painted green to conceal their activities. They both laughed over the camouflage attempt.

In fact, it was various groups in the Résistance and Colonel Michel Hollard, leader of the Agir[83] Résistants, who informed SOE of the launch base that Violette was now able to confirm with the added intelligence she had gained. Rockets were brought there by train on the railway line with a small branch line built to the caves and launch site. The site had its own diesel generators to produce electricity. Another exit for reaching launch ramps closer to the coast led to Saint-Saëns along a river and was not known by many people. Violette took in everything Pierre said, asking pertinent questions from time to time.

---

82 'Marne' is a kind of soft lime that is very easy to excavate. Often land will subside into natural caves formed millions of years ago. It is this very terrain that made digging the huge *Diables Noirs* complex hide-out possible as well as the caverns used and extended by the Germans.
83 'Agir' means 'to act'; a great name for a group of Résistants acting to free their country.

As the day darkened into late evening, Violette bade Pierre farewell with a fond kiss on both cheeks and grateful thanks from herself and her masters in England. She then hurriedly rode towards her hotel.

‡

A few yards from the hotel, she was stopped again, this time by a French police officer.

'*Mademoiselle*, it's very late. You should not be riding your bike on the streets. I must take you to the *commissariat* so you can explain yourself to my superior.'

'I'm so sorry. I was having a meal with a friend and we forgot the time. I'm two steps from where I live. There's two minutes to curfew and you can see the sign on my hotel from here.'

'Nevertheless, you will follow me, I insist.'

Fear stuck in her gullet, her heart pounded and her knees were unhappy carrying her slight weight. But she pulled herself together sufficiently to say with all the dignity she could muster: 'I'm most affronted by this. I shall not be treated like some little tramp!'

'I am sorry, *mademoiselle*, I am only doing my job and it is curfew. I must take you to my superior so he can make his judgement on whether you have violated the law of the land.'

'Oh, for goodness sake, don't be so pompous. Don't you realise how much dreadful damage has been done to this town and its people. I've lost my uncle, my aunt has died, another has lost her house and everything—'

'I understand, *mademoiselle*, but orders are orders. Please follow me. It won't take long.'

And so they walked to the police station not far away, the police officer having taken charge of her bike to prevent her from jumping on it and pedalling away.

‡

As soon as Violette was brought before the Capitaine de Police she launched her attack, 'I really do not understand this young sergeant, sir. I had just finished a meal with a friend where we were discussing the awful events of Wednesday before riding back to my hotel. I can't find my missing uncle. One of my aunts was killed and another made homeless. It's just too awful to bear. And now this.' And she burst into tears. It was easy: pent-up fears and tension from all that had happened brought the tears rolling down.

'Calm down, *mademoiselle*, and take a seat.' His eyes stared at her coldly. 'You must realise you are out late and committing an infraction of the law by being out after curfew. There's no excuse for that. Now tell me your name and give me your papers. I think I've seen you about. You will tell me exactly where you've been and why.'

Capitaine Le Roux was a large man. His cold unsympathetic eyes stared down at her papers. His lips were clamped shut. At that moment, another policeman entered. '*Bonsoir, Le Roux, vous avez les documents et les prisonniers?*'

'*Attendez, attendez Déterville!* This young woman's been seen around town the last couple of weeks looking for some relative, she says. Name's *Leroy, Corinne.* Secretary from rue Thiers in Le Havre. But I'm wondering how she can be living in a hotel for a couple of weeks on a secretary's pay, owned by an enemy sympathiser, by the way. Some silly old duck needing a good fuck! Ha, ha, see how poetic I can be, Déterville?'

'Sure, you'll soon make it to the *Académie française!*[84] Look, these documents need to be delivered to Alie in double quick time!'

'Okay, okay! First, I have to interrogate this pretty doll. I'll get the documents ready and the driver'll get me and them to Alie. We've caught a whole new bunch of *terroristes* and I want to get to the Palais and let the Chief deal with them.'

'Be quick about it, then. Ten minutes, no more. Then you get your fat arse over to Alie.' With that, Déterville stormed out. He hoped he'd not given that slug sufficient time to do any real harm. He'd wait around outside for the girl, whom he'd seen hustled into the police station by the arresting sergeant. He'd heard about the girl. Courageous and diligent in everything she'd done so far. She must have gained a tremendous amount of information; for that reason alone he must ensure she got out. There was nothing he could do at the moment without blowing his cover. As Alie's deputy, Déterville had been able to save many people from torture or death. He also provided valuable intelligence for London on Gestapo, Milice and military movements.

Back in the office, the captain continued, 'Now, *mademoiselle*, tell me what you're doing in Rouen.'

'I came from Paris about a week ago on my way home to Le Havre. I was asked to search for an uncle who's missing in this area. It seemed he might've got caught in one of the enemy raids that have destroyed so much. They've killed my aunt and made another one homeless.'

'Yes, yes. What's your address?'

'Here or in Le Havre, sir?'

'Le Havre, of course.'

---

84 The Académie française is the most prestigious academy in France, created in 1635. It has up to forty members, who may become 'les immortals', responsible for defining and defending the French language, awarding literary prizes, creating social benefits and advancing the dictionary. Its members included Jean Racine, Jean de la Fontaine, Jean Cocteau and Jean-Paul Sartre. In recent years the members include women writers of note including Marguerite Yourcenar and Assia Djebar.

'Well, it's on my identity card, sir.'

'Yes, yes, and here?'

'At the little hotel in rue Saint-Romain.'

'Did you find your uncle?'

'No. And worse still, an aunt was killed in the bombing this week. Another has lost her house and everything in it. I can't bear it.' She sobbed again, dabbing at her eyes with a handkerchief.

'Yes, you said. Stop blubbing! Now, why're you out at curfew?'

'Well, I wasn't r-really. I spent a few minutes too long in a c-café with a f-friend, deciding how to help my surviving aunt. Nobody has been able to help me find my uncle. I thought the authorities would be able to tell me something. But I still had time to get back to the hotel before curfew. After all, I was on my bike. Then the sergeant stopped me a couple of minutes before curfew and insisted I come to you when I could've reached the hotel in time. We could see it from where he arrested me. It's not fair, sir. I demand an apology. Because of him, I *am* out after curfew. I've no intention of breaking any law. And, honestly, I'm scared of more bombing.' And she wept again.

'Humph! Well, you should've been more aware of the time. I have more important things to do now, so you can leave. Ride straight to your hotel. I want you back in here tomorrow afternoon at four sharp. Do you understand? Better be questioned by me than Alie. Got it?'

It was clear from Le Roux's face that he was loath to leave off the questioning. But those bloody prisoners and documents had to be got over to Alie. However, he would need (and wanted, as she was a good-looking piece of skirt) more time to break the girl and would enjoy meting out rougher treatment. Tomorrow should do it. She couldn't get away between now and then, especially with all the checks at the stations and in the streets. Her name and description was already on all their lists, too. Still, as soon as he got back, he'd put a tail on her. Meanwhile the duty *flic*[85] could watch the hotel and arrest her on some trumped-up charge if she came out.

'Here's your papers. Four o'clock tomorrow!'

'Thank you, sir. I won't be late.' Violette picked up her papers and turned to leave. As she did, Le Roux added, 'And I suggest you don't try to leave Rouen.'

'No, sir! I certainly won't.' She gave a watery smile and said, 'I haven't finished here yet as I must try to help my aunt, if only by being with her for a few days more.' She opened the door and walked out, closing it gently behind her.

‡

As she left the building, a voice called her, *'Mademoiselle!'*

---

85 *flic* = copper (policeman).

She turned around to find the other police officer there. Again afraid of what was coming next, she mustered her courage and said a firm 'Yes?'

'Glad to see you weren't too long in there!' He gave her a wink as he said this. 'Follow me, please.' Violette was stunned and terrified.

Déterville marched her smartly to his waiting car. Before opening the door, he said, 'Mademoiselle *Corinne, the blossoms are lovely but the wind's blowing them away*, as they will your fears, I hope.'

Her surprise left her open-mouthed until she managed to reply, 'Yes, *spring's on the way*,' but she couldn't remember the phrase correctly.

He continued, 'I've heard interesting things about you, *mademoiselle*, and am honoured to meet you. However, you must leave Rouen. Is your work complete?'

'Yes, it is, sir. Thank you. I must retrieve my bike. I'm off to Paris. Are you really Alie's deputy? They call him and his team of henchmen the French Gestapo. I'm told he's utterly ruthless in getting information and trapping Résistants.'

'Yes, I am. And yes he is. It's a dangerous game but I have to say I enjoy obstructing that French Nazi. Now, I'll take you to your hotel. I know where it is. Friends have been watching out for you these last few days. You must leave tomorrow, if you can. Is that possible?'

'Oh yes, I should think so, by bike if necessary. I can't thank you enough, Inspector Déterville. I think you have saved my life or at least, saved me from a few very nasty sessions in there.'

'Sergeant, take this young woman's bike to rue Saint-Romain – Madame Thivier's hotel. She's coming with me,' he ordered the sergeant standing guard.

'Yes, sir.'

The sergeant had been just about to take a break. He came out cursing the order and saw Violette step into Déterville's car. He thought it odd, but knew Déterville had an eye for the pretty ones and wished him luck.

The black Citroën took a circuitous route back to the hotel. As they went, Déterville examined the young woman beside him and saw the strain etched on her lovely face. He told her quite a lot about Chief Inspector Alie and his deeds, warning her again that she must leave the hotel at dawn before the morning relief got there. Thank goodness, he thought to himself, that he had a fine reputation as a Don Juan. He would remember to a make some comment about the pretty woman beside him to satisfy the curious.

Five minutes later, he dropped her off, thanking her for all that she was doing for his compatriots. She thanked him in turn for his work and for saving her.

Violette walked into the safety of the hotel, relieved, shaken and weak with exhaustion.

‡

19

Back at the Hotel, Planning to Flee, Hasty Retreat to Paris

Night of Saturday 22 to Sunday 23 April 1944

It was time for Violette to return to Paris. She sat in the empty breakfast room of the hotel to plan her next moves carefully. If she remained any longer in Rouen, she would soon be arrested and forcefully interrogated. She very much doubted she would be as lucky as last time. The Gestapo and the French police attached to the Gestapo now had her on their records. She was expected at the commissariat at four o'clock tomorrow. Le Roux was bound to have at least one of Alie's henchmen watching the hotel, as Inspector Déterville had said.

Chief Inspector Louis Alie had formed an 'anti-terrorist' brigade whose sole responsibility was to entrap anyone suspected of Résistance activity. He was sadistic and enjoyed brutality. It was he who had arrested Isidore Newman and his co-conspirators. Later on in 1944, as the tide turned so decisively after the D-Day landings, Alie fled to Germany on 24 August with Gestapo archives. For some reason, he later decided to return to Rouen, where he was recognised and arrested. He tried to buy his freedom and a passport to Argentina, using the information he had retained on collaborators and the activities of the SS and Gestapo as a bargaining tool. Alie was tried and sentenced to death in November and executed on 27 December 1944.

If Le Roux mentioned Violette to Alie, there would be an immediate raid on Madame Thivier's hotel to arrest her and very likely Madame Thivier, too. Apart from Violette's cover and her courage, she only had Déterville's quick actions and Le Roux's lack of thought to thank for her present freedom. He should have slammed her in a cell but considered she was just a scared little rabbit caught in the headlights. Her act of fear and distress along with her cover had worked for now. However, she must be gone before dawn.

Her first thought was that she would go straight to *Marianne*'s house in the north and ask for help. She would hope to get a safe-house for a couple of days, then catch a ride with a Résister partway to Paris. Quickly she realised that this would mean putting them in very real and immediate danger.

How could she escape this town that threatened to become her prison? She was tired, tense and frightened but had to concentrate on the avenues open to her as she had too much information useful to the German authorities; they would stop at nothing to wrench it from her and prevent its transmission to London. This scared her more than anything else.

Her rendezvous with Philippe was from Tuesday 25 to Sunday 30 April in Paris. Tonight was Saturday 22 April; three days before the first day that Philippe would be waiting. She had planned to leave Rouen on the morning of the 25th by train. That way, final messages could be exchanged and loose ends tied, but there really was nothing more she needed to do in the area.

One option was simply to get on her bike and make her way slowly to Paris. Very dangerous, too, she knew. What would happen if she had an accident or the tyres blew? The distance was about 90 to 100 miles. She was fit and healthy, if a bit tired. If she did thirty miles or so a day, she would arrive on time. Not too bad; it would be relatively easy to sleep in the fields or find some guesthouse along the route. It would not matter should she be a day late; Philippe would be at the same spot each day in the Luxembourg Gardens, where he would wait for her for one and a half hours from midday. But wouldn't the roads to Paris be teeming with enemy transport in both directions? There would be some longer stretches where a young woman on a bicycle would look incongruous and therefore suspicious. Not such a bright idea after all.

Violette realised she *could* take the train from Rouen. She knew she would be stopped at the station checkpoints and that would be dangerous. But she would not endanger anybody else's life and could better protect the information she held. She would tell Madame Thivier that she was leaving and ask her to pass on her very real thanks to everyone. She would not tell her where she was going nor how she was travelling.

Then she remembered she had other sets of identity cards she could use. Of course, that is what she could do. Catch a train under another identity. She looked at her timetable and decided to break the journey. She could get a single ticket for Mantes-la-Jolie. There she would get out and go and spend any waiting time in the town or reading quietly with a coffee at the station. Then, after an hour or so, she would get a ticket to Paris. Yes, that was definitely what she would do.

At that moment, Madame Thivier walked into the breakfast room. '*Ma petite*, what on earth are you doing in here, in the dark almost?'

Violette told her what had happened and that she would be leaving just before daybreak. She did not say where she was going as she did not want to put this fine lady in any more danger.

'I'll be sorry to see you go, *chérie*. But I'm also glad. For your safety. You must be very, very careful wherever you're going. '

'Thank you. You've been so kind to me and I've enjoyed every moment here. Let me settle my bill now – not forgetting all those treats, by the way. You have made me as snug and safe as I could possibly be.'

‡

Violette took breakfast alone at dawn and then went to say farewell to Madame Thivier, who had got up especially early to see the girl had some kind of breakfast and a fond farewell from a friend.

That kind woman had made a generous pannier so Violette would not have to use a café-bar on her journey; Madame Thivier also gave her an old travelling blanket so she could sleep rough if need be or keep her warm during a train journey. She hoped the weather would hold out for that young woman.

She went off to get the basket and blanket while Violette went to her room to finish packing her luggage and make safe her rice papers, extra sets of forged identity cards and money. She was dressed in warm underclothes, nylon stockings and her smart navy shoes. She wore her silk blouse covered by the beige jumper over her navy skirt. Easy to move in. Winter scarf on. The blue cardigan had been returned to her and, still wrapped in brown paper, was tied to her case. She left her reading material in the room and carried her luggage down to reception. Once there, she tied the blanket that Madame Thivier handed her on top of the wrapped cardigan.

'Thank you very much, Madame Thivier. I shall never forget you. Please give Denise and Lise a big hug from me, to be passed on to all the friends I have made here. One day when all this is over, I shall come back and we shall have a wonderful time together.' She smiled so sweetly, it brought tears to Madame Thivier's old eyes.

'Now, you take great care, my girl,' she warned. '*Adieu*,[86] *petite!*'

'*Adieu, madame!*'

Violette took her suitcase in one hand, the pannier in the other. Her long jacket she draped over her shoulders and threw her bag over her left shoulder.

‡

She walked over the rubble, heading slowly to the north of town. Daylight had hardly reached the horizon. She had a timetable and a road map she had surreptitiously 'acquired' when she had bought her reading material. She was ready for the worrying journey on enemy trains. As it was Sunday, there would not be as much movement of civilians and military as on the other days of the week so extra

---

86 *Adieu* means [go] with God, similar to *vaya con Dios* in Spanish and equivalent to *farewell*. It means at the very least a long separation.

vigilance was required. She knew the police, and probably the Gestapo and Milice, would be on the lookout for her.

It was too early to go to the station, but Violette had something she must do first. She went for a last walk around the town. The duty police sergeant of last night was nowhere to be seen, nor his replacement. Ensuring she was not followed, she looked for an area free of people. She walked through the lanes towards the *Hôtel de Ville* and ambled unhurriedly along the side path into the extended gardens at the back, carefully looking for the space she needed. Shortly, she found a bed of mature bushes that seemed to have some sort of gap behind them.

Looking around carefully at the windows overlooking the park, Violette saw no snooping eyes. Quickly she pushed her way through the bushes and found just enough room for her purpose. A good hiding place, and dry. She threw in her luggage and ducked in. First, she unwrapped the cardigan. Taking off her jumper and jacket, she wrapped them in the brown paper that had held the cardigan, belting them to the suitcase. She put on the cardigan. It was lined and had pads to square the shoulders off, so it looked like a Chanel-type jacket. She removed her socks, stuck them in her bag along with her scarf, then brushed her hair into a fashionable style and put on a little makeup. Finally she placed a navy blue beret on her head.

She now looked quite different. She would walk differently too. Then she took out a new set of identity papers and hid her old ones in the name of *Corinne Leroy* in the lining of her cardigan (which she had prepared the night before). They may be useful again in Paris or when travelling back to England.

She was now *Madame Marguerite Blanchard*, née *Picardeau*, *veuve* – widow. Address in an attractive old quarter of Vincennes, a town to the south-east of Paris. Her cover was that her husband had been killed on the Maginot Line in 1940 and she now ran his small business in top-quality vegetables and charcuterie for the wealthier citizens of Vincennes. She had come, in the cover story she had constructed during the night, to Rouen to negotiate new terms with a farmer in Gournay-en-Bray, a *Monsieur Dubois* whom she had briefly met with *Joseph*. She would describe him as her main supplier of superior fruit and vegetables, explaining that all her supplies had to be the best quality as they were delivered by her carriage man to Château de Vincennes, requisitioned by the Wehrmacht.

Violette also had the pretext of seeking new suppliers in the region. Her identity papers included a special German authorities' pass containing the correct German stamps for such activities as visiting agricultural communities, even in the forbidden zone.

‡

Her new disguise complete, Violette walked purposefully and with dignity down the little lane out of the park. Turning right, she took the narrower lanes to the train station. She chose a street where she remembered posters of Philippe and Bob were affixed to a wall. After carefully glancing around she quickly ripped off two, stuffing them in her pocket for SOE in London, then quickly moved on. Later she could conceal them more securely.

The first check was at the entrance to the station. Violette joined the largest queue, head held high, slightly impatient while hoping the sentry's concentration would be lagging after a heavy Saturday night and the boredom of an early Sunday duty. As she came up to him, he looked at her carefully, then at her identity document with her photo. This image showed her in similar clothing to those she was now wearing. He also looked down a list that he held on a clipboard.

The name of *Corinne Leroy* must be on it, she was sure. With a description of her, judging from the careful scrutiny she was given. She had done her best to look different without a true disguise. Her cardigan-jacket was thrown elegantly over her shoulders and her beret slanted fashionably to one side. The guard checked every line of two of her documents, looked at her again, then let her pass. By this time, her hands were trembling but as they were holding her luggage it was not detectable.

She looked him in the eye and smiled offhandedly as he handed back her documents. Making her way to the ticket office, she purchased a first-class single ticket on the first train to Mantes-la-Jolie. This would bring her some forty-five miles towards Paris, about halfway there. Violette had chosen Mantes-la-Jolie on account of it being large enough that she would not stand out if she had to remain there for some time.

Her train would be departing in fifteen minutes. She decided not to go into the brasserie where she had met her friends. She doubted that 'her' colonel would be there at this time in the morning, but it was better to avoid trouble and to wait on the platform. At the platform-gate she was required to present her papers, which were checked again very carefully and then she was politely told to move on. Relieved, she walked smartly through.

Finally, the train crawled in, spewing smoke over the travellers. Although the platform was not full, there were enough passengers so that Violette could mingle and climb into a first-class carriage full of Frenchmen and women dressed in similar casual elegance.

The journey took just over an hour and a half. The gendarmes halted the locomotive at one station for fifteen minutes while they searched the carriages for two suspected 'criminals'. Another stop when papers were checked. Violette opened her pannier and snacked on the wonderful array prepared by Madame Thivier. Despite the delays, it was a relaxing and enjoyable journey.

Once the train pulled into Mantes-la-Jolie and she had disembarked with her luggage, she immediately went to buy a single ticket for Paris and then looked for the platform. Violette felt much less conspicuous here and not quite so tense. Her clothing was well chosen and although a number of men watched her as she walked past, her comportment discouraged any approaches. She wore her emerald engagement ring turned inwards as her wedding ring. She was elegantly dressed and every gesture was that of a woman used to conducting her own affairs.

Having checked the number of her platform, she bought a local newspaper, went across to the Brasserie Hôtel Terminus and ordered coffee, where she read the paper and glanced from time to time at the people as she waited patiently. She noticed that there were no Gestapo or police on duty. Two Miliciens were checking identity papers and German soldiers came in and out of the station. Outside in the forecourt, she noticed a number of military vehicles but nothing of great interest. This town had also been bombed on 19 April, as had many north-west and north-east of Paris. And, too, many of the other towns along the Channel coastline, with major roads, railway lines, canals and rivers, essential for the movement of German troops and weaponry.

The hour passed pleasantly enough and eventually she strolled elegantly over to her platform. A porter, whom she tipped handsomely, carried her suitcase and pannier. He was a happy man and winked conspiratorially at her.

Installed in her first-class carriage on the way to Paris, she noticed a few German officers further down her carriage. It was not full but there were the usual collection of businessmen and their wives going to treat themselves to Sunday in Paris.

A Gestapo officer took the seat across the aisle. Fear danced again. Her temples began to throb. She forced herself to calm down, reminded herself of her persona. She crossed her legs elegantly, picked up her newspaper from the empty seat next to her, opened it and began to read with a slightly superior air.

She tried to ignore his presence but could not, not entirely. He seemed absorbed in the papers he carried in a much used attaché case. Eventually, the train slowed to a crawl through the smoky outer suburbs of Paris until, creeping into St Lazare Station, it came to a leisurely halt in a hiss of steam and a loud double hoot.

‡

Part IV

20

Paris and André Malraux Once Again

Sunday 23 April to Monday 24 April 1944

Violette stepped down from the train with a huge sense of relief. The Gestapo officer had left his seat as they came into the station, jumping from the train even before it had come to a stop. Violette walked to the platform exit, passing uneventfully through the German security check and over to the Terminus Café, where she found a corner table and ordered coffee to think calmly through her next move.

It was afternoon on a quiet Sunday. Tomorrow she would have a full day in this anonymous city before her first chance to meet Philippe on Tuesday. Where should she go now? She could go straight to Tante Evelyn's apartment; she still had the key to the door. But she might put Philippe's aunt in real danger or possibly disrupt an operation, disturb a Résister using it as a safe-house.

Her instinct was to stay away until she had met Philippe in the Luxembourg Gardens. At some time, she knew, she would have to meet up with André Malraux[87] to let him know the fate of his half-brother, Claude. She preferred to talk to Philippe, her commanding officer, first. Not essential, perhaps, but correct procedure.

Her papers were extremely good forgeries and she had plenty of money. Violette knew of a small private hotel just off boulevard Saint-Germain-des-Prés, the Reine Marie, which Harry Peulevé had described to her. Discreet, established and comfortable. Under normal circumstances, it would have been way out of Violette's price range. She would take a quiet look first.

She hailed a vélo-taxi, a cycle rickshaw which was Paris's answer to the petrol shortage. Paris looked beautiful and it was clear that some parts of the economy were booming. Cash-rich Germans, military and civilian, frequented the myriad smart cafés, restaurants, fashion houses, elegant department stores and boutiques, brasseries, cabarets and concert halls. Yet for the Parisian working population food, coal, gas and petrol were in grimly short supply, with the Germans having every

---

87 Then Secrétaire générale des Groupes francs, part of MUR (Mouvements Unis de Résistance). Malraux helped Harry Peulevé's *Author* circuit. Roland Malraux (his half-brother) was Harry's lieutenant.

priority. The German soldiers had no trouble finding French girls to take to a *café-dansant*[88] or the cinema showing the latest films passed by the Vichy censor's office. Many cinemas were out-of-bounds to French citizens unless they were in the company of a German.

Since 1940, due to the Germans' lavish spending, there had been a cultural revival in *gai Paris*. Even *avant-garde* art and theatre were doing well, though many artists had fled the country. Germans and wealthy Parisians or provincial visitors enjoyed the performances of Maurice Chevalier, close friend and lover of Mistinguett, another famed and much-loved but by then ageing performer from the era of the First World War and roaring twenties. The growing popularity of jazz in wartime France was a less acceptable leisure pursuit to the German mind, who considered it mere decadent Jewish and Negro nonsense. So it was natural that jazz became a symbol of revolt and non-acceptance of Nazi tyranny.

‡

Violette needed shelter for three to five days, so she registered at the Reine Marie under the name of *Madame Marguerite Blanchard*, widow, as more fitting for a woman staying alone in a Paris hotel. Once registered, she unpacked in her pleasantly luxurious room. She decided to relax, have a bath and ordered coffee with pastry to her room. As the afternoon wore on, she opted to dress in casual, discreet beige and step out into the spring air.

She went for a long stroll through the boulevards. Paris is a small city and to walk from its northern boundaries to those of the south only takes about two hours. Paris was suffering shortages of everything from electricity to Métro trains to bread. All was much as it had been when she arrived three short weeks ago – an eternity. Some *débrouillards* were still getting rich on the black market while others with the cash paid dearly for little treats.

At 100 rue Richelieu, Violette met and spoke briefly to a number of people who had bought modestly priced prepared meals from the *Comité d'action de restaurants communautaires* (Community Restaurants Action Committee), set up for the purpose in 1944. They exchanged news of events in Rouen and this committee's work in feeding many Parisians.

She walked around the corner to rue George V and into Fouquet's on the corner of George V and the Champs-Elysées for a hugely expensive but authentic coffee with a real butter croissant on its terrace. The proximity of near-starving citizens to those Parisians with money to burn shocked her.

---

88 Café-dansant, a café where one could dance, having taken a table for coffee and snacks. A café-theatre is a place where one sat at a table ordering coffees and snacks while watching a play or spectacle.

Violette was amazed to see one group of Germans in front of a luxury hotel loading two large vans not only with bags and suitcases, but also crates of wine and spirits, furniture and silverware, all hurriedly piled into the back of vehicles without too much care or organisation. They seemed to her rather sheepish looters and she wondered if this signalled the beginning of the end. Were the non-military Germans abandoning Paris with as much loot as they could carry? Yet another piece of valuable intelligence for London on the German civilian and military frame of mind.

Being alone in Paris was proving useful in discerning the mood of the town. Violette was more receptive than when she had first arrived. Now she entered areas that would have been previously unwise. She blended in easily and she did nothing to attract attention to herself; the embodiment of demure anonymity.

How wonderful it would have been with Étienne beside her. Her heart cried out for him. He should have been there, in the hotel, lying next to her, holding her in his arms, making love to her. They should have bathed together, dressed together, both smiling with the look of love before dining and dancing somewhere swish and romantic. Violette had loved his laughing eyes, his tales of a legionnaire's life, his uniform, his medals for gallantry, even his battle scars and his obvious courage. She had missed him when his leave ended and he went off to war, but this searing of her heart was different. There would never be hope for tomorrow. Tears fell down her cheeks as she walked along.

She scolded herself for showing self-pity and dried her eyes. She clawed back her poise as she could not afford such emotions, instead allowing thoughts of revenge to sustain her. She hoped that in Rouen she had done sufficient to settle a score or two.

‡

Violette decided to climb the Butte de Montmartre, stroll round in a spirit of discovery and go to evening Mass in the Sacré Coeur. As she walked around, she found she adored the village atmosphere and the artists in their studios. She understood now her mother's and aunt's passion for the place. From impressionism to cubism and surrealism – it was all here. She watched artists working as young German soldiers asked for their portraits to be sketched, sightseers laughing and chatting as they strolled about and an occasional Gestapo or Milice casting fleeting shadows over the sunny enjoyment of the folk on the hill.

As she reached the Basilica she was impressed by the beautiful mosaic of Christ, his arms stretched wide in a welcoming curve. She walked into the Sacré Coeur, crossed herself with holy water from the font and lit her candles. She genuflected, crossed herself and then knelt in a pew to offer a prayer. The short sung mass was sweet and peaceful.

Afterwards as evening turned to night, Violette walked towards her hotel and on the way ate a solitary *cassoulet* at a bistro in one of the poorer districts around Clichy so that she could watch the people. She returned sad and lonely to her hotel.

Tomorrow, Violette would go in search of high fashion. She wanted to know all about *gai Paris* in wartime. She knew there was a strong Résistance movement here but it was not her present remit to contact them, nor would she. As she climbed into bed she picked up a book she had bought on her ramble this afternoon, André Malraux's *La condition humaine*, which she felt duty-bound to read. Soon, her eyelids drooped and she fell into a dreamless sleep, the book slipping quietly to the floor.

‡

Waking fully refreshed at seven the next morning, as she did not wish to mingle with the guests in the dining room, Violette took a leisurely breakfast in her room – not knowing if there were Germans, spies or collaborators staying at the hotel – and, spirits almost restored, decided to stroll across the river and up to the Madeleine.

Her confidence was still a little fragile from the grief that had struck her the afternoon before. Also Violette knew she must be extra vigilant not to let down her guard. She was feeling a little vulnerable, concerned she might be shown up as ignorant of some obvious local or widely known item of interest. That could prove dangerous in the breakfast room so she was out of the hotel by nine, walking into the gentle April sunshine.

However, her presence had already been reported to Rouen. The doorman of the hotel, a friend of Inspector René Déterville from the First World War, telephoned him. Déterville immediately contacted a like-minded inspector in the central police of Paris. He also spoke to friends in *Combat*,[89] the clandestine printing group led by intellectuals like Albert Camus and André Malraux.

Violette had been noticed as she fled Rouen. Déterville's driver had seen her at the station in Rouen. Unknown to her, as she was more concerned in passing the security check, he had come and stood just behind the officer checking her papers and, having read her new name, noted how thoroughly she had changed her appearance. He reported this to Déterville, who had immediately telephoned the doorman of the little hotel, asking him and his friends to keep a look out for *Madame Blanchard* on the off-chance she might appear there. The Reine Marie hotel in Paris was a known safe hotel for undercover agents although Violette was not fully aware of that. It had indeed been fortuitous that Harry Peulevé had mentioned it to her all those months ago in London.

---

89 The Paris *Combat* group was a different organisation from the Normandy communist Combat group.

Circles within circles. The three Malraux brothers, Claude in Rouen now arrested and deported; Roland in the south, second-in-command to Harry Peulevé, Violette's friend; André in Paris, although he had spent a great deal of time down south in the Corrèze with Jacques Poirier (*Nestor*), with whom Violette had trained in Arisaig and London and who had taken over Harry's *Author* circuit, renamed *Digger*.

As she was leaving the hotel, the doorman came to her and surreptitiously passed her a message. She read the brief note: André Malraux wanted to meet her in the Jardin du Trocadéro that afternoon. He mentioned *Charles* and Rouen. Violette was satisfied it was genuine, but was not keen to meet him again before she saw Philippe. However, she had little real choice. It would be discourteous not to meet him and Philippe may be delayed any number of days. She was obliged, simply from kindness, to let André know what she knew about Claude.

She mapped her day. Every inch the smart, discreet Frenchwoman, beret perched elegantly, gloves, shoes and shoulder bag toned with her outfit, she was going to visit some great shops, then the Madeleine and later, André. She looked young, brave and beautiful, although fatigue and tension had lightly marked her features. Her usually laughing eyes now conveyed an elusive depth of sadness, a new wariness and were quicker to reveal her hidden anger.

‡

As the meeting was later in the day, she would walk up the Champs-Elysées, strolling past the fashion houses on the far side where her mother had tailored ladies' garments during the First World War.

She had also promised my grandmother to light a candle in the Madeleine. Reine was sure that this elegant cathedral was where Étienne had said he longed to take Violette after the war. Violette, however, remonstrated that the Madeleine he spoke of was not in Paris but in the south of France, not far from one of the Legion's strongholds, with special significance for them. Nevertheless, she felt she must light a candle in the Madeleine of Paris for her mother, Étienne, her brothers and for me, too.

Thinking of Étienne and all she missed about him, Violette felt the weight of sadness afflict her yet again. She could not understand her sudden sorrow and despondency; she had not felt like this for a few months. Maybe the tension of Rouen suddenly lifting now she was back in Paris was like stretched elastic being released, she mused with a grim smile. She took in a big breath and resolved to get on with it.

Her thoughts turned again to me. Was I being well looked after by her friend Vera Maidment? Was I happy there? Lighting candles for her soldier brothers, her Tante Marguerite and the rest of her family and dropping coins into the donation box, Violette prayed. After a while she got up, genuflected again, crossed herself and, after a brief pause to look at the beautiful main altar, she left.

As she walked away, Violette looked back towards the Madeleine and saw somebody staring at her.

Waiting for his own meeting with André Malraux, a man strolled along the boulevards. And there she was. 'An adorable young woman who was part of the same service,' he wrote many years later. He went on to say he 'had taken her out a few times in London and had found her charming. But we were all preparing ourselves for our missions and, before my departure, I did not see her again … And there she was, in front of the church of the Madeleine.'

Against all the rules, as he knew so well, he approached her.

It was Jacques Poirier!

'God bless you, Violette!' he said softly as she smiled with warmth but kept a certain distance. He seemed to smile, turned and walked away.

She just had time to whisper, 'Ditto, Jacques – and take care!' That strange encounter brought her great cheer. They had, after all, trained together and enjoyed one another's company. Was it circumstance or had he been following her? They had exchanged a momentary smiling eye contact and then he was gone.

She would not follow him. It was against all the rules. But it was a wonderful feeling to have seen him. Violette was alone in a dangerous city, but not friendless, after all.

‡

Down the steps and into rue Royale, as she walked along she saw a beautiful black evening dress in the window of Molyneux. Ah well, she was young and beautiful and in Paris!

Edward Molyneux was an Irish designer of Huguenot descent, born in London in 1894. He was a close friend of Yeo-Thomas[90] who had worked for him in Paris. Violette had met Yeo-Thomas at London's social venues before and during her SOE days and so knew he was Molyneux's friend and manager of his store. Molyneux's style was extreme simplicity and perfect taste. He was renowned for his black creations. The evening gowns he designed were flowing and understated, often accompanied by soft velvet evening coats falling to the floor in long fluid lines. It was Molyneux who started the 'New Look', as it was later named by Christian Dior, whom Molyneux had trained along with Pierre Balmain and others.

She could not resist. The dress was sheer perfection. She felt she knew the salon after having chatted with Yeo about it, so walked in confidently as if she were a

---

90 F.F.E. Yeo-Thomas, GC, MC, CdeG, the *White Rabbit* (also the title of his biography), a superb agent and exceptionally gallant man. He was captured by the SD, taken to Avenue Foch and, as Michael Foot, says, 'appalling tortures followed; quite without useful results for the enemy.' He survived with Harry Peulevé.

regular customer of august establishments. She turned the wedding band to become again her emerald engagement ring. She eased out her *Leroy* papers from the lining of her jacket, slipping the *Blanchard* ones in. She needed to be *Mademoiselle Corinne Leroy* as she could hardly be buying such an evening dress as a young widow under Pétain's government. That would attract attention.

She asked somewhat aloofly about the evening dress in the window. Several German officers were making purchases and turned to look at her appreciatively; two were accompanied by well-dressed sophisticated German women who frowned at her, while the other women, mostly French, simply stared. Violette did not care, she just wanted that dress.

The rich crêpe de chine was heavy and fell in a sheer flow of blackness that needed no further adornment. With all the cheek in the world she asked to try it on. It fitted like a glove and she bought it while smiling charmingly at everyone around her.

As she was about to pay, she saw a crimson and deep-blue plaid dress, marked on her bill as 'en écossais'. With long slim sleeves, it was trimmed at the neck and cuffs in midnight blue velvet. She asked if it were her size. A sales clerk felt it needed adjustment so called over one of the fitters, who led Violette back to the well-lit dressing room where she helped her try it on.

It was beautiful. The material was soft and rich and the tartan pattern looked superb against her dark hair. The fit was good but the fitter insisted on making a few alterations, asking her to return in a couple of days. She agreed to return on Wednesday.

Another dress on a mannequin beckoned, a floral silk for summertime, small dark-blue flowers on a white background with short puffed sleeves and piping at the neck. It fitted beautifully and she bought that, too. The skirt came to the top of her calf, a little shorter than the present French trend, showing her shapely legs to advantage. The shorter skirts were a war-time economic directive.

The manager, noticing the very fine jacket-cardigan Violette was wearing, suggested she might like a superior yellow jersey, described as a golfing jersey. To Violette's mind, it was perfectly suited for any occasion, especially with the dark trousers that were becoming fashionable in England, even if much frowned upon by Pétain's France.

Violette had never felt so pampered. The staff of Molyneux danced attendance upon her. Complimentary coffee and biscuits were laid out on a tiny Queen Anne table – and there she sat with the enemy! Now that really was fun.

She cheerfully chatted that she was soon to marry and that her wealthy uncle had given her a generous advance wedding gift to buy a few outfits. This made everyone around her smile indulgently. Her bill came to a staggering 37,475 francs, ttc,[91] around £21,300 at today's rate of exchange. As she had reprised the role of

---

91 ttc = toute taxe comprises, including all taxes

Mademoiselle Corinne Leroy she smiled sweetly and handed over her identity card and the cash. The manager handed her a receipt with her name, *Corinne Leroy*, at the top and fussed around her. The money Violette used was, of course, counterfeit. Well, she thought, she did have a lot of money left and was on her way home. She smiled inside as she thought of the damage using such counterfeit money would do to the economy.

Violette walked out, hips swinging, smiling at the wealthy German clientele. Her Molyneux bag holding the black evening gown, silk dress and yellow jumper swung lightly from her hand. She was on top of the world.

‡

With her dangerously gotten goods, she went for a stroll through the Jardin du Trocadéro to meet André Malraux at the Varsovie Fountains, reflecting as she walked that apart from her initial meeting with him, and reading a few pages of his book, she had heard mention of him in one of the SOE schools and of that same book, *La condition humaine*. Glad she had at least read a few pages and got a brief glimpse into the measure of the man, she looked forward to the encounter. She was even a little intrigued by this serious writer of countless intellectual works.

She would give him an edited version of the events surrounding his brother, Claude (*Serge/Cicero*) and then chat about his life and activities, although she did not expect to discover much about this enigmatic man.

The Jardin du Trocadéro, covering the Colline de Chaillot,[92] was guarded by German soldiers on sentry duty. They met at the Fountains as planned. Malraux ushered her gallantly into a small café and found a table where they made themselves comfortable. After he had ordered chicory-laden coffee and a custard tart each, they spoke generally for a few minutes as they sized one another up.

Malraux thought her quite delightful and immediately decided to take her on as one of his *agents de liaison*. As he said in his post-war book, *La Corde et les souris*, he had heard she was 'the best shooter in the English army'.

He was in his early forties, she thought, perennial cigarette dangling from his fingers. His face was beginning to age and there was a depth of sadness covered by a sardonic veneer of aloofness and off-handedness. For all his charm, Violette saw anger or resentment below his urbane surface, or more likely a terrible *ennui*

---

92 Chaillot Hill – *chaillot* meaning stony; opposite the Seine with about the best view of the Eiffel Tower. Louis VIII wanted to complete the Villa Trocadéro, but never did, to commemorate taking the fortress town of Trocadero, defending Cádiz in Spain in August 1823 by his duc d'Angoulême. In 1878, the Palais du Trocadéro was built to house the 1878 World Fair but destroyed in 1937 in order to build the Palais de Chaillot for that World Fair. There are two aesthetically pleasing wings curving south with the Eiffel Tower and the Varsovie Fountain triangularly central. The English garden was also renovated by Roger Lardat.

towards the world. He was not a person she could take to immediately and so kept her own counsel.

André was coolly desperate to know about Claude. She answered his questions as fully as she could – how Claude had been caught, his Anne fiercely questioned, but that neither of them had been too dreadfully manhandled and not tortured at all. André was passably relieved and asked more questions. He continued to explain to Violette that he was deeply involved in the Résistance and would be going to the Corrèze in R5[93] as *Colonel Berger*.

In fact, he worked closely with Jacques Poirier (*Nestor/Captain Jack*), whom Violette had earlier seen outside the Madeleine. An intellectual, and behaving as such at all times, André was not well liked by Résistants and Maquis groups. Many had no intention of being commanded by some half-baked haughty colonel. He alienated people and did not give a damn. Yet Jacques, along with Ravanel, leader of the FTP, found working with him useful and enjoyable.

André went on to tell Violette that an inspector from the police in Rouen had been in touch with *Combat*. The inspector, he said, had informed them that she had done invaluable service for which they were very grateful. He then said that he would contact her before she left Paris, giving her some messages for London and further instructions that he required her to carry out. Violette pointed out that she already had a commanding officer, but that if she could do anything for him then she would be pleased to do so. She would certainly take his messages, either verbal or in written code. He felt duly chastised and smiling sardonically, thanked her, paid and they left together to go their separate ways.

Violette's high spirits did not diminish. She strolled, weary but delighted, down to the Seine and crossed the river. She had enjoyed her encounter with Malraux and hoped he was not too much put out by her besting him. She would not be bossed by someone she really knew nothing about.

After that meeting and her earlier shopping raid into enemy territory, Violette decided that there should be no more such shenanigans that day. But she passed a shoe shop and saw some wedged-heel sling-back sandals that would go very well with the silk floral dress. On the way back she also bought some books at one of the *bouquinistes* on the Left Bank. Three Maigret[94] novels were her choice – good light reading. She had a couple of days before picking up her *écossais* dress from Molyneux but was happy to wait. Tomorrow, all being well, she would rendezvous with Philippe. If not, she had reading material to pass the evenings away until he did arrive.

---

93 R5 = Region 5. This was centred on Limoges.
94 The detective stories of Maigret were written by Georges Simenon, a Belgian. He described the investigations of his protagonist Inspector Simon Maigret over a period of forty years, from 1931 to 1972.

21

Luxembourg Gardens, Rendezvous Philippe, Tante Evelyn, Transmits to London

Tuesday 25 to Thursday 27 April

Next morning, Tuesday 25 April, was the first day to wait for Philippe in the Luxembourg Gardens. Putting on her new silk floral dress and the new shoes, Violette decided to walk to the Trois Quartiers department store[95] in boulevard de la Madeleine to buy some gifts for her family as she had a few hours before her rendezvous.

The art deco store had almost twenty upmarket departments of clothing, perfume and cosmetics for men and women; even children were catered for. She enjoyed the modern elegance and sparkle of its interior white stone surfaces and black steel lines and gazed at the beautiful objects on show in bevelled glass showcases and gleaming counters. For her mother, Violette bought a Lalique-designed bottle of Worth's perfume called *Je Reviens* … 'I'm coming back …'. It had been created by Worth in 1932 and continued to be popular as a gift for soldiers' wives and sweethearts, not only for its fragrance but also for its evocative name of tender partings and joyful returns. She also bought a flacon of *Soir de Paris*.[96]

Continuing her spree, she bought silk-lined kid gloves and her mother's preferred rouge, 'Bourjois'. It was the first light makeup ever used by the theatre in France and Reine had used it when she worked in the Wardrobe of Paris theatre land before her marriage. It had replaced the heavy greasepaint of the times, to be dabbed on lips and cheeks from tiny bijou pink and cream pots edged with black trim and writing.

---

95 Trois Quartiers was a department store named after the three adjoining districts of the Madeleine, Opéra and Concorde.
96 *Soir de Paris* = Paris Evening by Bourjois was introduced in 1929. It was a classically romantic perfume of jasmine, Turkish rose and other fragrances, not as fashionably sweet as today's version. Ernest Beaux created it and Chanel No. 5.

Violette spent time searching the men's department looking for gifts for the boys and her father. She bought silk ties and linen handkerchiefs plus a fine set of brushes. She would decide later who would get what.

A gift for Vera Atkins was a must. Vera was a perplexing woman, yet Violette liked her. Severe and dismissive often enough, she could be smilingly kind. Her barriers would drop and out would pop a fascinatingly funny yet ever acerbic lady, until they slammed down again and she returned to strict working procedures. Violette appreciated it was good to be under a stringent regime unmarred by sentimentality. She liked the woman; there was something slightly un-English under the veneer of the 'Kensington lady'. She had no idea why, although they spent many hours together preparing for Violette's missions until, one day, Vera hinted to Violette she was not English. She was, in fact, Rumanian and had only recently been naturalised as British *after* becoming Buckmaster's assistant.

An unusual brooch caught her eye. She was sure Vera Atkins would like it so asked that it be wrapped as a small gift. It had a large cluster of red and green enamel beads and two smaller ones with a pearl drop hanging from each. Vera treasured it and showed it off at the première of the film *Carve her Name with Pride* where Virginia McKenna beautifully played the role of Violette.

Violette found the children's clothes department on the second floor, but the assistant was apologetic, telling Violette that there were not many children's clothes in Paris at that time. Most children had been evacuated so there had been a big run on clothes before they left, and stock had not been replaced as there was no real market for them by then. She asked how old the child was.

Violette replied that she would be two years old in six weeks, thinking how quickly she must be growing. The saleslady did not think they had anything left for children that young but would check. As she was doing so, Violette saw some beautiful silk and lawn dresses. She was drawn to the one with small blue and pink flowers with tiny green leaves. All very delicate.

Violette inspected it; even though it was for a child of about four she thought her mother could alter it or it could be kept until Tania was older. She was sure it would suit her pale complexion and hazel eyes. It had tiny puffed sleeves; perfect rows of hand-stitched smocking crossed the bodice with slim satin ribbons to tie at the back. Violette thought there could be nothing prettier for her daughter and determined that Tania would wear it to celebrate the war's end. I did wear it – to meet the King for her.

She bought a tiny ivory fan and a silk scarf of deep plum hues with just a touch of yellow for her mother. It was lovely. Reine adored scarves and would treasure a silk one with a hand-printed pattern.

Violette finally left the store and took the Métro back to the station near the Luxembourg Gardens. It was time to wait for Philippe.

‡

She strolled with her packages to the gardens, an active, elegant and sparkling woman, evidently going to meet her husband or lover.

The Jardin du Luxembourg is an extensive series of gardens and recreational areas spread over twenty-five verdant and tree-filled hectares. What an outrage, thought Violette, looking sadly at statues, defaced or destroyed by the occupier, but it did not stop the gardens being a beautiful place to relax on a lovely spring day. There were some unattended flowerbeds and miniature forests, but she also noted French and German gardeners tending vegetable patches. This activity was strongly encouraged by the occupying authorities to keep the conquered people otherwise engaged trying to 'grow their own'. German policy was to ensure that the French struggled on a daily basis to find sufficient nourishment for themselves and their families, leaving little time for organised resistance. In England, allotments created before the war continue to flourish, but in France their only use was as a tool to subjugate; they did not flourish after the war.

From their rendezvous point, Violette could see the Luxembourg Palace at the far end of the gardens. Even from that distance, the huge red and black square swastika hanging from the entrance of the palace offended the eye. The palace had been requisitioned by the German Luftwaffe as the Third Luftwaffe divisional headquarters. Today it is the seat of the French Senate, the upper house of the French parliament.

Philippe did not appear that day. She waited the one and a half hours they had appointed and then added another fifteen minutes. To stay longer would only be to invite unwanted attention.

As she walked off, Violette could see that the Germans had made this a secure stronghold, with bunkers dug into the destroyed lawns and Blockhäusern scattered between the trees. Violette saw signs that the Schutzstaffel, the SS, had placed several tons of TNT as mines in the gardens and palace area. Most frightening were the tanks aggressively arrayed over the twenty-five hectares. Well-armed sentries were ready to move instantly against any attack.

She sauntered back towards her hotel, stopping on the way in a *bistrot* for a coffee and a bite to eat. She returned to her hotel where the doorman warmly welcomed her. He asked if there was anything he could do for her. Violette smiled back, answering no, but saying thanks, as she was going up to rest and read quietly in her room. First, she said she would order coffee and sandwiches to be brought up at about six in the evening. He insisted he arrange it for her, having heard enough about her from Rouen that he would do his best to make her time in 'his' hotel more comfortable and safe.

‡

Wednesday morning rushed in on a strong gusting wind. After a leisurely breakfast in her room, Violette dressed in her floral dress with the cardigan from Rouen over it. On went the pretty new shoes, comfortable and smart. A little makeup, hair combed and she was ready.

She would pick up the tartan dress on the way to the Luxembourg Gardens to wait for Philippe. She took a vélo-taxi to Molyneux's salon. The manager eagerly greeted her; she was spending a small fortune there. Her dress was ready but she did not try it on nor have coffee. '*Non, mesdames, désolée.* I've an appointment and must rush. Thank you so much. *Au revoir.*'

Walking to the Opéra, she window-shopped, stopping for a coffee. She chatted with the waiter who saw her newspaper with a reporting of *terroristes* killing a Gestapo officer. He hoped there would not be too heavy a reprisal, wishing the Résistance would stay out of Paris. He bet that de Gaulle would be in Paris by Christmas. She studied him and saw he was absolutely sincere.

Violette took the Métro to Luxembourg Gardens. The electric trains were packed to bursting as services had been drastically cut so only a few were running on each line. There was no trouble, just the usual checkpoints where most people's papers were cursorily glanced at while tickets were checked.

She strolled from Métro Luxembourg into the Luxembourg Gardens to wait. Philippe was already sitting there, waiting patiently. He looked up and could not believe his eyes. She looked a million dollars. They rushed to one another and embraced as relief flowed through them both. Gradually they pulled apart, looked carefully at each other and walked away, arm in arm, looking like any other couple having rediscovered one another under the blue skies of Paris.

'*Alors, ma chère Corinne* ...'

'But I'm not *Corinne*, I'm now *Madame Marguerite Blanchard*, née *Picardeau*, widow.' Violette told him her new identity and cover story.

'Well, *ma chère Marguerite*, I'm astounded. Elegant and beautiful. You look and sound so much the part. I like it very much. Different from the young Le Havre secretary. You've done well.'

'Thank you. The new cover was necessary, otherwise I'd have been in a prison cell these last three days. Chief Inspector Alie's bunch arrested me. One of his thugs questioned me but Inspector Déterville managed to make that questioning very brief. I'll tell you all about it over dinner.'

Philippe was amazed by her matter-of-fact description of her arrest. 'First, let's get your things from the hotel and get over to my aunt's. Why on earth didn't you go there immediately?'

'Too dangerous for her, and perhaps for me, as I didn't know her situation or whether her phone is tapped. I was fine in the hotel. Turned out it's a safe-house. I bought a superb evening gown and a few other things from Molyneux ...' She giggled.

Philippe almost shouted, 'You did *what*? Molyneux's is loved by the Germans – officers and wealthy civilians. It is also run by Germans, as you bloody well know. What could you have been thinking of?'

'That beautiful dress, of course. What else? I was politely haughty and even smiled from under my lashes at some dashing German general! Only a few other things: a couple of dresses and a pullover. You see, Philippe, I had to do something innocent while waiting for you to appear ...'

'Innocent! You call that innocent? How did you pay?'

'Why, with some of the remainder of the money I had on me.'

'The cheek of it! Government property!'

'More cheek to the government, then! It's counterfeit, every last *sou!*[97] My little bit to destabilise the economy. Oh, and Trois Quartiers and a few other fashion boutiques.'

They made their way to the hotel, still talking about Violette's purchases, picked up her two suitcases, including a new and somewhat larger one of the best leather. Philippe sighed and paid the hotel bill while Violette said a fond farewell to the doorman and slipped him a substantial tip. They then got a vélo-taxi to the corner of the street where Tante Evelyn lived.

Tante Evelyn was overjoyed to see Violette safe and well. She had seen Philippe several times over the last three weeks but was eager to hear all Violette had to recount. Although Violette was delighted to tell her some of her tales, nothing she said impinged on the work she had done, intelligence she had gathered, nor activities undertaken or to be undertaken by those she left behind in Rouen. She would put no one in danger through her careless talk.

Philippe was so proud of her, amazed by what she had accomplished and that she had been able to meet so many people. Tante Evelyn had heard that some viaduct near Rouen had been blown. Violette grinned at Philippe. The three all clinked glasses. New landing sites had also been organised ready for drops of rifles and other weaponry.

Philippe said he would ensure transmission to London prior to their leaving just in case something happened to them.

Violette was happy; proud she had been instrumental in two strategic blows to the enemy, especially the Balentin viaduct. They discussed their plans to get back to London. Philippe explained they would take the train to Issoudun where a contact would pick them up there and take them to the airfield of Fay, a little south-east of the town. There they would be taken by Lysander back to England, probably Tempsford Airfield.

‡

---

97 A *'sou'* was at one time the smallest French coin. The first one appeared under Clovis, Charlemagne revalued the money while keeping the *sou* which was then equal to 12 *deniers*. (1 *livre* = 20 *sous* or 240 *deniers* until the French Revolution).

Part V

22

Back to London

Friday 28 April to Monday 1 May 1944

The train carried the two SOE agents to Issoudun via Les Aubrais about three miles north of the city centre of Orléans.

Before making their way to the station, Violette and Philippe had an early breakfast with Tante Evelyn. It was a happy breakfast, tinged by the sadness of reading in the Pétainist newspaper that Germans had taken reprisals against the population of Paris after a Résistance blockade ended in a gun battle in which about eight German soldiers had been killed or seriously wounded.

Still as the widow, smartly dressed for the journey, Violette had, as before, tucked socks and pretty rural scarf into her shoulder bag so that when she arrived at Issoudun in the heart of Berry, Indre, she could revert to the country girl before meeting their contact and being taken to a farm near Le Fay aerodrome, south-east of Issoudun.

She looked fresh and rested but lines of strain were etched on her face. She looked as if she was in her late twenties or early thirties when in fact she was not yet twenty-three. But Violette looked lovelier in her new maturity, a process youth alone does not usually bestow. Philippe, too, was looking a little strained after a hectic time travelling to meet groups in the south and south-east of Paris. At least he had on a fresh suit and shirt, shoes polished and tie nondescript but neat. Both of them were committed heart and soul to ridding their country of the pestilence of Nazi occupation. It was, however, quite impossible for fellow travellers to deduce that from their behaviour.

As it was a fine sunny morning, they sat on the small terrace of the Buffet Austerlitz and sipped 'national' coffee. At the appointed time, they joined the queue to pass through the usual checkpoints at Gare Austerlitz. The porter carried their luggage into their first-class carriage, hoisted it into the racks, received a generous tip and moved off smartly to find other customers. They took their seats and settled in comfortably.

‡

Echoing down the platform in a rapid-fire female French voice and a male Prussian one, the station tannoy announced the imminent departure of the train. The platform master strode along rapidly slamming shut any open carriage doors. Three piercingly loud, shrill whistles, and it was moving out.

People shouted and waved their last farewells, porters moved through the milling crowds, smoke billowed and the locomotive slowly chugged from the station, away from Paris towards Orléans. In peacetime, the journey took around an hour.

‡

En route, Philippe and Violette again discussed Violette's encounter with Malraux, referring to him by his alias of *Colonel Berger*.

'*Marguerite*,' Philippe said using her present cover, '*le Colonel* told me he heard you were back from your mission to Rouen and that he urgently needed to meet you to discover news of Claude. I'm glad you met up but your news was not happy.'

'He's a bit arrogant,' said Violette. 'But I was happy to help and enjoyed our meetings. In his sphere of the intelligentsia, he's well received. Otherwise, I believe he'd probably rub people the wrong way. Our third encounter, the day after you and I met again in Luxembourg Gardens, nearly ended in disaster.'

'Tell me again what happened with André,' asked Philippe.

'Certainly, I went to meet André at the given time to see exactly what he wanted of me. He was already there across the street. Just as I was about to go over to him, a hand grabbed my shoulder. I turned into the face of a police sergeant. He grabbed me, rather roughly, by the arm and pushed me into the police car. When we arrived at the police station, I was taken into the captain's office. He dismissed his sergeant with a thank you and asked me to sit down. My knees were knocking, I can tell you. Apparently, Déterville had been in touch with him – but I don't know this captain's name – and he warned me to get the hell out of town. The hotel had informed on me – but there was also a Résister, the doorman, as I told you, who contacted Déterville, thank God. They knew that I, as *Corinne Leroy*, had fled from Rouen and was hiding out in Paris. They even knew that I had another cover but not the name I was using. I don't know how. It was a blessing I left the hotel when we met on Wednesday. I saw our *Colonel*, André Malraux, turn away when he saw what was happening and walk off. Nothing else he could possibly do.'

‡

As they talked, there came a warning signal from the train as it pulled to an unscheduled stop after a steep curve. A small platoon of Gestapo troops rushed onto the train through the open doors of each carriage. An unsuccessful manhunt had already been made by German security police on the train for two Résistants who had apparently fled from one second-class compartment to another when their papers had not held up to the scrutiny of the conductor.

Gestapo double-checked every passenger on the train. Every wagon was also checked for stowaways. Voices were raised and chaos ensued. Once in the first-class compartments, the Germans worked more quickly and less conscientiously against the constant carping and complaints from passengers, including Philippe and Violette who acted like two harassed squawking hens. Later, shots were heard.

The train sighed, whistled and steamed off. Relief was palpable. Violette and Philippe stared grimly, nodding at passengers stretching necks to gawp suspiciously at everyone else. They were both shaken by the search, fearing it was for Violette.

Once they arrived at Les Aubrais Orléans, they had an hour's wait and decided lunch was a necessity. It was half-past two and they were peckish. As they walked along to find a brasserie or café-bar Philippe said Malraux was going south, no doubt to keep an eye on his other kid brother, Roland. He went on to explain what had been and still was happening in Orléans – a conservative and wealthy town rooted in age-old traditions. As Violette had seen, everyday life under occupation was much the same from town to town. The Germans requisitioned the best buildings to set up their occupying headquarters, the Feldkommandanturen. Normally, the PPF, Parti Populiste Français, i.e. the French collaborationist movement, was installed close by. Philippe continued that the German army had found few civilian clerical and housekeeping volunteers, fewer than thirty in 1942, but by then in Orléans many more were willing as wages were low elsewhere and they were fearful of unemployment. The rate of exchange, as Violette had discovered, was one Deutschmark to twenty French francs, making daily life even harder. Added to this, steeply rising prices and scarcity of goods caused more worry and distress.

Violette cut in, explaining that in London they were under similar restrictions, bombing raids and fires with incendiary winds; just not under Jerry occupation. Life was damned hard there too. Londoners coped, had their own sort of Système D. Everyone was trying to do their bit with the same skivers and racketeers as in France. Philippe went on to note that, like in London, shop owners all over France whose shops had been destroyed had erected temporary stalls in streets, squares and along the boulevards of the cities. Citizens in Orléans, like those of other towns, were forced to register their names with local suppliers for food. He presumed everyone in England had to do much the same. Even bartering. Philippe also noted that until 1943, German forces barracked in Orléans were mainly administrative. Repressive mobile forces only arrived this year.

The meal they had was measly but adequate, accompanied by 'coffee' with more carrot than chicory, never mind coffee; but they hardly noticed, engrossed as they were in their comparison of the two countries and discussion of events in Orléans.

SOE used the area around Orléans time and again, mostly through Henri Déricourt. He was a Frenchman and well-known pilot, but after the war he was never quite cleared of betraying his country and SOE, despite being acquitted by a French court. He was in a tortuous position as it seems he was faced with a stark choice: spy for Bleicher of the German security services, the SD and SS, or risk the life of his wife and maybe more. On the suspicion of agents whom he had transported to and from France, at least twice he was recalled against his will to Baker Street. Though they knew him, neither Violette nor Philippe knew what to think.

After paying the bill, they walked back through the station and boarded the train to Issoudun. There were no incidents, no unscheduled stops, and they arrived at half past four into a warm sun-filled afternoon.

‡

As they sat on a bench in the sun, their luggage at their feet, they chatted while waiting for Maurice Southgate's contact to arrive from the *Stationer* circuit further south. In the '*Dames – Damen*', Violette quickly metamorphosed from young city businesswoman back into pretty farming lass, hiding her widow's identity papers and carrying those of *Corinne Leroy*, secretary. She did wonder if the Le Havre papers were unsafe and maybe she should use her third set. No, they would soon be in the air on the way back to England.

Violette asked what she needed to know about the *Stationer* circuit, curious about this man with a fine reputation called Maurice Southgate.[98]

Philippe proceeded to tell Violette some background he felt might be useful to her.

‡

After a fifteen-minute wait, Philippe saw his contact rattle in noisily. Another gazogène running on vegetation. It was one of Southgate's men, well-trained and working as a young farmhand, delivering produce all over the region and further afield until the call for full mobilisation of Résistants and Maquisards took place. For this, he possessed the correct German *Ausweisen*[99] and French *permis*. With his old truck, he was a driver and messenger for the Résistance so his authorisations to drive long distances in this part of France were a real boon.

They piled their luggage in the back under boxes of vegetables and a few crates of chickens and climbed into the cab, where Violette sat cramped in the back part. After a noisy half-hour drive south-east along narrow country lanes, through a dark forest and across wide expanses of flat fields, they finally stopped at a small

---

98 Maurice Southgate, DSO, SOE leader of the *Stationer* circuit.
99 *Ausweis* in the singular. Mostly, German plural ends in 'en' as in *Ausweisen*. This is where we get ox/oxen.

farmhouse. They exchanged gifts, as was the custom. The farmer and his wife, the Dupuys, looked after them with great warmth and kindness. A couple of merry days passed, news exchanged, intelligence gathered and promises made.

As the two passengers had three suitcases, a large canvas bag and a few parcels, it was considered safer to walk them over to their departure field after twilight, pushing two barrows holding their luggage. They could hunker down in a small clump of trees and bushes on the edge of Le Fay, an ideal area for Lysander landings on a runway or in one of many fields surrounding it on the high plateau. They waited there until nightfall. Finally, the moon rose high, the reception committee arrived to set up flares in an L-shape for the approaching Lysanders.

‡

These tiny planes had no radio link or navigation system, relying on compass, moonlight and landmarks. They flew deep into occupied France with a 650-mile range on two full tanks, one under their belly, but no guns. The flights were extremely perilous.

Each aircraft, at a pinch, carried four passengers, with two lying across two seated passengers. Where both men and women agents were involved, straying hands, stern slaps, chuckles and giggles erupted. As well as agents, Lysanders carried politicians, downed airmen and communists, flying to Tangmere[100] in the south of England or, if they had orders and sufficient fuel, to Tempsford, further north in Bedfordshire. At both airfields, there were inevitable and often lengthy briefings and debriefings, with agents staying overnight in Tangmere cottage or Pym's Hazel Hall, an elegant Georgian manor house at Sandy.

Lysander pilots on special missions made these flights hoping not to attract enemy night fighters or flak from anti-aircraft guns on the ground. The pilots' flying and navigational skills were of the highest order as they could not rely on always having the moon and clear skies to light the landmarks below.

On the night of Sunday 30 April 1944, it was a 'double' Lysander mission. Even though it was cloudy, the half-moon still allowed the two 'Lizzies' a straight run. They took only one pass over the terrain to land so the aircraft were not short of fuel. They were delivering a landing-party of three, including *Dupuis* or *Pharaon*,[101] and collecting two – Violette and Philippe for Tangmere, where the two agents would spend the night in the cottage for initial debriefing.

---

100 Tangmere, near Chichester, is now the Tangmere Military Aircraft Museum with memorials commemorating the bravery of pilots and passengers alike and hosts various associated events, as does Tempsford in Bedfordshire, ten miles north-east of Bedford.
101 *Dupuis*, codename for an agent who had been brought to London for discussions, now returning under the codename *Pharaon*.

Those on the ground heard the slow but resonant drone of a Lysander approaching. Its pilot, Flight Lieutenant Robert G. 'Bob' Large DFC, Légion d'Honneur, gave the BN signal of a single beam for this operation codenamed *Organist* and received the correct AD signal of flashing lights from the ground. Torches lit the pathway so Bob Large banked the plane quite steeply to come in over a few trees, landed quickly and discharged his passengers.

Bob grumbled affably as he quickly helped his passengers out: 'Landing was bloody bumpy. Ridges the whole length from ploughing. The Lizzie vibrated like hell. The engine stopped as bloody fuel was thrown up. You know, if the fuel's over-rich, it gets damned difficult to restart a Mercury engine. Danger of the battery running flat in the attempt.'

He pulled the slow-running cutout – a control to stop the engine – a trick he expertly performed, to restart the engine.

'Who's the passenger? Woman, ay? In yer hop, then.'

The reception committee gave Violette a leg up, passing in her suitcases and canvas bag full of 'frivolous' things, plus a couple of boxy parcels. The whole operation was over within a few minutes. Bob, still grumbling happily, took off.

Flying Officer J.P. Alcock, on his first operational flight with the 161 Special Squadron, performed the second landing in much the same way, helping his passengers out and taking on Philippe Liewer, his one small suitcase and parcels. In his turn, he quickly took off.

The arriving passengers had disappeared from the field with their luggage, led away in the dark by members of the reception committee.

‡

The two Lysanders slowly made their way homeward at 150 miles an hour average speed. Suddenly they flew into a cloudbank and, without landmarks, Bob Large veered a little too close to an aerodrome with fighters on the ground used by the Luftwaffe, south of Châteaudun. Abruptly the sky lit up with criss-crossing searchlights. The tiny aircraft was being used as target practice.

'What the hell is all that?' shouted Violette. The noise of the engine made it very difficult to be heard or to hear even with the headphones and mikes. 'How come we're flying over an enemy airfield? We're being fired at?'

''Fraid so! Too close to a Luftwaffe base. That bank of cloud made us wander off course. Not much – but right into trouble. I'm turning off the intercom so I can concentrate and get us out of this. Okay?' Bob shouted over the noise of the engine. He thus avoided any smart-ass talk-back from some girl who shouldn't be over here anyway.

'Okay, understood and out,' shouted back Violette. Bob was a little surprised by her professional response. Fear certainly surged through her, but she kept quiet and concentrated on remaining in her seat. She saw from the window the puff-white flak and flying bullets streaming past as searchlights caught them in their beams.

Manoeuvring helter-skelter through the sky, Bob hoped he would not have some damned woman fainting on his hands when they landed, *if* they got out of this mess. He turned off the intercom so he could concentrate. Diving suddenly, swerving to the portside and then to starboard in quick succession, he avoided the worst damage. Violette felt like a rag doll. Although buckled in, her shoulders hit the sides a few times and her head struck the bulkheads as they careened through the night sky. Bullets slammed into them. Nothing had pierced the fuselage yet, at any rate.

Eventually they flew out of range into a clear, peaceful sky. The further north they flew, the more frequently they entered banks of clouds, making it impossible to see the land beneath them or reckon the distance to the coast. Violette could not work out where they were as they flew on, hoping for cloud cover over the Channel to prevent German antiaircraft guns on the French coast firing at them.

Suddenly they were descending. Why? Where? She could not understand why Bob had not put the intercom back on. They seemed to be coming down rather steeply. Were they crash-landing into enemy territory?

The next thing she knew, she was being thrown all over the place. As the plane touched down it crashed over to one side, sliding along on a wing, causing Violette to bang her head hard.

They screeched to a halt, sparks flying everywhere; there was more noise and Violette tried to get herself out. They must have crash-landed in France. She would not be captured alive. A piece of metal pipe had fallen to the side. A tall blond man in a uniform that she could not quite see approached and yanked open her side of the plane. She grabbed the metal pipe off the floor and threw herself out of the plane. She would use it to batter him with, or poke him one in the eye!

'*Haut les mains!*' she cried as she hit the ground, keeping the metal weapon levelled in front of her. '*Alors, garde les mains haut ou je tire, compris?*'

'Bloody hell, what the devil's got into you, you idiot!' shouted Bob Large.

'Oh – it's you! I thought you were a German. Where the hell are we? I almost bloody gave you one in the eye. I'm so sorry.'

'So you ought to be, dammed woman! I've got you home!'

'Your landing wasn't the smoothest. Almost knocked me out. You didn't turn the intercom back on the whole darned way after we almost got shot down. I had no idea where we were with the clouds and all, and then that landing – well, I naturally thought you were a flipping Kraut. I was ready to defend myself, and even you, if necessary!'

'Okay, okay. I'm sorry, too. Forgot to put the intercom back on. Let me get you a drink.'

'Easy to take you for a German in the dark, you know, Bob. Tall, blond and handsome! And in a bomber jacket and goggles. No helmet. I've seen the films, you know!' She grinned, gave him a kiss, and Bob burst into a spluttering laugh.

At that moment, the ground crew came over and looked at the plane.

'You guys are damned lucky. Tyre got shot to pieces and the undercarriage has all but packed up entirely.'

Bob and Violette looked at the wheels. He whistled when he saw the state of his plane, especially the smashed wheel. And they both laughed with relief.

Lysander wheels cannot be raised after take-off as the undercarriage is fixed and the left tyre had been shot up. It was in shreds. There was no way Bob could have known as he could not see the undercarriage while flying. They were lucky not to have been killed over France, or on landing, all due to Bob's clever handling. He was not the kind to panic and had dealt with the second-by-second events in cool, deliberate fashion.

'Where's the other Lysander?' asked Violette as they walked across RAF Tempsford and out over to the SOE cottage for debriefing and refreshments.

'It's landed and they're all in just about one piece in the cottage,' said one of the SOE reception people who had raced across with the crew, half-expecting the plane to blow. 'Alcock's propeller was holed by flak, bloody lucky to get back.'

'Darned good to be back and see you undamaged, Philippe,' said Violette when she saw him ensconced in a corner near the blazing cottage fire. Though it was nearly dawn, a hot meal was laid out on the table and everyone was helping themselves. Philippe opened the customary vintage bottle of champagne. The meal ended with fresh coffee and cognac, courtesy of Lysander, et al.

‡

23

Debriefing

1 May to 3 May 1944

Philippe and Violette bade one another farewell at Tangmere after arranging for Philippe to collect her in London after the first debriefing. Vera Atkins had wanted to do this herself but on reflection thought that they should spend time together after the initial debriefings, reviewing the events, joint experiences and insights of their mission, making notes of things half-remembered, forgotten, seemingly innocuous but useful. But at this stage, before the first debriefs, the less contact between them the better so their reports would be entirely free of the other's bias or memory.

They were driven to London separately. Vera Atkins had her driver run Violette and herself to the corner of Portman Square, where Orchard Court stood at the southern end of Baker Street. The initial debriefing took place immediately on their arrival.

Small flats in the building were available for agents to relax before the debriefs, which took place in one of a number of offices, or in Buckmaster's private domain, where careful notes were recorded from all agents' reports, including Violette's activities and conclusions. Her report was then later studied alongside the report provided by Philippe. Reports were often verbal, taken down in shorthand and typed up. Sometimes, they were handwritten by the agent.

Violette's report stated that, after being dropped at the beginning of April and with Philippe accompanying her to Paris, she had made her way to Rouen where, in effect, her mission was cut short by the Vichy police of Rouen, led by the infamous Chief Inspector Alie. She continued that, during nearly three weeks in the dangerous restricted zone, she had succeeded in establishing contact with the *Salesman* circuit's external members and with various Maquis groups and Résistance movements from Rouen to Le Havre and as far north as Calais and Dieppe. She also reported that, in her opinion, shared by Philippe, they had no chance of rebuilding this network, not only because the Germans had put a huge price on Philippe's head but because the German and French security police forces were much more active and had, over months, planned the capture of Résistants and members of the *Salesman* circuit while seizing arms caches. She added that they had no need to resuscitate *Salesman* as, by provisioning the group leaders noted in her report, they would increase their sabotage activities and supply intelligence on targets to be struck by the Allied Air Force.[102] The success of *Salesman* and its associated Résistance and Maquis movements was remarkable. Violette felt that the increase in enemy activity and erroneous estimates of where and when the Allies were to land was in no small part a result of the sabotage carried out by the *Salesman* circuit.

She recounted her unexpected brief meeting with Philippe in Rouen when she told him it was too dangerous for him to stay. She handed over the wanted posters of Philippe and Bob Maloubier that she had torn from the walls near the station and further reported all her findings on the rocket sites she had visited and on which she had been given information. This led to her being debriefed by the Ministry of Defence.

Violette concluded that she had to flee Rouen, not only for her own safety but for the safety of people she had dealings with. She had achieved all her objectives and more, and it would have been a mistake to stay longer. However, she said firmly that she was ready to return at any time with new papers and identity because, as a half-French woman, she could move around more freely and persuade people to join the Allied cause or wait for further orders. She had arrived in Paris a couple of days earlier than anticipated to rendezvous with Philippe and then they both returned to London via Le Fay.

The first debriefings were with Maurice Buckmaster and Vera Atkins. These meetings and debriefings swung easily between English and French.

Vera was also fluent in German and Rumanian and capable in other European languages. Vera Atkins' naturalisation papers had just recently been accepted. But she had proved her worth time and again as Buckmaster's assistant; some saying it was Vera rather than Buckmaster running the show. She certainly had mentally collated a myriad of details about the lives of 'her girls', their operations and those of male agents, radio operators and even codes, with not a word written down. Since the war, many questions have been asked as to her allegiances. I would suggest her total allegiance was to her adopted county and the Allied cause. As a Jew, she could have had no truck with the Axis. Vera might have had left-wing leanings but she was not alone. She might perhaps have given a helping hand to the US, where her brother chose to live. She had proved over the previous two years to be indispensable to 'Buck'.

Vera was promoted to F Section Intelligence Officer and could therefore use the abbreviation 'F Int.' giving her great satisfaction. She had suffered from anti-Semitism and was a victim of the general snobbery in SOE and her social life. This attitude was not at all unusual from the 'toffs' of the service – many refer to it,

---

102 Allied Air Force (AAF) = RAF, French, Polish, Dutch, Australian, New Zealand, American and Canadian pilots among others.

including Leo Marks. It had taken Vera at least four years from starting as a simple secretary to secure her merited high place in the service and to some extent she also adopted a haughty and often counterproductive attitude.

Violette understood this attitude, because in England she was working class, and it rankled when one was putting one's life on the line at the behest of such people. However, everyone knew their place, understood the system and got on with it.

Vera was at the peak of her abilities during these hard years of war and quite irreplaceable. After the war she would continue to do battle – always discreetly and totally dedicated – whether seeking the truth regarding 'her girls' who had been murdered by the Nazi regime or in her involvement in UNESCO and other world foundations.

‡

24

Rest and Refreshers, More Debriefs

Thursday 4 May 1944 onwards

'A rest I shall have, a sleep I shall have ...'
From a poem attributed to Leo Marks, code master

For four days and nights they were shut off from the world in the confines of Orchard Court, except for being chauffeured to Wigmore and Baker Streets. Philippe and Violette were thoroughly exhausted after separate and joint talks and debriefings, including those at the War Office and with Lieutenant Colonel R.A. Bourne-Paterson, SOE's F Section's second-in-command. Finally, they were able to join Vera and Buckmaster for an informal chat, then Philippe accompanied Violette to her parents' home in Burnley Road.

'Bed and sleep are the order of the day. You could both do with a good rest and certainly deserve it,' was Vera's parting shot.

As they sank back comfortably in the roomy, soft leather backseat of the Humber, Violette said, 'Philippe, would you ask the driver to take us to Mill Hill so I can pick up Tania. It's not too far away and not dark yet.'

'*Sacré bleu*,[103] Violette! You certainly pick your moments. All right.' Sighing deeply, Philippe turned to the driver and gave him directions.

Half an hour later, they drew up to a small house on a slight incline. Violette jumped out to fetch Tania. Vera Maidment had just fed her on bread and milk and was surprised to see them, but welcomed Violette in, helping gather a few of Tania's things. Back in the car, the tiny girl sat between Violette and Philippe yawning then dozing to Stockwell. It was early evening and dusk was falling.

The driver pulled in to the kerb outside 18 Burnley Road and helped Violette out as she was carrying the sleeping child in her arms, then unloaded Violette's luggage, taking it up the steps to the front door. No lights were visible; because it was blackout. Violette rang the bell and they waited.

After a while soft footfalls approached the door and an enquiring head peeped out from the door open a crack, 'Oh, goodness me, it's Vi. It's really you. Oh, how

---

103 *Sacré bleu* = literally 'holy blue', euphemism for *sacré Dieu* = 'holy God'.

wonderful. Come in, come in … and le Major Staunton is wiz you. Well, well, well … and little Tania, too? How did you …?'

'Oh, for goodness sake, Mum, give us a hug and let us in,' was Violette's laughing response to her mother's astonishment and delight. But she leaned back wearily against the door as Reine took Tania from her.

'She looks all in, poor girl,' remarked Reine, looking at her darling daughter.

'Just put her to bed and I'll be off,' said Philippe.

'Oh no, no you don't,' said Violette, suddenly coming to life. 'You must come in and have a cup of tea with us.' As they walked into the narrow hall, heads appeared from the kitchen and up the stairs. Reine had put her arm around Violette's waist, letting Tania climb down as she woke up to the excitement. Philippe brought in the luggage.

Pandemonium erupted in the little Georgian house. With her delightful French accent, Reine fussed around them all, to-ing and fro-ing from the kitchen, preparing tea and laying out biscuits, all the while exclaiming how good it was to see Violette and me, and welcoming Philippe. Charlie was in magnanimous mood and their youngest, Dickie, came in, wondering what was going on – he was growing fast – a strikingly good-looking lad and intelligent with it. Grinning broadly, he walked to Violette, kissed her on her right cheek and shook hands solemnly with Philippe.

Her other brothers, Roy, based in the south, and John, serving in the tanks, were on leave from the army while George had come on leave from the navy. The family was complete. Florrie Lucas, Charlie's sister, had come down from Hereford to see her son Norman, also on leave from the navy. They were all staying at number 18. A tight squeeze – but a happy one.

Violette, dying to distribute her gifts, shouted over the laughter and leg-pulling, 'Look, keep quiet a minute! I've got one or two little gifts for you. While I was down on the coast, doing my bit for the war effort, driving and the like, a couple of Belgians came over on a small fishing-boat loaded with hauls captured from German coasters off Belgium. Nobody seemed interested so we took what we wanted with the blessing of our superiors. They knew we'd been working damned hard and thought this would be a good way to say thanks. We thought so, too!'

Philippe sat in the background; his eyes wide at the easy story falling from her lips. He was happy to relax, seeing the pleasure Violette's parents and brothers showed at seeing her again. Her fatigue was pushed aside in the joy of giving out the gifts from occupied France, beguiling them to believe they came from some English field!

'Well,' chimed in Philippe. 'I'm off now. I have returned your errant daughter in one piece. She needs a rest. A car will collect her in two days to take her to FANY HQ as they want her to do advanced driving or mechanics or something,' he added wickedly.

Violette laughed. Reine looked up, smiling, wondering if they were romantically involved, while Charlie glowered at him, wondering what his intentions were with his only daughter. They both knew he was a French journalist married to a Frenchwoman. But his manners were impeccable and Violette treated him as her commanding officer. They concluded they were mistaken.

'Goodnight,' everyone chimed.

'*Major Staunton*, thank you so very much. I'm aware of some of what she's been through. Thank you for bringing her safely home to me and to Tania,' Reine whispered quietly to him in French.

'She did it all herself, *madame*. She is very clever and very courageous. And it's my pleasure. Goodnight,' he replied in French. He ran down the steps and into the waiting black Humber that carried him swiftly to one of SOE's special safe-houses.

Reine returned to her family and saw young Dickie with the small French Meccano set Violette had brought back for him. Violette gave Aunt Florrie one of her own bottles of perfume. She did not want her aunt and cousin to feel left out. Florrie was thrilled; it was her first bottle of expensive French perfume and she continued using it sparingly for years. Then there were lawn hankies and silk ties for the men; Violette had bought enough to give Norman, her cousin, a set. When her mother opened her gifts of cosmetics, perfume, kid gloves and beautiful silk scarf, she looked closely at Violette, who winked back. Her parents were not duped but the boys took her story at face value, admiring their gifts. Then Violette unwrapped her yellow jumper and the three dresses, shoes and handbag. 'That's a bit bright, Vi, that jumper, don't you think,' frowned her father.

'Oh, Dad, don't be so square!' was Roy's laughing retort, always coming to Violette's aid when Charlie Bushell grumbled at her modern outlook.

'All right, all right. Can't take a joke anymore, eh, Vi? It's a lovely jumper and you'll look like a summer's day in it. The dresses look pretty. Silk, aye? Might even write you a couple of verses on them and their provenance, if you're not careful.' Charlie Bushell knew when he was beaten and was, in fact, proud as punch of his daughter.

Reine frowned at the mass of contradictions that was her husband; sometimes rash and full of stories, sometimes taciturn and a 'bit of a tartar', as the boys liked to say. Charlie liked to consider himself the head of the household. He could and would protect his only daughter. He would never admit it, but he had known that she had been undercover in France since he found the parachute badge she had dropped after a flaming row over how she had sprained her ankle.

Perhaps his over-protectiveness was to compensate for the years he had to leave his two oldest children, Roy and Violette, with the French side of the family. More likely, it was the effects of serving on the frontline in the First World War and having experienced what he and everyone thought was the worst that mankind could do to itself across trenches of broken spirits, broken bodies, rotting flesh and cesspits. Those who survived would soon discover mankind could commit far worse.

Authoritarian as Charlie was with Violette, he was more so with Roy and the boys, who considered their father far too harsh. Hot arguments were no rare thing in the Bushell household, but they were often forgotten ten minutes later. There were also many happy moments full of laughter and fun. Reine was there to diffuse situations. She loved Charlie and so put up with his difficult nature. Her love was fully reciprocated, if taken for granted.

After the flood of gifts, Violette took out a special box and called Tania, who was not quite two years old, over to her. She gave her the box to open. It was full of lovely tissue paper and she pulled out the prettiest dress she had ever seen. 'That's for you, Tania, do you like it?'

'Yes, very much,' Tania said shyly. 'I want to put it on now.'

'You know, Violette, it's too big for her. It would be a pity, although possible, to alter it to fit her now. Better keep it in that box and it vill be lovely when she is about four, don't you sink, darling?' commented Reine. 'The material is beautiful. So smooth – zer best lawn comes from France, of course.'

There was a rueful look from Tania, who was desperate to wear it right then and there. Dickie called her over to show her how to put two pieces of Meccano together so the little girl forgot about the dress, losing herself in the magic of his box.

It was around nine o'clock when Roy, Norman, John and George went off down the pub for a beer or two. The door closed quickly so no light shone into the street. Violette said she was going to bed, taking Tania with her. Dickie had fallen asleep behind the couch so Charlie carried him to his tiny bedroom at the top of the stairs. Reine busied herself with clearing up, humming softly, glad Violette was back safe, knowing she had been in France, in dangerous places. Reine saw strain and fatigue in her eyes, hoping desperately she would take on no more dangerous missions.

‡

After she had put me to bed, Violette was so awake that she asked Reine if she could have a bath now the house was quiet again.

'*Bien sûr, ma chère* Violette. Let me run it for you,' said her mother, thinking that a nice warm bath would ease the tiredness from her daughter's young body. 'I'll put a couple of towels out to heat on the stove, too.'

'Come in and talk to me, or let me talk to you, Maman. *En français* so we can be discreet.'

'*Certainement, chérie,*' called Reine as she bustled to get the bath running. Florrie retired with a book into a corner of the sitting room, later sleeping on the divan Reine made up as a bed for the night.

The tiny bathroom was just off the kitchen so kettles of boiling water were brought in as needed and towels warmed over the stove. Violette poured a packet of luxurious French bath salts into the bath. She was feeling very tired but relaxed and free of anxiety.

'You sit on the stool and I'll tell you some really funny things,' went on Violette, entirely in French. She told her mother all about Paris, about the Grand Café with Philippe's aunt (whom she said was the aunt of a friend of Philippe's called Tante Eva, not Evelyn), touched on her trip to Rouen and Le Havre, about the train journeys, adding, 'It was so funny, you know, being on the Rouen train with German bigwigs kow-towing to an attractive young Frenchwoman, offering her a seat in their carriage, cigarettes and showing their photos to her.'

'Well, you *are* an attractive young Frenchwoman, dear,' commented Reine, speaking in English. 'Especially with zer beautiful accent you 'ave – very Parisian – you've lost your provincial Picardian accent. But it must 'ave been so perilous. Don't go again. It eez far too dangerous. You 'ave a daughter to think about.'

'*Maman*. I know. She's just gorgeous. But here's something I do well and it's for her and for you, of course for Étienne, for all of us and for Tante Marguerite all by herself under those damn Nazis.' She told her mother many things as she relaxed in the bath. 'You know, it was such fun going into those high-class fashion houses. I met André Malraux.'

'What was he like?'

'A strange man but doing his bit, quite a big bit, it seems. I'm about done now, pass me a towel, please, Mum.'

'I shall dry your back and then make you 'ot milk with 'oney. Like I used to when you were a child.'

Off she went to the kitchen and bustled about while Violette finished drying herself and put on her mother's dressing gown.

Ensconced in her narrow bed, pillows propped up behind her, hair damp and tousled from bathroom steam, Violette felt just like a child again. It was lovely. It was really her mother who kept the family together. I must think of making a will if I'm to go again, thought Violette, and make sure that Maman is guardian to Tania, not Dad, but Vera can look after her for as long as necessary. A light tap at the door and her mother walked in, bearing a tray with a glass of warm milk and honey and some tea biscuits.

'Gosh, it's good to be here. Thank you for everything, Maman. Tomorrow, I'll take Tania back to Vera Maidment as it's safer for her at Mill Hill and keeps her out of Dad's hair. I hope Vera is giving her good food. Mind you, I'm paying her so I'm sure she is, it's just that Tania looks a little peaky and seems to still have a bit of a cough. Anyway, at the weekend I'll pick her up and we'll come and see you. Meanwhile I'll be in the Pembridge Villas flat so I can get to meetings easily.'

'Yes, dear, I noticed her cough, too. But it should soon disappear now that it's springtime. I should think the weather's improved in Pont Rémy as well. You know, I just don't understand my sister, Marguerite. She's so stubborn; she wouldn't leave France when you and Dickie came 'ome. She should 'ave come to live 'ere with us.'

'She's happy there. You're the one who fell in love with an English bloke, not her!'

'You're right, Vi. But I miss her. And I'm afraid for her. Now, my dear, sleep. You'll wake up fresh tomorrow.' She kissed her daughter on the cheek, then turned off the light and went down the stairs after quietly closing the door.

‡

A further full day of debriefing took place at 59 Wimpole Street before Violette was summoned to be yet again debriefed, at a Baker Street office and finally at an office attached to the War Office. The meetings in Baker Street and the War Office bureaux concerned all she had learned about the V rockets, their sites that Violette had visited or acquired intelligence on and the German Naval Headquarters in Rouen. She was asked to draw ground plans. Question after question was asked to help her recreate the sites as accurately as possible. She gave details of military emplacements and personnel attending them and geographic and demographic intelligence on surrounding areas.

Finally, she passed on intelligence she had gained from her visit to the dangerous town of Le Havre and gleaned from Résistants and leaders of groups further afield.

Having a coffee in one of the canteens one day, she learned that, on their return flight from France, they just missed the bombing raid on Portsmouth on the night of 30 April, as they flew over the Channel. She and Philippe were truly lucky to be alive.

It was an exhausting four days and Violette went back to Pembridge Villas in the evenings, as it was central for her meetings with the Baker Street bods. Although she missed Tania, she knew she could not leave her alone in the flat at Pembridge Villas all day while she was being debriefed. She was happy to meet up with friends in SOE and go clubbing or to the cinema in the evenings. It took her mind off things.

At Orchard Court and Wimpole Street the main emphasis was on her knowledge of the networks remaining in the area around Rouen and Le Havre all the way to Dieppe, and the intelligence she had gained from further north to the Belgian border. Although they were coded and brief in the extreme, her notes from France helped her recall details of what had happened to the network, names or codenames of people she had met and their groups, towns and villages she had visited, the rocket sites she had seen and numerous other often tiny facts and figures which helped SOE and the War Ministry to build an ever improving picture of that area of France by comparing her intelligence with that brought back by other agents. She would be back the following day and then on to FANY[104] headquarters to report in.

Throughout the questioning, her reporting remained logical, fulsome and accurate. At each debriefing, another minor detail would emerge sometimes proving important. Her own understanding of all she had seen and done took on greater depth and slowly she perceived the bigger and, at times, more political picture emerging. These days, though exhausting, gave her intriguing insights into the machinations of government and war. It proved to her that daring did win so she would continue to dare carefully, as she had done with such good results.

Now Violette was free to relax until recalled for her next mission.

‡

It was time to take a complete break. In her WTS uniform, Violette decided to go to Hereford and breathe some country air for a few days. She enjoyed staying at the Old Kennels with her aunt and uncle. She took her two younger cousins, John and Brenda, to the fair, where she lost a very pretty earring and left the remaining one at Aunt Florrie's. In later years, Brenda took and treasured this earring as a fond reminder of that happy day. Violette went to pubs in the evening with Norman and helped Aunt Florrie with household chores. She spent a couple of afternoons with Uncle Henry grooming the dogs, survivors of the heartrending cull he had been required by law to make. On returning to London, she was much refreshed. The tired lines around her eyes had all but disappeared; she had put on a little weight and looked stunning in her dark uniform. She hardly wore the other clothes she had brought as she enjoyed being in uniform and the status it gave her.

‡

Most of FANY's personnel was absorbed into the ATS, formed as an auxiliary service of some 20,000 women during the Second World War. The women served in many different categories, including office duties, as mess and telephone orderlies, drivers, postal workers, butchers, bakers, ammunition inspectors, military police, gun crews and many other operational support tasks. FANYs provided most of the ATS Transport Section, called the WTS, to which Violette had been attached.

---

104 FANY – First Aid Nursing Yeomanry – was incorporated in 1909 with an HQ in London. It was an unofficial auxiliary of upper-crust women volunteers set up to serve mounted troops, by driving vehicles and giving nursing care, in the main! FANY is today a standalone service of women from teens to retirement with ongoing training to meet any emergency in urban and rural areas on the British Isles and elsewhere in the world. It provides excellent training, lots of fun, discipline where needed and, these days, lack of stuffiness. Service could be lifesaving, involving travelling to disaster areas around the world and so on. www.fany.org.uk.

Violette Szabó as a child of just nine. Reine Bushell, Violette's mother, my grandmother, fashioned this coat for Violette with fox fur collar while Violette still lived in France. *Author's archives*

Violette aged about eleven and her English life-long best friend, Vera Maidment; at Mill Hill, London, UK. *Author's archives*

The photo Violette gave to Manny Isbey. On the back were the words 'With all my love, Violette'.
Courtesy of Polly Isbey, Manny's sister, New Zealand. *Author's archives*

Violette aged sixteen with her brother aged seventeen at the Staff Ball of the Savoy Hotel in 1937.
Author's archives

Harry Peulevé looking weary, knowing and stubborn. He loved Violette. *Author's archives*

Winterfold House, north of Cranleigh, Surrey taken in 2015. Violette would have stayed at the top of the house with views towards Cranleigh and Dunsfold. *Mark Yeats*

Notice Violette is mentally translating from French to English, hence her French phraseology. Written to Vera, her best friend, while staying with her French Tante Marguerite and French grandparents. A teenager loving every minute. *Author's archives*

Honeymoon photo in August 1940 in our garden at 18 Burnley Road, Stockwell, SW8. *Author's archives*

Violette and Étienne marry at Aldershot Registry Office on 20 August 1940. l/r: unknown, Charles Bushell, unknown, Reine Bushell, Roy Bushell, Étienne and Violette, unknown, Georgian Prince Lieutenant Dimitri Amilakhvari, Colonel Kiss. *Author's archives*

A glamorous couple. *Author's archives*

Hazells Hall nr Tempsford; club where agents and pilots relaxed and slept over. Good food, fine wines/spirits and congenial if tense company. Since the war it has been converted into magnificent luxury flats. Great, as the Pym family told the author they were considering demolishing it. *Courtesy of Sandy archives*

At the Szabó Room in the Jersey War Tunnels a Sten gun with two cartridges and parachute silk – just like Violette would have used. *Author's archives*

One of Violette's false identity cards. She knew the area and went to school for a time at Noyelles-sur-Mer. *PF at National Archives and in author's archives*

SECRET   Report: 620   620

Squadron 36th A/C # 538   Date 8 June

Name of Operation STATIONER 110B   Alt.
Country FRANCE

Crew: Pilot FENSIER   Disp. HALL
     C.Pilot WARN   R.O. KINGLESBACH
     Nav. DAVIS, N.C.   Eng. THOMAS
     Bomb. YANCEY   Gunner GREY
     Pass.   P.ss.

	T	G	F	N	FH
Load Carried	4	12	10	5	
Load Dropped	4	12	10	5	

Result of Operation. COMPLETE

Time of Take Off 2214   Landed 0520

Was Exact Pinpoint Found? YES. How was point identified?
C-Type bte flashing "C." Identified ridge
leading towards threep a forest to NW.

Estimated Dropping Points
   1st Run — dropped 2 Jeé 12 C — 20yds to left of bte
   2nd Run — 2 Jeés Vernal package — right m
   3rd Run — 10 packages — in to bte
Bombardier and Dispatchers Report.
   Everything ok ok

.Target area. From 0134 to 0157 . Time Dropped 1st – 0149, 2nd – 0152, 3rd – 0157
.Height above ground   Course 300°   MFH
.Routes - Time. altitude and Point of Crossing English and Enemy
Coasts Batt Tail 2330 6000   Pt. Blanc 2359 6000
Pt. Blanc 0140 5000   Batt Tail okeu 500
.Leaflets dropped Guideuil Ambiance, Alloue,
Chatun, Cotte.

13. Load or part of Load Jettisoned; what was jettisoned:

Place   altitude   Time

14. Enemy Opposition (give A/C position, time and altitude, and what happened)
Saw Green yellow flare descend from above
plane at Ploerne (47° 57'N - 02° 23'W)
at 0020 hrs. 5000'.

15. Weather. How did weather affect mission: In route: Good.
                at Target: Fair.
Visibility 10 - 15 mile.

16. Captains personal report   Good reception at target
& at alternate. Poor coding of signal
letter at target.

_____ Deutch No 4 R.
(INTERROGATION OFFICER)

COMMANDING OFFICER,
CARPETBAGGER PROJECT.

SECRET

Jedburgh Fenster log of the Stationer Flight dropping Violette and team over Sussac in the Haute-Vienne. *Courtesy of the historian and dear friend, the late Tom Ensminger*

Flight Lieutenant Robert 'Bob' Large, DFC, LdH; Lysander pilot who safely flew Violette back to England from Le Fay in France while under enemy attack. *Courtesy of Bob Large*

The painting is *Loire Rendezvous* by Philip E. West. *Courtesy of SWA Fine Arts*

Tania Szabó and Bob Large, ten miles from where the latter was shot down in his Spitfire, pictured in 2014. *Mark Yeats*

Rouen devastated by German aerial bombing in 1940 and 1941 that Violette would have seen.
Author's archives

André Malraux smoking, south of France, as *Colonel Berger*. *Author's archives*

Colonel Guingouin knew how to win friendship of the Limousin country folk. Everyone knew and respected him. He wrote of Violette's courage and activities in his autobiographical book *Quatre ans de lute sur le sol Limousin* – Four years of struggle on Limousin soil – and to me when visiting with Paul Emile. *Author's archives*

Philippe Liewer aka *Major Charles Staunton*. A French journalist, founder and leader of the *Salesman* and *Salesman II* circuits as well as being Violette's commanding officer. *Author's archives*

Gestapo poster plastered all over Rouen in 1944 preventing Philippe Liewer returning. l/r: Philippe Liewer; Bob Maloubier. *Author's archives*

Huguette Dehors, a retired teacher, as a young woman a year or two after her ordeal in Limoges prison where she shared a cell with Violette. *Courtesy of Huguette Dehors*

Captain Isidore Newman (*Pierre*), Philippe's trusted wireless operator. *Courtesy of Martin Sugarman and JSTOR*

Albert Tisserand explains to Paul-Emile Holley exactly what he saw as a youngster of fourteen. He hid in the grange behind them. *Taken by the author in 2003*

The iron fence was where the German advance guard took up position and were shooting at Violette who, alone in the field to the left of the fence, was returning fire with her Sten gun. *Taken by the author in 2003*

The SS officer brought Violette, arrested, in his armoured car on June 10 1944 over the bridge to the house where Jacques Dufour (*Anastasie*) was hiding under logs to the right of the bridge opposite the house. *Taken by the author in September 2003*

SS-Obersturmbannführer Fritz Sühren, commandant of Ravensbrück, executed by the French in 1950. *Courtesy of Georg Schwab*

SS-Obersturmführer (1944) Johann Schwarzhüber. 12 January 1945 he was the Schutzhaftlagerführer of Ravensbrück concentration camp. He was directly responsible for executions and gassing of some 2,350 prisoners. *Courtesy of Georg Schwab*

The Walzroller was often to be pushed in the heat of summer or depth of north German winter until death. *Courtesy Ravensbrück Archives*

'Shooting gallery' in Ravensbrück concentration camp which led to a small execution yard, destroyed when the camp was liberated by the Russians in April 1945. *Taken by the author in 1995*

These cremation ovens show the long poles on which the women's dead bodies were placed before being pushed into the ovens. *Anon.*

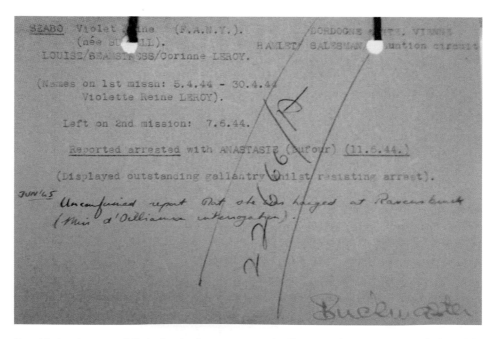

SZABO Violet ...ine   (F.A.N.Y.).   BORDOGNE ...TE, VIENNE
              (née BU...LL).   HAMLET/ SALESMAN ...untion circuit
       LOUISE/SEAMSTRESS/Corinne LEROY.

       (Names on 1st missn: 5.4.44 - 30.4.44
              Violette Reine LEROY).

       Left on 2nd mission: 7.6.44.

       Reported arrested with ANASTASIE (Dufour) (11.6.44.)

       (Displayed outstanding gallantry whilst resisting arrest).

JUN'45   Unconfirmed report that she was hanged at Ravensbruck
       (Miss d'Oilliamson interrogation).

                                                         Buckmaster

From Violette's personal file indicating her courage and gallantry as she saved Jacques Dufour's life and shot dead at least one German private and wounding a number of others. *Author's archives*

Country Sect. We agree
remarks on
SAB report

FG to MT.3 12.10.43.
This student is nominated for the course at
Group B commencing 17.10.43. Unfortunately
it is too early to indicate the area in which
she will be working as a courrier. She will
require 3 weeks plus scheme. She is bi-lingual
in French and English.
D/CE.M.1 to FG 13.10.43.
Is still under consideration.
STS HQ to Group B 13.10.43.
Will attend course commencing 17.10.43 at
STS 32C. Will act as a courrier in the field.

A/Lt. Shley STS 24-7.9.43.
I seriously wonder whether this student is
suitable for our purpose. She seems lacking
in a sense of responsibility and although she
works well in the company of others, does
not appear to have any initiative or ideals.
She speaks French with an English accent.
21.9.43.
For this member of the party one's feelings
are bound to be mixed. Character difficult
to describe:- Pleasant personality, sociable,
likeable, painstaking, anxious to please, keen,
mature for her age in certain ways but in
others very childish. She is very anxious to
carry on with the training but I am afraid
it is not with the idea of improving her
knowledge but simply because she enjoys the
course, the spirit of competition, the novelty
of the thing, and being very fit - the physical side of the training. She is very kind
hearted, although conceals it. The main reasons
for stating in my previous reports my doubt
regarding her suitability for this work are:-
1. When taking over a party, the first thing
I concentrate on is to win the students' trust
friendship and encourage them to ask me

8

A report in Violette's personal file with instructors' concerns – they clearly were unable to read this young woman! *Author's archives*

Telephone, Whitehall 3611 (4 lines) Telegrams. { Dracliffe, Parl, London
or
Tresag, Parl, London

RADCLIFFES & CO.
(RADCLIFFES & HOOD, ST BARBE SLADEN & WING)

G. E. SHRIMPTON.
H. EDMUND SARGANT.
S. F. T. L ROBINSON.
F. B. COCKBURN.

10, Little College Street,

Westminster, S.W.1.

| PLEASE REFER TO |
| B/D/MER |
| IN REPLYING |

3rd June, 1946.

Dear Sir,

<u>Mrs. V. R. E. Szabo, decd.</u>

We have to acknowledge the receipt
of your letter of the 29th May (reference
C.3.Army List) enclosing a certificate
of death of Ensign V. R. E. Szabo, F.A.N.Y.
We think that the certificate will be
sufficient for our immediate purpose, but
if any further point arises we will com-
municate with you.

We are, dear Sir,
Yours faithfully,

The Under Secretary of State,
War Office,
Golden Cross House,
Duncannon Street,
W.C.2.

Letter from solicitors Radcliffe's & Co to the Under Secretary of State on 3 June 1946. There was
considerable communications trying to establish a death certificate. *Author's archives*

RWL/F/INT/2156   12 NOV 1945   6th November, 1945.

To: Major HAZELDINE.   From: Flt/O. ATKINS.

         Thank you very much for your P/FH/B/861 of
1st November, 1945 enclosing copy of letter from Mlle.
Solange ROUSSEAU. I am still not certain that VIOLET,
LILIAN and DANIELLE were executed. It is so vague to
say "Nous avons su à notre retour qu'elles étaient déjà
execute le 5 fevrier". People like Marie DE MONCY and
Yvonne BASEDEN who were in the camp all the time
definitely have no such knowledge.

         I do not think it is any use pressing Mlle.
ROUSSEAU for greater details ie.e. how she got to hear
of this, who saw them or who gave her the information.

         Likewise the "précision donnée par un journal
anglais" can be dismissed as inaccurate and untrue.

         I am continuing the enquiries in all directions
and will let you know if any more information comes to
light at this end.

The writer of this document appears to me to be arrogant or lazy and thus unable to do a thorough investigation. *Author's archives*

COPY

LAST WILL AND TESTAMENT OF:

Violette Reine Elizabeth SZABO of 36 Pembridge Villas, Notting Hill W.11. made in London on 24.1.44.

I appoint:

> Reine Blanche Bushell, 18 Burnley Road,
> Stockwell, S.W.9.

to be my Executor.

I give and bequeath unto:

> My daughter Gania Damaris Desire Szabo,
> 59 Fernside Avenue, Mill Hill, Edgward, N.W.7.
> all of which I die possessed.

> (signed) V. SZABO.

Witnesses: R. A. Bourne-Paterson,
93 Chesterfield House,
London, W.1.

V. M. ATKINS,
725 Nell Gwynn House,
London, S.W.3.

Copy of Violette's last Will and Testament witnessed by R.A. Bourne-Paterson and V.M. Atkins. *Author's archives*

Violette's parachute badge which changed her father's views of her character. *Author's collection*

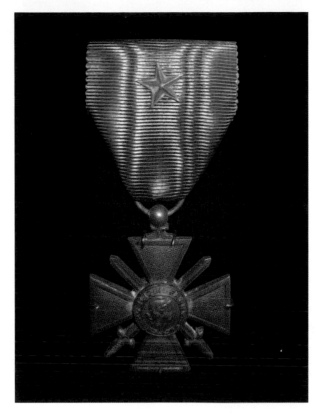

Violette's Croix de Guerre with Star. In Spinks cabinet with Violette's and Étienne's highest awards from their respective countries. This cabinet arranged for by Sotheby's in London. *Author's collection*

The enclosed Scroll is sent
by Command of The King
GVI RI

This scroll commemorates
Lieutenant V. R. E. Szabo, GC.
First-Aid Nursing Yeomanry
held in honour as one who
served King and Country in
the world war of 1939-1945
and gave her life to save
mankind from tyranny. May
her sacrifice help to bring
the peace and freedom for
which she died.

Violette's George Cross and scroll presented to the author as a child of four and a half in 1946. *Author's archives*

Some medals of Adj.-chef (13e DBLE) Étienne Szabó, Legionnaire. The Légion d'honneur, Military, Médaille Militaire, Croix de Guerre with Star and Palme, Médaille Coloniale. The Croix de Guerre is missing its two 'bars'. There were many other ribbons, too. These are in the same cabinet with photos of both Violette and Étienne. In *The Guinness Book of Records* they were named as the married couple with the highest awards awarded to them by their respective countries. Étienne is considered one of the Legion's heroes down in Aubagne, the Legion home. *Author's collection*

Not long after receiving the Croix de Guerre from the French Ambassador at a Gala evening at the embassy, Tania is wearing her mother's medals and her father's ribbons. All too heavy for her size and clothes so her grandmother made her a harness which embarrassed Tania very much! *Author's archives*

In memory of

Ensign Violette Reine Elizabeth Szabo

*Women's Transport Service (F.A.N.Y.) attached
Special Operations,
George Cross,
who died aged 23 between 25 January -5 February
1945
Daughter of Charles and Reine Blanche Bushell of Long
Jetty, New South Wales, Australia and wife of Lieut.
Etienne Szabo,
Remembered with honour
Panel 26 Column 3
Brookwood Memorial, Surrey*

Brookwood Memorial, Surrey, United Kingdom

*In the perpetual care of
the Commonwealth War Graves Commission*

The Commonwealth War Graves at Brookwood Memorial is beautifully designed and cared for. Often at Panel 26 (the day of Violette's birthday), next to her name, is a violet or a red poppy. *Author's archives*

In Morlaix, Finistère, Tania wearing Étienne's gift of a gold bracelet to Violette, later stolen, standing next to Mme Marie Lecomte, Breton resistance fighter wearing her Légion d'Honneur, Médaille Militaire, Croix de Guerre and one other. Marie was a huge source of strength and comfort to Violette in Fresnes prison, Paris, Ravensbrück concentration camp and the sub-camp in Königsberg. She wrote several letters to the author and her grandparents before they met in 1963. *Author's archives*

L/r: Charles and Reine Bushell, Violette's parents and the author's grandparents; Mme Marie Lecomte wearing the most precious gift Tania could give her, a gift from her guardian, Charles van Bergen. Tania wished to show in some concrete form how grateful she is to Marie for looking after Violette as best she could in those dreadful days. Marie survived but a skeleton of five stones and was very ill for many years. *Author's archives*

Marching with bands, steel band, many people, military groups with banners and the people of Brixton and Stockwell coming out of their homes or just cheering a few days after Brixton riots in June 1981. We were marching from Brixton Town Hall (where a plaque commemorates Violette) to 18 Burnley Road where the author and Mayor 'Johnny' Johnson unveiled a Blue Plaque on the house where Violette and Tania lived. *Author's archives*

This plaque is on the plinth topped by a sculpture of Violette by Karen Newman. The statue is before Lambeth Palace on the embankment looking directly at the Houses of Parliament!! *Author's archives*

IN MEMORY OF
MEMBERS OF THE SPECIAL OPERATIONS EXECUTIVE (SOE) F SECTION
WHOSE LIVES WERE TAKEN HERE
DENISE MADELEINE BLOCH
KING'S COMMENDATION FOR BRAVE CONDUCT, CHEVALIER DE LA LÉGION D'HONNEUR,
MÉDAILLE DE LA RÉSISTANCE FRANÇAISE (ROSETTE), WOMEN'S TRANSPORT SERVICE (FANY)
SHOT, JANUARY 1945
LILIAN VERNA ROLFE
MENTIONED IN DESPATCHES, CROIX DE GUERRE AVEC PALME, WOMEN'S AUXILIARY AIR FORCE
SHOT, JANUARY 1945
VIOLETTE ELIZABETH SZABO
GEORGE CROSS, CROIX DE GUERRE AVEC PALME, WOMEN'S TRANSPORT SERVICE (FANY)
SHOT, JANUARY 1945
CECILY MARGOT LEFORT
MENTIONED IN DESPATCHES, CROIX DE GUERRE AVEC ÉTOILE DE VERMEIL, WOMEN'S AUXILIARY AIR FORCE
GASSED, FEBRUARY 1945
AND THOSE WHO SURVIVED.

This plaque is on the Wall of Nations at Ravensbrück concentration camp and it is interesting to note that it also commemorates those who survived. Lest we forget! *Taken by the author*

This plaque is on a monument at the crossroads just outside Sussac and very close to where Violette parachuted in with her team on the night of 7/8 June 1944. *Taken by the author*

The unveiling of the stele in hommage to Violette on the 50th anniversary of Pont-Rémy's liberation by the Canadians. L/r: Paul E.F. Holley; Tania Szabó; Madame le Maire; Roy Bushell, Violette's brother who spent his young years growing up and being educated in France at the same time as Violette. *Author's archives, photo by Aimé Peltier*

l/r: Jean-Claude Guiet, SOE w/o, Tania, Bob Maloubier, SOE agent and his partner at the opening of the Violette Szabó GC Museum in Wormelow, Herefordshire. Each year on the Sunday closest to 26 June, Rosemary Rigby arranges for a picnic to celebrate Violette's life here, where as a young girl and woman she spent many happy years with her aunt, uncle and cousins. *Author's archives, photo by Steve Harwood*

The monument before Lambeth Palace with Violette looking towards the Houses of Parliament! *Author's archives*

Memorial stone in glacial granite. Unveiled at Winterfold in 2011 by Professor M.R.D. Foot – the official SOE historian. *Mark Yeats*

Tania, Mark Yeats and Virginia McKenna outside Winterfold House in 2013. *Mark Yeats*

Ex-French Resistance Mme Louisette Tanter, Odette Sanson GC, Virginia McKenna, whose starring role as Violette in *Carve her Name with Pride* still moves all who see that 1958 film. *Virginia McKenna archives*

All above: Stills from *Carve her Name With Pride.* © ITV/REX

What it was all for: preparing the barricades for the liberation of Paris, 23 August 1944.
Patrimoine Paris

She had, before joining SOE, worked at the Acton munitions factory, part of the Guinness Brewery sites and shifted over to military production, suffering frequent air raids from German bombers sweeping over London. At the factory she and her friends had had a couple of lucky escapes. When Charlie Bushell insisted she stop working there because it was too dangerous and upsetting to her mother, she joined the Land Army. After that spell of service, she joined the WTS on 11 September 1941 and was posted to Leicester after her initial training.

Violette did not find the work terribly appealing but made up for that in the evenings at pubs, dancing with friends in dance halls and going to the cinema. It helped keep boredom at bay for a while. Her tasks and that of her colleagues were to cook, waitress, plus chores of laundering a mass of sheets and shirts and similar drudgery. She muttered to the other girls that there must be something more exciting to do. She served in an underground Telephone Exchange until she was considered too ill with bronchitis caught in those cold, damp basements. She had enjoyed it for a short period but was not sorry to leave.

Why couldn't she join the armed services? She was a great shot with a gun and she was sure she could shoot any German soldier straight between the eyes from a distance. In October 1941, the 481 Heavy (Mixed) Anti-Aircraft (ack-ack) Battery was formed. Violette joined it with a group of men and women from Leicester. Another young woman, Elsie Gundry, came with a group from a training camp in Guildford. They had all been previously kitted out with uniforms, sat three examinations and committed to serve three years in the artillery. Other groups came from camps all over the British Isles. These diverse young women met on the barrack square in Oswestry in Shropshire and were introduced to their officers and NCOs.

The 481 Heavy (Mixed) Anti-Aircraft Battery was born – one of the first batteries to be set up to defend the British Isles from the airborne blitz.

'Violette, everyone tells me you were a member of the Free French. Did you take part in wonderful and daring escapes from behind enemy lines?' asked a wide-eyed Elsie one day. They were getting to know one another and enjoyed spending time in each other's company with the others in the ack-ack, or the A-A as these anti-aircraft batteries were also known.

'Good God, no! What on earth has got into the fools? I'm *married* to a Free French soldier, a French Foreign Legionnaire, that's all. It's him who's won all the medals for outstanding bravery. He's been all over the world, too, served a year or so in Indo-China, Tonkin, coming back to Europe in 1940.'

'Oh, I'm so sorry. I hope I haven't embarrassed you. I should have thought before opening my big mouth.' Poor Elsie, who was a very gentle and loyal soul, turned bright pink.

Violette replied, laughing, 'Not a bit of it. I'm glad you asked. I'm so damned proud of him.' She had also badgered her superiors to allow her to wear Étienne's Free French flash on the shoulder of her battledress blouse. I recall Commander

Minchin of the FANYs telling me how pleased Violette was to march with that flash! Violette was inordinately proud to be the wife of a Legionnaire, an NCO soon to be promoted into the officer class with an exciting future ahead for the two of them. Already well decorated, he had the scars to attest to his courage in battle. He opened up huge vistas of gallant war craft and dazzling chivalry in warm climes and sun-soaked living.

Violette enjoyed being part of the 481 Heavy (Mixed) Ack-Ack Battery, which was her first real taste of taking on the enemy with a weapon. There was also much fun with the other girls leading their NCOs and officers a merry dance, escaping through a gap in fencing to go to movies at NAAFI in the off-bounds camp next door; shopping or eating a meal in town, all the while on the lookout for those that might report them.

Violette and Elsie, plus four other girls, were detailed for fire piquet,[105] reporting for an hour's practice drill at six each morning. As Elsie and Violette had skipped camp a number of times after having been ordered not to, they were put on punishment duty cleaning windows with fire hoses that required two girls to handle them on full blast. Violette and Elsie worked happily enough, taking their time, laughing and chatting. At one window, Violette, holding the hosepipe to wash the windows, turned to say something to Elsie not realising the window was open. 'What the bloody hell! You bloody nitwits!' An orderly officer woke from his quiet snooze under a stream of freezing water from Violette's hose.

It seemed a good idea to vanish. Later, they were informed they had learned how to use the fire equipment and the team was changed!

After four weeks' training and parade ground drill, they were sent to Holyhead in Anglesey, North Wales, for gun practice. It was here that various talent competitions took place and Violette performed the Salomé dance in her blue striped pyjama trousers and a pink bra. At the end, after twisting and turning and swaying sexily to the music with a fine large handkerchief as a veil to cover her nose and mouth, her body sinuous as an Indian snake, she did a superb backward flip, only for her bra straps to snap in unison. Blushing deep crimson, she flew off the stage followed by gales of laughter and loud clapping. She had delighted the audience with her dancing. This was the icing on the cake for them – men and women alike!

In December they set out to Frodsham, near Warrington in Cheshire, where Violette stayed until February 1942. She was trained as No. 5 and worked the telescope following the angle of sight by elevating or depressing it. Elsie Gundry was trained as a No. 3 and followed the line of sight on the opposite telescope. The predictor then calculated the future position of the target to the guns by

---

105 Fire piquet = being on fire duty, stationed somewhere close. Two people are usually on duty and after midnight, the shift might be split. But, more likely than not, a mere two hours' sleep were had. Duties might include peeling potatoes, known as 'spud bashing'. The Piquet Commander was in the Guardroom.

means of electric cables after the height, position, range and fuse had been fixed by other members of the team – complicated but totally absorbing and interesting. Lieutenant Colonel Jim Naylor, Violette's commanding officer, described his Vickers Predictor operator as:

```
tiny, very slim and very attractive. Because of her height,
or lack of it, she seemed always to stand on her toes when
at her instrument. She was popular and her officers and NCOs
always spoke highly of her as a soldier and as a comrade.
She and another girl held French classes in the evenings
with excellent results. Whatever she did, she did it with
one hundred percent enthusiasm. She was always the example
and leading spirit.
```

‡

On her return from Herefordshire, Violette attended a final debriefing visit to Baker Street with a suggestion of a new mission in the offing. She decided to take Tania to show off her daughter to her many friends and acquaintances. She had let out part of her flat to help pay the rent. Violette was always in need of an advance. Vera Atkins did not approve in the least and never refrained from warning her of the dangers of advances far exceeding monies due. Vera was naturally very thrifty while it was obvious that Violette really did not wish to understand such a concept.

So Tania (me) went to Baker Street but hardly remembers it. I had been told the tale of the visit by my grandmother and was reminded of it by Yvonne Basedon, an SOE agent, in about 2005 when I visited her in London. Sadly, Yvonne did not like to recall such days – much of the war years have been tucked away in her mind and it distresses her somewhat to this day. One of Violette's friends, Sonia d'Artois, married to Major Guy d'Artois and living in Canada, remembers carefree moments together with Violette and Nancy Wake. The Terrible Trio, I have no doubt!

‡

25

Final Days of Waiting, Promotion, Preparation and a Night on the Town

Tuesday 16 May to Wednesday 31 May 1944

'Yours'
'Yours till the stars lose their glory
Yours till the birds fail to sing
Yours to the end of life's story'

Xavier Cugat, 1939

Everything seemed peaceful in London. The bombing had ceased and the buzz bombs[106] did not start to fall for another few weeks. But there was so much destruction – so many deaths and injuries.

Violette had been told plans were in progress for the next mission. She was itching to know more but did not press it – yet. Every day the heavily damaged areas of her beloved London increased Violette's determination to get back into the fray. Sharp, indelible images burned into her mind, along with the fresh images of Rouen and Le Havre. She reflected on the deaths of Étienne and of so many friends and acquaintances. Apart from Étienne, her own family had so far escaped death and the terrors of war. Even her mother, Reine, was assured that her dear sister, Marguerite, and the rest of her family in Picardy were alive. But Violette had lost Étienne and her and Tania's future with him. That still brought great rage to Violette's heart. As her little girl grew, how would she react? Would she grow whole or forever hold the feeling of loss? A new father could help, of that she felt sure, if she ever decided to remarry. But the right man for the two of them might never appear.

The overwhelming anguish had lost its sharpness since, almost three years ago, the arrival of the telegram in its brown envelope informing Violette of Étienne's death. Often enough now she had fun with friends and colleagues, going to the pub, dining and dancing, inviting friends round to her Pembridge Villas flat. Her mission to France had been exciting and successful and her confidence grew. Life was sometimes happy and full of laughter although dulled by time, the ache had not vanished. The disappointment and shock of loss had seared her soul but her

---

106 The VI flying bombs were variously called 'buzz bombs' and 'doodlebugs'.

natural exuberance would not be denied. She was enjoying the company of men, like the Scandinavian agent, Eric, Harry Peulevé and even her father's young friend, the second-hand car dealer Sidney Matthews, who had chased after her from well before the war, fallen for her and eventually had become a good friend. Violette found hitting the town, meeting friends, dancing to the big bands helped to heal the surface wound.

She flirted a little from time to time; thought of love again – but where was the glow, the sheer sparkling happiness that there had been with Étienne? She closed her mind to such reflections; it was dangerous to unlock those doors. Instead she concentrated on fun, excitement, her daughter, her friends, her mother and brothers – and another mission.

Violette went to Mill Hill to see Tania and spent a couple of nights there. It was a happy and fulfilling time for them all. She enjoyed visiting her friend Vera Maidment as well as being able to take Tania out for jaunts and up to London to do a little shopping for a few toys in Woolworth's, where she had worked before the war. This was her penultimate visit to Mill Hill and she decided to take Tania back to Stockwell, where she would stay until Violette left on her new mission. She said she would see Vera on her return from duty and, paying her, thanked her for all her help.

‡

One morning, in mid-May, without prior appointment, Violette arrived at Baker Street to see Vera Atkins.[107] She was surprised by the warm smile and solicitude from this normally taciturn woman.

---

107 Just about the very first question Sarah Helm, journalist and author, asked me when researching for her biography of Vera was, did I think that Vera had lesbian tendencies with regard to Violette, or, for that matter, any of the women in her charge? Not having ever considered this idea, I was somewhat at a loss. My curiosity certainly made me think carefully but on reflection, if Vera did entertain such notions she would have been extremely discreet. Equally, I know that Vera was attracted to a handful of men in her life with whom she had long-standing relationships, apart from the love of her life, a military man who had been killed in the war. On this matter, Violette and Vera had much in common. A year or so later, I met Sarah in her home, as she was temporary custodian to much of Vera's archives, on loan from Phœbe Atkins, Vera's sister-in-law, whose husband, like Vera, had changed his name from Rosenberg to the more English Atkins. I asked Sarah why she had thrown such a controversial question at me at the start of our interview. She told me that, very shortly before our meeting, a woman who worked within the same SOE offices as Vera had put the supposition to her so it was uppermost in her mind. We concluded there was not the remotest possibility as Violette clearly (and most probably Vera) preferred men as sexual partners. But, there was a strong mutual attraction of the platonic kind. They enjoyed their tentative friendship and their relationship of commanding officer to junior officer in SOE. Had Violette returned, she and Vera would doubtless have become firm friends, regardless of their many differences. Each had much to learn from the other.

'Well, my dear,' started Vera, 'how are you? You're looking much refreshed and the colour is back in your cheeks.'

There were files stacked in neat piles on a table under the dusty window, shelves full of box-files, books and ledgers, two filing cabinets securely locked. On Vera's desk was a roll of small cards in alphabetical order, two telephones and a file marked 'top secret'. Her chair was an ordinary one with a worn brown leather cover on the seat.

Violette blushed with pleasure and said she was 'raring to go'. And it was true; she felt a million dollars in her silk flowered dress from Paris, the sexy sandals and silk stockings. She felt a uniform was not needed on an informal visit.

She explained to Vera that the reason she had popped by was to say how she was dying to get back to France and that it happened that *Major Staunton* had mentioned at the last meeting that something was in the offing with him and Bob Maloubier in central France. He had asked Violette if she would like to join them and of course she had jumped at the chance and wanted to know when and—

Vera broke in by inviting Violette to a spot of lunch as she needed a couple of hour's break from her dreary desk and a good lunch to restore her equilibrium. Violette happily accepted and Vera asked Aida, her assistant, if she would get *Miss Taylor* a decent coffee and a couple of magazines so she could wait comfortably for about fifteen minutes while Vera cleared her desk of the task in hand.

Aida obliged with a smile, followed by a sharp about-turn to deal with the order. She was smartly dressed in her FANY uniform, tightly curled blond hair, not a strand out of place. No makeup, except a smudge of pink lipstick that suited her well.

Violette thought she was very young, probably not more than eighteen, not realising the irony when she herself was still merely twenty-two. But Violette had seen so much of life whereas these girls, a few younger, many possibly five or ten years older than herself, came from good middle- and upper-middle-class families, still lived at home or had just started on the new rage of 'sharing digs' that their fathers paid for. They were light-years apart in the ways of the world if not the social graces. Violette only ever vaunted her hard-won knowledge and intuition in moments of high irritation, or necessary defence of herself or a companion.

‡

Vera Atkins decided to give her a slap-up lunch at the Trocadero. Violette had eaten there before, having on occasion been invited by one of her brothers or some dashing officer. First they had a cocktail in the new and fashionable cocktail lounge, The Salted Almond. Then they went into the restaurant, where the waiters served their famous curry from the trolley. Violette loved it: the splendour of the venue, sumptuous *à la carte* menu and the pleasure of Vera's company.

Vera had a particular fondness for Violette for a variety of reasons. She found Violette's sparkle and love of life unendingly engaging and respected Violette's capacity to hunker down and work hard when, and only when, she was intrigued by a subject or project or mission to dangerous territories. Vera, along with those who trained her, were irritated to the extreme by Violette's frivolous and irreverent attitude when the subject at hand bored her or was so obvious as to be puerile – in her opinion, of course.

‡

During lunch, Vera broached the idea of the possibility of promotion to a higher rank and increment in pay that went with it.

'I've instigated a promotion for you, Violette. I thought you might like to know. You fully deserve it. It'll take a couple of weeks to come through, I should think. The work you did in France has greatly impressed, not only myself and Buck[108] but also other military personnel, including the air-reconnaissance branch of the air force and certain sections of the War Office. The Barentin viaduct blown and additional intelligence on the secret weapons are just two areas where you spectacularly accomplished your mission. Promotion to lieutenant. How does that appeal?'

With a broad smile, Violette replied, 'I'm stunned. As you know, I hoped they'd blow it but couldn't be sure as I had to scarper rather rapidly! Thank you, I will do my utmost to merit it. And, as you know, Vera, an increase in pay would be very welcome. I must also thank you keeping my affairs in order and sorting out my banking arrangements and all the rest.'

'It is an important part of my responsibilities to keep an eye on all my girls' financial arrangements and other matters.'

It was now Friday, 16 May 1944. Vera had told Violette at the lunch to report to Buckmaster's office in SOE HQ by half past four that afternoon. Buckmaster and Philippe were already present. Violette walked in with an air of expectancy and could see that they had been busy. There were papers, plans and maps all over the place.

'Congratulations on your promotion, Violette,' Philippe said as soon as she came in. His smile was warm, although he seemed a little tense and business-like.

Vera explained that plans were in progress for a new mission. Buckmaster put in, 'You don't have to go, you know. You've more than done your share.'

Violette smiled and then frowned in mock concern, 'What, don't you want me to go, then?' she asked.

'Well, yes. However, it remains up to you,' replied Buckmaster. 'Your courage and ability are not in question. Nevertheless, I feel you ought to know that this time it's going to be much more dangerous.'

---

108 'Buck' was the nickname for Colonel Maurice Buckmaster.

She smiled. 'Sir, you know that if I can be of any help, I shall be glad to go again. I *want* to go again. I understand the dangers and that it could be even more dangerous this time, especially as the Krauts must know we're up to something massive.'

Buckmaster turned to Philippe, 'Philippe, do you want to give Violette an idea of our plans and the area to which you'll be going? It seems as if nothing will stop her, so let's get on with it.'

'Certainly, sir.' Philippe laid a map out over the desk. 'Here you can see the small outlined area we would probably be parachuted into. On the other hand, the area of our planned operations is quite large – from Limoges down to Brive, at least, and as far north-east as Châteauneuf-la-Forêt. It includes the Mont Gargan and surrounding hills that, in the main, are heavily wooded and where the communist Maquis is well holed up.

'This is a zone full of Maquis wanting to fight; they have already created obstacles but equally have caused unnecessary reprisals because of a "do-or-die" mentality among certain members of the groups. This entire zone will be primed to explode in the face of the enemy once D-Day has taken place. That is our job.

'Our team consists of Jean-Claude on wireless to keep us in touch with London, Bob on reception committees, training in sabotage and warfare generally, you as liaison officer and myself as overall controller. We must get the various factions trained and working to an overall plan. In the Midi there are large numbers of Germans, including the SS-Das Reich Panzer Division led by Brigadeführer Lammerding. If they want to reach the Allied forces that will be landed along the coast, they will need to rush north along the two or three main north-south arteries. Once they get to Limoges on the N20, they could – depending on where our invasion takes place – branch out towards Dieppe and further north or towards the west of Normandy and into Brittany. The reason they're not up there already is that the Germans have to take into consideration that our plans could be to invade along the Mediterranean coast of France. If that did happen, then rest assured that the enemy has one of the truly crack SS military forces waiting down there.

'Late last year, a series of planned Gestapo, Milice and Vichy police raids on SOE and Résistance networks took place. The overall strategy of the German High Command is based on their conviction that the Allies will invade Europe over the Channel from England. They don't know where or when, but they do know it *will* happen ...'

'I'm sorry to interrupt, but would it not be possible to block the Panzers from leaving their base in the south?' Violette tentatively put forward.

'No, Violette,' broke in Buckmaster. 'It would require a huge force that is not at our disposal. They are being concentrated elsewhere at the present time and we cannot spread ourselves too thin, nor stretch our lines of communication too far.'

'*Alors, revenons à nos moutons,*'[109] cracked Philippe. 'We need to unite and supply the three main areas of Résistance before D-Day, as there will be a huge parachute invasion of Jedburghs just a few days after we're dropped. The Jedburghs are the first real teaming up of the American Office of Strategic Services and British SOE to parachute in joint effort into Nazi occupied territories all over Europe to assist in guerrilla and sabotage activities. Before they arrive, we are sending in teams of three or four, each team to include a French national. You and I and Bob Maloubier, who are French, and Jean Guiet, French-American, will make up one of these teams and parachute into the Limousin. It appears that I have no choice in the matter! I must jump!

'Our job is to unite, supply and train the Résistance in Haute-Vienne, Corrèze, Lot and the Dordogne. If you look at the rectangle of these four *départements* you'll understand just how strategically important they are.'

'What about the Auvergne?' broke in Violette.

'That area does not come within your remit, Violette,' interrupted Vera Atkins. 'That is covered by another circuit.'

'Yes, I see.'

Vera then went into their code names and other administrative details, saying, 'Violette, yours will be *Louise Leroy*, still the same surname, a seamstress this time, and Philippe will still be known as *Hamlet* and *Major Charles Staunton*, while the circuit will be *Salesman II*. And as Philippe said, Jean-Claude Guiet will take *Brave* and *Virgile* as required. You will all have three sets of identity and be clothed suitably for hot weather with a few extras for cold nights.

'This time you will be going over with a full moon on 6 June. Half-moon is not until 13 June, and 20 June is moonless. The 6th is a Tuesday so you have around three weeks to sort yourselves out. You should meet here every day or so to be brought up-to-date and to fine-tune your operation. You will each be carrying large sums of money and personal weapons. Violette, this is not like the solitary mission you were on in Rouen and Le Havre. You will be working as a part of a team under Philippe's overall command.'

'Yes,' said a very thoughtful Violette.

'You will all have to be very much on your toes,' stepped in Buckmaster. 'We know that the Germans down south are getting very nasty. They know they're losing the war. They're instigating brutal reprisals on the civil population right across southern France. Your safe-house will be in the tiny village of Sussac. Madame Ribiéras has a small grocery shop there; her husband is a POW in Germany. She's experienced and she'll do everything she can for you.'

---

109 '*Revenons à nos moutons*' literally means 'let's get back to our sheep' and derives from a farce of a trial regarding sheep in the sixteenth century. It is the French way of saying, 'let's get back to the matter in hand'. Quoted often by Rabelais.

A knock on the door heralded the entrance of a young French-American, Jean-Claude Guiet. Introductions were made and a quick drink to wish them all luck – or '*merde*' as Vera would say.

It was late by the time they took their leave. Philippe offered to drive Violette home to Pembridge Villas. They had all pored over the maps. Bourne-Patterson had come in to talk finances and they had all once again discussed ideas and the people on the spot in each of the areas.

Once in the flat, they continued going over details until two o'clock in the morning, both yawning and deciding to call it a day. Violette offered him her divan, threw a pillow, a clean sheet and a blanket over to him from the airing cupboard and said goodnight. They were both exhausted.

‡

In the morning Philippe invited her to a little Italian coffee house in Notting Hill Gate to have a decent breakfast. Violette accepted with alacrity. As they arrived there, a young man approached Philippe. 'Ah, Jean-Claude, glad you could make it. You remember Violette. She'll be our courier, in fact, our liaison officer.'

The three of them breakfasted on strong coffee and continental breads while Philippe told them both that they should make any remaining personal arrangements over the next few days. They would also need to go over their cover stories carefully, double check their clothes and all the small items they would be taking to France again. Lastly, he reminded them not to forget to go and get new codes for use in the field.

'I'll have my driver take you, Violette, to the code officer, Lieutenant Leo Marks, you remember him from last time, I should think. The driver can take you wherever you want after that.'

'I've already been,' Jean-Claude stepped in before Philippe could turn to him on the matter. 'Strange fellow, but a good code man, I reckon.'

Earlier in the year, when choosing her other codes, finding her WOK[110] and LOP no problem, Violette discovered this codemaster was a decidedly strange man: young, terribly intense with a sharp and funny wit. She had been warned he fell for each female agent he met, weaving odd little tales and webs, trying to ensnare them. She had found him somewhat comical and could not believe people would fall for his yarns. Nevertheless, they did.

‡

---

110 WOK = Worked-Out Keys in codes, e.g. memorised poems. LOP = Letter One-Time Pads, usually in columns of four or five digits, printed on silk or paper. Initially on tiny pads so that once used the code could be destroyed, and the rest kept.

During this period of rest and refreshment, training and promotion, Violette did not forget her mother's birthday on 22 May. She bought Reine more French perfume and a pretty scarf and insisted they go to a fine restaurant. It was a lovely afternoon spent talking in French and then an evening at home in Stockwell with her father and mother. Charlie had written yet another love poem for the Frenchwoman he had married in 1918.

‡

It was time. Violette began preparing for her departure and saying farewell to friends. She realised her fellow agents must be on similar missions to hers and saw few people apart from Sonia d'Artois and Nancy Wake. And of course, those people she was working with – Vera, Buckmaster, Philippe, Bob Maloubier, Jean-Claude Guiet and a few others. A girlfriend of Harry Peulevé told Violette he had gone overseas but did not know where. Violette was fairly certain he was somewhere down south in France. She wondered if she would be instructed to rendezvous with him as part of the co-ordination process. The area was large and there were thousands of Frenchmen and a good few hundred Frenchwomen involved in this crucial project through which Harry directed a great many Résistants.

She had some studio photos taken of herself, which she asked her mother to keep for her return to start her portfolio. Reine looked at Violette for a long, hard moment, apprehension in her eyes. 'Look Maman,' said Violette, reading her mother, 'I needed some. I'd like to try my hand at becoming an actor in films. Although I could always take up the career of cat burglar after all my training, acting would be sheer delight after the war.'

'Yes, darling, I know. But, I'm afraid for you.'

'No need. I'll be back soon, giving Dad a few more grey hairs!' She smiled at her mother and moved forward and hugged her. 'Look, I also have to put my affairs in order. But I really don't want you to worry. Most of the bods I know come back safe and sound. Just a little crazier, that's all.'

'All right, Vi, what would you like me to do? What about Tania? Is she all right with your friend? I'm just a bit doubtful, I don't know her very well.'

'She should be all right with Vera. I've given her enough money to look after Tania, and I took Tania to buy a few extra clothes, which she enjoyed. But, should anything happen to me – which is highly unlikely – I want you to bring her up along with Vera Maidment. That is, if you don't mind. I have given Vera a letter stating that she take care of Tania but that's just a protection.'

'Well, I've been looking forward to the freedom of having only grown children, except for Dickie – and he's growing up fast.' She laughed, trying to play down her daughter's request. 'You know, Violette, I would look after that little child of yours. I just don't want to have to. I want you back here, safe with us.' The idea that Violette, her only daughter, might not come back, was close to breaking her heart. She had watched bemused while her exuberant, intelligent and fun-loving girl grew into a beautiful, brave woman.

‡

At home, the following day, Violette again broached the subject of her affairs. 'Mum, I've made my will. I'm leaving everything I have to Tania. Not much, I'm afraid, but everything that's mine, including a couple of hundred in the bank – from Étienne – and my meagre wages. These'll be paid quarterly into my bank account. Vera Atkins takes care of all that. I want you to look after my wedding ring for Tania too and the gold compact (I know the mirror is cracked but it's special), vanity case, gold bracelet and Étienne's ribbons, military blanket, old leather suitcase and the other jewellery he gave me. That should all go to her, of course. There's a knife and a small pistol that I won't be taking either. What I think I'll take again is my engagement ring. It just might bring in some cash in a tight corner or I can use it as a bribe. It's worth quite a lot.'

'Violette, you're frightening me!'

'Yes, I'm sorry, Mum. I should have done all this before I went last time. I just didn't want to worry you. Miss Atkins gave me a real dressing-down for leaving everything in a mess. So, if I don't want her coming down on me like a ton of bricks, I've got to do it. Don't you doubt it, I'll be back!'

'I understand. So what else?' said Reine with evident relief.

At that moment, Charlie walked in, 'What's going on here then? Coffee on the go again. You two up to something? How about a nice cup of tea for an old man, then, and one of those biscuits you've been hiding, eh Reine?' He was relaxed and in a happy mood. It seemed the right moment to get him to agree to a couple of things.

'Look, Dad, I'm going to be away for a while and I don't see the point of keeping on the flat in Pembridge Villas. Costs too much. Vera Atkins is sending you ten quid to cover the rent, but then it should be let go. I need the money to cover Tania being looked after by Vera Maidment. When I get back in a few weeks, I can look for something else. So, would you get rid of it for me and sell the furniture? There's still something to be paid on the fridge and furniture but after that's all settled, there should be some over to put in my account. The address is on my statements along with my account number.'

'What the bloody hell, Vi? What's going on?'

'Don't start now! I've been told that I was most remiss in not attending to these things by Miss Atkins, my commanding officer. She's just an old fusspot so it's her who's scaring the living daylights out of Mum. Now, will you help me or do I go to someone outside the family?'

'Now, now, all right. Just a damn shock, that's all. I've hardly sat down and you want me to sort out your tangle, is that it? Right, yes, I'll do all that. Anything more?'

'Thanks, Dad, you're a brick! That's about it. Mum will be executrix for Tania, and everything I possess is going to Tania, too. It's in the will Miss Atkins had me write. So, I think that's it. And thanks, Dad, I do appreciate that. Somehow, though, I think you'll enjoy disposing of the flat.'

Violette smiled fondly at her father and mother; they had concern written all over their faces.

'Now, if I don't appear for a while, don't go trying to find out where I am, will you? Vera Atkins has asked me to be sure to impress this upon you both. Even once the war's ended. I just might be helping out somewhere under some other name or something. Nothing dangerous but it might be undercover in some way. Okay?'

'Well, if you say so,' grumbled Charlie Bushell, most unhappy at what was unspoken. Bloody wars. All they did was damage everybody, he thought to himself. He was going to have to be careful with Reine; she'd worry no end. He'd try and cheer her up with a few car trips, she liked those.

For the last few days of her tenure in Pembridge Villas, Violette decided to invite her friends around for drinks and to listen to records, perhaps dance a little. Bob Maloubier was a regular visitor. The flat had been for her, Étienne and Tania, and she knew she would get over emotional if she stayed there alone.

So, her friends came to party. The flat was full to bursting, blackout curtains were pulled across securely, soft lighting cast a soft glow all around and music filled the room, cigarette smoke curled in spirals towards the ceiling. Bob came into the kitchen, where Violette was preparing more bowls of Smith's crisps, nuts and raisins to accompany the drinks. She had made a huge saucepan of mashed potatoes with cheese and onion to feed everyone a little later in the evening.

'Listen, Vi, put on "I'll be Around". It's a great song,' said Bob.

Violette started to hum as she went back into the living room. She found the record and put it on the turntable.

'Your favourite, isn't it, Bob?'

'Keep me in your mind, maybe,' Bob said a little wistfully.

'Yes, Bob, how many girls' minds do you want to be in?'

'Just yours!'

Violette laughed merrily, knowing Bob was charming company but fickle. 'Well, I wonder if you'll be around in June, should I need you, in those fields of wheat and cognac grapes?' whispered Violette into his ear.

That sobered up Bob very quickly, thinking of the dangerous task just days hence. Someone else said, 'How about "La Vie en Rose"? Sonia just told us that you've got it.'

'Okay. And my two choices are "Begin the Beguine" and "The Lambeth Walk",' Violette stated firmly, smiling happily.

It was an evening filled with warmth and laughter.

‡

Back in London, after spending a night with Tania in Mill Hill, Violette returned to her flat in Pembridge Villas. Most mornings she had donned her dark blue WTS uniform and made her way either to FANY headquarters in Chelsea or to SOE in Baker Street to see what instructions were waiting for her. Most were to keep her on form in clandestine activities and ensure she was not wasting time and herself in idle pursuits.

One task was that of tracking trainees without being spotted. She never was. Another was to meet up with a trainee agent at the offices, while in uniform, or a club in 'glad rags' and find out some detail they were instructed not to divulge. She might be briefed to persuade them to say where they were living, or to give away their real name. Each agent had a cover name[111] from the day they started training at SOE offices and Special Training Schools or mixing with SOE backroom and field personnel. Violette tried to discover any other detail about those she was testing or their family, or some new piece of military information. She was surprisingly adept at getting the trainee to reveal what he or she knew,[112] surprisingly having most success with the women. On the whole, it was an exercise she enjoyed.

She continued target practice in amusement arcades and at a gun club near Fleet Street. She felt this was absolutely essential; not more than two days would pass without her having shot with a rifle or pistol.

It felt like deep summer during the hot, mostly sunny days. Violette decided to again visit her relations in Herefordshire for a brief quiet and restful break. She took Tania with her on the train to see her aunt and cousins. It was wonderful to be back in the beautiful Hereford countryside.

‡

On Wednesday 24 May, Violette picked up her issue of one pair of boots, the first part of her kit, and her promotion. She was now Lieutenant Violette Szabó. Her field pay had been increased from £300 to £325 per annum, paid quarterly to the Trafalgar Square branch of the National Provincial Bank. She was so excited

---

111 Each agent is supplied with many codenames, plus their cover name while training in the British Isles. As there is an overabundance, for easy reading I have used them as sparingly as I possibly can.

112 When a trainee agent was failed at any stage of training, he or she was sent to work in a remote, secure location and supervised closely for the duration of the war and not informed of his/her potential security risk.

when she told her parents that afternoon that she was babbling half in French, half in English.

'Well, I'm proud of you, my girl, damn proud of you. You've done bloody well. I'm too old to go to battle but I'm doing my damndest as an ARW.[113] John's doing a good job in the REME[114] and Roy's in the army. George is risking his life on the high seas in the navy and now you, chit of a girl, climbing the bloody ranks. Well, I bleedin' never!'

Reine looked on with pride and sorrow in her eyes. Her quiet but stubborn courage had been the backbone of the family since 1918, and now she must show greater stoicism in the face of imminent threat of serious injury or violent death to her three boys and daughter, as well as worry about her parents and sister in France. She was not immune either to the fear of being bombed, of Charlie and young Dickie being caught in bombing raids.

Violette tried to take her mother's mind of these things by taking her window-shopping, walking through shining department stores. Her mother had done so much for her family. A little bit of pay-back time was due to her. It worked – for the time being.

‡

Next day, Violette returned to the issuing office to collect her battledress top and trousers with two shirts, one with collar attached, and two extras, a pair of socks, two ties and one pair of gloves. After some discussion, a pair of shoes was handed over. She signed for them, was issued a receipt and took them back to the flat.

A few days later, in the afternoon while John was still on leave, Violette was sitting at home, wondering whether she had made the right decision to meet Eric for a night on the town in Soho. She did not know him very well and had not spoken to any of her SOE chums about him. She knew he was an agent for the Norwegian Section of SOE but not much more. So she decided to persuade John, to join them. He was decidedly reluctant,

'Oh come on, John. I'll take you to the fanciest joint in Soho and we'll paint the town all the colours of the rainbow. I'm meeting a friend in the forces, a Norwegian, Eric,' pressed Violette. 'You'll like him. He's a friendly guy, plenty of spirit and funny.'

'Yeah, well, I'm off on a pub crawl. Not sure I want my sis cramping my style.'

John was in the REME because since childhood he had been intrigued by machines. The fascination stayed with him his entire life – especially in electronics and space. He read science fiction with a passion – all of which, to a small degree, he passed on to me. John took advantage of the excellent training, earning the

---

113 ARW = Air Raid Warden.
114 REME = Royal Electrical and Mechanical Engineers.

practical and professional qualifications that set him up for life in Australia and then the US. It led him into the danger of war on which he thrived and survived, like his father, physically unscathed.

'Well, I can drink you under the table any time, brother John. But I prefer to dance. Anyway, he'll be company for you! It'll be fun. We can dance and a drink, perhaps a bite to eat. What d' you say?'

'Aw, okay. I guess so. Don't see you that often. What've you really been up to, ay sis?'

'Nothing much, really ...'

'Don't answer; keep mum as the posters say! I can bloody well guess – you be damned careful.'

'Always careful, Johnny boy. Don't drink too much, don't smoke too much, dance and play a lot, shoot and ride as often as possible. Eat well. That's a careful life, now isn't it?'

'Yep!'

'Let's say half past seven here. I'll pay the taxi to and from Soho and you two can cover the rest. Celebrating my promotion. Section leader to lieutenant. I'm now a commissioned officer in the army. So, watch your step.'

When Eric arrived, Violette had to look up high as she did with John. They were both over six feet in height while she was a mere five feet three inches tall.

She introduced them. Eric was not much older than Violette, which meant that they were all in their twenties and very ready to enjoy a great evening. Eric, like John, was the quiet type, but a good sense of humour bubbled under the surface. Intelligence gleamed from his crinkly eyes and he was good-looking. John had a wicked sense of humour and could not resist, 'I better go and put a dress and bonnet on if I've got to chaperone you two!'

'John, you're just the bloody limit! You're on leave; I was feeling sorry for you and didn't want you to be lonely, sitting here at home, all by yourself – so there!' She retorted angrily, knowing he was not far wrong.

'Humph!'

Eric fell about laughing at this brother-and-sister sparring.

Charlie came in, looked at the trio and grumbled, 'Who the bloody hell are you?'

'I'm Eric and I've come to take your daughter out for the evening.'

'Oh, have you just? Where the hell do you think you're going to, then, huh? Vi,' he said turning to her, 'if you're not careful, I'm warning you, you'll come to a bad end.'

'Dad, you are the biggest pain!' Violette swung around crossly. 'If you were a little bit civilised you'd welcome my friend. Eric, John, and I are going out. If you bloody go on like this, I'll be back at Pembridge Villas before you can say Jack Robinson. Don't forget, don't drink too much! It upsets Mum!'

Charlie swung round and stormed out of the room.

A couple of minutes later, Reine came in and said, 'What on earth 'as got into Charlie now? Did you say something to 'eem, Violette?' Her French accent rose with her concern.

'Yes, I told him to bugger off and not to drink too much,' retorted Violette, still smarting from her father's attitude and words.

Eric stood smiling broadly alongside John, who had whispered something in his ear about their father and his unwarranted and unwanted protectiveness of his only daughter.

'Now, you go out and enjoy yourself, Violette. You mustn't always fly off zer 'andle with your father. He's only trying to protect you, dear.'

As they reached the door, Violette turned round and grinned at her mother. 'We won't be back until the wee hours, but I'll take care of these two brutes and bring them back safely. Bye.' They all laughed, said goodbye and the three young people tumbled down the stairs to the waiting taxi driven by Sidney Matthews, their family friend.

John understood Eric was a naval man who had joined the Norwegian freighter M/S *Vestmanrød*. This ship was to be the first to deliver supplies to the Normandy beaches on D-Day. John was intrigued by Eric, as he knew next to nothing about Norway and Norwegians. He asked many questions for which Eric did his best to supply the answers. He told them that the Norwegians were politically united under their new monarchy, unlike many other European countries. And in spite of Vidkum Quisling's activities and his traitorous broadcasts, a high degree of patriotism was prevalent.

Eric described how King Haakon VII had escaped with the Royal Family and the government in 1940, bringing with them the gold reserves of the Bank of Norway. Violette said this must have been at the time when Étienne was fighting in Norway. The British, along with the Free French and many in the Norwegian navy, army and civilian population withdrew from Norway as their positions became untenable.

‡

For the rest of that night, war was a distant ghoul; Eric, John and Violette had a great time wandering the streets of Soho and into Great Windmill Street, where the Windmill Theatre played on, closing not once during the entire war. The three young people moved through a throng of musicians carrying their trombones, violins and other instruments, congregating in the street hoping to be picked by one of the major bandleaders. Finally, they entered a nightclub where they stayed until the early hours, the boys drinking heavily, all three singing, laughing and dancing to a three-part jazz-band and singer. John and Eric were the worse for wear, unsteady on their feet, singing foolish songs and, in a boozy haze, wondering how to get home.

'Couple of twits. I'm going to flag down a cab,' said Violette. She pushed their hulks into it and arranged them onto the seat where they fell into one another's arms, guffawing and giggling all the while. When they arrived in Burnley Road, Violette paid the driver, clambered out and reached in to yank them out and then put an arm from each man over her shoulder, struggling up the steps, tiny between them. She was the only one sober having drunk very little. She hardly ever drank very much – a crème de menthe, a shandy, a Guinness and possibly a gin and tonic or half a pint. It was her nature to be in control of herself, even while she was having fun, dancing and generally enjoying life.

Reine came to open the door and smiled broadly, putting her fingers to her lips to keep them quiet, 'My goodness, Violette, what a state they're in. Let me help you.'

After having hauled them up the steps, Violette let her mother take one of the boys into the sitting room while she pushed the other inside and into a chair in the corner.

'I see zat you are all right, Violette. Didn't you enjoy yourself?' asked her mother.

'Oh yes, immensely, but somebody had to stay sober or we'd never have got back!'

And they both giggled over it, being mindful not to wake Charlie who had gone to bed early, grumbling about the lack of morals of the young today. He was snoring peacefully after Reine had tucked him in like a child, kissing his forehead and tucking the blanket more firmly around him.[115]

---

115 For his contemporary biography on Violette, Violette's mother wrote to R.J. Minney: 'Violette did not like drink and she smoked very little. One night she took her brother John, who was home on leave from REME, and a young Norwegian named Eric, who was a secret agent, to a nightclub in Soho. Both boys were over six foot tall, and you can just imagine Violette having to bring them home in the small hours of the morning with one boy on each side of her, holding on for support to this tiny girl. All Violette told me afterwards was: "Somebody had to stay sober or we'd never have got back."'

26

Hazells Hall, Fun and Delays

Friday 2 June to Monday 5 June 1944

'A lie gets halfway around the world before the truth has a chance to get its pants on.'
Sir Winston Churchill

'In wartime, truth is so precious that she should always be attended by a bodyguard of lies.'
Sir Winston Churchill

On the night of Friday 2 June, Violette sat with her mother and father. Again she implored them neither should attempt to find her, 'Things may get difficult out there. I could be on the run and the Germans may be looking for me. It may be impossible for me to get back as planned – or to write. But you really mustn't worry if you don't hear from me. I'll try to get messages to you, I really will. There's always a way.'

'Just you take damn good care of yourself. We know more or less what you're up to and won't do anything to jeopardise your work or your safety. Vi, please be careful,' admonished her father. 'I know we don't always get on but you know I love you, your mother loves you and so do the boys.' He was remembering with embarrassment how he had shouted at her when she returned from her second course at Ringway, near Manchester, yelling that all she was up to – apart from driving ungainly lorries – was clearly 'servicing' the military and she would end up in the gutter.

Violette, outraged, had grabbed her bag to storm out, but the contents had spilled over the sitting room floor. After shoving everything back in, she stalked up to her room, utterly furious with her stupid father, while he remained downstairs, fuming. A glitter under the settee attracted his attention so he bent to pick it up. It was her parachute badge, earned on completing her parachute course. Charlie had realised immediately what it meant; he went to her and apologised. They talked, 'Mum's the word, uh?' he had said. He never mentioned it to anyone except his wife.

Now here she was, and he in utter anguish, but he listened.

'There's one thing I must insist you do not do: never try to find out where I am.' Violette rushed on, not wanting to upset them but feeling she had to reiterate these things. 'Just wait until the end of the war. It's not going to be long now, anyway. If I get caught, I'll be doing my damnedest to get back, you know that. I've been trained in all that sort of thing. And you'll find me at the door, just like last time.'

Reine held back the tears, whispering, 'I'm so frightened for you. Please be so, so careful.'

'Of course I will, Maman,' Violette said softly. 'I'm dead scared of being captured and beaten by those thugs, you know …'

'Oh darling …' cried Reine. Charlie went white at the idea.

'People do get through it. I suppose I would too. I've been well trained. And anyway, it's rather unlikely to happen. I'll kick them all up the bloody arse and run like blooming hell!' She frowned hard in mock-anger.

Charlie laughed and Reine couldn't help but smile – a tiny smile. Violette knew she should not have spoken of her fears, but they were her parents and she felt … well, somehow that there was a kind of message she had to leave … but she'd done it all wrong, she knew. Although her father was loquacious, she had never known him to divulge a confidence, so she knew she could trust him. Her mother likewise; Reine was naturally discreet and hardly accepted the concept of 'gossip', never mind taking part or talking out of turn.

They talked on a while. Charlie told them some anecdotes about buying and selling old bangers. The wireless was playing songs sung with poignant sweetness by the young and lovely Vera Lynn. They laughed, relaxed and eventually Reine stood up, pressed her face against her daughter's and told them it was getting late and they should retire to bed. The next day, Saturday 3 June, Reine took Tania back to Mill Hill, accompanied by Dickie, who years later remembered his mother's anxiety and reluctance to leave her granddaughter in Mill Hill. But before that, Reine and Tania had seen Violette off at Stockwell tube station early in the morning.

They had walked to the tube, and Tania's grandmother picked her up just outside the station, and held her in the crux of her left arm. Tania noticed that Violette had a beret or funny pointy hat on. Violette was laughing. After a quick kiss on each cheek and a smiling farewell to her mother and Tania, Violette, in her neat dark-blue uniform, looking so smart and slim, went down the stairs into the station. They watched her go into the dark tunnel. As she descended, she turned one last time with a smile on her face and waved lightly to her mother and Tania. It was the last time. They were never to see Violette again.

‡

Violette made her way to SOE headquarters, where a car was waiting to take her to one of SOE's comfortable serviced flats for the night while they sorted out her final plans.

Once there, Violette went over to the wardrobe and carefully checked every article of French clothing hanging there. In the chest of drawers, she found French underwear, including two pairs of silk stockings from Germany, wondering how SOE had acquired them and feeling chuffed that she was the recipient of these, for which an agent had risked his or her life. Another agent had brought back a very attractive bra, pant and suspender set in handmade Belgian black lace and another set in cream from Belgium. Then she checked the shoes. On the dressing table, she found a small bottle of *Soir de Paris*.

The following morning, Sunday 4 June, the Humber rolled up and Vera knocked at her door.

'Come in,' shouted Violette, 'The door's not locked. Is that Miss Atkins?'

'Yes, are you ready? The car's waiting. Have you got any last messages for your mother or for Tania?'

'Yes, loads and none! Can't really think of anything specific except I love them both and miss them.' Her mother and Tania were now locked safely away in her heart while she concentrated on the tasks ahead. Violette was sure they both knew they were in her mind – at all times and forever. She did not need sentimental messages and nor did they, she felt sure. They had said everything they needed to say and made their farewells.

Violette and Vera sank into the plump beige leather seats of the limousine while the driver drove them to the Georgian mansion house, Hazells Hall in Sandy, Bedfordshire, which was being used as sleeping quarters and clubhouse for agents and fliers leaving for France on undercover missions. Woods and fine grounds surrounded the house. It was a peaceful place to try to relax and keep things in perspective while waiting for the right weather conditions or pilots and aircraft to wing them away to danger.

The RAF had requisitioned this already-decaying but lovely house, so amenities were spare but adequate. There were, however, plenty of alcoholic beverages, much brought over from occupied countries, and reasonably good food. There was just enough hot water for showering or shallow baths. The bedrooms were clean and basically comfortable. Unfortunately, perhaps, the wooden floors, creaking and groaning, kept naughty activities to a minimum.

‡

The final preparations for D-Day were heating up as Violette readied herself for her mission. June 5th was chosen for D-Day but the invasion had to be delayed for twenty-four hours due to bad weather. The mighty armada was to be dispatched

the night of 5 to 6 June starting at 00.16 hours with the gliders to land along the
Normandy coast. On this momentous Tuesday 6 June, in very poor weather, both
strategic and tactical surprise was achieved, as the Germans had not expected the
Allied invasion force to cross the Channel in such appallingly bad weather conditions nor along the western Normandy coast. While the forces were readying to
strike on the beaches, the small team of four agents was about to fly out on an RAF
Halifax and jump out over the high fields of the Limousin on 3/4 June.

‡

The westerly winds were the strongest they'd been since 1917. Although it was
dull, no rain fell. Violette, Philippe, Jean-Claude and Bob finally met up at RAF
Tempsford. Violette was looking forward to parachuting once again. Although
tense at the thought of the danger, she found it relatively easy to push it all to
the back of her mind. Here she was again, about to jump out into the sky after
a noisy but exciting flight in an English bomber. More exciting than the movies
she wanted to be in: this was stark but endlessly seductive reality – no props; the
real thing.

'Let's go and have dinner over at the hall,' announced Vera Atkins in her clear
ringing tones. As they arrived at the entrance, she came up alongside Violette and
said quietly: 'You're the only girl going across.'

'Oh? Lucky, aren't I, to be surrounded by such a fine group of men?'

'Judging from their expressions, I think it's they who are lucky.' There were
many men in the dining hall of the mansion, with what seemed like a colony
of Jedburghs from the Special Arm Service. A group of men turned to look at
Violette. Surprise, admiration and disapproval flitted in quick succession across
various faces. It was still a time when many felt 'a chit of a girl' was in need of
protection, not going out under the nose of the enemy.

'These boys are embarking on perilous operations so there's a great deal of tension,' commented Vera quietly to Violette as they relaxed after dinner. 'But you are
perfectly calm and composed. I'm astonished.'

'Not really, Vera. I'm looking forward to it.' As Violette said this, she suddenly
understood: these fellows knew they were going into battle, whereas she was not.
Yes, what she was doing was just as dangerous – the idea of being caught, questioned and tortured, even killed, was still at the back of her mind, but she thought
it did not have the same immediacy that going directly into battle would.

Most of the Jedburghs had left in groups. At last, Violette, Philippe, Jean-Claude
and Bob set off in separate cars to the airfield. They pulled down the blinds in the
cars as they left so ground staff could not see them. None of them was in uniform.
Philippe, Bob and Jean-Claude were in velvet corduroys and jackets while Violette
wore a French-cut leather jacket and slacks. As was the essential custom of strict
security, each had had their clothes, pockets and suitcase thoroughly inspected for

anything even slightly suspiciously English, but they were French from head to toe, inside and out, looked it, smelled it and sounded it.

The Halifax was standing ready with its crew of British fliers. 'Suits on please,' ordered Philippe. 'And don't forget to load those zipper pockets with your essential gear. Small arms, ammunition, compass, maps and rations!' Violette and her team struggled into their parachute suits while the pilots were completing their checks.

'Just double check, if you would, you haven't inadvertently placed anything not entirely French in with those things. No English cigarettes or matches. No photos. No keepsakes,' ordered Vera Atkins in a cold military voice. 'No room for sentiment. Could kill you.'

Jean-Claude took the admonition calmly, Violette with a grin followed by a sad moue at having no photo of her family, Bob frowning impatiently at Vera, and Philippe just got on with it. By their varying cool reactions, they each revealed something of themselves.

'Time to move,' came the command.

Vera shouted '*Merde*'[116] in time-honoured salute of farewell as they all climbed aboard while Vera moved off to her waiting driver and car to whisk her back to London.

The bomb racks at the back of the plane did not hold their usual complement of bombs but containers filled with arms and explosives. The four were sitting behind the racks, cramped, along with the rear gunner and dispatcher who would control their jumps. It was already loaded with the larger airborne-troop parachutes like the ones Philippe and Violette had used in April, rather than the standard service ones. As the Halifax taxied forward, the team tried to make themselves comfortable.

Ground crew removed the chocks. The aircraft's engines revved up. Imperceptibly, it began to move and slowly taxied towards the runway. The pilot looked out to check for unexpected obstacles. He saw a member of the ground crew waving his arms as he ran across the apron.

'Message just came in. Stormy weather ahead has already closed in. Orders to return to base.'

'Bloody fucking arseholes!' roared the pilot.

'What the bleedin' hell!' said one of the crew at the back.

'Nothing we can do about it. Bad weather, better drinks, hey mates?'

It was impossible to fly. Winds were gusting up to sixty-six miles an hour. Worse, over Dorset, Dartmoor and Somerset, there were thunderstorms and torrential rain more than 200 times the average for the time of year.

It had been decided higher up that they would instead go the next night, the night of 5/6 June. They piled out of the plane, the feeling of anti-climax and

---

116 *Merde* = shit, but it is a much less offensive sound than in English, and Vera used it in the way of Theatreland 'break a leg' knowing, and they all knew, they were going into a nasty place.

disappointment making them edgy and bad-tempered. A return to Hazells Hall was the only ride they would get that night.

Vera, who was informed by the guard at the gates that the flight had been postponed, sympathised, saying that she had arranged accommodation for them back at the Hall.

They traipsed into the Common Room. Violette was unperturbed. A damned nuisance, but no use going on about it, she thought. Enjoy the company, food and perhaps an outing somewhere tomorrow. She suggested they go for a drive the next day as Jean-Claude had probably not seen much in that area. She wondered if they could drive to Cambridge as it was such a lovely old city to which Philippe agreed.

Vera bade them all farewell again, but this time with an ordinary 'goodnight', and said she would be with them tomorrow to go through the procedures all over again. She returned in the black Humber to London.

‡

On the next morning, Monday, 5 June, in the pouring rain, with gusts sending swirls of water into faces and trickling down collars, the Famous Four borrowed a car and drove the twenty miles into Cambridge for a day out. They were going to enjoy themselves and forget all about the flight planned for that night.

'It's a pity they're not holding the college balls because of the war,' said Violette. 'They put on these marvellous balls in the gardens of the colleges and punt down the Cam – for that alone, I would have chosen Cambridge above all other universities.'

'No punting and no dancing on the grass. That's war for you. I'm cold, so let's get to a local pub and have a decent lunch for Chrissake,' growled Bob, sounding just like the thunder overhead and still just as gloomy as the sky.

'No, let's all go on the river, as it's almost stopped raining,' said Violette. 'First, we are to go boating!'

'Punting's been stopped. Don't you ever listen?' grumped Bob.

'Bet we can.' And they did, Violette laughing as she showed she could punt just as expertly as any of the men.

After the first half-hour of frantic punting to outdo each other, they gave themselves up to the peace of the river. It was utterly relaxing. Now that the rain had completely stopped they could have done nothing better. They took it in turns to punt while the others leant back comfortably in the flat-bottomed boats, watching the banks drift by. The fragrance of wildflowers caught the wind as the current moved them along.

Later, Jean-Claude pointed out a very traditional-looking pub and said: 'That's where we should go. Real English ale and – what do you call it – "hangers and bash"?' He smiled in anticipation while the other three burst into laughter.

'No, Jean-Claude, bangers and mash – not hangers and bash – although you could hang an overcoat on some, and bash them with a hammer, they're so large and tough.'

They went in and were hit by the warmth coming from an open fire. Sheer bliss. The food, as Jean-Claude had endeavoured to inform them, was indeed bangers and mash, and the men drank pints of decent ale – Jean-Claude the French-American agent was polite about the fact that it was lukewarm. Violette ordered just one half-pint to keep them company. They sang and chatted about everything except war. They asked for a pot of coffee while they all smoked.

As they came out into the grey mid-afternoon they continued to sing as they strolled down the ancient streets.

‡

27

Flight to Sussac

Monday 5 June to Thursday 8 June 1944 (D-Day was Tuesday 6 June)

Violette and the team returned from Cambridge refreshed and in good spirits. When night fell, they had a light snack at the Hall, made final checks on luggage and plans, then back to Tempsford airfield – sure, this time, their flight was on. The weather had eased somewhat and a second RAF Halifax waited. *Salesman II* was authorised to prepare again.

The usual checks on all issued equipment done and farewells given, the aircraft took off with a roar, curving steeply onto its given course.

'Seems a pretty smooth ride,' commented Jean-Claude over the din to whomever might be listening.

A general round of nods while the dispatcher handed Bob a pack of cards, 'How about a game of blackjack to pass the time?'

'Jolly good idea.' Violette cleared an area, moving aside a couple of items.

'Didn't Vera Atkins supply us with hot chocolate?' asked Philippe.

'No, crew's canteen, and there's plenty,' commented the dispatcher. 'Help yourselves, mates. It's damn good stuff. Made with real milk, plenty of sugar, plenty of cocoa. Won't get another chance like it.' The rest of the crew bent down to the task of winning at blackjack.

Three hours passed uneventfully. They chatted quite happily and heard some funny stories from the crew and each of the team.

The morale of the team, Jean-Claude later told me, was high. There was very little tension, except, as he said, *Staunton* (Jean-Claude only knew Philippe as *Staunton* at the time, so continued to call him thus) seemed nervous. Philippe was considered a veteran and Jean-Claude, very young, was unaware that Philippe was only making his second jump. He felt reassured that his team leader showed a certain trepidation; it seems his other missions had been landings by Lysander.

Three hours later, the navigator picked out the landmarks and confirmed they were above the drop zone. The reception committee was absent. Neither pilot nor co-pilot saw signalling lights. They circled the area ground repeatedly, but no lights signalled to them.

'Sorry, folks, no landing lights, no sign of life. We're returning to base now,' came the pilot's voice over the intercom.

'How could they 'ave fucked up,' growled Bob. 'Buckmaster got all the messages transmitted to the reception committee, everything was set. What the hell happened to them?'

'Any manner of things, Bob, so just calm down, will you?' said an exasperated Philippe. 'I'll go find out what the bloody pilot thinks he's doing. Maybe shed some light on the business.'

Philippe argued heatedly with the pilot, who concluded, '*Major Staunton*, no way am I dropping your team and containers over a landing zone that could've been compromised. I'm sorry; we're turning back!' The pilot felt he had no option. He would not drop his passengers and cargo into a death trap. They turned back.

A noisy three-hour return flight in the back of an uncomfortable and windowless aircraft was excruciatingly boring and another huge anti-climax. Philippe and Jean-Claude tried dozing the time away. Philippe found no relief whatsoever in not having to jump. His only thought was that his mission was compromised perhaps beyond recovery by these delays. It certainly would be if this continued. Twice foiled in their attempt to reach mid-France.

At the same time, one of the pilots drew the other's attention to the fantastic sight of the invasion below them. The Channel was covered in boats – all kinds – all sizes – warships – tugs – huge lumps, could be containers – landing craft. Damn well everything the Allies had must be on that strip of water. They joked that Jerry must be sleeping! They were not.

The card players in the back of the Halifax knew nothing of this. Not the pilot, nor co-pilot, nor any member of the crew who witnessed the amazing scene told the team what was happening below in the choppy waters of the Channel. The portholes were all blacked out with reinforced material.

Six tiring and utterly depressing hours after they had left, they landed back at Tempsford, fagged out, hungry and thirsty. Even the crew had long faces.

It was nearly dawn. The team felt grey as they got in the cars and returned yet again to the clubhouse. They had a drink, ate a sandwich or two then climbed the stairs to the same rooms, undressed and got wearily into bed.

‡

Short hours later, the door to the room the men were sharing shook to purposeful knocks. The batman entered.

'Time to rise and shine, sirs! It's now five o'clock.' He said firmly, used to the general cursing always directed at him whenever this duty befell him.

'What the bloody hell!' Philippe jumped out of bed.

'Sir,' repeated the batman, 'It's your wake-up call. Five o'clock as directed. To make sure you get up immediately, sir.'

'What the hell do you mean, "as directed"?' was Bob's furious bark.

'Well, sir, you did leave a notice on the door, saying you wished to be woken without fail at five this morning.'

Chaos reigned. 'The devil we did?' was Jean-Claude's surprised comment. He had not heard anything about early morning calls.

'What's the big idea? We're not wanted till tonight. You know that.'

'Well, gentlemen, the note I found on the door just after you retired states: "Urgent. Please call us at 5 a.m. sharp, without fail – and see we are up."'

They looked at one another angrily. Understanding spread over each face. 'That bloody woman!' muttered Bob.

'Let's pull her from her slumber! See how she bloody likes it,' stated Philippe as he marched past the nonplussed batman and strode down the hall, yanking open the door and pulling Violette roughly from her bed, sheet and blanket tangling around her as she fell.

She had already woken up at the rumpus and angry shouts, and giggled like a child as Philippe dragged her from bed, then pummelled her with pillows. She was helpless with laughter on seeing their outraged faces, hearing their volley of oaths and curses. It was hugely successful. The batman had followed the men and now stood just outside the door with a grin spreading across his face. He'd had to get up early to ensure he obeyed the order but he didn't mind one jot. Most amusing. Something to tell the other batmen. Not often a wee lassie got the better of male officers! The men stormed back to their room, slamming the door behind them ordering the batman not to let *anyone* near them until ten o'clock in the morning.

Violette, still keyed up, got dressed and went downstairs to stoke up on strong, hot coffee, scrambled eggs and a slice of bacon. Vera arrived just before nine to commiserate over the failed drop and to announce over the coffee that the invasion had taken place, saying she must return to London immediately and would send her assistant, Nancy Frazer Campbell, to see them off tonight if she couldn't make it back. She asked Violette to tell the team about the invasion and that the reception committee had sent a message during the small hours as they were flying back. There had been German patrols on the prowl so no landing or danger signals could be given. Violette turned on the news then flew upstairs into the men's bedroom, shouting, 'The invasion. We've landed. Come on. Get up! We've landed.'

'Get back to your blasted bed,' from Bob with an accompanying pillow thrown at her head and just missing as she dodged it.

'No, it's not a joke! Honest! It's true. Miss Atkins has just told me before she drove back to London. Put the wireless on! We've invaded. They must've been sailing across as we flew back. We didn't see a damned thing.'

What made them immeasurably angry was that on their aborted flight the pilot had not told them of the astounding sight of the Allied armada crossing the water in the moonlight's gleam with fighter pilots overhead, protecting their progress. They had missed seeing for themselves the picture that was now spread across the morning newspapers. Violette, Bob, Jean-Claude and Philippe were deeply, deeply disappointed and absolutely furious with the pilot and co-pilot; the navigator, too.

'Miss Atkins has also briefed me on our departure. She didn't want to wake you again so she asked me to pass it on to you. We go tonight. Last night, Germans were prowling so the committee thought it too dangerous to light up. They got a message through while we were flying back. Same arrangement tonight. Won't be the Halifax as it's on other duties. Probably a US Liberator with a US crew.'

'Well, go back to blasted bed for an hour or so, Vi, and give us a bit of a break.' said Philippe wearily. 'We'll all meet downstairs at around eleven.'

'Okay. To make up for this morning, I'll take you all rowing on the Cam and a late lunch afterwards. Same pub, if you like. My treat.'

'I should bloody well think so,' grumbled Bob. 'You owe us.'

She laughed and left them in peace.

Later, they went for a long, lazy row on the Cam. Violette looked gorgeous in the yellow golfing jumper from Paris, grey slacks and short tousled dark hair. The water was icy but the day hot and sunny. They lay on the grass and chatted a while as they caught the sun. A little later, they lunched in the pub, returning to the clubhouse relaxed and looking forward to the night flight.

‡

Vera was disappointed to have to send her assistant in her place to see the team off, but she needed to attend to urgent matters in London. She regretted forever having missed her '*Merde!*' to Violette; she liked to see off all 'her girls' – it was her personal ritual, appreciated by the agents.

Her assistant, the neatly uniformed Captain Nancy Frazer Campbell, was moved by Violette as she saw them off. Violette seemed so tiny next to the men. Nancy shouted to them the customary '*Merde!*' by way of farewell, deafened by their shouts back of '*Merde!*'

This time they were not flying from RAF Tempsford. Instead, after a light dinner accompanied by a little wine, they travelled to RAF Harrington, used by the US Air Force. They drove the forty-five miles in two black Humbers with hooded lights; a long hour's journey winding through narrow country roads in the deep black of night. Not a light glimmered from farm or village.

‡

The Liberator[117] stood ready for take off at 22.26 hours on the night of 7 June and everyone climbed aboard. The B-24 crossed the English coast at Bolt Head in Devon at 23.30 hours, at a height of 6,000 feet, reaching Port Blanc on the Brittany

---

117 The Liberator was B-24-D 42-40538 K.

coast at 23.59 hours. Maintaining its height, it continued to fly south-east between Paimpol and Guingamp, keeping to the west of St Brieuc and away from enemy guns. So far so good.

Again the team and crew members in the aircraft's depths saw nothing but the backs of the heads of the pilot and co-pilot. The Liberator was huge, easily transporting the agents and containers to be dropped. Its interior was stripped down: wooden sealing and protective plates were placed under the portholes and cargo door. The din excluded all conversation except that shouted in the ear of the listener. It was supremely uncomfortable but no one seemed to mind.

The target for the American Liberator mission carrying Violette and her team was the coded location of Stationer 110B. Manned by the eight-man crew of Pilot Marvin Fenster of Squadron 36 No 538; their load was four 'joes' (people), twelve containers, ten packages and five Ns ('Nickels'[118]). There were no PHs (pigeon hampers). They completed their operation successfully.

Gunner Darwin Grey kept his eyes peeled for the enemy; any time they could be hit by anti-aircraft fire. Enemy airfields and military complexes armed with gunners and flares littered the port areas and all France. A time for nerves to become ragged or be kept under crisp control. This team of three men and one woman controlled their nerves by playing cards, gin rummy and blackjack.

Twenty-one minutes later, after crossing the French coast, at 00.20 hours, they flew over Ploërmel, where an enemy green and yellow flare-dropping plane descended from above, lighting up the entire region in an eerie glow. They were flying at 5,000 feet at the time, but not a single gun boomed. No flak rose to pierce the fuselage. Clearly, the enemy on the ground was fully diverted by the invasion east along the Normandy beaches where Americans were taking Cherbourg and the Brits, Caen.

No enemy activity was directed at the Liberator and the weather remained 'good' en route with visibility at ten to fifteen miles. Pilot Marvin Fenster, co-pilot Richard Warn and navigator Rick Davis identified the ridge leading to the target plus a forest slightly north-west, and Davis verified the precise drop zone.

The bombardier, Avery Yancy, in place of the original bomb pit, had a hole through which joes dropped. The retractable turret with its guns had been removed to provide a circular 'joe hole' for parachutists and containers, covered with a slab of wood until they were over the drop zone. Their dispatcher, J.W. Hall, radio operator John Ringlesbach and engineer Richard W. Thomas kept busy. Seats were placed around the hole for the agents and dispatcher. The usual line and lights were installed.

‡

---

118 RAF code for propaganda leaflets to be dropped – originally in nickel canisters.

Fenster announced their approach to the drop zone. The team prepared to jump but heard the pilot over the loudspeaker report he saw no coded lights. He would circle three times. If no lights appeared, they would return to England. Violette's heart sank. To have come so far. Again. To be over the target. Again. To be forced to turn round and make the long tedious journey back. Again. All because the reception committee was not there, or warned of enemy presence, or arrested, perhaps even dead. It was not an option – not this time. Philippe was incandescent.

‡

Fifteen minutes later, they approached the drop zone for the third time. Fenster noted the coding of the signal letter at target was there, but poor, and he considered going to the alternate target. Philippe, as commanding officer of the group, had already instructed the pilot to ready the aircraft to drop them whether or not coded lights showed.

'Captain, it is essential we arrive this night as we have already been delayed by bad weather for two days. The Allied invasion has already taken place. We're late and a huge task awaits us and time is running out fast.'

Taking Philippe's previous comments to heart, Fenster decided that 'poor' signalling was a damned sight better than 'non-existent' and continued the mission to drop over the *Stationer* zone. Successfully.

'I understand. On your head then.'

'Right. D-Day's done. We *were* supposed to be on the job two days ago.'

'No problem. Get ready to jump,' ordered Fenster.

'Be glad to be anywhere else except near that damned hole!' grumbled Philippe as he wiped his sweaty hands down his overalls. 'It's a damned long way down with a wind blowing.'

The C system of lights has three torches, usually red, in a row with a white flashing signal light set up at the downwind end of the row, to indicate to the plane the approach needed in order to land upwind. But they were not all alight as the aircraft approached. The reception committee, needing to ensure that they signalled to the expected plane, waited for sight of the aircraft before setting the white signal flashing.

Over the target the weather was fair, no longer good, visibility was down, but that did not affect the drop of joes and containers. The reception according to Fenster's report was 'good'.

Flight Lieutenant Fenster pulled the heavy craft up and round. It rose and curved through the dark sky like some prehistoric bird. Scarred by shrapnel and too many near-misses in other ops, the Liberator circled smoothly, responding to the lightest touch of the controls by its pilots.

'Course 300°,' Fenster shouted to his co-pilot. It was now 01.34 hours in the morning of 8 June.

'650 feet,' responded the co-pilot.

Philippe and Bob jumped first at 01.49 hours. Next, bombardier Yancy and dispatcher Hall dropped twelve containers that landed just twenty metres to the left of the light.

The Liberator swooped off to make its second run.

The co-pilot confirmed to Fenster: '600 feet.'

Three minutes after Philippe and Bob had jumped, Violette and Jean-Claude jumped. It was now 01.52 hours on 8 June. Yancy and Hall pushed out the ten personal packages, which landed to the right of the light. These packages included their suitcases, along with Sten guns, pistols and GM machine guns plus ammunition, a great deal of money, maps, plans and other equipment required for this urgent mission.

Pulling up again, Fenster brought the plane in for the third and last run at 450 feet at 01.58 hours and his crew dropped the ten remaining containers.

Just six minutes later, the five nickels were dropped on the plane's return path, as it flew over the towns of Excideuil, Ambernac, Alloué and two villages. It crossed back over the enemy French coast at 03.40 hours at a lower height of 5,000 feet arriving back at RAF Harrington at 04.10 hours.

‡

As Violette parachuted down, a sudden gust very slightly affected her landing so that she came down a little harder than expected from the fairly low jump. She fell onto her right side as her left foot, already having suffered torn ligaments, fell into a slight pothole. She picked herself up quickly enough and, although a little sore, she ignored it. She did not limp – it did not hurt sufficiently, although Philippe saw her rub it as he ran over to her.

'*Ça va, petite?*' Philippe whispered loudly, hoping she had not hurt herself thus jeopardising the mission.

'*Oui, oui, pas grave!*' was Violette's muffled reply as she extricated herself from her harness and pulled the parachute towards her, ready to discard it safely. She stood up, winced briefly to herself and walked off without the least limp. She knew how an injury could cause a mission to fail or be ineffective. Given twenty-four hours, it would be as right as rain.

'*Allons-y!*' shouted the leader in a loud whisper to his reception committee and his four 'guests'. His group had to collect and take into the trees all the containers and packages, ready to be loaded onto bikes.

'*Vite!*' cried one of the reception committee. 'Before *les Boches* find out just where the plane was circling.'

'We gotta get rid of all the containers.'

The men and women rushed to get the containers off the landing field and into the truck hidden in a large, dark thicket.

Violette was introduced as *Louise Leroy*, Philippe as *Major Staunton*. Jean–Claude was kept in the background with his wireless set. The less people saw of him, the better. Bob, so tall and a little bombastic, stood out and so Philippe made the most of it by pushing him forward, introducing him as instructor and leader of sabotage ventures.

They were driven to the tiny village of Sussac, just north-east of their landing zone. Madame Anna Ribiéras hated the Germans who made her husband a prisoner of war, so from 1942 to the liberation of the Limousin in August 1944 she had offered a safe-house to agents from England. She was trusted and took very good care of her 'guests'.

‡

Part VI

28

Arrival in Sussac

Thursday 8 June 1944

Sunlight was filling the tiny attic room when Violette woke up. She had wearily climbed into bed just after five o'clock in the morning. Reflecting on her arrival here in this tiny village, Violette wondered about the unnamed Maquis member who had led the reception committee last night. He was married to an Englishwoman; that seemed a darned good reason for him to liaise with the British agents on the evening of the Normandy landings. This man had arranged for Madame Anna Ribiéras, who lived with her young son, Jean-Pierre – nicknamed Pierrot – to prepare bedrooms for the new arrivals: *Louise*, *Major Staunton* (*Hamlet*), *Captain Mortier* (*Clothaire*) and the *Virgile* (or *Brave*). It had also been he who had arranged with the Maquis that the parachute drop of the four agents and the containers should take place over the large piece of farmland called Le Clos, just a few miles from Sussac.

It had been around three o'clock in the morning when he and his reception committee accompanied the team to the safe-house Madame Ribiéras provided. Violette was unsure of his real role; perhaps it had been he who had helped Harry Peulevé on his first jump when he broke his leg. The moon had given the only light as they arrived in the village. They had been driven along the village square and stopped around the corner at a shoulder-high wooden gate. A low gleam came from the Ribiéras' store at the back of the building. Once inside, they walked across to the opening into the kitchen where a few greetings were quickly exchanged as Madame Ribiéras, accompanied by her close friend and constant companion, Mademoiselle Géry, ushered the four new arrivals quickly through into the living room.

Anna Ribiéras' hatred of the Germans matched her fear for her POW husband Jean. She was fiercely independent and wanted her and her people's full liberty restored, so she entered into clandestine activity and acted as a safe-house. Violette could see she was plucky and indomitable. She fed everybody well and fussed over them as if they were children.

Madame Ribiéras said that the reception team leader had arranged for the people from London to liaise with the Maquis groups in the area. She went on to explain the layout of the house and that the English could take their things to their rooms.

Turning to Violette, she clarified that *Louise* would have a room to herself and the three men could share the other one at the back and after they had settled in, to come down and meet everyone. Violette and Philippe simultaneously thanked Anna very much.

Violette though that Madame Ribiéras was quite surprised that her team spoke French with varying regional accents just as well as those in Anna's village. Once she decided they were *sympathique* and spoke French like the French, she could not have been kinder. She called Violette *la p'tite Anglaise*.

Philippe was keyed up and ready to start planning. So, shortly after three o'clock on the morning of 8 June, the team from RAF Tempsford set to work with the neighbouring Maquis chiefs who had arrived to make contact. One was Charles Gaumondie (*Colonel Charles*) with his aides who, unknown to the team, acted as a front for Georges Guingouin who survived with his men because of his great caution, strong discipline and security measures, but still accomplished more than most other Maquis groups.

'I live in the village of Magnac-Bourg, strategically placed to do repeated damage to the rail link halfway between Brive-la-Gaillard and Limoges, about fifteen miles north of Salon-la-Tour,' explained Charles Gaumondie. The rail link was on the west side of the main highway, the Nationale 20.

'*En effet*, it's well situated between the *auto route* and the Limoges–Toulouse railway line. Madame Marguerite Lazerat runs her grocery shop there, right beside the Magnac-Vicq station.' He went on to insist that Philippe, whom he knew as *Major Staunton*, meet her. She resolutely acted as a 'letter-box', in spite of the great risks involved. Many people used her grocery shop to meet up, leave messages and prepare for sabotage activities with special emphasis on this railway. Georges Guingouin took shelter there whenever he was in the area. 'My group, *Bistrot*, acts as the reception committee for most of the arms dropped from London. The first drop was 18 August last year.' Gaumondie then went on to describe their sabotage to communication links and destruction, sometimes seizure, of German matériel, with attendant adventures and even comic events. There was much laughter, but Philippe wanted only to get down to business. His journalistic disposition kept his curiosity alive although, like all the team, he was tired. They needed some shut-eye before getting stuck into the real nitty-gritty.

He then bent over to Violette and spoke quietly in her ear, 'I want you to pedal over later in the day to Madame Lazerat in her grocery shop – take some explosives – and get an idea of what, if anything, can be done. See what she's made of. First, I'll sort out which instructions to pass to her.'

'Great,' said Violette. 'I'll get moving late morning, after a sleep and checking with you to see what else crops up.' She would endeavour to find out more about Madame Lazerat and, if it felt right, pass on the instructions from London that Philippe had given her. The woman certainly seemed ideally placed, reflected Violette. She was looking forward to the ride, discovering the layout of the area and meeting more people. She loved this job, she thought, even as fatigue crept over her. But she knew how to disguise her tiredness with smiles and the right questions. To yawn on the job was not an option.

They drank Pernod, chatting animatedly, and then partook of a glorious ome-lette *aux fines herbes*, salad with baguettes and charcuterie, while surreptitiously trying to judge each other's mettle. After the shortages of London, even though SOE agents fared better than most, it was still wonderful to eat food that was truly fresh. Every now and then laughter burst forth – a good sign of co-operation to come, perhaps, thought Philippe.

They made provisional plans and it was generally agreed that Violette would go the next day to the neighbouring groups on a circular trek east by bicycle or car to meet with leaders of smaller cells. Jean-Claude would be found a secluded but high safe house to keep in contact with London. Philippe wished to meet with Georges Guingouin. *Colonel Charles* said they would first meet his own group, the *Bistrot* Maquis and take it from there. Philippe explained that they would also broaden their zone of activity to include Montauban, Brive and Tulle in the south and certainly Limoges, possibly Châteauroux and La Châtre towards the north.

‡

Charles Gaumondie was a neat man in his mid-forties with a small pointed face, blond hair with thick darker brows and a long aquiline nose. He welcomed the SOE team with a warm smile. Seasoned Maquisards, with confirmed successes behind them, he, his brother-in-law, Albert Faye, and Paul Renaudie had been involved with the Maquis since 1941, when they had organised one of the first Résistance groups operating from Magnac-Bourg from September 1942, with Georges Guingouin keeping a close eye on them in the early years. A year earlier, using grenade sticks they had made in Léonard Lornac's forge, they had blown up the *botteleuse*, a wheat-packing factory in Croisille-sur-Briance.

Colonel Charles was the leader of the local Maquis. He was a saxophonist in a *bal-musette*[119] by trade, and a *soldat de deuxième classe* but with no war experience. He was in the FFI for the Limousin area and had a wider brief than was first apparent to Philippe.

Philippe was utterly put out by the man, and over the weeks to come became deeply suspicious of him. He reported angrily to Baker Street that *Colonel Charles*

---

119 *Bal-musette* – a local dance with small accordions – akin to a barn dance. '*Bal-musette* is a style of French popular music which arose in 1880s Paris especially the 5th, 11th and 12th districts, where Auvergnats had settled in large numbers in the nineteenth century, opening cafés and bars where patrons danced the *bourrée* (a French court two-step dance) to the accom-paniment of *musette* (an accordion) and *grelottière* (a leather strap with tiny bells strapped to the ankles of men and women, as with English Morris men and other groups over Europe.' (Musée archives, Mémorial de Caen).

was acting as a decoy for Georges Guingouin, who was head of the local FTP (the 'feared' communists). I wondered about the word 'decoy', but realised that, although Philippe's English was near perfect, he phrased some sentences in a French style and tended to use some unexpected words that did not quite fit. Probably, he just could not think of the English expression 'front man'.

It seems that, at this time, Charles Gaumondie did all of those things. In addition, he was the only area contact for Maurice Southgate (*Hector*), who had been captured as Violette and Philippe flew back to London on 1 May, as well as for *Anastasie* (Jacques Dufour) and *Samuel*.

Georges Guingouin seemed to have steered well clear of *Anastasie*, considering him too much of a loose cannon.

‡

Violette looked at her cheap French watch and saw that it was almost half past eight. She was surprised that she was fully awake and refreshed after so little sleep. The rest of the house was still quiet. She could hear the subdued chatter of people across the square and the bell of the shop below, tinkling each time someone entered. A horse and cart rumbled by, someone shouted as a bicycle bell rang out.

There was a quiet tap on her door. '*Entrez!*'

The door was pushed open and a small head peered in. It was Pierrot, Madame Ribiéras' son, about seven years old, maybe eight. '*Maman* asked me to bring you your breakfast, *mademoiselle*.'

'Oh, *merci*. Breakfast in bed!'

The youngster laughed softly and placed a tray on the bed and, with a shy smile, quietly crept back out. Violette heard the other bedroom door being opened and trays taken in to murmurs of sleepy men saying thank you.

Violette did finally get out of bed, washed, brushed her teeth, and dressed in a simple short-sleeved summer dress and wedged shoes. As she dressed, she suddenly remembered the date: 8 June. Her daughter's birthday. She hoped that Tania was with Reine and Charlie in Stockwell and that the same sun was shining down on them all. Violette sent a birthday wish on the gentle breeze wafting northward. And then she pushed such thoughts to the back of her mind. She had much to do and great distances to travel to do her bit to win the war.

At around nine o'clock she went downstairs into the kitchen. Anna Ribiéras was on her own and greeted her with a warm smile, pouring her another cup of coffee.

Anna and the reception committee were impressed by the uniforms as all the agents who had been through SOE training schools and dropped that midyear into France were given British military ranks and therefore uniforms, including the French nationals. This was done to help protect them should the enemy take them. Holding military rank should have ensured they would become prisoners of war and not tortured or shot out of hand.

Looking around, Violette asked where the men where. Madame Ribiéras told her they were still enjoying breakfast in bed and thought they would soon be down.

‡

The weather had given an inauspicious start to the Normandy landings but the British, American, French and Canadian contingents had still successfully established a strong foothold on the beaches and were now advancing on Cherbourg and Caen. Rommel was rushing back to France to take control of his ground forces, having ordered troops to converge on Normandy from wherever they were stationed.

SOE had been preparing for D-Day and its aftermath since early 1943. The SOE sections had also joined forces with SIS (British Secret Intelligence Service), the fledgling SAS (British Special Air Service) and the American OSS (American Office of Strategic Services); sometimes with good grace, sometimes with petty bickering. The job in hand for these services was to confuse, obstruct and slow down, if not prevent, the German rush into Normandy. So, during the months of April to July intensive effort was put into hampering and harassing in all directions: enemy troops from the Belgian border to Paris, enemy bases in the south of France along the Mediterranean coastline and those installed a little north of Toulouse at Montauban, and the SS-Das Reich Panzer Division endeavouring to manoeuvre north.

The overall plan for D-Day, code named *Overlord* and *Neptune*, was ingenious, intricate and superbly jigsawed into neat interlocking pieces. Not everything went to plan, nor were all operations intended to fit into this neat jigsaw. Many operations were mere *trompe d'œil*, stratagems, decoys, or diversions to hoodwink and confuse German intelligence.

Weaponry and ammunition, money and other supplies, as well as daring agents, valuable aircraft and priceless pilots were expendable to defeat an implacable enemy. However, the idea of suicide missions was anathema to the British. In their training, agents were psychologically tested to ensure they had no suicidal tendencies. A dead agent is, after all, a useless agent.

Violette and the rest of Philippe's team in Sussac had a pivotal role in that overall jigsaw, as had her mission to the *zone interdite* in April. Was her solitary April mission part of the jigsaw, but only as a diversion devised by the British and Baker Street to confuse the Germans? Was Violette one of the decoys? The *Salesman* circuit was clearly blown; it was a dangerous area to enter for as long as she did and was almost impossible to find the remnants of the circuit, difficult to compensate damaged families financially and persuade Résistants there to plan attacks and sabotage co-ordinated specifically to *Operation Overlord* and the Allied invasion. Yet she did these things and discovered new intelligence on the V rockets, getting out alive with a great deal of information and delivering it safely to London. These important successes make it seem more likely to have been a genuine mission rather than a red herring.

If Violette had been considered 'expendable', then her masters did not know her very well. She was a small but perfectly honed cog in a very large and complicated machine. But what of this new mission?

Would she be betrayed this time?

‡

The swathe of land from Cherbourg, south through the western Loire valley, Vendée, Bordelais and the hinterland to Montauban, was the major danger area for the Allies. So first they flew in SOE agents, liaison officers, wireless operators, instructors, food, clothes, arms and ammunition to prepare the ground.

From Châtellerault to Tulle and east to west Clermont-Ferrand to Angoulême was the large area Violette's team was to work in, sometimes criss-crossing and extending into areas of other SOE agents doing similar work. Lines were indistinct; co-operation all-important. More agents and couriers were dropped with Jedburgh teams with further detailed plans for obstructing enemy communication lines – roads, rail, telephone and telegraph. Then the American, British and Canadian airborne troops followed shortly afterwards.

‡

Among those at Madame Ribiéras' corner shop at ten o'clock on the morning of 8 June were the communist commandants Fernand Philibert and Roger Magadoux of the OS.[120] Philibert, a stocky man of about thirty-five, perhaps forty, with dark hair, high forehead and a square face, was the very epitome of a seasoned warrior.

Also there was Rousselier's (*Rivier*'s) right hand, *Capitaine Annick* (real name Lliane-Annick Bojekowlska), of Russian Trans-Caucasian descent. After being introduced, she listened intently without saying much. She reported back to *Rivier* on the events of the night and the team from England. She and Violette immediately took to one another. *Annick* thought *Louise* exquisite, especially her magnetic eyes. She had heard a rumour that *Louise* had done some pretty extraordinary things in the north of the country but did not know quite what. Colonel Rousselier (*Rivier*) was a polytechnicien who had been an active officer.[121] He was a good-looking man in his thirties. In 1942, he had first commanded the AS – the Armée Secrète of Region 4 (R4) in Toulouse before taking over the leadership of the FFI in R5, then much later, the 12th military region in April 1945.

---

120 OS = Organisation spéciale created by the Communist Party in France prior to setting up the FTP.
121 *Polytechnicien* = one who has graduated from one of the highest and most prestigious French educational establishments – a polytechnic or 'grande école' – that have huge prestige.

Another one present was Jacques Dufour (*Anastasie*), a risk-taking Pétainist gendarme committed to the Résistance. He was somewhat akin to Bob Maloubier in personality but without Bob's training, discipline and slower-burning courage. *Anastasie* flitted from one group to another with great but dangerous bravura (dangerous for others, more than for himself, some say), but doing his best and somewhat petulant in his demands to London. London kept a very British 'cool' in its replies and supplies to him, much to his voluble disgust. *Anastasie* was flanked in the kitchen by Maquisards in his group.

Also present were part of Georges Guingouin's initial team: Adrien Meymerie, Adrien Petignaud and Raymond Barre,[122] who all lived in Sussac and were all committed communists. Pierre Magadoux arrived too, a seasoned Résister who would also participate under Philippe in the battles of Mont Gargan, and the seizing of an SS-Das Reich division armoured car on 9 June. His brother Roger was very close to Colonel Guingouin, a fully seasoned Résister but not a Maquisard. He often took on dangerous missions with his own unit.

‡

The team of Violette, Philippe, Bob and Jean sat in the courtyard of the grocery shop. The others gathered and joined them. Roger Magadoux, Barre, Petignaud, Meymerie, *Anastasie* and *Annick* milled around and pulled up rickety chairs and stools. A couple remained standing, pacing the yard.

Jean-Claude Gulet stood up, 'I need to go up to the room, sort out the radio. Last night was not a good enough reception and I want to try and improve it.' He did not like to be in such a crowd. It was time to make his excuses and leave. 'Need to find a safe-house on higher ground, *Charles*.'

'Will do. Are you going to send my message, *mon Brave*?' Asked Philippe.

'Yes, Major. I'll repeat your last night's message just to make sure everyone knows we're here and safe. I'll send it before this one. Neither is too long so there should be no problem.' He turned and walked to the door.

'Thanks, *Claude*,' called Philippe as Jean-Claude left. Violette smiled as he passed her. Damn sweet girl, Jean-Claude thought as he looked down into her sparkling eyes.

He went quietly up to the room to set up his wireless set in a new position. Reception was not good enough from the room the three men were sharing. Concerned that he might need to move somewhere else if he could not get a decent reception in the upper floors of the shop, he decided to try the wire in Violette's room to see whether that would help. He had some difficulty attaching the wire so it travelled unobtrusively around the wall joint and ceiling to the window, but after

---

122 This was not the Raymond Barre who later became prime minister of France from 1976 to 1981.

fiddling a while, he finally managed. Jean-Claude fixed it so well that Violette used it after he had left for his safe-house. It was still in place nearly twenty years later.

Once Jean-Claude had erected his wire, taken out his silks[123] and laid them next to his radio-set on the bed, he worked meticulously, coding the messages Philippe had instructed to be transmitted to London, informing their masters of their arrival and that meetings were already taking place with the various Maquis groups to pass on instructions and that plans were progressing. Bob was immediately sent to begin training units in weaponry, sabotage, use of explosives and security. While Jean-Claude was working on his messages, the others made plans in the cool of the shaded yard.

‡

'Look,' explained Philippe yet again to their most loquacious visitor, Jacques Dufour, 'we've got to get these plans and directives, along with some personal messages from London, down to Arnac-Pompadour, a short hop from Tulle, as soon as possible. But *Louise* has to go on a couple of other sorties before meeting with *Captain Jack* and *Colonel Berger*.[124] However, she needs to see them no later than the 10th, two days from now. It's absolutely imperative.'

'No problem, easy! I'll do that. Leave the lass here, out of danger's way. I don't think you'll be getting much joy out of *Colonel Berger*, though,' was Jacques Dufour's supremely confident and dismissive reply. He had no idea who Violette was or of what she was capable, and had no idea that she knew the two men rather well.

'As it is,' continued Philippe noticing Violette's eyes raised to the sky. 'We were delayed trying to get here by the bloody weather, then the German patrols prevented the reception team from receiving us a couple of nights ago so we had to fly all the damned way back!

'*Louise*, not you, *Anastasie*, must meet with *Captain Jack* after she's completed a couple of other runs for us to co-ordinate activities from Poitier, Châteauroux down to Brive-la-Gaillarde. You will act as her escort and bodyguard. Do you understand that?'

'*A vos ordres, mon major!*' said *Anastasie* with a sarcastic curl to his mouth.

'You can then take her on to meet other leaders in the region, as *Captain Jack* will probably be too busy to do that. But let him guide you as to whom she should meet. Right?' Philippe cocked his eyebrow towards *Anastasie*.

---

123 Leo Marks created the worked-out keys printed on silk. After an operator used one key of five characters and sent the message, he or she would immediately tear off the strip.

124 *Captain Jack* (or *Capitaine Jack*), alias *Nestor*, alias *Digger*, was Jacques Poirier, Violette's friend and co-student. *Colonel Berger* was André Malraux, representing de Gaulle to gather assorted political and military groups loyal to de Gaulle in preparation for a peaceful transition to democracy after liberation.

'*Bien sûr.*' The curl was turning into a slight smile.

'The SS–Das Reich has left its barracks in Montauban and already caused a lot of trouble,' continued Philippe. 'Today, you, *Anastasie*, should go east while *Louise* goes to meet a Résister, Madame Lazeret, about fifteen miles from here. She can go on one of the bikes.'

'There's a bike just out front,' replied *Anastasie*. 'But it's very dangerous because the Germans have forbidden cars and bikes to the population unless they have proper papers. Shouldn't she be accompanied by one of us Maquis?'

'That is a problem,' sighed Philippe. 'Anyone around the table able to provide papers for *Louise* to ride a bike? Maybe as a delivery girl for farms or a travelling milkmaid or something?'

Laughter burst forth at this, but *Annick* said she actually had some identity and pass papers on her. She took the papers from a compartment in her bag, hidden behind a lining that opened with a concealed zip.

'Here you are; *Isabelle Durand*, laundry woman. Curzac. How's that?'

'Just perfect. I'm *Isabelle Durand*, laundry woman from Curzac. Where's that?'

'It's actually on your way from Sussac so you can ride through and get an idea of what it's like in case you're stopped. A tiny village with a pretty château in the hills.'

'Great. It won't be necessary for me to be accompanied. You all have more important things to do and I'll be better on my own, anyway. I'd like to make a move now. Can someone draw me a map and show me on the maps you've got? That way I'll have a pretty good idea of the route and any major buildings or landmarks. It all helps, not only to get there, but if I'm stopped or need to make a detour. It'll only take a few minutes and then I'll have memorised the route and landmarks.'

They talked on for the next twenty minutes, showing Violette the route and each giving their knowledge of places to note as she rode along. Philippe then took her aside and discussed how to approach the woman in Magnac. Violette listened carefully, asked a few well-chosen questions and then stated, 'I've got a small revolver that a Pole gave me in England and I'm going to tuck that away in the back of my belt with a light cardigan over it. On this mission, I do not intend to go anywhere unarmed. If I'm stopped, I should be able to get through with a sweet smile and perhaps a worried look. Does wonders, that does!'

'All right,' acquiesced Philippe with a frown. 'You know what I usually think about arms. However, down here the situation is quite different. I, too, shall be armed at all times. Here we are in danger of attack from ambush and unexpected SS–Das Reich units on patrol. You should leave as soon as we finish here. Go carefully. Don't rush, and keep your eyes peeled.'

‡

29

Sussac

8 June 1944, SS–Das Reich Panzer Division, Maquis, Tulle, Oradour

'The political situation at the time of our arrival and departure from the field was the same. The entire region is communist … However, there was no political outburst at all during our stay; only consciousness that France should be freed – before starting politics again.'
From a 1944 report of Jean-Claude Guiet – accurate if one discounts minor but often heated arguments and individual hot-headed actions

One of Violette's tasks on this mission was to travel to and fro between leaders of groups of Maquisards as well as between Philippe, *Colonel Charles* and *Anastasie*, carrying messages, wirelesses, money, plans and instructions – the last two being memorised. This was intended to unite the distinct and often adversarial groups while preventing the SS–Das Reich from reaching the battlefields of Normandy. Another of her tasks was to help where necessary in sabotage activities, primarily in disrupting and incapacitating rail and road communications.

In the central zone where the *Salesman II* team had dropped, three key groups were to be brought together to pledge allegiance to de Gaulle. Since autumn 1940, many groups had been created and merged in the south. At the start of 1944, non-communists in the southern and northern zones regrouped yet again. In the south, they were *Combat*, *Libération* and the non-communist Franc-Tireur (FT). These three groups became the *Mouvements d'Unité de la Résistance* (MUR). In the north, *Défense de la France*, *Lorraine* and *Voix du Nord* fused. It was one of *Salesman II*'s tasks, with André Malraux, to fuse these groups and the communist groups – such as the FTP – into one national cohesive whole.

The Armée Secrète (AS), divided into four battalions, remained the military wing of the MUR. The AS had been founded and directed by Jean Moulin.[125]

---

125 'The SS staff in France were comparatively, but only comparatively, human. Many were inexpert and brutal interrogators, and Jean Moulin, the most important man SOE and the BCRA[M] (Bureau Central de Renseignements et d'Action [Militaire]) sent to France they ever captured, was interrogated by them so brutally and so stupidly that he died in their hands without saying a word (not that he would have said anything had he lived).' 1940–1941, Foot, *SOE in France*, p.109.

Moulin, an iconic French Résister, was under direct orders from General Charles de Gaulle as a prime member of de Gaulle's Comité national français in London to create an administration to organise common services for the disparate movements and networks. This pledge of allegiance was accomplished with the eventual active help of the SOE F Section and de Gaulle's SOE RF section.

The Résistance was tightening its grip around Brive-la-Gaillarde while Guingouin's FTP continued its work of disrupting the railways through relentless sabotage activities. These communication networks were also pounded by Allied aircraft diving to drop their bomb loads precisely on railways, depots and yards. Strict instructions were given to avoid hitting the civilian populations at all costs.

It was now imperative, and the major purpose of *Salesman II*, to create more confusion and cause damage and destruction to enemy forces, further distracting them and causing the SS-Das Reich Panzer Division to slow its progress north. Already, the SS-Das Reich had split its forces so that they were able to detour around heavier concentrations of Maquis. The Germans were finding it decidedly tricky to avoid ambushes and sabotage.

During the war, bombing raids over towns reduced to cinders trillions of French banknotes, not only in businesses and homes but also in bank branches. The Bank of France and the Treasury wrote off these losses simply as 'notes not presented', but there were other disappearances reported discreetly as 'withdrawals' for the Résistance, the Wehrmacht and the Milice. The Résistance was permanently short of funds and as the Allied invasion arrived, caution was abandoned. An audacious hold-up at the station of Clermont-Ferrand on 6 February 1944 delivered 1 billion francs in 1,000-franc notes and more than 3 million in 20-franc notes in over forty sacks into Résistance hands.

Then there was a train carrying around 50 billion francs. The wagon was derailed, German soldiers killed and the money disappeared. A rogue Maquis group, decidedly communist, had allegedly done the deed. On the other hand, rumour also had it that *Anastasie* and possibly even *Paco*[126] and the *Soleil* group had been involved. Whatever group accomplished this act of daring, it did not share the spoils with other groups.

On D-Day, a Bank of France wagon containing almost 3 billion francs in new banknotes from the mint's printers in Chamalières was coupled to a passenger train in Périgueux and attacked between Périgueux and Bordeaux on the Neuvic stretch. Close accounts of these monies were kept by the Dordogne préfet, the departmental head of the FFI and the treasurer Monsieur Latappy. Many such hold-ups took place.

Throughout the regions of Corrèze and the Haute-Vienne, the many disparate groups of the Maquis fighters were slowly being harnessed into a hard-hitting, well-trained and well-armed force. It was an extremely difficult task as the Résistance – all over France – had instantly grown by thousands after the Normandy landings.

---

126 *Paco* and *Bob Mortier* = field names for Robert 'Bob' Maloubier.

Those who had been undecided, the '*attentistes*' or wait-and-see brigade, suddenly saw an Allied victory and wanted to be part of it – on the winning side.

‡

'Listen,' said Philippe, catching the attention of the group bent over the maps. 'With your groups, *Colonel Charles* and Roger Magadoux, and Fernand's OS, we must pull the Maquis movements into a force to be reckoned with, ranging from Châteauroux in the north to Brive in the south – together you must number a good few thousand, I shouldn't wonder.'

'Well,' jumped in *Anastasie*, 'tell me what you want to do and where you want to go and I'll have the car brought round so you can travel just about anywhere you like.'

'Okay. Just make sure it's not a car but a truck. Something unobtrusive, please. The first person I want to speak to is Georges Guingouin – I want to do that today. Can you take me?'

'Sure, but I don't …' started *Anastasie*.

'I don't exactly know where he is,' butted in *Colonel Charles* rather too quickly, 'but I can take you over to various groups who probably know how to get in touch with him. He keeps himself and his men well-hidden.'

Anastasie tried hard to hide his humiliation at not being in the know. He had so much to learn.

'Thanks, *Charles*. The sooner I meet him the better. I also want to take a look over his territory,' Philippe responded. 'We've got to get hold of that chap – imperative!' He turned to Violette. 'I think you should come with me later on so you get an idea of the geography and topology here about. There are huge expanses of very hilly wooded land and flat bare terrain. There are, as I understand it, some huge fields on fairly high plateaus suitable for parachute drops of men and equipment. I need to know exactly where they are and what they offer. I also want you to meet as many people as you can before travelling down to *Digger* the day after tomorrow.'

'Madame Ribiéras was telling me that somewhere just north of here,' commented Violette, 'to the north of Mont Gargan, there's a farmer who would be happy to have our agents and containers parachuted over his fields. I think it's where we landed last night. Do you know it, *Anastasie*?' She saw his self-esteem had been wounded and, although that was probably a good thing, thought it wouldn't hurt to mollify him at this point.

Anastasie laughed warily, 'Yes! It's exactly where you landed and, as you now know, it's not very far.' He stood up, and then announced, 'I'm off to find Alain and his *camionnette*. As soon as I'm back, we can be off.'

'*Merci, Anastasie*,' answered Philippe, thinking, he could be a real asset if he curbed that damned enthusiasm and conceit.

Violette and Philippe sat back down with the others and the maps that were laid out in front of them.

‡

'*Claude* also needs a safe-house, reasonably high up for good reception and transmission and so that he can be well away from us. It would also be useful if he could be supplied with a bicycle,' said Philippe to no one in particular.

'*Pas de problème*,' one man replied. 'He can accompany me when I leave. There's an ideal place not too far from here and a choice of five or six bicycles. A relative of mine.'

Jean-Claude stood up and moved towards the door onto the yard. 'I'll go and sit in the square until you're ready to leave,' he said. He turned quietly to Violette, 'You know, *Louise*, you said in Cambridge that you were just a little concerned about your French after being back in England. Well, let me tell you. It's fluent and perfectly normal. There is a slight tonal variation, which under normal conditions would go undetected except for someone on the alert for it.'

Violette smiled. She had wanted someone knowledgeable to endorse her French. It was satisfying to have it corroborated. 'Actually, I think the "slight tonal variation" is Pas-de-Calais, the area where I grew up and went to school.'

'Ah yes. That's it, for sure. In fact, at the moment, it's more current than mine – and,' he laughed, 'you know a damned sight more slang than I do.'

And off he went, with a wave of the hand after pecking Violette on both cheeks and shaking hands with the men in true French fashion.

He preferred to be seen as little as possible and was more than happy with his own company. Naturally a bit of a loner, he was a good judge of character and could spend hours observing people as they moved through the routines of their day. The little village of Sussac was not particularly busy but Jean-Claude, in old farmer's trousers, disreputable hob-nailed boots and a beret pulled well down over his face, bought the local newspaper and sat on the edge of the market square in a half-hidden corner under a large tree, where he rolled a thin scraggy Gitane, struck a match and puffed the cigarette into life. No one even noticed his presence there. There was not a German in sight but farmers and farmhands from the surrounding countryside came into town. Farmers' wives also came to town to buy a few extras from the market and Madame Ribiéras' grocery store, which always seemed to have something interesting in stock, even in these hard times.

Jean-Claude noticed a few gendarmes strolling around. Pétain had about 200 of these country, semi-military police in the area. *Anastasie* had been one of them before he became a full-time Maquisard. Jean-Claude felt uncomfortable with that young man; he felt he was just too boisterous, too lacking in prudence, a know-all who knew quite a lot but not enough. Jean-Claude felt that *Anastasie* had not divested himself of his extreme dislike of the pro-communist elements in Sussac that had been instilled in him in the gendarmerie. However, *Anastasie* had started working for the Maquis long before leaving the military police and had helped out in any way he could from within the gendarmerie, sometimes disposing of police or enemy reports, sometimes handing over to the Maquis identity papers and other documents that could be used. So, even before the mass movement of the area's gendarmes over to the Maquis, *Anastasie* had already participated in and led some pretty daring exploits that caused the Germans based in Limoges to the north-west of Sussac to consider him 'the greatest bandit in the Limoges area'. However, *Anastasie* had no time for security and the Germans already knew his real name as well as his *nom de guerre* and he had a sizeable price on his head – dead or alive. The Germans had arrested and questioned the hotel-owning Dufour family in *Anastasie*'s hometown of Salon-la-Tour, only to discover that they were not related. This merely incited Jacques to further acts of bravado. He could not understand, even after the arrest and interrogation of this family, that his uncontrolled and unconsidered actions could needlessly put other people in great danger and cause considerable misery and fear, if not torture and death.

‡

To the south of Sussac were the Corrèze Maquis and to the east, the Creuse Maquis, while other Maquis groups extended westward across the Dordogne into Cognac country. In addition to French Résistance and Maquis groups of deep country folk, in the Limousin and Périgourd were the Brigardistes, Spanish Republicans who had fought in the Spanish Civil War and were now escaping Franco's regime. There were also the Polish officers demobilised in 1940 who formed the *Réseau F2* (F2 network). Now D-Day had arrived, uniforms of all descriptions abounded. The men resembled – often acting like – a motley crew of pirates, not well-trained guerrilla fighters. Feathers fluttered in hats and berets, jackets sported gold epaulettes while khaki shorts or corduroys with khaki berets at jaunty angles did double duty as farming clothes and Maquis disguise.

From Sussac to Châteauroux some 3,000 Maquis – many still untrained – roamed freely and hid in huge expanses of woodlands. From time to time heavily armed German detachments made raids into the hills and forests; a skirmish would take place – a few men being lost on both sides.

Frustrated in the extreme by the lack of security and discipline that he found on his arrival, Philippe sent in a stinging report to Baker Street:

```
When I left London I was given to understand that I would
find on arrival a very well-organised Maquis, strictly
devoid of any political intrigues, which would constitute
```

a very good basis for extending the circuit throughout the
area. On arrival, I did find a Maquis, which was roughly 600
strong, plus 200 French gendarmes who joined up on D-Day.
But these men were strictly not trained, and were commanded
by the most incapable people I have ever met, as was
overwhelmingly proved by the fact that none of the D-Day
targets had been attended to and that each time it took
me several hours of discussions to get one small turn out,
either to the railway or the telephone lines.

He is likely referring to *Anastasie* and Charles Gaumondie. His exasperation
is evident.

On receiving arms and explosives, the men had donned their fighting clothes,
put rifle to shoulder and hung cartridges, explosives and grenades from their
belts to rush off with no discipline or training, provoking the enemy into battle.
Consequently, they suffered heavy casualties. They had no campaign plan but went
on wild quests, only to flounder and reap terrible reprisals on their families and
neighbours. Bob Maloubier as assistant instructor had his work cut out for him.

Had Philippe been able to start from scratch, as he had in Rouen, he might
have succeeded in mounting a controlled, disciplined and well-trained number
of Maquis cells – each separate from, and unknown to, the other. However, these
bands of Résistants were disorganised and frequently rejected instruction – and,
he thought angrily, under the leadership of a man he presumed to be the remote
figure of *Châteauroux*, Georges Guingouin. Rivalry between civil and military
Résistants or between FTP and Secret Army heightened London's distrust, fearing
spontaneous uprisings.

In his later report, Philippe explains:

The Chief of the Maquis … a man who calls himself Colonel
Charles, was by trade a saxophonist in a Bal Musette; a
soldier of the second class with no war experience. He had
been for Hector, Samuel and Anastasie (the leaders of the
separate sections) their only contact with the neighbouring
Maquis, which none of these leaders had ever really visited,
relying on Charles for their information.

‡

The main road to Normandy, the N20, ran from Toulouse through Limoges,
which the Germans had made their regional stronghold. They had taken over the
town's prison and set up a Gestapo headquarters a kilometre or so from it in the

Impasse Tivoli.[127] The Wehrmacht headquarters and barracks for the soldiers spread across the town. To hear of someone being taken to 'La Tivoli', or to be taken there oneself, was to instil fear and loathing.

Since 27 April 1944, the SS-Das Reich Panzer Division had been stationed in and around the town of Montauban, between Toulouse and Limoges. The battle group consisted of 2,500 men commanded by Heinz Lammerding. Many of them had fought on the steppes of Russia, where they had committed innumerable atrocities on the Russian army and people. On 3 February 1944, the Sperrle Orders had been issued to SS-Das Reich Panzer Division, ordering harsh reprisals for terrorist attacks and tasking officers to place the welfare of their men ahead of that of the civilian population.

The Panzer Grenadier regiment was mostly equipped with trucks and halftracks. Germany was not able to keep up the production of tanks to supply all the Panzer divisions, but this SS-Das Reich had a full complement of men and armoured vehicles, including tanks. It had begun to move on 8 June 1944, starting along the N20 and then deploying its advance units along the D902 at the same time that Violette and her team were planning their next moves. Philippe knew time was short.

Some elements of SS-Das Reich that were not yet fully mobile remained near Bordeaux at Montauban, but the main body of the Division then set out north from its assembly area at 08:00 hours on 8 June. It planned to reach its destination of the Tulle–Limoges area that evening. The distance between Tulle and Limoges is about forty-five miles or so. The troops divided and travelled along several routes, spreading their lines far behind them. The SS-Panzergrenadier Regiment 4 'Der Führer', made up of four battalions, was ordered by Sylvester Stadler to take the lead of the vanguard.

Hitting hard over the next months, the Allies unleashed hundreds of tons of bombs in air raids all over France, damaging, even obliterating, rail and road communications used by the German military, destroying railway stations before the enemy could utilise them to amass their forces. Bridges were bombed, major radio and telecommunication centres used by the Germans were attacked and concentrations of enemy vehicles were shot up.

The side effect of this was extremely painful and endlessly sad for the French in the loss and wounding of thousands of French civilians and the destruction of their fine towns and villages. For the Allies, it was akin to going in to destroy a

---

127 Today called *Impasse [Antoine de] Saint-Exupéry*, named after the author of many bestsellers including *Pilot de Guerre* and the delightful allegory *Le Petit Prince*, written during the war in the US where he was sent against his will to assist with propaganda as he was a bestseller there too and pilot extraordinaire.

virulent cancer with massive bombardments of radiotherapy, destroying much that was good along with the incurably bad.

‡

As de Gaulle put it from Radio London to his people on 4 June, 'For the sons of France ... the simple and sacred duty is to fight the enemy by any means available.' That is exactly what the French did – valiantly and for as long as was necessary – as did the Allies.

The Germans had nicknamed Region 5, where *Salesman II* was operating, *petit Russie* or 'little Russia' as it was heavily suffused with communist beliefs, dogma and training. Marcel Godefroy (*Rivière*), a dedicated fundamentalist communist, was the commandant of the FTPF for this region. Georges Guingouin, communist in training but independent in thought, was decidedly disillusioned with his communist comrades and their constant meddling in his plans. He found it particularly unacceptable to put the civil population at risk and was quietly making overtures to the FFI, the Gaullists, and even London, along with politically more moderate groups, eventually and especially, the *Salesman II* circuit led by Philippe.

From D-Day the entire region was in revolt. An entire series of military operations was implemented, greatly supported by Allied drops of armaments and agents.

‡

SS-Panzergrenadier Regiment Der Führer began its ponderous approach to Brive, between Cahors and Limoges, along the N20. A reconnaissance group detached itself from the Brive column, deviating towards Tulle, where the Maquis had been only too successful in creating havoc amongst the enemy troops.

Among seven of SS-Das Reich Panzer Division submissions, General Lammerding's submission number 6 to his superiors, accepted and passed to his troops, translated reads:

```
To let it be known that for every German wounded, three
terrorists will be hanged (and not shot) and for every
German killed this will be ten terrorists - and get on
with it.
```

And they did so with gusto, along the entire route with the first mass hangings in Tulle. The barbarism of a demented ideology gone rabidly mad, trying to shake off Résistants snapping at its heels. Ninety-nine civilians were hanged in direct reprisal of Résistance activities along the streets of Tulle on 9 June as Violette was cycling across the countryside, just a little to the north. One hundred and forty-nine other civilians were deported to concentration camps. Just over 100 never returned.

The advance reached the tiny village of Oradour-sur-Glane on 10 June at about two in the afternoon, some four hours after what would turn out to be a fateful roadblock at Salon-la-Tour for Violette. Insisting, without a shred of evidence, that the town was infested with Résistants, the Nazi troops herded the civilians into the small pretty village church; in all, 642 people, including 100 children. Then, Kommandur Adolf Diekmann ordered the troops to pile straw inside and out, to pour gasoline over the whole village and the church and set them alight. Among the people rounded up, only two Résistants were found and hanged and a handful deported. The others were simply townsfolk.

All those people were burned alive; there was no escape from the growing inferno in the church. Just one woman of all those men, women and children escaped incineration. Some inhabitants who happened to be away from home survived. But not many. The ruin of the village remains testimony to this most dreadful deed, along with the atrocity of Tulle.

The SS–Das Reich Panzer Division continued its way on the N20 to Bellac and Poitiers.

‡

It was indeed fortunate that the British SOE agents acted neutrally with regard to political factions, or acted with circumspection when aligning themselves to one faction or another. By this process, British agents prevented loss of life through infighting and were able to help a great deal in the melding and welding of small units into a greater force shortly before D-Day and in the following months in the push to defeat the enemy.

Most importantly, during the last two weeks of June and all of July, Philippe was skilful in organising about 10,000 men. Guingouin, who eventually accepted *Salesman II* aid, had around 8,000 men. They all trained hard, London sent material, new and larger terrains were found for the American paratroopers.[128]

Colonel Maurice Rousselier (*Rivier*), regional head of the FFI, liaised with the regional military representative (DMR).[129] The legendary figure of Georges Guingouin, '*le Préfet du Maquis*', operated in Corrèze. His was a tough, well-trained and disciplined group of young men. He kept them isolated in Maquis country, not allowing them home so they became inured to discomfort and were rarely a security risk. During the month of June alone, nearly 800 railway lines were severed in the Indre and not one plan for sabotage failed. All railway communications were interrupted and long-distance lines sabotaged, with the exception of that between Clermont and Tulle. The technicians of the telecommunications group, *Groupe*

---

128 Finally Philippe took the German surrender in Limoges signed by Gleiniger on 22 August 1944.
129 DMR = Délégué militaire de région (Regional Military Representative).

PTT, had been shot dead just before they were able to report where exactly to cut the lines.

The work of the Résistance and *Plan Tortue* provoked heavy reprisals, from Carzac to Oradour-sur-Glane. The objective of *Plan Tortue* was the sabotage and disruption of enemy road transport. Three more French 'plans' existed to deal with disrupting other spheres of enemy activity.

‡

30

Magnac, Madame Lazerat and Meeting the Maquis

Thursday 8 June 1944

Violette pedalled along in a happy frame of mind through lovely countryside. There were few people about in the tiny hamlets she cycled through and she did not see one German, not even a Milicien or Gendarme, and yet there had been talk of the SS–Das Reich Panzer Division moving north from Montauban, a huge force of some 23,000 men with tanks, armoured vehicles, packed with weaponry.

That was what these virtually untrained, unruly, unarmed Maquisards were up against. It was the job of the *Salesman II* team to help obstruct the force every way possible. Bob had already started work, training men in the forests. Jean–Claude was moving to a safe-house high in the hills to relay messages back and forth to London.

She stopped at a little café–bar in Curzac to buy a bottle of mineral water. The woman who served her wanted to chat a little. Saying she had come from way up north, Violette asked about the rumours of a huge force moving towards the north. A worried, scared look crossed the face of the waitress.

She spoke of how they had had enough of war and now these dirty Boches were ransacking and burning their way north. Thousands and thousands of them. She had heard some dreadful things and was so frightened, not sure at all that she should keep her family in this little village – but what else could she do? Where else could they go? Violette recommended that she stay put as it was out of the way and very unlikely the Panzers would roll through there as they had no reason to, even for advance detachments. Violette advised her not to wander too far to which the woman nodded gratefully telling Violette to take care of herself.

She left and pedalling fast much of the way, it took Violette just over an hour to reach the little railway station of Magnac-Vicq. The grocer's shop stood close to the railway. She could see no Milice or other obvious enemy. It seemed so calm and devoid of danger but she had learned that appearances could be deceptive. She walked around a while, looking as if she were waiting for someone and finally she went in.

'Madame Lazerat?' Violette had entered from the bright sunlight into a dark interior and walked straight over to the rather severe-looking woman behind the counter.

'*Oui*,' was the suspicious reply. 'What can I do for you?'

'Albert says you have *the best vegetables for miles around*, madame.'

'Ah, does he now? Now, *just which Albert would you be talking about*, mademoiselle?'

'*Votre gendre*, madame.' As Violette mentioned the second part of her code of the son-in-law, after the first: '*the best vegetables for miles around*', Madame Lazerat smiled thinly and gave the second part of the code, *Just what's he up to now?* Simple, appropriate but just different enough not to be confused with everyday exchanges. Violette was assured she had the right person and Madame Lazerat was happy to trust the young woman, for now.

She led Violette into a back room where she offered her chicory-laden coffee while they quietly discussed all the instructions from London that Violette passed on and supplies that Madame Lazerat and her son-in-law could call upon, and how many other leaders of small groups there were in her area. Mostly the leaders only met here in the grocery store to finalise plans, or dropped in singly with messages to be passed to others who would also come in singly or pairs, ostensibly to buy produce and goods.

About an hour later, they had gone into some depth about what was to be done and whether it was possible. Madame Lazerat was quite pleased with the care taken in the instructions and the way they were delivered by this young, but self-assured woman. She asked if Violette would accompany her to her friend's house just a couple of minutes away. There she was introduced as *Louise* to Léonard Lornac (*Raoul*), a wheelwright from Monceau, *Robert* and two women who seemed to be very much on the periphery of things. Cautiously, Violette chatted with them for a good ten minutes. Feeling greatly reassured, she asked many questions, including what London could do for them, and then she passed on instructions from Philippe for sabotage activities to take place during the next seven days, with the admonition that to fail would be to put liberation in great jeopardy but success would hasten its approach. As they returned to the grocer shop, a man stepped out and hurried away. Marguerite Lazerat pointed and said, '*Celui-là, c'est le Préfet des Maquis*.' It was none other than Colonel Georges Guingouin, who, it turned out, was being given shelter at her grocery shop.

Violette felt she had done all she could, convinced of the woman's ability, and the others, their patriotism and loyalty to liberating France. She stood up to take her leave, hoping they would meet again. It was noticeable how a certain resilience was reappearing in the people now that liberation was expected in months rather than years.

She got back to Sussac in mid-afternoon, reported on the great deal of useful information she had gained, on the fact that Madame Lazerat and the two men promised to follow Philippe's instructions to the letter, and that she had almost bumped into a man she was sure was Georges Guingouin, referred to as *le Préfet du Maquis*. Madame Lazerat and the two Maquisards kept her son-in-law, *Colonel Charles*, informed of the activities and plans of the groups in their areas so that over the next few weeks they would concentrate on keeping the Paris–Toulouse railway line out of order and cut the telephone lines everywhere and as often as they could.

Philippe was delighted. Violette was a perceptive liaison officer. Her intuition had not failed her in Rouen. It would not do so here, he was convinced. She was vital to his operations until Limoges was liberated. She had natural ability to get on with people, see things from their point of view and in that way could persuade them to do what she had been instructed to ask them to do.

Philippe smiled, praising her on a job well done. He continued to tell her that she would accompany him so that she would know whom he had met and what plans they would all make. The figures and general intelligence she had given him on the Lazerat groups would be reported to London and useful in their discussions that evening.

After they had eaten, Violette freshened up and came down the stairs just as an old gazogène drew up. They both climbed in and were driven off.

‡

The truck rumbled and bumped along the highway. The driver, *Adrien*, talked non-stop all the way to their destination, giving them a full rundown of events, groups, plans and general Maquis positions. He stressed they were communist to the core but still lauded the Gaullists who, he felt, would bring in democratic government after liberation, as de Gaulle had promised when speaking over the BBC. Although the communists were doing a great job, he had heard stories of breakaway groups caching arms and money for their own use after liberation. He was sure it was not Guingouin who was doing this: he was far too prudent and was working for a peaceful socialist revolution once liberation arrived. Guingouin had become seriously disillusioned by the communists. Philippe and Violette listened to this very carefully. They asked *Adrien* how they could contact Guingouin but only received evasive answers.

It was going to be difficult to get the various networks and groups working along the same lines, particularly where a group's activity overlapped that of others. Violette and Philippe would be walking on eggshells. As it turned out, that evening they did not get to see Guingouin, but did meet Maurice Rousselier under his name of *Colonel Rivier*, regional head of R5[130] of the FFI, directly under the

---

130 Région 5 for the FFI, comprising the Haute-Vienne, Creuze, Indre, Dordogne and Lot. From April 1944.

control of General Marie Pierre Koenig who had, coincidently, been Étienne's commanding officer in the Legion in Africa.

After D–Day, SOE F and RF sections with the Jedburghs were brought under the overall command of Koenig, as part of the FFI. In 1942, Koenig had led the heroic stand of the 136th Brigade of the 13ème French Foreign Legion at Bir Hakeim just south of Tobruk. Now, two years later, Violette was under the same overall commander as had been her gallant husband. In March 1944, Koenig had been appointed delegate of the Provisional Government of the French Republic, at the side of Eisenhower and *commandant supérieur* of the French Forces in England and *commandant* of the FFI. *Rivier* was soon to become General Rousselier, on 28 June 1944 and awarded Violette her Croix de Guerre avec Étoile in absentia during August.

Violette and Philippe were also to meet *Rivier*'s second-in-command, Roger Lescure (*Murat*),[131] who, as a very active member of the French Communist Party, had been arrested and escaped in September of 1943 to rejoin his group in the Corrèze.

The road entered the forest of Châteauneuf-la-Forêt, and finally the truck turned off, bumping and rattling rather alarmingly along a small lane. An isolated clearing appeared ahead, far from enemy patrols. As they approached it, they could hear barking. Guard dogs, thought Violette. Good idea.

Two Maquis aggressively stepped out, pointing Sten guns at them. *Adrien* shouted at them to let them through. One of the guards, Michel Boulestin, was only sixteen years old and came from the town that seemed to grow out from the forest, Châteauneuf-la-Forêt. His comrades in the township's Maquis FTP had given him the small dog that yapped at his heels since Michel was so very young. Without youths like Michel, and without the many families from the Limousin who fed, hid and cared for the young and older Résistants, they would not have been able to maintain their forest life, living in shacks and abandoned hovels and cottages that were often not even watertight. The farming people of the Haute-Vienne were, like so many, a micro-society with a strong identity based on their old language, Occitan, and an old tradition of rejecting central power (power emanating from Paris). It is from these tough, courageous country people that the Résistance found the solid base on which to build.

'Good,' said Philippe. 'This is just about the first time I've seen any kind of half-decent security and men with some training.' Once the two Maquis had recognised *Adrien*, they had saluted smartly to Philippe, in British uniform as *Major Charles Staunton*. The Maquis present were wearing uniforms of a sort: crumpled

---

131 Roger Lescure (*Murat*), was appointed lieutenant colonel alongside his colonel, Rousselier (*Rivier*) in the FTPF. He was colonel in the FFI, Compagnon de la Libération, Légion d'Honneur, Rosette de la Résistance. He ran the '*école*' that continued to produce well-trained Résistants, well after the German attack.

khaki shirts and trousers held on their skinny frames by old belts or string, boots in need of repair and probably no socks.

They went into the clearing where a dilapidated *cabane de bûcheron*[132] was standing. A few metres away, forest vines were beginning to scramble over an old *scierie* or sawmill. A few men and two women were busily doing something. In the barn, three small storm lights were hanging from a rafter, shedding flickering light onto a long makeshift table.

'*Entrez, entrez mes chers co-conspirateurs!*' waved *Colonel Rivier*. '*Bienvenue, Mademoiselle Louise! Bienvenu, Major Staunton!* We have much to discuss and not much time to do it in.'

They spent the next three hours going over plans and arranging scouting parties to look out for new fields for parachute drops. They also decided that the fields already in use were to be reconnoitred again. Philippe asked how many men were involved in each of the reception committees and what training they had had to date. He also asked for numbers of men in each Maquis group.

As they talked, it emerged that, a few days before they had landed, Georges Guingouin had categorically refused to liberate Limoges so, on 5 June, an autonomous group of communist FTP decided to encircle and liberate Tulle instead. The small German garrison of 1115 Feldgendarmerietruppe,[133] two companies of 95th Regiment plus the Maintien d'Ordre[134] forces, consisting of the French Milice, Garde Civiles and Groupes mobiles de reserve[135] had been blocked in, unable to flee the town. The next day, as news of the Allied landings filtered through, the FTP group was again galvanised into action. This prompted the Germans to order Préfet Trouillé to get the Maintien d'Ordre to co-operate with the Wehrmacht stationed there and fight their way out together. Monsieur Trouillé, a secret member of the Résistance, had refused and that night the Germans moved into the girls' school while the Milice, Gardes mobiles and reserves put up ineffectual barricades at the town exits.

On the evening of the 7th, the FTP group led by Godefroy known as *Rivière*[136] and Jean-Jacques Chapou (*Kléber*) attacked the town. Frenchman against Frenchman. The Vichy MO group hid in various buildings, only for the FTP to send mortars in, killing and wounding some of them.

Préfet Trouillé begged the FTP to let the 'poor buggers go' and they were allowed to flee. The Germans held out, incurring heavy casualties until a group of fifty tried to break out. There were some forty or fifty dead Germans and

---

132 *Cabane de bûcheron* = woodcutter's hut, '*bûche*' is a 'log'.
133 Feldgendarmerie = German field gendarmes or field police localised in German-occupied towns.
134 Vichy Maintien d'Ordre (MO) = Vichy Maintenance of Order.
135 Groupes mobiles de réserves, known as the GMR, the Vichy reserve mobile security police.
136 *Rivière* and *Rivier* are two separate cover names. The first is for Godefroy, the second for Rousselier who became a general on 28 June 1944.

twenty-five wounded as their stronghold in the girls' school fell. Monsieur Trouillé then had to protect them from the fury of the FTP who had seen a good many of their own civilian population shot against a wall by the Germans. The FTP celebrated their victory, but the Préfet warned that the Germans might come back.

Jacques Poirier, SOE co-student and a friend of Violette, whom she had met so briefly in Paris at the Madeleine, had instructed his team and other Résistants to implement London's *Plan Vert* (green plan), successfully causing chaos on the railway lines. However, no bridge along the Dordogne had been destroyed nor had been included in the *Plan Tortue*, so the SS–Das Reich Panzer Division, even while striking out in desperate skirmishes with the Maquis and SOE teams en route, was able to march into the Limousin.

Under orders from Paul Guérin and Anthème Besson, *Alliance* network treasurer, the telecommunications group *PTT* in the Basses-Alpes had extended branches of its telephone line to Gap and Grenoble. Many Résistance telecommunication lines, especially in the centre and south of France, were funded by Banque de France, exiled in London. As the SS–Das Reich Division set off, a Cahors employee of the postal and telecommunication 'repairs and faults' service sent a warning signal by safe telephone line to Besson in Brive, warning that the division was approaching. The message was not passed on to the FFI of R5. Guingouin reports that none of the Gaullists, Giraudists, or communist leaders was informed. He goes on to say that faults had developed in the network, whether by design or accident is hard to say. On the other hand, a little later, the regional head of the Milicien in Limoges, Jean de Vaugelas, was warned of an imminent Maquis attack and decreed a state of siege, barricading the town. Units of SS–Das Reich, already with a bloody reputation for civilian massacres, readied themselves.

On the morning of 8 June, as the *Salesman II* team were waking in Sussac, Monsieur Trouillé, the *préfet* of Tulle, had awakened to the stamp of Nazi boots above as units of the SS–Das Reich Panzer Division took over the Préfecture. The SS–Das Reich deported 149 men aged eighteen to sixty, of whom a mere forty-eight returned. To further exact their revenge, ninety-nine civilians and Résistants were executed by hanging; from lampposts and balconies. Friends and family could only watch as the victims were dragged to ropes casually thrown up along the streets.

Tulle straddles the Corrèze river. It is a small picturesque town with a road following the course of the river on either bank and many small streets and lanes with historic buildings, and now a single monument to the ninety-nine citizens hanged by a revengeful German regiment.

‡

Apprehension increased as news spread that the Panzer division was on the move. All motorised transport was forbidden to the civilian population, so news was sketchy. The German authorities went so far as to forbid bicycles, but the Vichy police and Feldgendarmerie did little to prevent cyclists who were needed to keep local production going. All other forms of transport required special permits from the German authorities. Papers were always thoroughly checked when holders were stopped and their vehicle searched for stowaways, weapons or contraband.

As those present at the forest meeting considered the rumours and facts to hand, it was clear that the utmost discretion was required by everybody. Philippe uncharacteristically and rather starkly announced that he wanted little to do with hotheads like *Anastasie*. He was surprised by the lack of adverse reaction, which he rightly took as a good sign. He then turned to Violette and asked her to relate her visit to Madame Lazerat. She gave her impression of the elderly woman and what they might expect of her. She recounted that she had met two more Résistants, *Robert* and *Raoul* at the home of Madame Lazerat's friend who lived a couple of hundred yards away. She was sure that they would perform and do so discreetly. She had passed on instructions and the explosives she carried on her bike to use on the railway line to Madame Lazerat, who immediately started to enlist the assistance of the *cheminots* on her part of the Toulouse–Paris line as well as gathering together the small groups of Maquis in her area – Magnac-Bourg to Viqc-Breuih and as far north as Pierre-Buffière. *Colonel Charles* was likewise engaged with his other Maquis groups through his main *Bistrot* group. Violette also reported her stop in Carzac and the fears of the people that the heavy tank division was approaching from the south.

These two people from England impressed Roger Lescure. He warmly thanked them and London for all that they were doing to help bring an end to the horrors, atrocities and occupation.

Maurice Rousselier,[137] *Colonel Rivier*, was impressed by Philippe's generally diplomatic manner, his insistence on tight security, training and discipline plus his desire to move things at a cracking pace. *Annick* had already reported on them and he had been eager to meet them. *Rivier* found Violette quiet and unobtrusive, and when she had something to say it was to the point and informative.

Louis Godefroy, alias *Rivière*, directed his FTP[138] to conduct operations from Eymoutiers in the Haute-Vienne, just a few kilometres away, from Egletons and from Tulle in the Corrèze, where he had previously dealt with Jacque Poirier, *Captain Jack*, in his *Nestor/Digger* territory. It had been *Rivière's* rash operations against the Germans in Tulle that had roused the SS-Das Reich to inflict such terrible reprisals upon the population there. Philippe was aghast at such bad planning,

---

137 Colonel Rousselier (*Rivier*) cited Violette for the Croix de Guerre with Star reporting that she had killed at least one German at the site of the ambush. She had wounded many more.
138 *Rivière*, that is Louis Godefroy, not to be confused with Rousselier, alias *Rivier*, became second-in-command with Roger Lescure from 11 June.

insisting no more actions within townships should take place against the enemy. *Rivière* agreed he would lead his group along London's planned line of harassment and sabotage, and they discussed a series of plans in the Lot and Corrèze regions to continue this work.

'Look,' said Philippe, 'I really want to get the FTP involved. Communist or not, we're all here to get the Nazis out – once that job is done we can consider the politics. Meanwhile, it's essential that everyone hunker down and abide by our rules.' At this, he looked deliberately at *Rivière*.

'Yes,' said Violette, not too sure where Rousselier (*Rivier*) and his men stood. 'We're not in the least politically motivated. As far as we are concerned, there is plenty of time for that after liberation. We won't achieve that liberation unless we all work together now and use the best people available.'

'Absolutely,' confirmed Philippe, 'We'll work with all parties, the more the better. But we must get some of these younger men trained and instil some discipline into them. Little training and too much bravado puts civilian lives in danger. I don't give a bloody monkey's balls for any of your politics. I insist on and expect bloody discipline. We're planning on a large drop of munitions and SAS paratroopers very shortly – as soon as I can let London know that we not only have a suitable field for a large drop, but that we also have a bare minimum of Résistants capable of fighting and it is absolutely imperative that we keep up the sabotage.'

‡

After discussing the activities for the following day, it was suggested that Violette should go to Figeac to establish just what condition the Maquis was in, how many groups and number of Maquisards in each group and their needs, along with estimates of civilian Résistants in the town and surrounding area. In the end, though, instead of Figeac, a shorter circular route east was decided so she could visit a number of villages. This was fortunate for her as the SS–Das Reich Panzer Division arrived in Figeac that day, taking reprisals.

As the night drew on, they all relaxed a little more, having combined their intelligence, plans of action and instructions from de Gaulle's men and SOE. Finally, after genial goodbyes and handshakes on all sides, *Adrien* drove them back to Sussac, arriving back at Madame Ribiéras' in Sussac at about two in the morning.

‡

31

Domps, Le Clos, Michel, Dog

Friday 9 June 1944

Friday 9 June dawned as another beautiful day. Long lines of the SS-Das Reich Panzer Division were slowly mounting towards Normandy, as it spread out over a huge expanse of the Dordogne, Creuse and Haute-Vienne, crawling along the approaches to Tulle to the east and Brive to the west, with offshoots protecting the flanks. The convoys were a good two miles in length and terrifying to behold. The long rumble of their passing shook houses and distressed the inhabitants. March A of SS-Das Reich moved towards Tulle via Figeac, while March B, which included the SS-Der Führer battalions, pushed towards Limoges through Cahors and Brive. This latter route would prove particularly ill-fated and tragic for Violette.

The task of the Panzer Division, in the first instance, was not a 'forced march' to the front. It was, as per Sperrle's orders, to destroy resistance, to annihilate the key armed groups of Frenchmen in the zone, and Brigadeführer Heinz Lammerding had orders to deal with armed militants. Lammerding voluntarily admitted that the actions of the Résistance delayed the Panzer Division's march to Normandy and one of its main sections was seriously strafed by Allied bombers, between June 7 and 11 when its various battalions reached the area between Angoulême and Poitiers. It was not until a few days after the invasion that Sperrle's orders to annihilate the Résistance were retracted and the Panzer Division began its real race north. The Limousin Résistance, aided in every way by SOE agents, slowed the division's progress by a good week, whereupon they were delayed yet another week to overcome their exhaustion.

‡

Jean-Claude signalled London:

```
All targets satisfactorily covered. All road, rail and
phone traffic stopped since D-Day. Too, too easy. Country
strictly yours. Bistrot Maquis growing fast. 1,000 strength
with latest joined recruits 300 Corrèze gendarmes. Also
```

up to 2,000 local men willing to join up. Pump deliveries
in fastest.

Jacques Poirier had been as worried as Philippe. Jacques knew his *Nestor/Digger circuit* group was convinced of final victory but if the Allies had delayed the invasion and the Germans launched a huge attack against the Résistance, he doubted his men could hold out against an efficient army. Although new recruits were flooding in, he remained apprehensive: these recruits were inexperienced, caused security problems and there was the maintenance of supplies to be considered by agents and Maquis leaders.

‡

Violette set out on her bike at just after eleven o'clock on 9 June, accompanied by the young guard Michel and his dog. Michel was a healthy young lad ready to take on the world, but a bit bemused and bedazzled by his task to accompany this beautiful woman. They both had much to accomplish and many places to visit so Anna Ribiéras had given them a picnic basket each. Hidden at the bottom of the baskets were packs of explosives, grenades and detonators, and much-valued cigarettes to pass to the leaders they saw through the day.

Around Violette's waist, under her skirt and short-sleeved blouse, she carried a huge amount of money in 1000-franc notes and a map of the entire area. She had instructions to determine the needs of those she met: what their plans were, the numbers in each group, their specialities and whether sufficient training had taken place. The London instructions she gave were to be adapted to suit the conditions she found. The principal instruction was to cause as much damage to communications and rail links, petrol stores and any other enemy installation that was relatively easily reached. She was to instruct everyone she met to stay clear of towns to reduce reprisals, to take their time and not act rashly.

General Marie-Pierre Koenig had instructed that the supply of weaponry and ammunition be restricted and that the Maquis should hold back, concentrating on sabotage. They were not, under any circumstances, to try liberating towns as had been so disastrously attempted in Tulle.

Cycling to their first rendezvous, Violette and Michel talked about the rumours flying around that the most feared of the enemy's forces were crawling all over the region. They had heard that splinter units had dropped out to roam the countryside – punishment corps, reconnaissance units and snipers as well as advance patrols and vanguards. And yet, not one rumour had been substantiated. Some thought it was no more than the Feldgendarmerie and bands of Milice prowling around.

It would not do to take chances. They agreed on a brief and plausible cover story that Violette had come from up north and she wanted to stay a few weeks as she was too frightened to go back to the *zone interdite*. Michel was her cousin twice removed and was taking her to meet relatives she had never met. He also wanted to introduce her to some of his mates. He looked innocent and young enough for this to be easily believed and the little dog, wagging his tail happily, just added to their tale.

Violette went over with him the established routine for protecting one another's retreat if they needed to run. He had had one training session in this strategy, in the woods, about a month previously, but that was all. Violette told him that she would introduce him to Robert Maloubier when they got back or leave a message for Bob to ensure Michel joined his sessions wherever practicable.

They got off their bikes while she demonstrated exactly what she meant by protecting one another. She made him copy her. Agile and quick thinking, he mastered all she showed him. Now he felt more confident and somewhat more of a soldier. They practised the routine a few times. One of them aimed at the imagined enemy while the other raced behind for some sort of cover. A bush, a log, a hole, or small rise in the ground. The one under cover would then cover the other, running back for new cover. And so the relay would continue for as long as necessary, or until severe disablement, death or capture. There was much laughter in their practice while the little dog barked and chased and thought it was a wonderful game to play.

Half an hour later and puffing from exertion, they set off again. After thirty more minutes, they were in Champs. Their tour was a circular one. Their next town would be Domps and on the return loop, Le Grand and Le Petit Bouchet, Reberol, Meillac, Murat and back to Sussac.

‡

As they left Champs, a number of racing Feldgendarmerie vehicles passed and Violette made a note of the direction they were taking and how many vehicles. Michel took note of ranks from the German uniforms. The German soldiers did not even look at them, so intent were they on reaching their destination. A few minutes later Violette and Michel were in Domps. Michel guided her to the tiny *estaminet*[139] where a few elderly men were playing cards in the corner. A large scowling woman came in, but her face lit up in a beatific smile when she saw Michel. She brought over two coffees and a snack, sat beside him while he whispered to her and then introduced Violette as his distant cousin from the north. She leant over to Violette and said she would do whatever she could to help. The local Maquis group was in the forest somewhere but she was seeing '*le chef*' tonight. Violette asked a great many questions. Glancing sideways at the men, with suspicion at one or two, the woman answered her as best she could. She hesitated on just two questions and

139 *Estaminet* = a modest tavern. More frequent in north of France and now considered an old-fashioned term.

avoided giving the name of the man who commanded not only her '*chef*' but also a good number of others. Violette was sure that this unnamed man was the '*Préfet du Maquis*' – Georges Guingouin.

The men in the corner were clearly in an unfriendly mood and one sauntered over and asked what was going on. Michel ingenuously told him that his distant cousin *Louise Badeau* had arrived here, running away from the dangers of the north, and that he was now showing her his 'beloved' Limousin. He asked him and the other men if they could help as she wanted to work on a farm and be safe from the Germans. Once they saw this young woman looking a little unsure, they as good as patted her on the head and intimated they would be happy to help. The woman smiled to herself as she slipped quietly back behind the bar.

After thirty minutes or so, Violette and Michel set off from the hamlet of Le Grand Bouchet to its smaller namesake, the pretty Le Petit Bouchet. Again this was a small commune and they merely dropped in for a quick coffee and gave out some information to one man who, Michel explained, belonged to another group that often worked for Commandant *Rivier*. Violette also handed him some cash and explosives, explaining what was required and how he could help to bring a number of leaders together to plan a few concerted actions for later in the month.

They started to retrace their steps but further to the south than planned, through Reberol and Meillac, after which they would go through Murat and back to Sussac. At each village and a couple of farms along the way, Michel introduced Violette as *Louise* with as little detail as possible. During every stop, Violette was able to learn more about the various groups, although it seemed to her it was just one big headache with each group fiercely at war with the next. On a few occasions, she passed over money to help families in difficulty or for special requirements. Most would not take money for themselves. Again, she left explosives.

They came across two more small convoys of Germans and heard some shooting in the distance. As one convoy went past, the little dog barked and growled. A very large German turned to look at the dog, pointed his machine gun at it and then laughed as he roared away. In Meillac, the Feldgendarmerie was out and about checking identities. Michel and Violette kept to the back of the houses and cafés until they had discovered all they could and left quietly in the late afternoon.

They arrived in Murat to find that a large number of Maquisards were gathering in the café–bar, talking loudly and clearly planning their next moves. Michel went up to them and in his most imposing voice asked that the commandant come to be introduced to Violette. They sat down together for a good half-hour over coffee and Ricard, going over plans for sabotage and Violette reminded them of Koenig's orders to keep out of the towns. No town was to be liberated – even if it looked easy. It was too early at present, she clarified. Considerably more planning was needed and the formation of reception committees for arms, ammunition and paratroopers was more urgent. She assured them it would not be long, perhaps two or three weeks, and all their plans would be ready to implement but only after careful preparation.

‡

It was well after seven o'clock when they finally got back to Sussac, stiff, and with legs like jelly. Philippe came in not long after and Violette recounted their day and all the information she had gleaned on numbers, group names or aliases, leaders and weapons required. She told him how much money and explosives she had handed over and to whom, and passed on the request, so often repeated, for an instructor. Bob Maloubier was in great demand and kept busy, quite apart from the sabotage forays he would lead or join. He was already training the Spanish Résistants with success.

Then she gave her impressions of all those she had met, the confusion of groups and the infighting that existed. It seemed especially fraught between the communists in the FTP and those of the far left of centre, who considered it inappropriate to be politically exclusive. She explained she had some feeling that these inclusive sentiments applied to Guingouin in particular. Violette had not actually met him, nor had expected to, however she had heard quite a few allusions to *Le Grand* or *Le Préfet du Maquis* or his area the enemy had nicknamed *la petite Russie* and a leader who would not allow his men home, trained them hard and hit the roof if they attacked Germans near a town.

Then it was Philippe's turn to go over his day in some detail. He was finding it extremely frustrating not being able to get to grips either with Guingouin or some of the other leaders. He felt they were testing him. He did not like it and, anyway, time was of the essence.

He reminded Violette that tomorrow she was going down to Arnac-Pompadour to meet up with Jacques Poirier. She was to spend time with him and, if possible, Malraux and Commander Robert (Jacques' father). It was essential to bring his large group into the picture, as they knew they could rely upon him.

‡

32

Going South, Ambush, Chase, Capture

Saturday 10 June 1944

'If there is one thing upon this earth that mankind love and admire better than another … it is [the one] who dares to look the devil in the face and tell him he is a devil.'

James A. Garfield

The Parisian Committee of Liberation (CPL) called the *cheminots* to a general strike and to acts of sabotage; the German police had arrested the president, the former vice-president, the director-general along with with nine other top executives of the SNCF.[146] On this day, Saturday 10 June, they would be released. The citizens of Tulle were burying all those whom the SS–Das Reich Panzer Division had executed by hanging along the streets of the town.

Limoges was now swarming with the leading elements of the Panzer Division, after considerable delays on their move north to Normandy as bands of Maquis had harassed them on all sides through the Lot, Dordogne, Corrèze and Creuse. However, the Maquis in the Haute-Vienne were being restrained by their leaders, especially by Georges Guingouin, from blazing into action. The French Gestapo had saturated the entire area. The level of danger to civilians and Résistants alike travelling the roadways and byways of the Limousin had risen hugely.

SS–Das Reich was forced to move its 209 tanks, assault guns, ancillary repair units, accompanying troops, reconnaissance advance and vanguard along two-lane pre-war roads as sabotage had made railways impassable. Under normal conditions, it would have taken them a mere three days to reach Normandy, but the Panzer Division did not arrive in any great number in Normandy until 23 June – a journey of fourteen days! Even then they were weak and exhausted in morale.

The night before, as Violette and Michel were returning to Sussac, Major Helmut Kämpfe, a popular senior officer of the division and close friend of Kommandant Heinz Lammerding and Major Adolf Diekmann, had been captured and executed by the Maquisards under Georges Guingouin. Kämpfe had either been too impatient to wait for backup in his desire to destroy the Maquis or, for some other

---

140 SNCF = Société nationale de chemin de fer – the French national railway company.

unknown purpose, had ignore protocol and gone alone in his armoured car into Maquis country. In a frenzy of patrols and roadblocks, the SS-reconnaissance and sniper units were racing about the towns and villages and along the country roads searching for the Maquis group that had 'kidnapped' him.

From 9 June, all road, rail and telecommunications traffic was stopped for several days. Some 600 Frenchmen in the immediate vicinity were poorly armed, and more particularly, ill-trained. However, after the hurried meetings that had taken place, and inspired by Philippe, Violette and Bob, groups in deep rivalry in the fight against the occupying enemy showed immediate and exceptional fighting spirit that went on to deal devastating blows to the German military juggernaut.

‡

Late into the night of 9 June, there had been heated exchanges between Jacques Dufour (*Anastasie*) and Philippe, with Violette acting as mediator. In the end it had been decided that Violette would leave at around half-past nine in the morning to travel to meet Jacques Poirier in his safe-house in the Château de Virolle, Limeuil, between Tulle and Arnac-Pompadour. Her tact and good humour helped keep those late-night discussions reasonably temperate most of the time.

'It's too far. Fifty kilometres at least. *Sacré bleu!* It will take too long and a girl travelling alone along some of those isolated stretches could raise suspicions. I've got my grandpapa's *traction avant*[141] up and running,' insisted *Anastasie*. 'It's full of petrol filched from the German military supplies last week. It would be much better if I drive her halfway and she can cycle the rest of the way. I'm going there in any case to liaise with my *Soleil* group. It's easy enough to attach the bike to the passenger side of the car.'

'Well,' cut in Violette. 'That could be a good idea. You do have a valid point about a girl alone on the longer stretches. However, I'm sure girls have to do that all the time. It just requires a sensible story if stopped and appropriate papers – which I've got. Our job is to stop the Germans getting to Normandy, or at least hinder their progress so they hardly know which way to turn. Now, it seems good work was done today, judging from reports coming in. Bob's cutting himself in half, training fledgling Maquis members from all over the region. *Capitaine Jack* must get the instructions we've received from London so he can co-ordinate activities. I know I'm fast on a bike but I'm not a champion of the Tour de France!' This brought a smile and cut the tension. Philippe knew she was right.

'*Anastasie*'s idea sounds dangerous; all cars are banned without German passes.' Violette went on. 'On the other hand, yesterday's *randonnée à vélo*, pleasurable

---

141 *Traction avant* = front traction. All French cars with engines in the front were, at the time, called '*les tractions avant*'. This one was a large black Citroën, a model that was a favourite not only of the Résistance and Gestapo but also of war films set in France.

though it was, was pretty exhausting. The country around here is not exactly flat. Perhaps a lift halfway has its advantages.'

She smiled at *Anastasie*, who nodded at what he considered was more than self-evident, seemingly oblivious of the danger his large black Citroën could cause.

Violette continued, '*Major*, I had a chance to have a good look at that land owned by the Charials called Le Clos on the right coming from Sussac and, you're right, *Anastasie*, it's quite perfect for landing Allied paratroopers and loads of canisters. It's on the D30 halfway between Meillac and Forêt-Haute. On the left going up the hill, you have the farmhouse and outbuildings, usual farm clutter with plenty of room to hide all manner of things, and then those huge fields. We landed there the other night, in one of the smaller, closer fields. Michel and I made a short detour to meet the farmer and have a little Ricard. They are really good people and can be trusted. In the middle of the high plateau there, there's a grove of chestnut trees, where Charial said the parachutes could be hidden. His young son's clamouring for the job. The land is high, large and not easy for the enemy to get to quickly. It could handle the largest drops of paratroopers.'

'That's good,' commented Philippe, impressed yet again by Violette's capable work and her ability to use her own judgement to good effect. '*Anastasie*, you see *Louise* agrees entirely with your assessment of Le Clos. I'll get *Claude* to report its details to London ASAP. Then we wait for the BBC's message of the drop date while we continue sabotage on all enemy communications. I insist that *Louise* or I lead, or second, some of these activities. It will help us understand the thinking of the various Maquis groups and see what more we can do in the way of finance, training and arms. Just sort out the reception committee. But I guess you, *Charles*, already have that in hand?'

Charles, the colonel, smiled a *bien sûr*. He looked over at Violette, not sure whether he was resentful of her solo visits yesterday or impressed by her good thinking. He decided in her favour and gave her a wide smile.

Philippe continued, 'Well, our imperative orders are to delay and obstruct the Germans from getting to Normandy. We, all the Maquis, FTP, and so on have been entrusted with one of the most important tasks there is: to stop that Panzer Division from getting north too soon. I'll bet it was *Nestor*'s gang along with *Casimir*[142] giving them a bloody nose. We might not be able to knock out the Panzer Division but we can damn well slow them up!'

'We've been deprived of weapons, told not to fight or liberate the towns without firm instructions from London, in other words, Koenig – and now you go insisting we get out there,' grumbled *Anastasie*, 'I've been out there every day, risking my neck. You know I've got a big price on my head, don't you?'

'Yes, but if perhaps you had been a little more prudent—'

---

142 *Casimir* was the cover name in this region for Peter Lake, who led or took part in the sabotage.

'What the bloody hell do you mean? Prudent …! If I'd been more prudent, as you say, there'd be no great influx of new recruits.'

'That's another worry.' Philippe frowned. 'We need to keep security tight and recklessness at arm's length to avoid losing any of our people or, worse, inviting reprisals on civilians.'

'Yes, Major. But …'

'I know, I know. Total security is total inactivity. But we've got to plan carefully and we've got to keep hitting the Boches where it hurts – and that's in their lines of communication – rail, phones, roads, ambushes, derailments and so on.' Philippe saw impatience glinting in *Anastasie*'s eyes and stopped to reflect on the best way to tackle this impetuous young man.

Before he could, Violette stepped in, 'We must also co-ordinate our activities with those of other groups. After I meet up with *Capitaine Jack*, you and I will meet again down there so you can introduce me to other group leaders. This Panzer division doesn't move in one big mass, nor in just one direction – north.' The Germans had been deploying large and small patrols all over the region to set up ambushes and they were having some success. Other battalions had orders to keep the passage north as clear as possible; some were staying in the Montauban–Toulouse area to ensure replacement equipment and vehicles were in good running order and to deploy fighting forces all over the south. That was the intelligence Violette and the rest of the team were picking up – another reason Violette had to get to *Capitaine Jack* as soon as possible.

'Yes,' continued Philippe, somewhat irritably. 'It seems young *Capitaine Jack* is doing a damn good job over the entire region.'

'*Ouais*, he is. Except he keeps in a bit too well with the commies!' grunted *Anastasie*, peeved by Philippe's taking charge, irritated that the leftist bastard *Capitaine Jack* was getting too much praise, especially as he seemed to be in cahoots with those Bolsheviks. They were as much a danger to the country as Hitler and Pétain, as far as he could see.

Violette had met up with Jacques Poirier a few times in London when she was with Harry Peulevé. She had also done part of her training with him, along with Cyril Watney (*Michel*), Sonia d'Artois and Nancy Wake, in Scotland, Winterfold in Surrey, Beaulieu in Hampshire, Wanborough Manor near Guildford and Ringway near Manchester. They were on good terms and enjoyed one another's company. Cyril was Jacques' wireless operator. Having trained with these people, Violette understood their thinking and they could interact and make plans swiftly and non-combatively. After the brief 'ships passing in the night' meeting in Paris, it would be so good to see him again.

Harry, as she now knew, had been arrested along with Roland Malraux by a maddening piece of bad luck at a house near Brive on 20 or 21 March and badly tortured. They had given nothing away. They were deported to concentration camp. Roland died there but Harry survived, although he never really recovered.

Harry's adoration of Violette is clear from his copious handwritten notes and reports at war's end, and in some measure helped to sustain him. He had known for some time that she, too, was an agent and understood some of what she would be going through. He did not really approve of women being allowed to risk their lives in enemy territory. Whether this love would have stood the test of time cannot be known. Nor do we know how Violette really felt towards him except that she was clearly very fond of him. He was another important reason for her to fight on. She might not love him, but he was her friend and she was always fiercely loyal to her friends and family.

‡

Looking forward to meeting Jacques Poirier again, Violette intended to help him continue Harry's work in any way she could. His *Author* circuit had been blown; it had been the Corrèze offshoot of the old *Scientist* circuit created by Claude de Baissac in Bordeaux, where Harry had started out as Claude's wireless operator. He then acquired his own *Author* circuit, which he ran with great success until he was caught at his wireless set along with Roland Malraux. When Harry was arrested, Jacques took over the circuit and London renamed it the *Digger* circuit.

The three Malraux brothers seemed to be a constant at the shadowy edge of her activities. In unhappy circumstances, too. Peulevé had received the message of 12 March 1944 from Rouen (probably from Broni Piontek, as mentioned in the Rouen chapters of this book) when Roland Malraux was with Harry. The reason for sending the message to Peulevé was to tell Roland of his brother Claude's arrest. Then Violette had heard from Vera Atkins that Roland had been arrested. Before too long, the same fate awaited their half-brother, André, but he was only briefly imprisoned, not tortured, and not deported.

André Malraux was just beginning to posture, as some French historians are inclined to describe it, as *Colonel Berger* from SOE. However, Harry Peulevé and Jacques Poirier both considered he was doing a first-class job in trying to bring the disparate Maquis groups under one umbrella organisation. Already a celebrated writer, he had not seemed inclined to involve himself in the fight to liberate France until March 1944 on discovering the fate of his half-brothers. Nevertheless, he had strong and enduring links with the Paris *Combat*, Albert Camus, Gide and many other left-wing intellectuals of the time who used their skills in producing newssheets for the Résistance and offering refuge to those that needed it.

In the Corrèze, the two lieutenants–colonels, Guédin and Vaujour, largely aided by Jacques Poirier and the members of his *Digger* circuit, had already received clear and distinct instructions from London and the Allied high command. Over the next three days, these men put a severe brake on the progress of the Panzer columns. The Armée secrète and the FTP – mostly led by Georges Guingouin – started a real '*travail de sape*', a constant sapping of the enemy's strength and intelligence, and further destabilising the enemy by attacking the railways and destroying trains and road convoys.

‡

Although Walter Watney, being well acquainted with Jacques and his family in France, had discreetly passed him the address of his brother, Cyril, in London, Jacques felt it would be decidedly imprudent to contact his friend's brother and family, considering the sort of training he was about to receive.

A few days after his arrival in Inverness for sabotage training, he met a young English officer who introduced himself as Cyril Watney. Jacques, although stunned, had sufficient *sang-froid* to reply using the cover name of *Jack Peters* that he had been given in Orchard Court. Jacques thought that this could well be one of the tests that all agents encountered before and during their training. They could even pass or fail on the name they used in a pub. Very soon, though, as Cyril was complaining about not having the luxury of using his brother's powerful cars, Jacques was encouraged to say he knew that his brother would have lent him a superb Delage. It was the start of a great friendship that led to Captain Cyril Watney being chosen as Jacques' radio operator in the Dordogne under the code name of *Michel*.

At Mallaig in Scotland one day, Jacques left the SOE school there to seek whisky and took with him '*la petite vedette de l'école*', Violette, 'the little star of the school', as Jacques recalled she was teasingly called. On the train, she and Jacques simulated a train sabotage operation and hold-up. There was much anger and fear engendered but also some mirth.

On another occasion, a few weeks later, he was on a training mission in Sheffield to play the secret agent and set up a circuit. Tails were sent to follow him and blow his circuit. They did not succeed as Jacques cleverly decided to create his network from people not on the list given to him by the school. The police in Sheffield were eventually sent to arrest him by somewhat red-faced instructors. Violette and Cyril, who had been paired together by their instructors, caught all those they had to tail. When their roles were reversed and they had to set up a circuit, they were never caught by other fledgling trackers.

They had all learned survival skills such as silent killing, the use of codes and wireless transmitters, parachuting at night or in the day, rowing boats, the use of many kinds of plastic explosives and detonators along with grenades, guns, rifles and pistols. Physical training was important and weeks were spent on learning various cover stories and withstanding interrogation under fairly harsh conditions such as sleep deprivation, to break those same stories and intelligence they had been given to learn. Violette annoyed her instructors for not taking it all seriously enough but she did not fail any of these 'exams'; under her sparkling fun-loving attitude was a steely determination to succeed, plus the inherent abilities to do so.

‡

'Okay, *Louise*, if you're sure. Now, you'll need the money belt as well as memorising all London's instructions for the groups. I cannot tell you how important this is,' were Philippe's directives and comments to Violette.

Violette and Philippe had taken a long walk, far from prying eyes and ears, to recap their brief and Violette's new task. The *Salesman II* circuit was to take over part of the *Stationer* circuit after Maurice Southgate (*Hector*), its leader, had been arrested. *Hector* reported three active Maquis organisations under his network and the possibility of using about 2,000 men in the Indre. *Samuel* was his second-in-command and a radio operator. *Anastasie* was his lieutenant for Haute-Vienne and Creuze; Maurice Southgate had asked for officer status for him in March 1944. Finally, among some very good people was *Marc*, personal assistant to *Samuel*, and his wife, *Samuel's* courier. Since the arrest of *Hector*, the circuit was divided up by London so that the south and south-east of the Indre into Haute-Vienne to Limoges would remain under the command of *Samuel* (with *Tutur* as radio) and the Haute-Vienne south of Limoges would be the area of the *Salesman II* circuit.

'Now, *Louise*, we've arrived late but things seem to be working out. *Claude* is doing a superb job as radio, we're slowly getting somewhere with *Samuel*; he's given us Marie to help out, which leaves you free for liaison work.'

'I'm looking forward to seeing Jacques and assessing the position in the Corrèze. From rumours, it's worse than we expected.'

'Yes, and it'll be necessary to change points of attack since some target details were captured with *Hector*. But I'll get stuck into that north of here while you're down south. At Châteauneuf, we know there're at least 600 Maquisards, a small group at Terrasson thirty miles south of Périgueux and 250 in Brive. It's the Châteauneuf Maquis that we need to be in close contact with and supply their needs ...'

'That sounds like Georges Guingouin, doesn't it?'

'Yes, but he's crafty and won't let us get too close until he can trust us. We have to work with that. They stand between two roads and two railway lines that are strategically useful and used by the Germans.'

'And our B messages will tell us what guerrilla activities to implement so we can harass the Jerries to the maximum but without any frontal encounter. London really does not want us to get up too close as yet, do they, *Charles*?'

'No, we need to keep in reserve the main striking force for more important and larger-scale attacks which'll be required later.'

'So, it's my task to go down to *Captain Jack* and agree with him and André Malraux on a division of spheres of responsibility. I see no difficulty with that, as they have no particular political or personal axes to grind. Don't you agree?' ended Violette.

'Yes, I do,' replied Philippe. 'But exact details must be worked out on the spot. London thinks it best that I become responsible for Malraux's FTP connections in the Creuze and in the Haute-Vienne.'

'I think that's absolutely right. The FTP is far too communist to deal comfortably with André and his more middle-class intellectualism.'

'Now, *Louise*,' said Philippe, looking intently at Violette. 'As far as the Corrèze and the Dordogne are concerned, it will be a matter of assessing which group would be the better able to deal with them. If this can be agreed, the contacts in those departments can be passed over to a single head. Can you handle that?'

'I'll do my best, sir!' saluted Violette. It was a large and important task but she felt confident that she could handle it. Might take a few days.

'Yes, I'm sure you can. Both *Samuel* and *Nestor* have done sterling work here and our approach must recognise that at all times. The only way, London suggests, of further dividing these areas is on the basis of military necessity. Difficult communications make it essential that units must now be concentrated into smaller, compact units capable of close control and with good communications with Allied HQ. And, for God's sake, don't forget to convey to *Nestor* HQ's appreciation of the work they're doing.'

'Of course.' Violette smiled. 'And first pass instructions that *Nestor* needs to target the railway lines converging on Bergerac and Uzerche.'

Let's get back to the others and get you ready for your journey!' laughed Philippe.

‡

'We've got to prevent or at least slow down that Panzer division making its way north from Toulouse.' Violette, who was actually directing her comments to Jacques (*Anastasie*), looked toward Philippe as she spoke.

'Ah yes, *Louise*,' *Anastasie* broke into her thoughts. 'We have already caused much havoc. Our Maquis further down south have been harassing them every step of the way with sabotage, even capturing enemy troops, including officers, but it hasn't stopped them. The reprisals have been particularly vindictive. It's a pity *Hector* was taken. As his lieutenant, I did a helluva lot of work. He put a promotion to officer in the pipeline for me. London doesn't half take its time.'

They had laid out on the long table a detailed map of the entire region from Brive-la-Gaillarde in the south to Châteauroux in the north. Underneath it was a more detailed local map.

'Now, *Major*,' *Anastasie* used Philippe's rank to cajole Philippe for more money and arms, 'My *Soleil* group is in desperate need of weaponry and could do with some financing. How can you help?'

'At the moment,' replied Philippe, somewhat tartly, 'there is far too much work to do checking out exactly what Maquis groups there are and how well trained they are.'

'Mine are trained as well as can be under the circumstances. But that's not exactly the point.'

'Oh, but my dear fellow, it is *exactly* the point. I need to know just who and what we have here. It seems to me the first thing you need is for *Clothaire* to come and lick your men into some kind of force to be reckoned with.' That was Philippe's last word on the matter.

Philippe was not at all sure he approved of this young Frenchman. Plenty of courage but not to any degree security minded, it seemed to him. Too political, as well.

The difference between the seasoned security-minded and somewhat left-of-centre Gaullist journalist and young, spirited right-of-centre gendarme and Gaullist fighting against his Vichy masters was too big for a congenial working relationship.

Anastasie was tempted to storm out, angrily denouncing the bloody British as arrogant, left-wing and lacking any understanding of the valour of his men. No, he would swallow his pride and stay, for the moment. This British major may be a closet communist but he was in a position to import good equipment. He would make sure he and his men got a proper share of it, not only to kill Germans and sabotage their installations but also, by taking some of the parachuted equipment for himself and his men, he deprived the communists and thus weakened their position. He would not see his country be freed of the Nazis only to be dragged under the yoke of communism.

Sussac was generally a communist stronghold, but the people were also very loyal Gaullists. Many had been recruited by the 'arch-communist' of the time, Georges Guingouin. This man had set up one of the most successful Maquis groups through hard discipline and tough training. Throughout his long life, he remained staunchly to the far left, but in the early years of the war he had eschewed militant communism and was, in fact, a dedicated pragmatist, keeping his idealism strictly within bounds.

‡

It was time to set out. Violette had packed her small suitcase. She wore a white blouse and light summer skirt and jacket; her coat was rolled up on the back of her bike. Her money belt was firmly around her waist, under her shirt and skirt. 'Has someone checked the Sten gun, *Major*?' she asked Philippe as she threw her luggage into the passenger side of the Citroën, where her feet would rest on it.

'Yes, it's been kept in good condition and was thoroughly cleaned and oiled last night. Here're a couple of extra magazines in addition to the one that's already loaded.' Violette knew the Sten intimately; especially this new version, knowing it could fire automatic or single shots up to 200 yards.

'Thanks. Can you fix the bike to the car for me, *Anastasie?*'

'Of course, *mademoiselle*.' *Anastasie* smiled lazily. 'I've got to pick up a pal up in Croisille so we'll attach the bike to your side of the car. That way, he can climb in from my side at the back.'

'Now, look here, *Anastasie*,' interjected Philippe. 'This isn't a picnic. It's a dangerous journey you're about to take. Isn't Croisille out of your way? *Louise* needs to get down to Arnac-Pompadour quickly; you do realise that, don't you?'

'Of course I do, *Major*. But I want company for the ride back. It *is* pretty much on our route and he'll be outside waiting.'

'I'm still not happy about the use of the car, *Anastasie*. It's not as if you're going any great distance. Why couldn't *Adrien* come along in his gazogène? Far more appropriate. There're far too many Germans about the place: patrols, ambushes and security checks. You just be damned careful and keep to the lanes, the *routes blanches*. There's less likelihood of you running into some reconnaissance or advance unit.'

Adrien, apparently, was ferrying sabotage equipment to another group. As Jean-Claude Guiet later stated to the author, 'The whole trip was pushed by *Anastasie*, especially the use of the car. Cars were fairly common for upper echelon and people who knew how to work the angles. *Anastasie* was happy go lucky, terribly sure of himself. Maloubier can furnish more info: they were great friends. If time had not been of essence, Violette would have gone by bike.'[143]

'Okay, we'll be off. Take us about an hour. The car has a full tank and is in tip-top nick. Pinched it right from under the Boches' noses, we did. I have a gun, but perhaps a couple of grenades, *Major*? Just in case. I'll bring them back again – unless I need to use them.'

The Maquis had a rather good supply of the Marlin submachine gun and *Anastasie* brought his. It was heavier than the Sten and more accurate. The Sten was light and easy to carry but also known for sticking and lack of accuracy.

'Don't think you'll need any grenades on this trip.' Philippe frowned. *Anastasie* had a good gun; it would suffice.

Anna Ribiéras stood beside her friend, Mademoiselle Géry, who was very excited by all this and impressed by *Anastasie*. Anna, eyes glistening, gave Violette a hug and a kiss on the cheek telling her to take great care.

Violette and *Anastasie* got in the car. Bob Maloubier arrived at that moment and stood beside Philippe as they waved the car off. Violette turned and waved a cheery goodbye, smiling happily, hiding a niggling feeling of misgiving. Something was definitely out of kilter. She shook her head and tried to dismiss the thought by considering where she would start the journey on her bike. Uzerche was the best place, but if necessary she could get out before that.

---

143 From Jean-Claude's correspondence with the author.

She felt unbelievably conspicuous in this large black car running on German petrol. She also felt decidedly uneasy, as the bike had been strapped to her side of the car, making escape from that side impossible. She would be relieved once she was on her bike, alone, a quiet country lass going about her business. She had a woman's bike this time with a nice round wicker basket on the front, deep and large. The loaded Sten, safety-catch on, was at her feet with her luggage. Two magazines were in her pocket.

In this vehicle, they would certainly not be considered quiet country souls. If they were seen they would undoubtedly be stopped, she thought, and probably shot at. Apart from the Germans and Milice, only the Maquis had cars like this. The sooner she was out of it, the better. It had seemed reasonable when they had discussed it, but not now. Every nerve in her body was alert.

‡

Philippe went back to the others. He needed to check out all the information he had. Violette did just great yesterday, he thought. Extraordinary girl. Women were very adept at this sort of work – nearly all the circuits had women working as liaison officers or couriers. *Colonel Charles* said she had worked wonders on Madame Lazerat. Things were beginning to come together elsewhere too; some good meetings, even though they took such a long time around here. The meeting in the forest had been instructive and good groundwork had been laid there. Two days in and things were happening. Violette would soon be down in the Tulle area and she would do a great job passing on instructions to *Captain Jack* and other circuit and Maquis leaders, bringing back Jacques' and Malraux's assessments, plans and requirements and those of other organisers. She had an important task to perform but she had she had bags of tact and the necessary stamina and had proved her talent. A great boost to have her with them.

‡

The sun glinted off the Citroën as it went along the narrow roads. It was hot and they wound down all the windows. Violette's window was a bit stiff as the bike's pressure made it a little difficult to wind down. After about eight kilometres, chatting as they went through the pretty countryside, they reached the D43, where they bore left.

Anastasie told Violette he came from a little village called Salon-la-Tour of which he was extremely proud. The N20 that still runs alongside it was the major highway for north–south traffic. 'Look, it's on our way to Arnac-Pompadour, after Croisille, as I told the *Major*. I'll take you through it. You'll love it.'

'Oh, I don't think so, *Anastasie*. We must get on. We don't have time for sightsee-ing, much as I'd like to. I've got quite a ride from Uzerche to Pompadour and maybe onto Tulle.'

'No, I really mean it, *Louise*.' Without waiting for a reply, he went on, 'We have to go through Salon-la-Tour to turn on the route to Uzerche so we'll just pass through.' He laughed gaily so sure of himself. He was certainly good-looking, thought Violette, just not my type. Too boastful, too loud.

A few minutes later, they were in Croisille-sur-Briance. They screeched to a stop outside the shop that his friend's father owned. *Anastasie* jumped out. 'I'll just go and check he's ready. Won't be a mo.' About five minutes later, he came out with his friend, Jean Bariaud, who was about the same age as *Anastasie*.

'Come on, Jean, jump in,' *Anastasie* shouted. 'Get in the back, will you. *Louise* can stay in the front with me. Jean, meet *Louise*!'

'*Enchanté, mademoiselle*,' was the somewhat oily response from Jean Bariaud.

'Heard anything new, Jean?' asked *Anastasie*.

'Well, there seems to be some heavy movement of Gestapo, Milice and they even say the Panzer Division is on the move all over the *département*. All the lighter stuff got up to Limoges yesterday with Lammerding. There've been a few ambushes apparently set up by advance units. Guess it's to keep us from ambushing them!' Jean said with a grunt of a laugh.

'Don't think we have to worry, anyway.' *Anastasie* was driving fast. Violette was surprised Jean knew so much. She felt danger in the air. Just silly fears, she thought to herself. She still preferred to keep a lookout, just to be on the safe side. She had put her Sten across her knees and kept her eyes peeled on the road ahead and along the sides, especially on the bends.

'Are you armed, Jean?' asked Violette, turning to look at him, wondering what he would do if they were stopped.

'No, never carry 'em.'

'Look, *Anastasie*. I'm feeling pretty conspicuous in this car. I think it's safer for all of us if I get out and ride the bike. Easy enough to put the suitcase on the back and the Sten can be wrapped in that old coat. I've memorised the entire route and I'd feel a lot more comfortable.' She looked at *Anastasie*, who looked back at Jean and winked.

'Come on! Don't be so independent. It's great having such a good-looking "*nana*"[144] with us. I want to show you off to Salon-la-Tour, and I can do a lot to help you. It's only a few minutes to Salon, where we can get to the café my friend owns and see what more we can find out. I think you're worrying for nothing. The Boches are all up at Limoges and towards Guéret to the north-east of Limoges. And the tanks are still way down south. I won't hear another word about you getting out before time.'

---

144 *Nana* = dolly-bird, babe.

She could not. She was trapped by the bike strapped to her door.

The road twisted through verdant fields. The small trees along the bushy embankments allowed some shade as *Anastasie* whizzed along, singing at the top of his voice. Jean Bariaud joined in the singing and then Violette did too. They would not understand if she did not and it would do her good. She loved the songs; her fears began to melt away.

Suddenly an old wheezy tractor loomed towards them. *Anastasie* hooted and waved as it lumbered off in the direction they had come from. But it brought back Violette's unease. She felt she must persist with her concerns.

'On Thursday and yesterday, I heard a lot of people talking about patrols and ambushes,' commented Violette, casting a wary glance at *Anastasie*. She raised an eyebrow as if testing him. 'They can't all be wrong.'

'Only a few more minutes and we'll be in Salon. You'll see, all clear of Boches – all the way.' Had he forgotten that the local Feldgendarmerie[145] had taken over the town hall in Salon-la-Tour as their headquarters, with a small contingent of SS-Feldgendarmes in their grey-on-brown uniforms? He must have known as it was his hometown. It is possible that neither Philippe nor Violette was aware of this military stronghold in Salon-la-Tour, but surprising.

There was no point in discussing it further. However, she made up her mind that once in Salon-la-Tour she would not get back in that car. She would ride her bike the rest of the way. She felt the worry disperse now she had made a decision. She smiled at them both and joined in the singing again. The songs she had learned in France as a child lifted the foreboding from her shoulders as the car rushed on.

✝

A few farm buildings were coming up on their left. A dog barked a warning and came running to the roadside. As they crested the hill across road appeared at some distance. Something glittered and caught Violette's eye. 'I think we've got trouble at that crossroad. It could be an ambush, *Anastasie*. Do please slow down!'

He did so. There was some command in her voice that could not be so lightly ignored this time. He peered ahead but saw no movement.

Then he saw two soldiers erecting a roadblock, just as they saw the car. It was probably a platoon from the SS-Feldgendarmerie, stationed in Salon-la-Tour, with orders to secure the main highway for the advancing Panzers headed by the

---

145 Feldgendarmerie = Field police. The Feldgendarmerie of the Waffen-SS had its own SS-Feldgendarmerie, known by the sinister nickname of '*Kopfjäger*' or 'Headhunter'. This was a reference to the SS '*Totenkopf*' or 'Death's Head' skull emblem on their caps, but also to their severe reputation as strict enforcers of military law. They frequently carried out route reconnaissance as an integral part of their overall duties.

SS-Der Führer Battalion. Two more soldiers came out, brandishing their rapid-fire Schmeissers. 'Halt! Halt!' One of them shouted.

Immediately *Anastasie* pulled over to the left, in slight shelter, and shouted: 'Run for it, Jean. You haven't got a weapon. Get out, away from cross-fire and behind the tower!'

Jean did exactly that. Not a shot was fired at him. No one chased him. He ran as fast as he could into Salon-la-Tour, disappearing into the lanes behind the tower.

Both Violette and *Anastasie* started firing from the car.

Anastasie had jumped out first and lay beside the car. Violette had to clamber across from the passenger seat to the driving seat, lugging her Sten and the two magazines of bullets. The windscreen shattered and she fell back against the driving seat. She felt searing pain in her shoulder and blood ran down her left arm. She climbed out and fell beside him, Sten gun in hand, continuing to fire at the soldiers a couple of hundred yards away. Violette and *Anastasie* were in a slight ditch near a farm building that afforded them a little protection for a moment or two.

'Keep firing, *Anastasie*,' shouted Violette as she let rip a volley, hitting at least one soldier. She did not think she had killed him. 'Make every bullet count, if you can. We don't have much ammo. As soon as you're ready, lead the way to give us a chance at escaping. I'll cover you. When I get up to follow, cover me. Proceed as you've been taught by *Clothaire*. Okay?'

'Okay. I'm going through the maize field behind the farmhouse. It'll give a bit of cover for a minute or two.'

They were under strong fire and as *Anastasie* leapt up and made a run for it, Violette aimed and fired a short burst of automatic. Bloody thing's not very effective but it'll keep their heads down while *Anastasie* gets clear, she thought. 'Now!' she shouted as she now leapt up, scooted into the field behind the farmhouse. *Anastasie* covered her. She fired another volley as she reached the field.

The Germans heaved up from behind the crossroads. There were about forty of them. Some remained at their lookout post. The others raced up the road, automatics firing. But Violette and *Anastasie* had a good start and the soldiers were running uphill with heavier weapons. As Violette ran, she heard engines being revved up. She ran on; the Sten gun was heavy and awkward in her hand so she threw the strap over her shoulder without breaking stride.

'God! They've got armoured vehicles, *Anastasie*!' she yelled. 'Quick, deeper into the field. It'll be difficult for them to follow in vehicles. The corn's getting fairly tall, get down on your belly and we'll crawl.'

'Already have,' shouted back *Anastasie*, annoyed by her instructions. He was, after all, no debutant. He was a damned seasoned fighter.

Further down, Madame Marie Verdier, seventy-three years old, emerged from her barn. She was immediately killed by a volley from the nearest soldier. They delayed a few more seconds, unsure how many were in the barn. A sergeant ordered soldiers to get in there and shoot to kill anyone on sight. No one there; just that poor woman. Some people say she came out of the barn hoping to distract the Germans. That is very possible. They shot her anyway.

It has been mooted that the ambush was a company of about 400; probably from Diekmann's SS-2nd Battalion 'Der Führer', but some believe it may have been a company from SS-1st Battalion 'Deutschland'. Both were part of SS-Das Reich Panzer Division and had been looking for the kidnapped officer, Kämpfe.[146] But it appears likely to have been an SS platoon from the Feldgendarmerie stationed in Salon-la-Tour deployed to protect the passage of the SS-Regiment Das Führer and Das Reich Division as it endeavoured to race to Normandy with new orders.

Violette and *Anastasie* crawled through the maize field parallel to the road. It was stifling as they weaved between corn stalks, half-crawling or bent double, running and stumbling through sharp stalks, machine guns heavy in their hands, ready to fire. The corn tore at Violette's bare legs. They maintained their tactic of zigzag, turn, aim, shoot then zigzag again. As she ducked and hid, *Anastasie* did likewise. At the field's border, they stood and ran headlong between the field and the farmhouse.

Violette stumbled into a half-hidden hole. Her ankle gave way painfully. She fell and staggered up, only to fall again. She also became aware of the bullet wound to her shoulder that she'd received as she was escaping from the car. She now noticed blood streaming down her left arm. Her ankle could not support her and she fell again.

'*Anastasie*, my ankle's gone. Can't go much further. Here – take my money belt. Hand it to *Major Staunton* or, if absolutely necessary, *Captain Jack* and no one else! Got it? No one else! Get moving and tell everyone what's happened. Tell them all and especially the *Major* and *Captain Jack* that my mouth will stay firmly shut. Those bastards won't get a word out of me. Tell the *Major* he'll have to get new instructions to *Captain Jack*. Okay?'

'Come on, *Louise*, you can make it. I'll keep you covered. Follow the same pattern – we'll make it!'

'No we won't – but you will. You can see my bloody ankle – it's already swollen! Stop wasting time. I can't keep up with you in this state. I'll get as far as I can. I can still lurch ahead a bit. I'll cover you until I'm out of ammunition. Now, get the hell out of here!'

Crawling proved no use. It was too slow now enemy armoured vehicles were hurtling through the field. *Anastasie* did not know what to do. It was pointless for them both to get killed but how could he leave a girl there to defend herself, and *him*? He ran on and turned to cover her slow stumble, but he could see no alternative – she was right.

---

146 Kämpfe was Diekmann's friend and the much-valued commandant of the SS-Das Reich who had been kidnapped by Guingouin's Maquis and eventually killed.

'Get going, you bloody fool! Don't look at me like that. You look stupid. You know I'm right. Don't even think about it. GET GOING! I'll cover you. I'm going to get down as far as that little tree in the middle of the field. You keep running from behind me. Don't look back.' She laughed then. 'Don't worry, I'll be just fine. You don't have any idea how tough I am. Get back to the *Major*, and tell him what's happened. He'll need to go to *Captain Jack* and *Colonel Berger* himself, as soon as possible. Okay? *Go!*'

So he left, running for his life. He jumped a small brook and ran, stumbling and out of breath. He knew where he was going: to his girlfriend over the other side of the railway bridge, on the high plateau. They wouldn't think of looking for him there. He ran on and on towards the country lane where her parents lived. He could hear the shooting in the distance and then it stopped. Everything was still and quiet but for the rasp of his breathing. He sobbed as he stumbled forward. He arrived on the top road and ran, barely catching breath. He reached the house and shouted, 'Suzanne, It's me. Hide me. Please. Boches are after me!'

His girlfriend came running out, as did her younger sister. Their father and mother followed. They heard vehicles start lumbering up the road from the town in the valley, approaching the bridge across the railway track.

'Quick, quick, Jacques, hide under these logs and faggots,' shouted Suzanne, her eyes large with fright. They all helped to move them; he lay down and they covered him over. He was sobbing uncontrollably at leaving Violette.

‡

Meanwhile, Violette limped and hopped, stumbling and falling, and then ran into the field behind the farmyard belonging to the Montillet family where young Albert Tisserand was staying. Today, it is his farm. He was about seven at the time, playing in the yard when he heard running feet, soldiers shouting in German, shooting, and heavy vehicles snarling through the field of maize. He ran and hid in the barn that looked directly out over the field leading to the orchard.

‡

German soldiers rumbled up to the farm, jumping down into the farmyard from their vehicles. The old iron fence and gate acted as a support to their machine guns. They fired at Violette, their spent cartridges falling around them as she ran, fell, got up, hopped and stumbled and picked herself up again. She made it to an apple tree, far across the field, isolated in a small dip. All the while, she turned and fired to protect *Anastasie* as he ran to the edge of the field and disappeared.

Now she was on her own. She was blisteringly angry. Had that passenger, Jean, or even *Anastasie*, given them away? She thought not. Just bad luck. But she had been right: it really was stupid to be in that great car rather than a truck or on her bike. With a gazogène, they would have had the excuse of travelling with livestock or vegetables. Had it been *Adrien*, he carried all the necessary German documents to get through any roadblocks. They should never have come near a crossroads in a town. Stupid. Stupid. Stupid. She would pay for not listening to her own inner voice. She wondered, fleetingly, why Philippe had sanctioned the car. Same reason as she did, she supposed. She was damned sure, too, that most of these weren't SS-Panzergrenadier. They were Feldgendarmerie – she knew all their bloody uniforms. So how come her team had not been informed where these Germans were stationed? And how come there'd been no intimation of roadblocks in the area? Was it a roadblock or an ambush? Forget it. She had to fight on – and bloody would.

The apple tree wasn't very big, but it gave her some shelter and something to lean against to steady her aim. One or two smaller vehicles and a good number of soldiers had arrived in the farmyard. Larger armoured vehicles blocked the roads and were still trundling about in the fields. An SS-Das Reich forward unit rolled in, wondering just how large the enemy Maquis force was. The soldiers rushed over to the iron rails and gate and took careful aim.

And so, they fought it out. A young woman dressed for summer against grey-green-uniformed military might.

The girl behind a small tree, blood pouring down her arm, running out of bullets and in pain with an ankle that had crippled her. She felt like a trapped animal but she was full of energy, determination and quiet, burning anger. She would not surrender until she had no ammunition. Violette took careful aim and started firing, one bullet at a time. A soldier near the side barn was down. Her spirits soared.

The soldiers fired and missed. Shells were scattered all over the farmyard. They were using rifles now. Her boyfriends had scarpered.

Violette continued taking careful aim with her final magazine of thirty bullets – two bullets were often removed to give added stability to the gun. She husbanded her strength, controlled her breathing and fired only when she was sure she could keep still enough. A few of the bolder men were just beginning to crawl through the grass in front of the farm towards her, but her aim was too good, as evidenced by the wounded men, so most of them waited. The armoured vehicles returned to the roadblock, as did most of the men. About a dozen remained, trying to get closer, their commanding officer overseeing this wasteful endeavour.

Finally, the Sten gun fell silent.

Violette breathed deeply, calmed herself and stood leaning against the tree. And waited. Not one soldier lifted his gun to such an easy target. She had guts, they thought. They edged over the grass toward her, ready to fire if she produced another weapon.

She had no other. Her bag, her suitcase and the bike with a few other things were still with the car. The pistol had disappeared during the chase. Her clothes were filthy and bloody. She calmly waited, her hands at her side, her head held high.

Finally, two or three soldiers stood up and approached her. One grabbed her, pulled her forward and slapped her hard on the face.

'You bitch. You wound some best men. You killed other. This you pay many times,' he said in broken French. He got behind her and started to push roughly her towards the farm. She stumbled forward until they reached the outhouses and barn, from where Albert, the young lad, had seen a good deal. The enemy soldiers shoved her towards one of the remaining vehicles and awaited their commanding officer.

As he arrived, the enemy officer ordered Violette into his armoured car, which already held her suitcase, and they raced along the road on the ridge. When they reached the plateau and as they crossed the bridge, the officer ordered a halt in front of the farmhouse to talk to the farming family standing nervously outside. He jumped down and asked if they had seen a man running.

'Yes,' said the mother, Madame Montintin, a tiny woman of about four feet ten. 'We wondered what was going on so we came out to look. He went down the road, clambered over the railway track and disappeared into the hills.'

'We don't like these young fellas gettin' all excited and bringing reprisals on the likes of us, you know,' complained the diminutive farmer, an inch or two taller than his wife. The two girls looked at one another but they remained silent, not wanting to draw attention to themselves.

Anastasie's girlfriend, Suzanne, suddenly noticed from the corner of her eye that his foot could be seen. His worn boot and part of his ankle were in plain sight through the woodpile. She sauntered over to the stack and she calmly sat on the pile near his foot, covering it with her skirt.

'You'll never catch him now, you dirty scumbags!' shouted Violette, distracting attention from the girl and her movements. Violette was elated at the thought that he had made it and that she had made that happen. They would never find him. She had been exhilarated by the gunfight, knowing she had bested some crack troops. She saw that the ones that weren't local SS-Feldgendarmerie were from the SS-Panzer Division. She'd got through that battle. At least one dead and some badly injured. Herself – only a gunshot wound in her shoulder and a damned useless ankle. That, and running out of ammunition had been all that had stopped her. She had the nasty feeling that something else had led to her capture, though. But what, exactly? She hoped *Anastasie* would report to Philippe later that day what had happened so that new plans could be put into immediate operation.

Violette desperately hoped Philippe and the others would not worry that she would talk. She knew she would not. Just as when she was a child and got hurt she would never cry, merely say she wanted to go *dodo*, the French equivalent for 'sleepy-byes'. The same was true now. She would not surrender any part of her: her loyalty, her mind, her capacity to act, her body. They could take by force the last three, but not the first.

The SS officer looked at her in open admiration, offering her a cigarette by gently placing the filtered end in her mouth. He was sure she could do with one. Her shoulder and foot must be giving her hell. She was dishevelled and dirty with drying blood down her arm and over her legs, but her eyes were shining and she was undaunted.

She spat the cigarette out. And then spat the disgust of years full into his face.

'You're a fiery little thing, aren't you? Can't help but respect your pluck, *mademoiselle*.' He clicked his heels in salute, bending slightly towards her. Finally, he said, 'You will come now with us as our prisoner to the Tivoli, the Gestapo headquarters in Limoges.'

‡

33

Arrested, Maison d'Arrêt de Limoges, the Tivoli and Huguette Deshors

Friday 10 June to Wednesday 15 June 1944

'Women were not exempted from torture. Usually upon them the tortures were most odious.'

From *Inside SOE* by E.H. Cookridge (1966)

After running from the car, Jean Bariaud heard the shooting continue for a good twenty minutes. It seems he had to walk the fifteen miles to Anna Ribiéras to warn Philippe so that the local Maquis could try to do something about:

```
freeing Szabo and Dufour. The only thing he was positive
about was that he had heard firing going on for over half-an-
hour while he was escaping through the woods …
```

as reported by Philippe in his PF.[147] Jean's trek would not have completely exhausted him, as he was fit, but he may have experienced some discomfort for, as he told the author in 2004, he had been in the French army on the Maginot Line in 1940, and, apparently wounded, sent home to Croisille to recuperate. He remained there, helping his father. What else he did is hard to say. It was many hours later that he reached Philippe in Sussac to tell him of the disastrous turn of events.

Anastasie stayed hidden under the logs until after nightfall, afraid that the Germans might return if they decided the farmer had not told the truth. They would not have been gentle to the farmer and his family. When *Anastasie* emerged from his hiding place, they all discussed his predicament while he gulped down food and coffee. He was still dirty and sweat-stained from the exertion of running and crawling through the densely growing maize, then running for another two miles over very rough terrain, mostly uphill.

The mayor of Salon-la-Tour, Monsieur Montelly, had been compelled to hand over the *Hôtel de Ville* to the Feldgendarmerie for its local HQ prior to June. The mayor's son, a child of ten at the time, saw the mêlée in the town on that hot

---

147 PF = Each agent had a Personal File. Many are held at the National Archives in Kew.

afternoon, when, apart from the presence of the SS-Feldgendarmerie, part of the SS-Regiment 'Das Führer' swept into the town square. German ambulances were in attendance and a number of injured German soldiers were on stretchers or standing and sitting around. *Colonel Rivier,* later to become General Rousselier, recipient of the Compagnon de la Libération medal, reports in his citation to Violette that she had certainly killed a German corporal. It was obvious to him that the casualties in the square were the direct result of the encounter between Violette and the SS platoon.

When Philippe later spoke to some of the people in Salon-la-Tour he was told that the Germans had taken *Anastasie* prisoner as well as Violette. The Germans had deliberately passed this piece of disinformation around, and Bariaud also told those he met that that was what had happened. Reports have it that the Germans broadcast it about that, 'We caught the lad later in the woods. We've certainly got him.'

Philippe waited anxiously for *Anastasie's* report but when he did not return from what they believed would be an uneventful journey, he became seriously concerned. There was not a lot Philippe could do but wait for news while he continued implementing his plans. Losing Violette was a major disaster to the *Salesman II* circuit's activities and Philippe knew he or one of his men must get down to Jacques Poirier (*Capitaine Jack*) as a priority before going to the north of the region.

Why did *Anastasie* not, as was his first duty, immediately report to Philippe or at least get a message to him? Instead, he spent a few days hidden in the warehouse of an uncle's timber and machine business not far from Salon-la-Tour railway station. Monsieur Montelly, the son of the mayor, explained to me years later that *Anastasie* hid for an unknown number of days in amongst farm equipment in a large barn. He mentioned that, if he recollected correctly, it was the huge warehouse and timber yard at Salon-la-Tour railway station that belonged to Jacques' father, Jacque. *Anastasie,* was acutely aware that Philippe would be furious at his abysmal failure to drive Violette safely at least to Uzerche, a little over half-way to Arnac-Pompadour. He did not reappear for about four or five days, not just one night, justifying it by saying the Germans were still on the lookout for him and he already had a price on his head.

However, the first and most basic task that was expected of him was that he report immediately to Violette's commanding officer in the Sussac safe-house, indirectly through a third person if necessary. In Sussac, he would have been afforded all the protection possible. Was he too ashamed to face Philippe, as *Major Charles Staunton,* his military superior?[148] Had he decided to put a deadly spoke into the communist wheel? No one has clarified what exactly had happened.

---

148 It happened that, years later, Jean Bariaud, the man who had run away, told my companion, Paul E.F. Holley, and me in his family home in Croisille-sur-Briance, *'J'ai honte! J'ai honte! On aurait dû la sauver.'* That is, 'I'm ashamed! I'm ashamed! We should have saved her.' Maybe, as Huguette says, the two men ran away together and only Violette was there with her Sten gun! Maybe I should ignore the supposed verbal report. Maybe …

Anastasie would not have wished to speak to Philippe again. He had sent a hot-headed report to London, listing his deep dissatisfaction with Philippe and complaining how Philippe only helped the communists. He left the area, he wrote in his report, to go south to join other Maquis groups. The village people told us that after the war, he went to Vietnam, Cambodia and Laos, where he was killed. He was later buried with honour in Salon-la-Tour.

Philippe, in one of his debriefings after the war, reported that *Anastasie* only gave him a verbal report, which he wrote down later from memory. His memory did not serve him well in that the report stated that *Anastasie* said Violette was exhausted, or *Anastasie* was clearly not telling the truth. Hot as it was, Violette had far more stamina than twenty to thirty minutes' racing through maize fields. However, the word in French for 'exhausted' also means, 'short of' or 'out of', in this case, ammunition. Philippe's written English is very good, but often has areas of French syntax and wording.

Philippe received information the day after Violette's arrest, that is, the afternoon of Saturday 11 June, from two men in the Limoges Résistance force, who came specifically to see him. Bariaud eventually did meet with Philippe to recount his story. They told him that she had indeed been arrested – along with *Anastasie*. Jean-Claude Guiet reported the following, 'We also sent our courier, *Corinne*, [i.e. *Louise*] to contact the organiser of Dordogne. The day after she left we received news that she had been captured by the Germans.'

Jean-Claude makes no mention of *Anastasie* being arrested, although he does say that they all moved out of Limoges into the hills after Violette's arrest, as it would be safer for them. It was the Maquis and Limoges Résistance who suggested that a rescue attempt just might be possible. When Philippe asked about *Anastasie*, they replied there had just been the young woman. They reported to him that they had seen her 'limping badly', being dragged along by her assailants. For all that, as the 'beautiful girl' was pulled along, they said, she carried her head high and with dignity.

For the next several hours, two French Résistants from Limoges and a few of the local Sussac men in the Résistance talked with Philippe about how they would plan her escape. Philippe was distraught. He knew he should not have let Violette go in that damned car. He was also desperately angry at the delay in their plans caused by her arrest. Apart from Jean-Claude Guiet assiduously sending messages to London from his safe-house, he had lost his most valuable team member; Violette, as his courageous liaison officer would have achieved much in unifying the Maquis forces, leaving him the time to orchestrate instructions from London. He would now have to travel down to Arnac-Pompadour himself, as well as try to spring some sort of rescue attempt. He was not hopeful of success.

It was the two French Résistants who did most of the planning for a rescue attempt. The men all knew it would be extremely difficult if not impossible to realise. Jean-Claude Guiet explained years later, 'What Philippe Liewer's final statement to Dufour's [verbal] report does not state was that for several weeks we were in contact with one of the French jailers who led us on to believe she was still in Limoges and accepted money to help Violette and provide information. It brought back some bitter memories.'

Limoges prison was full and held important resistance leaders who had been captured. They were all dragged back and forth for interrogation sessions to the Gestapo HQ in Impasse Tivoli. Harry Peulevé suffered a similar horrendous fate to Violette's, here in Limoges.

The first step was to set up a watch of the Gestapo headquarters and the prison to check on her journeys between the two. Philippe asked the Résistants to deal with the escape plan as new and unfamiliar faces such as his and Bob's could attract unwanted attention. Bob was given the task of staying in very close touch with them while he contacted other local groups for further armed backup in the rescue attempt.

The distance from Gestapo headquarters to the prison in Limoges is roughly a kilometre. High walls, depressingly blank and grey, the prison is forbidding in its ugliness, even today. It faces onto a paved square with a few scrawny trees.

On some days at eleven in the morning and four in the afternoon, Violette exited from Limoges prison by a side door escorted by German SS soldiers and was taken by car or frog-marched across a kilometre of town to Gestapo headquarters at the end of the Impasse Tivoli. The Limogeois have changed the name of the cul-de-sac to that of Impasse Saint-Exupéry and demolished the house of horrors. It was a substantial three-storey house, guarded by the Gestapo twenty-four hours a day.

The SS-Hauptsturmführer questioned Violette on each visit. These visits would last from one to two hours, sometimes more. Then she was returned to the jail. They already knew that her name was *Vicky Taylor* and that she came from London and an agent for SOE. She therefore continued to give her name as *Vicky Taylor*. How did they have it? From London or France?

Opposite the prison was the Wehrmacht HQ for the German army and close by the French Milice premises. Although only two guards accompanied her, any rescue attempt faced the problem that there were always German soldiers, Milice, Gestapo, SD officers and armed personnel going about their activities in the square itself or passing through.

‡

Having had his platoon of experienced, SS soldiers so ignominiously held at bay by the accomplished shooting and spirit of Violette, the SS officer did not relish reporting the event to his superiors, nor that his dignity had been roundly attacked on the railway bridge in front of his men by this mere slip of a girl. He would have been loath to admit that Violette had, with her one shaky Sten gun and ninety bullets, held up for around half an hour an SS-Feldgendarmerie unit of at least forty men possessed of machine guns and a unit of an advanced guard of the SS-Regiment Das Führer with armoured vehicles. Nor would his superior officers have been keen to report the incident. Soldiers might bear being shot and wounded by a sole individual under combat conditions, but by a young, lone woman, and clearly wounded – that was shameful and intensely discomforting. Better forget the incident ever took place. All over the region, too, the Germans were constantly under sniper fire, sabotage and inveigled into deadly skirmish after deadly skirmish. Most incidents were never reported by the Germans, and often not reported by the French or British either.

It was the country folk who filled in the details of the actions of '*la p'tite Anglaise*' against some of the best troops of Nazi Germany. They told not only Philippe but also many people who came after the war to discover what had happened, including R.J. Minney, her biographer in 1956, Squadron Leader Edward 'Ted' Crawfurd and my grandparents with me in 1963 and my later visits including with Paul Emile. During those early post-war years the still young or middle-aged villagers and farmers were alive and only too happy to talk of the remarkable '*p'tite Anglaise*' and her courageous demeanour and actions.

Georges Guingouin and Jacques Valéry were instrumental in ensuring a monument to Violette was erected. Jacques Valéry's father had been in the Résistance, and he has dedicated his own life to ensuring that the Maquis of the Limousin will be remembered for the courage they showed and battles they fought to return France to freedom; many other folk of the Haute-Vienne campaigned until they had a monument erected to Violette close to Mont Gargan, the spiritual home of the Maquis. Every June, the people of the Limousin commemorate her life and courage, as they do all the Maquis, first at her monument and then by climbing to the top of Mont Gargan for their final commemorative ceremonies.

There were many extremely courageous Résistants in the Haute-Vienne, willing put their lives on the line. Their brave acts tend to be neglected or overlooked because they were mostly communists in the Haute-Vienne.

It took Violette's father, angry and distressed, agonising for months to get any information at all from the authorities on the fate of his daughter, while his wife suffered great anguish. Vera Atkins considered him a danger as he went to the newspapers, trying to discover what had happened or where she might be. Vera even described him as a 'despicable little man'. Charlie Bushell went to the press simply because the Red Cross had provided no information or help, nor had any of the agencies of the armed forces, or the government and its bureaux, nor any member of SOE. They simply did not want to disturb the status quo. At last, Vera Atkins was moved to try to discover what had happened to 'her' missing girls. It must be said that it also suited her career and ambitions to visit the Nuremburg prisoners awaiting trial for crimes against humanity. But she did a superb job and with great sincerity, being utterly dedicated to it.

The Maquis group in Limoges did plot a rescue plan. Philippe agreed it and arranged for Bob Maloubier to go to Limoges to meet with the four men who had done all the groundwork and would deal with the guards. Tommy guns supplied by Bob were essential, as was transport. Bob arranged for a second car with six armed men to deal with the soldiers at the exits of the town. They expected a fight.

The day chosen was Thursday 16 June, six long days after her capture, arrest and incarceration in Limoges prison. That morning, early, she was gone. To Gestapo headquarters in Avenue Foch in Paris.

To this day, Violette's daughter, the author, remains bemused. Why has Bob Maloubier refused to tell her what he knows, but does talk to the media on Violette's capture? Has he spoken, faintly, through Huguette Deshors?

‡

I met Huguette Deshors, a young Résister and now a retired school teacher.

This is what she told me of Violette's time in Limoges prison and I translate her words into the third person. From 1 April 1944, Huguette and her mother had shared a cell with eight other women in that part of Limoges prison reserved for the use of the Gestapo. She was about sixteen years old. She knew her brother was doing something in the Résistance and she had helped. It was not unusual for the young to be involved in some way, usually delivering verbal messages. Huguette told me very little of why she was there, nor anything about her suffering and that of the other women. Violette was her companion, her friend and her sister and that is about whom she wished to speak.

One morning in June 1944, she is not sure when, but probably the 8th, she was separated from her companions by two impressively armed 'verts-de-gris'.[149] She was alone after that, in a filthy narrow cell. The only 'luxury' was a bedstead with one single blanket, a jug of water, a sort of hollow plate and a lavatory hole. No towel, not even soap. The casement was solidly barred but no glass; it was terribly chilly at night. The only thing to look at was the high grey wall, not the slightest bit of sky.

It was there that Violette arrived. Huguette does not remember exactly for how many days because in prison the notion of time is very quickly lost. Huguette says they shared everything, the same concerns, the same humiliations, and the same suffering. Huguette had only been subjected to two interrogations (the word 'only' is hers, not mine), just after she had been captured. The Gestapo were not

---

149 Verts de gris = in French slang for the Germans. Vert = green, ver = worm (both pronounced the same). Gris = grey (the colour or Wehrmacht uniforms).

really interested in her, 'I was only small fry.' For Violette it was quite different. Violette was interrogated every day. The two jailers were nicknamed the 'two robots' by the inmates and they would take Violette away and bring her back during the afternoon.

Huguette says she remembers Violette's arrival perfectly, two days after her solitary confinement began. One afternoon – this would have been the afternoon of Saturday 10 June 1944 – the dreaded footsteps stopped outside her cell. This pounding of boots governed the prisoners' lives; they were always on the alert for them. What a relief when they moved on, 'Phew! It's not for us!'

When the stamp of military steps came to a halt and the door opened, Huguette got up and turned to the wall, looking down. That was the rule. This humiliating stance had become a conditioned reflex. In the crack of the half-opened door, Huguette could glimpse a navy blue skirt. She says she almost collapsed with fear, expecting insults and blows from the navy-uniformed guards. But no, the door had already closed again and she heard someone say, '*Bonjour*, I've just been arrested by the Gestapo'. The SS and the Gestapo were twin servants of horror and both names were used by those outside the occupation forces quite indiscriminately.

'I'm *Magda*,[150] and who are you?'

Huguette had great difficulty hiding her emotions. A pretty young woman held out her hand. She wore a dark blue skirt, Huguette said, and added that Bob Maloubier would be pleased to hear that detail on clothing as he had completely forgotten it.

Huguette was so relieved it was not the fearsome Panther[151] but this new young woman she would soon be calling Vicky and become a real friend to. The navy suit that Violette wore was of very light material, under which she wore a white shirt. She did not wear stockings but peep-toe slightly wedged sandals. Huguette remembers them as flat-heeled and that it had rained. The two women immediately sat side by side on the bedstead and started to get to know one another.

‡

The door soon opened again, but without the awful warning from the boots. This time it was Satan in person who came in; black-uniformed, perhaps an officer – Huguette was not sure. This was, in fact, SS-Hauptsturmführer Aurel Kowatsch,[152] who had returned from overseeing the ninety-nine hangings selected by SD official

---

150 Magda Valetas was the name of a pharmacist in Tulle at that time and although it seems doubtful that Violette had been there, she may have acquired this woman's identity as an extra cover. Maybe Violette had simply seen the name and decided to use it.

151 Panther = one of the more ferocious female guards, silent when wishing to inflict a surprise attack.

152 SS-Das Reich 1c (3rd General Staff officer, responsible for intelligence).

Walter Schmald and carried out by the Pioneer platoon of SS–Panzer Aufklarungs Abteilung 2 in Tulle the day before.[153]

Without saying a word, he planted himself in front of Violette, who remained seated. For an endless moment, they measured up to one another with a stare. Huguette says she was terrified, how could she make '*Magda*' understand that she should stand up, not remain seated? Huguette was hypnotised by the enormous revolver the officer carried on his hip. The scene was so intense that it is still just as clear to her today as it was then.

He leaned towards Violette with a sardonic smile, that of the victor before its prey. Very proud, seemingly very calm, Violette never moved a millimetre away; she seemed to defy him. After this incredible and silent confrontation, he left, as he had entered, without a word.

Huguette muttered, 'Oh, I'm so scared … for you. You've to stand when they come in, otherwise they just hit out.' Her new friend simply shrugged her shoulders and smiled at her without comment, but Huguette felt the pressure of Violette's hand on hers. During Huguette's moments of discouragement and fear, Violette always gave her that comforting touch of the hand. It was more eloquent than any words could be.

A little later, a fat young woman came in – as wide as she was tall (*la Bonbonne*[154]) – full of jokes, seemingly delighted to be there. Her totally relaxed attitude was so surprising in such a place that she was immediately suspect to Huguette. She had, the woman said, been arrested for no reason in a street in Limoges. She then questioned them rather clumsily so Huguette knew she was a mole. No doubt Violette was of the same opinion.

Almost immediately, laughing, with her loud vulgar voice the fat woman burst out, 'Hey girls, have you been raped yet? No? That's a surprise! Girls like you! You're going to be put through the wringer. All the women are, at the Tivoli. Do you know about the Tivoli? It won't be long.' She did not get the tiniest response from Violette, even though she persisted. The horror and panic she instilled into Huguette clearly delighted her.

Huguette brought up this detail, she says, because she thinks rape is the worst possible sort of torture. It is possible that such a 'mole' was inserted to do exactly what it did to Huguette but on the surface failed to do to Violette. Courage, after all, is the defeat of fear, and Violette had proved many times she was very good at that. Huguette wanted me to understand why she believed, the evening Violette

---

153 This information on Kowatsch I received from the author of *Das Reich*, Philip Vickers, in his fax to me on 19 June 2000. I have since researched this back to discover the SD man Aurel Kowatsch was sentenced to death in 1951 in absentia. Philip provided me with much information when Paul Holley and I stayed in his lovely French home not far from Angoulême.
154 Bonbonne = carboy, i.e. a large globular glass or plastic corrosive liquid container, usually protected by a wooden casing; a large flagon.

came back later than usual, that she had been subjected to that very cruel assault. Violette *never* told her that, Huguette said. Huguette then begged my forgiveness for having recently revealed this to someone who then betrayed her confidence.[155]

She went on to say that the fear of sexual violation was why the sound of the boots made the female prisoners' hearts leap into their mouths. If what Huguette has written to me in all the above seems obscure or vague it is because she did not wish to admit, even in writing to me, that Violette might have been sexually violated, raped, on her forced visits to the Gestapo headquarters sometimes twice a day, sometimes for the entire day. It would have been unusual had she not been subjected to some sort of sexual humiliation. As Cookridge said, 'Women were not exempted from torture. Usually upon them the tortures were most odious.'

One night Huguette was lay awake waiting for the mole's snoring, then she gently shook Violette. Violette was deeply asleep and woke up with a jump. It was the only time Huguette saw fear in her eyes. 'She's a mole, you talked too much,' said Huguette.

Violette replied, 'I know.' She shrugged her shoulders and went back to sleep.

‡

The next day this fishwife, as Huguette called her, left and Violette surprised Huguette by revealing, 'I didn't tell her anything that the Gestapo don't know! They know perfectly who I am ... there's a traitor in the circuit!' She sat down next to Huguette in the corner, which became 'her' corner.

'I can still see her there. Like that, we were almost face-to-face' Huguette said to me. When Huguette was taken back to the cell in recent years for a television interview about Violette, she said she could see her so clearly in her imagination, sitting there in 'her' corner, that Huguette broke down and cried.

Violette told Huguette that she had been on a mission, accompanied by two men. She had been going as far as Pompadour. When she saw the '*traction*'[156] at the T-junction she immediately understood that they had been expected. The three of them jumped out, she said to Huguette. The two men fled on one side. She started shooting and went on shooting. She had to protect them and hoped they'd been able to get away.

Huguette learned years later through Bob Maloubier that Violette's ankle had been injured and therefore forced her to capitulate. Violette, Huguette says, 'never told me, she never complained, yet she must certainly have been suffering. The

---

155 Huguette is referring here to a television programme that did not take sufficient care in how they filmed her, the questions they asked and her responses along with their voice-overs. I was informed that there was no recording preserved of what she actually said in French. Where it is translated, it is unclear and is very upsetting and distressing to Huguette.

156 '*Traction*' = light armoured vehicle during the war. Today, a 4×4 or jeep.

cell was so narrow that you could hardly move around in it so I had never seen her walk.'

Bob Maloubier may not have known that Violette's ankle had been severely damaged at Ringway when she was practising her parachute jumps. It was so severely injured that she had to convalesce in Bournemouth in a wheelchair. That ankle gave further trouble when she landed at Le Clos on the night of 7 to 8 June, but it was not too severe so she was able to hide it. It was this ankle that let her down as her foot went into a hole running across the field.

Huguette listened to her. She often saw Violette deep in thought, taking her head in her hands and murmuring as if she were convincing herself, 'There's a traitor in the circuit.' On one of the days, Huguette says, Violette confided that she had travelled around in Corrèze with the identity of a pharmacist from Tulle: *Madame Valetas*. Huguette knew the chemist's shop well, but not the chemist. 'I'd really like to know if I look like her,' Violette said.

After the Liberation, when Huguette had been freed, she made a point of going into Tulle and, of course, to the chemist's shop. Madame Valetas was dark haired, but she did not look like Violette. Huguette said she should have asked the pharmacist, 'Do you know *Magda*? Or *Louise*? Or *Corinne*? Or *Violette*?' But she did not dare. Everyone was still very circumspect, said Huguette, and so they remain today.

In their prison cell the women were woken at dawn by shouts from a loudspeaker. They were meant to get up immediately but they obeyed the call only when they heard the pounding of boots stop before their cell and the first bolt drawn. After the warder had passed, they got back on the bed and went back to sleep.

They shared the same bed (the mole's palliasse had disappeared with her); a bedstead for one person. They slept back to back against one another, forced to sleep on their side. Huguette only realised much later that Violette probably had the worst place, between Huguette and the wall, where it was impossible for her to stretch out to relieve any stiffness.

They kept their clothes on; Violette would take off her jacket but kept on her skirt and white blouse. They spread the only blanket over the bedstead; it was summertime and although the nights could be cold, they had the warmth of one another's bodies to combat the chill.

They did not have the same tasks as the other prisoners, so they were very isolated. Huguette goes on to say that a jug was placed in a hatch in the door. They got four boiled potatoes a day delivered by the two 'robot' staff, who were wooden faced and silent. That was all they had to sustain them. They shared a bowl to drink from. One day they received an unexpected supplement: a sort of sticky greenish slice of bread. They tasted it, and it was utterly disgusting, inedible even for someone starving.

During one interrogation, Violette protested about their conditions. She had, she told Huguette, obtained a metal mug, some linen and soap. It was wonderful news. Huguette was already dreaming about soapy foam and a good scrub to get rid of the filth as she was terribly aware that she smelled bad and felt humiliated by it. She had worn the same clothes for three months. She did have a piece of cloth that her mother had torn off a shirt to use as a flannel. That simple rag was a precious thing; it allowed her to have the meanest of washes over her body. With no soap it had become yellow, dirty and smelly. Violette had a handkerchief to wash herself with. So as not to dirty the water in the jug, they wet their 'precious rags' over the lavatory hole, wringing them out carefully to spread over the jug's top.

The day they were separated, they both received a *quart* –a sort of iron mug that army people carry on their belt – a piece of soap and a towel. When one of the 'robots' presented these longed-for items, the two girls immediately got undressed to use them, but were soon disappointed. The soap was like a beach pebble and the towel was coarse and hard. It was apparently a gift from the Red Cross.

Huguette had already noticed that, like her, Violette had a few red wheals – marks, she assumed, from the Panther's riding crop. They simply said to one another, 'You, too?' That second feeling of emotion shared was powerful; it made them fellow sufferers. Huguette assured me that she had not seen any deep wounds or sores on Violette. On the other hand, Violette may well not have revealed how wounded or painful any particular part of her body was. She might have done this not only to appear brave and keep up Huguette's spirits, but also because diminishing the importance or ignoring pain does make it more bearable. They were not allowed to join the circular walks in the yard. Huguette would have loved to catch sight of her mother, even at a distance.

In the afternoon, when the clicking of boots stopped in front of their cell, Violette pressed Huguette's hand. 'That's for me. Don't move!' She said. She was standing even before Huguette could react, to minimise Huguette's fear. Huguette just sat worrying until Violette returned. She followed Violette in her thoughts and could not help imagining the most monstrous of things. When Violette returned, she looked just as calm, still just as impenetrable and silent.

'What did they do to you?'

'They interrogated me.'

‡

Their long hours of solitude were filled with conversations, but also with long periods of silence, each of them isolated in their thoughts.

Violette never told Huguette that she had a daughter. That hurt Huguette's feelings when she finally discovered that fact, when she saw me on a television programme. It made her feel that Violette had never truly confided in her. Poor Huguette, still a teenager, had not yet learned that some things were not for telling, that Violette was protecting her child and her family. She would have been remiss in telling Huguette too much, things that maybe the Germans did not know. All she told her were things the Germans already knew. But Violette would have been grateful to Huguette for her company during those six days of hell. Huguette thought that it may have been longer.

Huguette was unsure whether to recount the episode that follows. It was so unexpected but genuine, as unreal as it was.

One evening Violette was returned to the cell rather later than usual. Huguette had not waited for her to eat her two potatoes; she was just too hungry. As Huguette apologised, Violette put the remaining potatoes in Huguette's hands, saying, 'Take them, you can eat them without feeling guilty. I'm not hungry! Eat them ...' The offer was so tempting that Huguette readily admitted that it was difficult to resist. They decided instead to hide the two precious potatoes under the blanket for a time when they might really be starving. So as not to crush them while they slept, they put them in the bowl. The very next morning the potatoes became their breakfast and, of course, they shared, one each.

Violette had, it seemed to Huguette, lost a little of her usual calm that night. She shrugged her shoulders, 'Something unimaginable happened to me! He was furious tonight, crazy and furious, unbelievably worked up.' Violette only called him *he* or 'the interrogator'. 'He yelled, "I admire you, I admire you and I cannot stop myself liking you, but if tomorrow I get the order to execute you I will do it without any soul-searching."'

By her quite extraordinary courage, by her heroic resistance and by her beauty, Violette had troubled a monster.

Violette never told Huguette what the officer did to her during those many interrogations. But women are always vulnerable in certain areas.

‡

At dawn one day, even before the loudspeakers called, they were roused from their sleep and dragged to the ground floor, pushed without ceremony up against one of the casements to look out onto the yard.

Suddenly, in the silence, steps rang out in the yard – marching soldiers. In the space of a second, Huguette felt irrational hope leap up, 'They've landed. The Americans have landed!' The hope that US paratroopers had landed in Haute-Vienne quickly dissipated.

Male voices sang the '*Chant du Départ*'[157] 'Do or Die'. Violette took her hand, holding it very tightly. In the same moment, wrote Huguette, they had both just understood what was happening. Silhouettes passed in the hazy gleam of dawn. Five Résistants were lined up against the wall. Five young people could just be made out in the gloom. In front of them, a machine gun. A soldier kneeling.

They cried out, '*Vive la France!*'

---

157 *Chant du Départ* = Song of Departure.

Huguette closed her eyes. An enormous explosion resounded from the spitting machine gun. This new and terrible image, impossible to erase from memory, shook them to the core. Even today, Huguette cannot bear the noise of firearms, or firecrackers or a car backfiring.

It was not their turn. They were returned to their cell. They never touched on what they had witnessed. No need for words to share the horror. But Violette held her hand.

One of the warders – who was from Lorraine, Huguette learned later – went off, muttering, 'Frenchmen are killing Frenchmen – it's not the Germans!' Not all guards were German but the Nazis drafted Frenchmen from Alsace and Lorraine.

This was indeed the case. Some of the communists and Gaullists did waste life, energy and ammunition fighting each other. The preparations made by people like Charles de Gaulle, *Passy*, Jean Moulin, André Malraux and Georges Guingouin helped to bring the many different factions together in order to form a Gaullist government after liberation. Throughout the following years they had many tough political fights with the communists. Here, in the prison yard, it was the French Garde Mobile or Milice executing their fellow citizens.

Three days, Huguette thinks, before they separated, Violette came back very subdued. She just dropped next to Huguette in her corner. Huguette asked the usual question, like a ritual,

'What did they do to you today?'

Violette closed her eyes and passed her hands across her face.

'It's horrible! Tonight they found the way to make me talk. They tortured a young man to death. He was one of ours.' She also said that she had so far not given any word of truth to her interrogators. Bob Maloubier does not agree. 'She did not know anyone,' he told Huguette. However, Huguette says she had written her account of this in the notebook that she wrote in December 1944. In that month, her memory was still very fresh; she couldn't have fabricated this. It seems to me that this victim could so easily have been a young Résister like Michel. Violette did not need to know him personally, just that he was 'one of ours'. There were so many like him, including Huguette's own brother.

Bob was mistaken in saying that Violette did not know anyone. How could she not? Violette had had two days full of meetings with the Maquis in the surrounding areas. She knew not only her own team but also a couple of dozen Maquis members, and the Maquis reception committee.

Huguette recalls Violette saying, 'They did not stop whipping him, hitting him with gun butts. They pulled out his nails. His face was streaming with blood. He no longer looked human, but his eyes were begging me. What were they telling me? "Speak, speak I beg you" or "Don't speak"? I don't know. I just don't know.'

That night they did not sleep. They stayed for a long time just sitting together. Huguette heard her murmur, 'London has surely been warned now. It's more than a week; they've had time to change their code. It can't be important any more. It's just unbearable, that kind of horror. They'll start again tomorrow. Will I be strong enough to hold back vital information like that?'

Several times, she asked Huguette, 'Do you think that London's been warned?'

She replied, 'I don't know, *Magda*. I'm not in a position to know.'

Violette understood that by asking Huguette she was seeking comfort but she felt she should be stronger than that. She knew that Philippe would have warned everybody. Although she carried very useful information, most of it would have already been useless to the Germans within forty-eight hours or so. At each question, she had told a close approximation to the truth, but with times, places and activities all jumbled up so that German resources would be used in one place uselessly while sabotage took place as planned elsewhere. This was a tactic she had learned as a student at the SOE schools – and she was particularly good at it.

Bob Maloubier told Huguette that London had been warned the morning that Violette had been captured. It was one of the first things Philippe ordered Jean-Claude Guiet to do, as Jean-Claude's messages show. However, it would have been much later in the day, not the morning after Violette's capture that he could get the message across to warn all the circuits. Nevertheless, Violette knew that she had to keep silent, no matter what, for at least forty-eight hours. She would try for longer, as extra time for her people could save someone's life. She had refused to carry the L-pill – the pill containing a lethal dose of cyanide that kills instantly, an eternal release from either intense fear or intense suffering. Those that took it usually had it fixed into their mouth in a special pouch. Violette had made her decision, had to do without. She plumbed the depths to find enough courage to prevail.

The next day, when Violette came back for the last time, she seemed very serious but perfectly calm. She had just signed her death warrant, she knew that immediately. 'That's it. They have what they wanted. There would have been other tortures, other useless deaths. They're taking me to Austria. To a fortress. They'll shoot me. They don't shoot women in France.' Her words to Huguette were not quite true but protected her people.

Huguette, after reporting Violette's words, said, 'She didn't have time to sit down next to me as usual. The warders were already there, marching her off, still mute, but without violence. The second one moved aside to let her pass.' She was struck by this attitude and added, 'Perhaps it was true, that he felt a certain respect, a certain admiration for her.'

The two girls hugged one another hard. Violette muttered, 'Courage!' In the doorway, she turned round. She smiled at Huguette and very discreetly waved.

Huguette was all alone again, completely isolated, terrorised by the clicking boots, for three or four days – she was no longer sure how long – she was forgotten even, no food. She broke her nails on the *cordes* of the bedstead trying to make a noose to hang herself from the bars of the window.

‡

Huguette told me what it felt like facing death in such circumstances. She said, 'Ah well, when there was gunfire, for the dawn execution of five Maquisards, I trembled at first, but when I thought the fatal moment had arrived, I felt nothing, no fear. Totally accepted it. Absolute calm. A sort of anaesthetic perhaps, by the grace of God, I should think.' But she had not faced that gunfire herself.

Afterwards, she was taken to another cell, with 'Simone la Marseillaise', a big-hearted prostitute, for company. Condemned to death these final days, they both escaped the execution wall by an unbelievable miracle, it seemed to them.

Huguette said that she had been able to hold on to her sanity, thanks to Violette's fine example. She had, in some way, inoculated Huguette with some of her pride, and stoicism. Huguette told me she accepted every moment of suffering, every humiliation thinking about her – without tears. Nor are there from me as I write this – but very nearly!

She closes by saying that Violette had sacrificed herself even when she was sure that she would not be putting her circuit in danger. She wanted an end to the poor boy's agonising suffering and to save others' lives.

‡

34

Limoges to Avenue Foch and More Interrogation

Friday 17 June 1944 onwards

At dawn on 17 June, Violette was taken to a communal shower room of Limoges prison, given back her belongings, told to shower, dress and comb her hair. The shower was heaven, even though the water was cold and the soap hard. She felt clean for the first time since 10 June. Imprisonment had not been a great shock, nor had Violette expected it to be.

She had been conveyed to the prison, that hot afternoon of Friday the 10th, in a staff car of the Waffen-SS (SS militarised unit). SS-Sturmbannführer Kowatsch, stationed in Limoges as an interpreter with the SS-Das Reich Panzer Division, had also been in the vehicle.

Violette was delivered over to the SD or Gestapo. At the Kommandandeur des SD in Limoges was a good-looking man in his forties, SS-Obersturmbannführer Nummer-73073, August Meier. This man spoke no language other than German, having been educated at a trade school, became a young businessman and then, after normal military service, entered the ranks of the SS. To interrogate his prisoners he used the interpretation skills of his colleague and friend Kowatsch, who later claimed that SOE agent *Louise* had been treated with respect and supplied with clean clothes before being handed over to the SD. This may have been true briefly; however, once with the SD, things were different as Huguette's account attests, along with those of so many other men and women who suffered under their hands in Limoges, including Harry Peulevé.

Her lack of shock and her calm demeanour was due in no small part to the fact that, at the SOE training schools, potential agents were duly warned and trained under pretty rough conditions for such an eventuality. No, not shocked after her six days' incarceration but nevertheless deeply distressed and in considerable pain from internal contusions and ripped skin. Her shoulder was healing but remained sore. The welts from the Panther and interrogations were still an angry red.

Violette found it laughable that Kowatsch, Schmald and Meier would think her shamed and intimidated by being stripped naked before them and then savagely questioned. She dealt with their physical offences against her with stoicism. She bore the degradations that followed with great dignity while giving nothing away.

The three men, on the other hand, knew that they had instantly lost their dignity before her. They knew, too, that she knew. They had to face the scorn flowing from her beautiful eyes. It roused them to rage and immense frustration. They could not help but wonder, albeit subconsciously, who truly had the upper hand.

The rather grand Gestapo office used for interrogations was part of the process to diminish these 'peasants' in the face of grandeur and power. In the photo, you can see the arrogance in Meier's eyes. During these interrogations, seated behind a large, overly ornate desk, he explained gently at first that he wished to know what plans were being implemented by the Maquis to prevent the free movement of the German SS-Das Reich armoured forces through the region. On the wall was a large map with pins of various colours over the entire region from Châteauroux through the Haute-Vienne and down as far as Montauban. The roads and railway lines were well marked and Meier invited Violette to join him at the map and show him where the Maquis, parachute troops, SOE agents and Jedburghs would strike and where and when the Allies would fly bombing raids on the installations used by the Germans.

She refused.

Confronted by her silence and disdain, some of the frustration and strength of feeling of these three men against Maquis activity was vented on this brave young woman.

She endured.

The beatings and other indecent tortures were harsh but not unendurable as her tormentors wished to leave no permanent evidence of their assaults upon her. However, when SS-Obersturmbannführer Meier, Kommandatur der Sicherheitspolizei in Limoges, had failed so miserably he found a way almost to crush her. His minions were ordered to bring in a young man. They forced her to watch that poor boy being beaten to within an inch of his life. The thought of another youngster being brought in had all but destroyed her. Still, Violette knew that she had given nothing of substance away, and she took strength from that. She endured, even though it was well after the forty-eight-hour period agents should endeavour to withstand, after which they were permitted by their SOE masters to give way if things were unbearable.

The SS officers had not succeeded in their given task. They were subsequently ordered, none too kindly, to have her taken to 86 Avenue Foch in Paris. There she would be questioned by the SD. No doubt that would produce something. Once they had finished with her, if she was still alive, she would be sent to the firing squad, to be hanged or left to rot in Fresnes prison some twenty miles south-east of Paris until they decided her fate.

This was by no means an unusual pattern for men and women Résistants who had been caught. It was unusual that this young woman had come from England and defended herself and those around her from their crack forces with a Sten gun until her ammunition was exhausted. That she had been captured in a gunfight was de facto confirmation to her tormentors of her Résistance credentials. But what exactly did those credentials consist of? Whom was she helping? She was too self-possessed and aggressive not to have been well trained. And what an accomplished shooter she was – disciplined in her carefully measured firing and retreat, even though injured, isolated and alone behind a small apple tree.

Violette had found it relatively easy not to reveal a single name or acknowledge that she knew any, even though many names were thrown at her. Invention was her tactic to buy time for her comrades and, for a while at least, slightly less pain.

'This hothead *Anastasie* – is that who was with you and ran away leaving you to the Gestapo's tender mercies?' they gibed.

'We know that his real name is Jacques Dufour. A common terrorist with a price on his head.'

'You don't wish to be likened to such riff-raff, an intelligent young woman like you.'

'Where is this *Préfet du Maquis*?'

'Who is *Colonel Berger*, and where is he'?

'How many men and women are involved?'

'Where are the safe-houses and what are the names of the people staying in them?'

'Where have you been staying?'

'What are the names of the Maquis groups and networks?'

'Give us the names of the leaders and names of the SOE circuits.'

On and on it went, hour after hour, day after day. Saturday became Sunday and Sunday became Monday and then Tuesday, and still the questions and treatment continued for another three days. From 10 to 16 of June, Violette went back and forth from the filth of the prison cell to the relative opulence of the Gestapo headquarters.

It was when they brought the boy in that she decided to speak.

She proceeded to throw them off the scent. She told them she knew very little about this man '*Anastasie*', had never met him and would not wish a 'hothead', as they claimed he was, to be associated with her.

Perhaps, she murmured with great weariness, *Colonel Berger* was the *préfet* they were talking about, but she had not met him either. She was simply going to Angoulême to hand over some money; the money they had found in her suitcase and confiscated.

Who was she to hand it over to?

Violette did not know exactly, but someone there would see her in the square in front of the *Hôtel de Ville* and on meeting they would exchange a coded message. She was surprised that she had not been given any sort of name but the coded exchange would be sufficient. At that time they would exchange names, was all she had been told.

Where was the square?

She didn't know as it would be her first journey to the town, but it would be easy enough to find, she said. After all, there must only be one *Hôtel de Ville* even in a big town.

What was the coded exchange?

Inwardly, she thanked her lost dream, her lost husband, Étienne, for giving her the memory she offered up in homage to him. It had been Bastille Day, 14 July, and her mother had sent her out to bring back a French soldier for tea, wanting to give a homesick soldier a little mothering and a taste of home. Unsure how to go about it, Violette enlisted her close friend, Winnie Wilson, to accompany her. Finally, feeling somewhat ridiculous, they went to Hyde Park and sat on a bench, looking at every French soldier passing by. One, a dashing Legionnaire, went past rather too quickly, glancing at the two girls. A few steps later, he returned to ask Winnie in halting English what the time might be. Violette, in a flash, leaned forward, pushed his sleeve up, and read the time to him from his watch in faultless French. They all laughed and Violette and Étienne fell in love.

Well, she told her tormentors, the person meeting her, a man, she thought, would ask her the time of day, as if he were flirting with her. And she, flirting back, would bend forward, push his sleeve back, read the time off his watch and then laugh right into his eyes. Even if he were the ugliest son-of-a-bitch, that was what she had been instructed to do!

She recounted these things haltingly, seemingly reluctant, she even managed a tear.

The boy was spared further punishment but every time she held back a bit he, and therefore she, were threatened anew. And so it went on.

At her penultimate session of interrogation at the Tivoli with the Limoges Gestapo, she was informed they had checked her story and found nothing. They presumed that it was all fabrication. But she insisted it was not and that they obviously were not fast and wily enough to find the people concerned.

In a curious way, this story provided her with relief and some sort of escape. Violette knew there would be further torture now they had checked all this out, but she had decided to cross each bridge as she came to it. She continued to plan each story so that it contained enough truth to be reasonably authentic and flexible enough to mesh into their interrogations and the information they dropped. She was also aware they were telling her things that could be useful to London if she managed to escape or, most unlikely, to be freed. It was not difficult to stammer, refuse, cry out and go a step further in her story, seemingly under duress. Each story, each lie, each small fiction was dressed in enough fact to be seductive and seem authentic.

‡

The drive to Paris from Limoges was a long three to four hours, Violette thought. She was beginning to lose the ability to judge the passage of time. She was handcuffed in the back of a black Talbot and treated well on that drive. Another softening-up process, she surmised. Or a 'last supper' before execution. A cigarette was proffered and light extended from a fashionable gold lighter by the Milice officer seated beside the driver. In the back, on either side, were two Miliciens with loaded pistols holstered. She accepted the cigarette. She had taken her stand and was not broken. Now she must garner her strength and avoid undue confrontation.

She had to admit it was good to be out of Limoges prison, to be on the road in the fresh air, to be relatively clean and relatively intact. The surface weals and other marks from the 'robots', Panthers and interrogators were hardly noticeable now; the other injuries were hidden from sight, some so internal that she might now never have another child, should she survive.

She knew that what was in store for her in Paris would not be pleasant. But for now, she was content to be on the move, out of pain for the most part, and on the receiving end of a little courtesy, arrogant and dismissive though it may be. The Milice officer even ordered a stop on route in a tiny village for a coffee and snack. The officer apparently had a lady-friend there and spent some time in an upper room.

It was hot and Violette had taken off her jacket. Her suitcase had been placed in the boot. The lining had been ripped apart and there were signs of interference with the leather casing where attempts had been made to discover hidden recesses where maps and documents could be hidden. They must have found her identity papers, because they had gone. Luckily, she had no maps or notes in her possession as she had memorised everything. Not even a code key sewn into her clothes or shoes.

‡

As they approached Paris, Violette saw there were barricades up everywhere, far more than when she had last been there just six weeks ago. Things were changing and hope was rising in the hearts of Parisians as they looked towards liberation in the not too distant future. Hope even stirred in Violette's heavy heart.

They arrived in rue Pergolese and turned into Avenue Foch. Not far along, among other imposing *maisons*, was 82–85 Avenue Foch, Gestapo headquarters for the Nazi security services throughout France. The four buildings were all used for Gestapo counter-intelligence services, the SD, while Americans and diplomats from other countries lived in houses close by.

They entered the rather gloomy and forbidding hall, where the guard led Violette over to a desk and the uniformed receptionist entered her name meticulously into a ledger while confiscating her suitcase once again. A large female SD prison officer dressed smartly in grey led her to a cell. To reach the cell on the fourth floor they first had to pass through a long underground passage, which was cold and damp. This passage actually led them from 84 Avenue Foch to the adjacent building where the cells were. Warder and prisoner then climbed an iron staircase that rang its complaint from the heavy steps of the warder and creaked alarmingly at

Violette's lighter step. Three floors could be reached from this staircase, but only via an iron cage that had to be unlocked to enter, then the first door was relocked before they crossed to the opposite side, where the second door had to be unlocked to gain the corridor of that floor along which ran the cells. It clanged shut and was locked by the warder as they left it.

On the fourth floor, they traversed another cage where a security warder opened and locked each side after their passage. They walked along the corridor until they reached the cell into which Violette was unceremoniously shoved. It was small and dark, about four metres long by two metres wide. The plaster peeled from the walls and the sole window was a series of small squares of frosted glass covered in grime and dust. A couple of panes were cracked and a tiny sliver of fresh air entered the dark cell if the wind was in the right direction. A fraction of light penetrated the dim interior. The guards had long ago removed the handles and renewed the cement so the window remained firmly closed.

Violette saw that her sleeping arrangement was yet again another rusty old iron bedstead, folded, this time, against the wall. However, here a lumpy, bug-ridden palliasse could be thrown on the bedstead when lowered. The second luxury was a rickety chair. The third luxury was a lavatory seat, not just a hole in the ground; with a tap above it.

Many female and male SOE agents had passed through the cage doors. Some jumped from Avenue Foch windows to their death or injury and recapture, including Violette's friend Harry Peulevé. He was injured and recaptured to later be deported to Mathausen concentration camp. On 12 May 1944, eight women were brought from Fresnes to Avenue Foch. They were: Diana Rowden (*Paulette*), Eliane Plewman (*Gaby*), Yolande Beekman (*Mariette*), Madeleine Damerment (*Martine*), Vera Leigh (*Simone*), Odette Sansom GC MBE (*Lise*) and Sonia Olschanesky (*Tania*) and one other. Only Odette survived; she famously said of Violette, 'She was the bravest of us all.'

Violette spent about two weeks in the cells at Avenue Foch. Here, she was severely beaten and subjected to all manner of humiliating torture and sadism, as so many others had been. She did not give away any of her comrades nor any plans or other information entrusted to her. The Gestapo knew exactly who she was, that she had a daughter in England staying with her mother and that her husband had been a Legionnaire and killed at El Himeimat during the second El Alamein battle, on 23 October 1942. From this, Violette surmised there had to be a traitor in the camp.[158] Her interrogators used this information to show her how helpless she was before their intelligence services and how small her own knowledge; hence she might as well be amenable to save herself unwanted suffering.

---

158 Déricourt told Jean Overton Fuller in interview for her book *Double Agent* that SOE top brass were fully aware the organisation had been penetrated by the Gestapo and that men and women were deliberately sacrificed in order to distract attention from other activities.

Who was the traitor? Was it her commanding officer, Philippe Liewer, or Buckmaster, head of SOE F Section; Charles Boddington, his deputy – perhaps also known as Nicholas Bodington – second-in-command under Buckmaster of F Section (later accused of being a double agent, he lost his post in SOE, was sent to lecture the Allied troops on French politics)? Vera Atkins, even? Of all of these people, it seems it may have been Boddington/Bodington as he had been sacked on suspicion of handing secrets to the enemy. No one has ever been publicly acknowledged as having betrayed Violette.

The agent Odette Churchill/Sansom, GC, spoke of being in Avenue Foch:

> We talked about when we were captured, and what this one thought about it, what that other one had to say about it. I remember what one of them said because I had the same feelings. She and I, we had a feeling that something had been wrong. The others thought they had been captured because of the work they were doing or the people they were with. She had the feeling, because she had been arrested as soon as she arrived in France, that there was an informant. And I did too.

This other person that Odette speaks of was unlikely to have been Violette, although she was arrested very shortly after arriving on her Sussac mission. There were a number of men and women who were, indeed, arrested *on* arrival, that is, on landing in France – whether by parachute drop or by Lysander. The Germans were waiting. No satisfactory answer has ever been supplied as to how and why this could have happened. From Huguette we are told that Violette said it was a 'circuit member'. That means someone in *Salesman II*, the principal members of which were Philippe Liewer, Bob Maloubier, Jean-Claude Guiet and Violette. It was obviously not the latter two. Jean-Claude hardly knew her, and although the first two knew a considerable amount about Violette, having spent time with her in London, it is unthinkable that Philippe or Bob would have betrayed her. Was Violette sent out as a decoy?

We have two women, Andrée Borell, an agent, and at least one other women she was with who were sure a traitor was operating at a high level in London, in SOE. And if Huguette's memory is faulty on this point, perhaps Violette was referring to all circuits or Baker Street, as later, another woman, Madame Meunier, reports that Violette was convinced there was a traitor in Baker Street.

It is interesting to speculate whether there was an infiltrator or traitor higher up the scale. Perhaps a 'back-room' member of staff or an agent in the field? Possibly both or more. All agents could have described the schools, the training, the cover names of trainee agents and instructors and so on. But not many people would have known that *Vicky Taylor* was Violette Szabó who had a child in London.

Over the war years, and especially towards the end, informers were common in occupied countries, seeking safety for themselves or their families, not able to withstand torture, or selling secrets for money. I can understand all these motives, except the last. Informers and traitors existed at all levels of every secret service, too.

Sometimes betrayal was of another sort entirely – where information was unintentionally left that the Germans discovered and used. When Roland Farjon was captured in 1943, his apartment in Paris was searched and the Germans found lists in clear and in code of agents throughout France and much other information useful to the enemy. Another case was when the unlucky Southgate (from the *Hector* and *Prosper* circuits), arrested on 1 May 1944, had not destroyed his handwritten notebook. This and other papers, including various BBC messages and material on his circuit and sector of activities, were picked up by the Gestapo at the safe-house where his radio operator *Aimé* was living. He and another agent, wrongly supposing after the first forty-eight hours that they would better be able to save lives, then led Vogt, interpreter and interrogator at Avenue Foch, to parachute grounds, weapons dumps, giving names of their comrades and where they worked.

It has never been made public who might have been the traitor in SOE, although there has been much speculation. It is reckoned, although not verified, that only thirteen percent of SOE files remained after the devastating fire in January 1946. *That* is, indeed, interesting.

‡

During the many interrogations Violette was subjected to, the questions were repeated over and over. Sleep deprivation was one of the minor softening-up processes. Food was grey soup and a hunk of greyer bread. No washing facilities. Toilet – with a seat with a tap above it, but without hygienic paper or even newspaper. It was solitary and disgusting. She remained in isolation for days at a time without interrogation during her stay at Avenue Foch.

Women or men were frequently thrown into a cell together, with perhaps a 'mole' or walls that had ears. Prisoners who had given in and given information to their interrogators had special treatment, better food, reading material and so forth. While she was incarcerated in Avenue Foch, Violette survived and grew mentally stronger and more resistant through the strength of her deep hatred for the Nazis. Her health suffered, though. She had grown thinner and her hair hung in lank strands. Under the grime her face was pale, her eyes sunken. The glaze of pain extinguished practically all vestige of sparkle, but anger continued to grow. She remained sardonic at all interrogations, under all circumstances. It was her shield against all they could do to her. Violette had like most prisoners been subjected to the cold bath, a favourite pursuit at Avenue Foch and a little electric shock treatment to coax her stubborn mouth to spill out what she knew. Eventually they tired of her; they had new sources to drill for information. She was sent to the notorious prison at Fresnes, south-west of Paris.

‡

Violette had a pretty good idea of what to expect before her first visit there. She had heard of Fresnes prison. The car taking her there drove sedately through a long avenue lined with tall poplars. On the right-hand side was a series of buildings, each with gates leading into their separate outer yards. The gates were slowly opened by armed sentries, allowing the official car to pass through to the female blocks only after a thorough check. The men's block was adjacent, with similar gates and outer yard.

The prison stank. It was high summer and, after four years of war, resistance, occupation and normal criminal activity, it was overflowing with far more than the stipulated 1,600 inmates. By 1 July 1944, when Violette arrived at Fresnes, men grossly outnumbered women and were crowded five or six in a cell intended for one or two. There was still space for a good number of the women to be kept in solitary confinement. Violette shared a cell with a much older woman and later a third cellmate until she left for Saarbrücken on 14 August 1944.

During the harsh interrogations, Violette had remained defiant before the questions, threats and promises, answering, 'What do you take me for: a halfwit?' and something along the lines of, 'It won't be long before the tables are turned. Then you'll be where I am, and our men will be in your chair. What will *you* do then?'

She was not far wrong.

‡

While these interrogations were taking place, the Maquis, all the French groups, the SOE agents, the SAS, the Jedburghs, the paratroopers and bombers of the Allied air arm, all were making huge inroads, sweeping the occupant aside throughout France.

Railway lines were blown up or torn out, trains sabotaged or derailed, telephone lines destroyed, fuel dumps blown, the enemy harassed at every crossroad, in every town. They were slowly but surely being defeated. Another nine months, more or less, had yet to be endured before capitulation and unconditional surrender, but long before then, small and large pockets of land were liberated.

After Violette's capture during June to August, Philippe Liewer secured the loyalty and huge effort of Georges Guingouin, who met every target and never once let Philippe and his team down. Philippe liaised with groups across the entire region from the Atlantic to the Alps, from Châteauroux to Toulouse, making it sheer hell for the German troops; they might be lucky to escape one ambush, only to fall victim of the next. Their nerves were raw, ragged. They shot hostages, but this deterred not one jot the Résistants and citizens, who were going all out to destroy the German army.

Philippe organised the surrender of the German armed forces, Gestapo and Milice in Limoges, and Guingouin was fêted, as was his due. As Philippe reported to his London masters, 'We piled up in a deep cutting two kilometres from

Salon-la-Tour two successive passenger trains. This produced an effective block for six weeks, the Germans being short of heavy cranes.' That was just one of the successes for the *Salesman II* circuit.

Jean-Claude Guiet, the fourth team member of *Salesman II* who kept London fully informed, was never caught, never questioned. In a flurry of messages, he let London know of Violette's capture and the plans to secure her rescue, and finally their failure to do this. It was, after all, an almost impossible task, not least amid the increasing momentum of planning, training, sabotage and so on. Jean-Claude was constantly receiving fresh directions to pass on to Philippe.

Jacques Dufour (*Anastasie*) had left the groups of Maquis in the Haute-Vienne, angry with Philippe for supporting what he considered dangerous communist elements that were ready to put France under a new occupation.

‡

Now it is time for Madame Marie Lecomte, Légion d'honneur, Médaille Militaire, Croix de Guerre avec Palme to speak. She was from Morlaix, sixty kilometres from Brest, on the most western tip of Brittany, where she had first been imprisoned and tortured. She first wrote to my grandmother and then me in Australia, when she discovered where we were after the film *Carve her Name with Pride* had been shown in 1958, and we later met.

Marie Lecomte had promised Violette faithfully to contact us at war's end and at last, after the years had passed, was able to keep her promise. This is an extract of Madame Lecomte's first letter, translated by my grandmother, concerning her meeting with Violette in Fresnes prison:

No. 75386[159]   Morlaix, 19 April 1958.

Dear Mr and Mrs Bushell

You will be surprised to hear from me in faraway Britanny. Please excuse me writing to you, but I have to do my duty. With all my heart must I give you the message, which now comes from the grave. It is from your darling daughter Violette, she was of the heart and the flesh to you, to me she was a daughter of the heart and I loved her very much. Violette and I were inseparable.

---

159 75386 was the number Marie Lecomte bore from the time it was tattooed on her arm in Ravensbrück until she died. The high number is a silent testimony of the number women who had gone before her. I wonder what Violette's was and which arm?

I was arrested by the Gestapo, horribly tortured, put into prison in Brest 60 km from Morlaix. After being condemned to death, I was transferred to Fresnes prison in Paris, arriving there at 11 o'clock at night. Everything I had was taken away from me, then up to a cell on the third floor, No. 24 – already in this cell were an old lady of 69, a portrait artist, and your dear Violette. She was looking at my face, covered with bruises, lips cut, etc. She understood why I was there; we were both in prison for the same cause.

I was 40 years of age and your daughter 23. She looked upon me as a second mother. Maman Marie she used to call me. She told me about her parachute jumps and how, on the first one, she could not get out of it. Had to keep very still when she heard heavy steps approaching. She thought, Germans. But they were only gendarmes talking French to one another. She was then saved to join the Maquis. After her second jump, she stayed at a farm,[160] she was to meet her chief at a certain place and by car to Salon-la-Tour to pick up a young man *Jack*, when they came to the T-junction, they saw Germans on each side of the road. They started firing on them, so a terrific battle took place and ended only when their ammunition ran out. Violette and the other man were[161] taken to a guardpost and brutally assaulted. From there Violette was taken to Fresnes, where I met her ten days later.

We both suffered terribly, morally also because the stairs in the prison were made of iron, very noisy to walk upon.

Each day several women were taken away, we used to listen to the steps coming up, wondering if it was for us they were coming today, and in an instant open our cell door, but when we hear those steps going away noisily, we knew we had another day to live.

Violette was always hoping to escape, so she kept doing her P.T. exercises to keep as fit as possible. Alas, one day someone came for her, she was going, we were in despair to be separated; it was 13 August 1944. She left, and myself two days later, the 15th, the day of our Virgin Mary, also my own birthday.

Ah, I almost forgot to tell you about the small hole we made in the windowpane, so we could watch the yard below where the men prisoners were kept in iron cages.

Each morning they were allowed one hour for exercises. With a piece of meal bone from my corset, we made a small pin sharp enough to pierce the glass. We were only able to put one eye to it and see what was going on down there.

One day Violette saw a man[162] she had worked with. She made me look at him too. 'We must send a message somehow – you are much taller than I,' she said. 'Get on the head of the iron bed and use the stiff curtain as a funnel. Shout loudly through it, 'All is well, V. All is well V.' Violette looking at the hole saw him looking up. He had heard our message.

160 Violette stayed at a farm with Philippe on the first mission, not the second, but this could be to protect the Ribiéras family in the grocery shop at Sussac. Violette needed to talk but she could still talk with inaccuracies where necessary.

161 Unsurprisingly, Madame Lecomte has not quite remembered what happened. Or, perhaps Violette deliberately misled her, planning what she would say if interrogated further. Or maybe there was truth in the SS–Das Reich assertions that the man was arrested as well.

162 This was Harry Peulevé.

Among others whom I have spoken with over the years, two Frenchwomen, Huguette Dehors and Marie Lecomte who are witness to Violette's incarcerations did not know one another but there is a distressing sameness in the way they describe their imprisonment and a heartening similarity in the way they describe Violette.

Marie Lecomte does not go into great detail of the dank awfulness of Fresnes, but what she says is evocative. As Marie wrote, it must have dredged suppressed memories. After her time in Ravensbrück and her liberation from Buchenwald on 25 May 1945, skeletal at seventy-four pounds (five stone four pounds) and an invalid of war, this extremely brave lady was plagued by long-term ill health. She died at the age of sixty-two, a hero of France, leaving children and grandchildren.

She had fought first for her family then her hometown of Morlaix, Brittany and finally for France in the Résistance as a *'caporal des FFI du Finistère'* – a corporal in the FFI in Finistère, the region on the very tip of Brittany. She was of tenacious and fiercely independent Breton stock. It may have taken her many months to garner the courage to keep on living. It was very painful for her but she wrote so she could keep the promise she had made in hell.

‡

When Violette recognised Harry Peulevé, down in the yard below, she could see that he was limping badly and his face was ashen. Lines of pain streaked his face and his eyes were sunken into deep grey hollows.

In Fresnes, some of the women – Violette among them – did much to enliven things, constantly planning escapes and finding ways of communicating from cell to cell and across the distances, even with the men. Companionship came from the raised voices of women singing the songs of France, Spain, Poland, England, and other countries. It was moving and joyful and brought tears of consolation to many eyes. Women shouted out, *'Vive la France!' 'Courage ma fille!' 'Bas les Boches!'* Veritable conversations took place through the walls, especially cursing Laval and Pétain and hailing de Gaulle. Violette was soon part of this. She joined in the old French standards and sang some of the English ones like 'Run Rabbit Run', with the 'Rabbit' often replaced with 'Hitler'. It was not many months later that Pétain and Laval were imprisoned in this same building. How those women would have rejoiced!

Food came on trolleys trundling exasperatingly slowly along the corridors. They each received 100 grams of bread a day – a chunk of about two inches. Very occasionally, they got a small piece of mouldy cheese, or a thin slice of margarine, perhaps two ounces, would come through the hatch. On rare occasions they had a sausage of meat and bread, apparently salvaged from bombsites as they contained dust and bits of brick or concrete.

Nothing more than slops accompanied the bread. It was called 'cabbage soup' and contained a few beans. It was poured through the peephole from into the rusty bowl placed by the prisoner on the inside ledge. This bowl would have held perhaps as much as a large mug would today. Everyone was very, very hungry.

Violette was no longer in isolation. Within a few days of incarceration the elderly artist joined her, as the prison became ever more crowded, then Marie Lecomte. Violette kept doing her exercises to keep fit, always hoping for a chance to escape. She did not understand why she had been put in Fresnes prison. Why had she not been deported or executed? On the third day, she understood.

She was taken into the forecourt, put into a prison van and realised she was going back to Avenue Foch. The van was windowless and hot, with only a small grille on the door to see through. She caught fleeting glimpses of Parisians seated around tables on sunny café terraces enjoying coffee. The van smoothly pulled up at the gates of 84 Avenue Foch. The gates swung open and armed guards waved them through. At the dark gaping hole of the entrance, Violette got out and was led back into this forbidding building, arms manacled behind her back, flanked by guards.

Unlike the grey, awful prison of Limoges, this house had been a palatial and beautiful private residence. Strange, Violette thought, how the Gestapo turned things of light and laughter into things as sombre and grim as this. Her heart beat quicker from the trickle of fear of the unknown hours ahead.

SS-Sturmbannführer Kieffer was the commander of 84 Avenue Foch. He sent a young, good-looking and very smartly dressed man as inquisitor – Herr Vogt. After selection for this type of work, his training had been rigorous. He was, supposedly, an interpreter. Vogt spoke French, German and Italian with a smattering of English. Polite and calm and with great assurance, he began to question her. He truly did offer her tea and 'English' cake, as he did to each of his British victims. Violette laughed bitterly in amazement and sardonically accepted.

After a long day spent patiently questioning Violette, Vogt, Kieffer and August Sherer, a civil auxiliary to the SS and a schoolmaster by profession, were tired. They found the girl too stubborn. Hatred blazed from her eyes, sarcasm dripped from her lips. She needed a lesson. She would get one on the morrow, they resolved. For now she could damn well go back to Fresnes and in the morning before coming back she would hear the firing squad outside her window.

The following day, his expression bleak and determined, Sherer looked across the desk and noticed her sullen expression. Maybe at last she was cracking. Another man was standing in the corner of the large ornate office, ready to provide a little extra persuasion. He had put on his desk an array of devices, his preferred instruments to help encourage an informative chat with his prisoners. This one proved decidedly recalcitrant with her 'I won't!' 'I won't!' each time he said, 'You'll talk to me now, won't you? Your silence isn't doing you or anyone else any good, you know,' with Vogt interpreting and therefore doing much of the interrogating.

After some hours, face contorted from pain, eyes glazed, voice no more than a murmur, her frequent childhood defiance of her father sustained her. 'I won't!' she whispered. Violette eventually staggered from the room, refusing any help, brushing aside an extended hand. How dare they, after what they had done!

Back in Fresnes, she lay in great agony on the dirty mattress. She forced herself to drink her broth with an occasional bite of bread. 'I must. I must sustain my strength.' She ate every morsel, drank every drop, lying there thinking, singing songs until she felt a little better. One or two days later, she started her exercises, three times a day. She even persuaded her cellmates to join in. The elderly artist was very solicitous but Violette was careful in what she said, just in case. But with Marie Lecomte there was an instant rapport, recognising in one another the same stout fighting spirit and the same scars from the treatment that had been meted out.

She was elated she had given the bastards not a word to help them. Oh, yes, Violette had continued to tell them stories, wilder as the pain got more intense. Often she thought of Étienne, dying for freedom, and knew she had to endure as much as he. She fought for her daughter, for her father who had done his best in the Great War, her mother, her brothers and Tante Marguerite; and her King and Queen and their children.

Yes, Violette was glad she had given nothing away, except fantasies. It was all so worthwhile. She knew that victory was theirs, maybe not today or tomorrow – but soon enough. She hoped she would be there to enjoy the celebrations and parties, and then to watch her daughter grow and to take part in normal everyday life. Good thoughts, they were. Good dreams, as she drifted in a peaceful sleep far away from the pain that had racked her body.

‡

Philippe and the remaining team could not get the loss of Violette out of their minds. It added anger and strengthened their resolve to move the Maquis to ever more actions against the enemy.

‡

Part VII

35

Fresnes Prison to Saarbrücken

Wednesday 13 August 1944, Charlie Bushell's birthday

'A word to young historians – when we read your studies
about our underground world, they appear a bit cold.
Without wishing to be pretentious, you should not be afraid
of dipping your pens in blood: behind each set of initials you
describe with such academic precision,
there are comrades who died.'

Pascal Copeau

By early August 1944, the Résistance throughout France was creating ever more
havoc to German plans and movements, with weaponry and agent assistance from
the American OSS and the British SOE; General Patton, commanding the Third
United States Army, and General Leclerc leading the Free French forces were
almost upon the capital, where the Germans were panicking more as each day
passed. By 19 August, Patton had reached the Seine.

The Germans were having great difficulty acquiring sufficient fuel as the battle for Normandy ended and the US 21st Army Group advanced. In September,
Limoges, Paris, Brussels and Antwerp were liberated. Good Allied planning had
been an absolute catastrophe for the German fuel supplies.

Hitler and his High Command could not accept that defeat was rushing towards
them. They continued their frenzied fight. The Nazi High Command ordered that
all foreign and some French agents should be moved out of Paris and into Germany
so that they would not 'become available' to the Allies. They could be used as
slave labour if they were sufficiently alive to be active. Those Nazis responsible for
'crimes against humanity' would be in fear of their own lives now. These Nazis and
their creatures knew that the foreign agents and Résistants who had seen and been
subjected to inhumane horrors would readily give evidence against them. It was
time for their potential accusers to disappear one way or another.

The Résistance was now focused on blowing up railway lines. Trains to and
from Germany were held up, even blown up, all over France. German troops were

killed or wounded and supplies destroyed. The roads remained the least difficult means of transport for the Germans, but they too were dangerous, with many ambushes set up.

Over Le Clos, where Violette and the team had landed, 864 containers packed with hand grenades, machine guns, rifles and revolvers, ammunition, explosives, other stores and money filled the summer air on 25 June, dropping by parachute from a force of eighty-six US B-17 and B-24 Flying Fortresses. On this same day, Violette was surviving the SD cells of Avenue Foch under intense interrogation, just fourteen days after her gunfight and capture. The next day, 26 June, would be her twenty-third birthday.

At Le Clos, 300 Maquis and thirty trucks were required to haul all the equipment off to designated areas, with every road used blocked and guarded by Maquis. Wave after wave of parachutes descended onto the high plateau with the countryside alive with the sound of cheers and song from the country people in the area. Three hundred Maquis became 3,000 overnight.

‡

On 19 June, Denise Bloch, Benoist's[163] wireless operator, was arrested. She was a Frenchwoman and, like Jacques Poirier and other French agents trained by SOE, had been sent into France by SOE as an English agent, carrying a uniform so that in the event of her capture she would come under the international laws covering prisoners of war.

According to a report written by Vera Atkins when she was seconded on 13 March 1946 to the Judge Advocate General's Branch Headquarters BAOR (the British Army of the Rhine), Denise was seen not only at 84 Avenue Foch, the SD headquarters, but also at another interrogation centre at 3 Place des Etats-Unis in Paris, where a number of the women were taken, perhaps including Violette. Denise Bloch also spent time in Fresnes, as did Christiane Wimille. When Christiane was about to be deported to Germany, she had the great good fortune at Gare de l'Est to see one of her cousins driving a Red Cross van. She managed to slip over there unseen by her captors, put on a white coat and served sandwiches. In this way, she evaded recapture. It is quite possible Christiane, Denise Bloch and Violette made contact in Fresnes prison, as Morse code and singing in English and French were common. Prisoners could also get messages to each other just by shouting. Lilian Rolfe, who had been George Wilkinson's wireless operator for the *Historian* circuit, was caught in July and also ended up at Fresnes Prison, as did

---

163 Jean-Pierre Wimille, part of the old *Chestnut* sub-circuit that Roger Benoist (French world champion racing driver) revived along with *Clergyman*, had been arrested, as had Benoist, who managed to escape on 18 June. Christiane Wimille, Jean-Pierre's wife was also part of the *Clergyman* circuit.

Yvonne Basedon, who early in the year had been wireless operator to Bondages de St Geniès, a determined and very patriotic French nobleman.

Vera Atkins clearly and publicly stated that there had been a betrayal, although this was quickly quashed. However, it seems that from 1 January 1946, SOE had been terminated, with records and people certainly expunged with great rapidity. There was also a now-infamous fire that destroyed so many records. It appears that it is only by delving deeply into German, French or American archives that one might find any kind of answer to the betrayal question. Nevertheless, while the other secret services continued quietly in the background of British post-war international activities, SOE was a constantly newsworthy subject, in the face of perhaps less-than-vigorous remonstrations from Buckmaster, Vera Atkins and others.

It was clearly strongly felt that no good would come in seeking and punishing the traitors. Europe and the United Kingdom were in great turmoil, so these matters were not investigated with all due vigour, if at all, and, to all intents and purposes, remain unresolved. Maybe there is merit in the argument that there is no point pursuing this, but for the survivors and those left behind it is extremely unsatisfactory. It also creates fertile ground for any kind of conspiracy theory and unfair aspersions to be cast on the wrong people. In addition, it should be remembered that betrayal after torture is one thing, and can be absolved: everyone has a breaking point. Violette withstood all that was meted out to her, but not everyone could.

‡

Most sources have it that Violette was moved on 8 August. Marie Lecomte, though, is sure that 13 August is the date of Violette's departure from Fresnes prison. It was two days before her own birthday, on Assumption Day, 15 August. The difference is easy to understand as incarceration confuses the comprehension of the passage of time.

A number of records, including notes from Madame Rossier,[164] state the date was 8 August. The following extract is from a document she wrote, which is in my archives; I first received it from the SOE advisor at the Foreign and Commonwealth Office, Sir Duncan Stuart.

At least four other women were moved from Fresnes on 8 August 1944, including Diane Rowden, all marked for execution, not at Ravensbrück, but at Natzweiler concentration camp where two men, Dr Guérisse, a French Résister, and Brian Stonehouse, both witnessed the arrival of the three young women and, later, their execution. These women did not include Diane Rowden who was killed later at Natzweiler.

---

164 Madame Rossier was an inmate of Ravensbrück and talked to Paul Holley and me at my studio in Jersey.

Madame Rossier wrote:

... on 8 August 1944, seven girls left Fresnes chained together. They passed through Neurenn [sic][165] near Saarbrücken, and arrived at Ravensbrück on 25 August 1944. One of the three English girls was described as *Corinne* or Violette, small, dark, large eyes, said to have been arrested in a Maquis at Limoges.

‡

So, some eight and a half weeks after arriving in Paris, incarcerated in Avenue Foch and Fresnes, Violette, along with Denise Bloch and Lilian Rolphe, was brought down from the cells. They were each told their suitcases or bundles with their small collection of personal possessions (but no papers, no jewellery, watches and no money) were being loaded into one of the vehicles from a trolley just outside the prison doors while the prisoners were led into the prison's great hall.

Cuffed at the ankles, Violette was shackled to Denise by a chain running from her ankle to Denise's. All the women were joined in pairs in this way. A group of men were similarly chained. The prisoners were crowded into the front hall and then out into the waiting covered lorries for the journey to Gare de l'Est.

Violette and Harry Peulevé saw one another across the hall as they were all pushed into the yard to waiting vehicles. They had spent two months in different sections of Fresnes. This was their third sighting of each other: there had been their first recognition from the cell, followed by another where shouts were exchanged and heard. They could see one another clearly now, and each was surprised by the sorry state of the other. They had both suffered extensively from battle injury, torture and incarceration. Wing Commander Yeo-Thomas was also among the male prisoners.

As the prisoners were being assembled, every so often a voice would ring out in patriotic verse momentarily picked up by other male and female voices. Angry and nervous, the German guards indiscriminately shot a few prisoners but the spirit of hope and resistance could not be so easily exterminated.

As the vehicles were about to leave, every prisoner was handed two days' rations from the Red Cross. When they reached the railway station they were given their belongings. Violette received her bundle – her suitcase had been destroyed while the Gestapo were trying to find secret compartments with incriminating evidence. She had her silk flower dress, white blouse and blue linen suit plus one pair of wedge shoes and a little underwear.

They were entrained into two third-class carriages by mid-morning. The prisoners had sufficient water for about one day. The train was not long but was heavily

---

165 By Neurenn she means Neue Bremm, a suburb of Saarbrück where the industrial area once held a concentration camp.

guarded, including an anti-aircraft gun mounted on the roof. Three hundred or so wounded German soldiers were in the other carriages. The train did not leave until late afternoon, by which time they were very hot and weary sitting in the fug of the over-crowded carriage. Optimism about the course of the war was very high and this helped them all through those hours of waiting.

Finally, the train moved out. Including the long wait, the journey took over twenty-two hours instead of the normal time of just under two hours to reach what was then called Châlons-sur-Marne but has since been changed to Châlons-en-Champagne. This township is not far from Compiègne, Carrefour Bellicart de Compiègne to be exact, where one of the French concentration camps of deportation stood and where Claude Malraux, Jean and Florentine Sueur, Isidore Newman and all the others had arrived in March, a month prior to Violette's reconnaissance mission in April 1944.

Cattle wagons, packed tight with male prisoners, met up with that train on the northern side of Châlons-sur-Marne. There had been 1,250 men at the Royallieu internment camp. They were regrouped that day in Camp C, where they were provided with a very small amount of food and water and loaded into lorries. The convoys set off to Carrefour Bellicart, where the cattle trucks were waiting on the railway line.[166] The two trains were quickly combined. Harry and Yeo-Thomas' group were shoved roughly into the cattle trucks and the women's carriage attached to the same one.

Each livestock truck could reasonably carry eight horses or forty men. But there were never fewer than eighty men in these, even as many as 120 on this day of crushing heat. Immediately chains, irons and bolts clanked closed, ensuring they were entombed behind the locked doors. Night fell, and Wing Commander F.F.E. Yeo-Thomas tells us in his biography *The White Rabbit* by Bruce Marshall that before they left Compiègne, not a breath of air had arrived to bring the least relief to the prisoners, who were trying to get sufficiently organised, at least to use the empty cans as a communal latrine. The stink flowing from so many grimy, sweating male bodies mixed with the heaviness of the hot, stale air ensured that the old and the sick were already cursing, groaning and moaning, calling for non-existent water to drink.

The night passed slowly for these poor men stacked together, exhausted from standing hard against the next man or trying not to stand on the sick and dying, trying not to hit out in panic, trying to avoid those hitting and screaming in panic around them. Fights, more curses, knives originally fashioned to dig out floorboards to create small gaps to freedom struck flesh not wood.

---

166 Pierre Bur, a Résister of eighteen years of age, arrested on 11 June 1944 near Azat-Châtenet fighting a detachment of the SS-Das Reich Regiment, supplied much information on the men in cattle trucks.

At dawn, the train moved off, slowly clattering down the line with its human livestock. A cooling flurry of air penetrated the slats before giving way to stewing heat. As the miles passed under the chattering wheels, the 'latrine' cans filled and overflowed, slipping and slopping everywhere with the train's motion.

The drone of Allied planes could be heard, high in the sky. As the train crawled through one station a woman cried, 'You will not reach Germany, they have made a pact!' But the train rolled on, continued to roll on and did not stop rolling, ever onwards towards the east.

At Vic-sur-Aisne and at Soissons station masters and nurses from the Red Cross tried to stop the train but in vain, Jacques Vigny[167] tells us a 'furious madman was commanding the convoy'.

As they travelled on there was nothing they could do about filth slopping all over the wagons. Thirst was so rampant that many licked the sweat off the back of the man nearest them. Dead men were shoved into a corner, the corpses taking up more space than when they were alive.

As night fell, firing could be heard all around. The train stopped. Still no water. An escape attempt. The *schupos*[168] raced into the countryside with their police dogs. Several of those who escaped were quickly caught again and shot. Five of the youngest prisoners were forced to dig a grave in a bomb crater, then coldly shot in the head as reprisals. The prisoners who had been detained with them were brought out of their wagon as it was no longer secure and distributed in the other, already cramped wagons.

They continued to wander along French rails. The detours that could have saved them merely prolonged their agony and when, finally, they reach German territory, all hope had faded. Somewhere along the journey, this cobbled train was bombed by the Allies, thinking – quite rightly – that it was an enemy troop transport.

The heat was intense, men screaming and cursing and crying and dying had had no water for days. They were sick and dehydrated and no doubt Harry, when he saw Violette, thought that he was hallucinating, except Yeo-Thomas saw her too.

She and Denise Bloch, whom she was shackled to, had struggled out of their carriage, where the women were piled in more comfortable conditions than the men, but still basic and with hardly any food. Violette could not bear the suffering she could hear – maybe the image of the young man in Limoges being tortured moved her to action.

She said to Denise, 'Look, we've got to help those poor buggers.'

'Yes, yes, I agree,' said Denise. 'But how can we?' She looked pale and ill.

'Well, we can damn well get them some water!' shouted Violette above the cacophony of bombs dropping, fires crackling, the anti-aircraft guns firing and the uproar coming from the wagons of men. 'The bloody Bosch have all run for cover

---

167 Jacques Vigny lived and worked in Compiègne and has a web page dedicated to him as has Pierre Bur.

168 *Schupo* = familiar abbreviation of *Schutzpolizei*.

except those on the guns. They're too busy firing at our boys in the skies to think of two scrawny girls. Come on, Denise. We've got to get to the water supply, fill up as many cans or anything we can find and slip it through to the men.'

'Okay, Violette. I'm with you. Got no bloody choice really, do I? Chained up as I am to you and you so bloody stubborn! But I'm only too happy. Poor blokes.'

So they struggled along the corridor, found the water, filled a couple of cans and went back to the wagons, carefully lifting the cans as high as possible, wondering how on earth to get the water inside.

'Violette, is that really you?' was the voice of Harry Peulevé, full of wonder.

'Who the bleedin' 'ell d'yer think I am, matey? Look, how do we get this water through to you? Put your thinking cap on quick. Once this bombing raid stops, they'll be onto us like a ton of bricks.'

'Yeo,' shouted Harry to Yeo-Thomas. 'Get your mugs over here. Vi's got water for us.'

'What? Christ, that's bloody wonderful!'

And so, oh-so slowly for the men, Violette and Denise poured the water through the slats into the mugs. They repeated this many times, giving sustenance and life to a good number of men in two wagons. It was exhausting. Poor Denise was almost dropping and Violette was keeping her going with words and a helping hand, taking the weight of the large can they found and refilled over and over again from the water closet used by the soldiers.

The bombing stopped, the soldiers returned from their hiding places in ditches alongside the railway track. They shot some dozen prisoners, beat ten half to death. Violette and Denise also caught the butt of a rifle each, sending them hurrying back to their carriage knowing that by their actions alone many of the men were somewhat refreshed.

The courage and example of those two dirty, starving girls gave the men more courage to endure their own agonies and kept some of them alive for a while longer. Some lived until old age thanks to the two young women and their simple courage. The sights and sounds that Yeo-Thomas and Harry suffered were terrible. Scared and dehydrated, unable to throw themselves down on the floor, some of the prisoners threw themselves on top of each other, they were stacked so tightly. It was steaming hot in those filthy cattle trucks. Even Harry and Yeo-Thomas, who were trained to withstand, would have had a hard time suppressing their fear. A few were frothing at the mouth. Yeo-Thomas says in *The White Rabbit*:

> We all felt deeply ashamed when we saw Violette Szabó, while the raid was still on, come crawling along the corridor towards us with a jug of water which she had filled in the lavatory. She handed it to us through the iron bars. With her, crawling too, came the girl to whose ankle she was chained. [...]
>
> This act of mercy made an unforgettable impression on all. She spoke words of comfort, jested, went back with the jug to fill it again and again.

'My God that girl had guts,' says Yeo-Thomas. 'I shall never forget that moment,' says Harry Peulevé, 'I felt very proud that I knew her. She looked so pretty, despite her shabby clothes and her lack of make-up – and she was full of good cheer. I have never under any circumstances known her to be depressed or moody.'

The journey to the German frontier took the best part of a week. From the attack they were transferred into lorries. After a gruelling journey through Reims and Verdun they finally arrived at Neue Bremm. It had been exhausting, frightening and the conditions were diabolical.

‡

The train's route and then the lorries had been circuitous for three reasons. First, Allied bombing had destroyed or damaged many of the lines. Second, continuing sabotage of lines made detours even more necessary. And third, it is quite possible that the Germans were happy for these detours to take place, knowing the agony of the prisoners and therefore knowing a good proportion of the weaker ones would be dead on arrival. The wounded Germans were taken good care of by nurses and doctors in carriages roughly adapted as medical areas. There was plenty of drinking water and food for them. And kindness. But for the prisoners, the more that died, the fewer that needed to be fed even meagre rations of watery soup and mouldy bread in the labour camps. Those still alive would be farmed out at Saarbrücken to work in one concentration camp or another, with a few to be executed on arrival or summarily thrown into the gas chambers or hung and cremated in the ovens.

‡

On reaching Metz, our shackled prisoners were 'billeted' in stables for the night. Martin Sugarman, archivist at the British Association of Jewish Ex-Servicemen and Women (AJEX), says that one agent, Bernard Guillot, reports that he saw many of the female prisoners while he was being moved from one prison to another. In his debriefing of 12 April 1945, Guillot mentions that he had seen and talked to Denise Bloch.

It was extremely crowded. They were there for about two days with little food but adequate water. Violette was even able to wash out her white blouse and underwear. Yvonne Basedon particularly remembers, as she told me when I met her, seeing Violette washing her blouse in a bowl on what seemed to be a stack of crates.

Just as for the horses attached to the barracks that had once dwelled in these stables in great comfort, straw was provided for the prisoners in the loose boxes. Horseboxes ran down each side of the stable, with a walking area and a drain running down the centre. The guards pointed their rifles at the men and women with the threat of instant death if they approached one another, but they were able to talk during the day. There was so much talking, in fact, that it was hard to hear what anyone was saying. When night fell, things quietened down, men and women moved closer together as they lay across the straw- and sawdust-covered floor so they were able to touch and talk to one another across the drain. However, they remained chained by the ankle to their companion, as they had been the entire journey.

Violette and Harry managed to move right up close to one another and spent the day and night going over everything that had happened to them. Harry recounted to Rubeigh Minney, writing his biography of Violette entitled *Carve her Name with Pride*, the dreadful suffering that had befallen Violette. He was diffident in relating such things to another man for a book her daughter would surely read and he only briefly and so eloquently touched upon the horror.

Harry had this to say:

> Violette and I talked all through the night.
> Her voice, as always, was so sweet and soothing, one could listen to it for hours.
> We spoke of old times and we told each other our experiences in France.
> Bit by bit everything was unfolded – her life in Fresnes, her interviews at Avenue Foch.
> But either **through modesty or a sense of delicacy, since some of the tortures were too intimate in their application**; or perhaps because she did not wish to live again through the pain of it, she spoke hardly at all about the tortures she had been made to suffer.
> She was in a cheerful mood. Her spirits were high.
> She was confident of victory and was resolved on escaping no matter where they took her.

She would have wanted her family, including me, to know something of what had happened to her under interrogation. However, Violette may well not have wished to go into detail with Harry. She would not have covered herself in shame and embarrassment. If she were here today she would have stood defiantly proclaiming that by remaining silent while her body was used and abused she had given no useful information to the enemy at any time. In fact, she did not impart hard information to her cellmates and travelling companions, shackled and thirsty and hungry and in pain. Just in case. Only now, to her friend, Harry, who had suffered as she had without speaking, could she speak – but lightly – of what had been done to her. She would want it known that she had not given in. Harry's words to Rubeigh Minney are so kind that they soothed Violette's mother, Reine Bushell's, troubled spirit on reading what her darling daughter had suffered. These two men, the author and the friend, did well.

‡

The two days in the stables provided much psychological sustenance to Harry and Violette. They whispered many things together in the darkness of the night and laughed together in the daylight with the others. Although everyone was weary and distressed there was still singing, and jokes and stories. Nor did it prevent the guards coming in and slamming rifles and belt buckles down onto the shoulders or back of any they could reach to give a salutary lesson to these 'sub-humans'. The doctors and nurses actually came among the prisoners to check as best they could all those who were ill or appeared to be getting ill. They called the guards to take those who were desperately ill to the infirmary.

Sometimes they did and sometimes they didn't.

Sometimes they took ill men and women – but not to the infirmary …

‡

Harry Peulevé's report written on 23 April 1945 was for official purposes and has nothing to do with the feelings that were stirred a few years later when he was talking to Rubeigh Minney. As it should be, that report is coldly calm. All SOE agents are trained to give impartial and particularly uncluttered reports. He says:

> I left Fresnes on 10th August and was taken from solitary confinement to a cell where I met other agents. In all we left Paris 37 strong, mostly from Fresnes but with a few who came from avenue Foch or Compiegne …
>
> We travelled all night until two o'clock next afternoon when the train was bombed by allied planes and brought to a standstill. Luckily we had no casualties either amongst the women or ourselves, but seventeen German soldiers being evacuated to Germany were killed and one British prisoner of war.
>
> I believe we were in the vicinity of Châlons-sur-Marne and from there we continued our journey in a requisitioned lorry to Reims, having been told that should one escape everybody would be shot. I nevertheless made every attempt to free myself from the handcuffs and had agreed with the other man to whom I was handcuffed, whose name was Barrett, that we should attempt to escape. Unfortunately, the majority of prisoners saw that we were attempting to escape and said that we should not as we should be endangering everybody's lives. We stayed the night in large barracks in Reims and the next morning continued our journey in the lorry and here I managed to get my handcuffs off.

Although he does not mention here that Violette had offered water to the men, this does not mean, as has been suggested, that he was cold and calculating and therefore there was no warm friendship between Violette and himself. Nor does it mean that he was not in love with her. He was, as is fully evidenced by his handwritten notes. Harry came back in very feeble health. It took him many months to come to some sort of terms with his life and what he had just endured. The fact that he says,

'Half the men who met Violette Szabó were probably in love with her; she was after all an exceptionally attractive girl' does not mean Harry was not truly in love with her. And it might have been something he could cling to while he tried to recover his lost health. But after he finally escaped Buchenwald concentration camp, he commanded his two prisoners, SS guards, to empty their pockets. He wanted their papers to hand over to the Americans when he reached their lines. A new and terrible image, a photo, of Violette assailed him. Photos dropped from the SS guards' pockets showed twelve women being forced to jump naked through the snow. One of them he was in no doubt about. As he states in his handwritten notes (in my archives), it was Violette. With great bitterness and anger he stomps the photos into the snow which he later regretted as it was yet more proof of SS barbarity.

‡

Later, the women travelled northward to Saarbrücken. They were now truly on German territory. Neue Bremm is on the southern outskirts of the city of Saarbrücken, very close to the French border, about 160 miles from Paris. It remains a transitory stopover for visitors of all kinds. A memorial area acknowledging the men's and women's camps existed there. Here, as in so many places in Germany and Nazi-occupied countries, the Gestapo had established a collection point from which prisoners were sent elsewhere to larger concentration or extermination camps. It was also a camp for disciplining conscripted workers of the STO[169] programme. The Nazis called Neue Bremm in Saarbrücken an 'expanded police prison'. Here, men and women were brutally disciplined, undernourished and killed. The prisoners who were transitory and to be sent on elsewhere were treated no better. The Germans today call such places *Orte des Schreckens*, 'Places of Horror'.

This place at Neue Bremm was the camp in which Mademoiselle Monique Level,[170] a French prisoner, saw Violette, Lilian and Denise. She thought that Lilian looked quite ill; both Denise and Lilian were, by this time, worn down into illness.

‡

---

169 STO = service de travail obligatoire = compulsory work service instigated by the Pétainiste government. Not a wise move by Maréchal Pétain. Those young men, their families and friends were suddenly the enemies of Vichy France. Many had scampered to the hills and thus the Maquis was born.

170 Monique Level says the girls went to Gestapo HQ and later she saw them in Strasbourg and Saabrücken and they finally arrived in Ravensbrück on 25 August 1944. Eighteen days from Fresnes to this camp in north Germany. I first saw this detail from the BBC page written by Martin Sugarman, but have corrected the date. They were also in Strasbourg *after* Neue Bremm in Saarbrücken.

36

Saarbrücken to Fürstenburg and a Walk through the Forest

August 1944

'… that camp of awful fame.'
From 'Ode to Violette' by Charles Bushell, 1946

The days spent in the town of Saarbrücken, or rather the suburban area of Neue Bremm, had again rendered the young women prisoners from Fresnes prison dirty, hungry and thirsty. They were weary but at least they were not being tortured; manhandled perhaps, even receiving the odd brutal blow from a '*gummi*'[171] on the whim of a guard, but the girls simply scoffed at such random and wanton bullying.

Violette's cheerfulness and soft voice distracted them from their desolation. Others sometimes noticed a deep sadness in Violette's eyes and came to comfort her. Mostly she consoled herself with the firm conviction that in her tiny part of the war, she had won her battles and would continue to do so. Even her capture had been a victory of sorts. It had diverted the SS–Feldgendarmerie and the SS–Das Reich patrols from more pressing duties prevented them from torturing somebody else while they wasted their time on her.

It never failed to surprise the women and their SS jailers when, on the receiving end of bad treatment or when one of the other girls was being roughly treated, Violette showed steel. Immediately laughing eyes turned hard and cold; hot anger lashed out. She did not flinch to insert herself between guard and prisoner, standing there swearing at them roundly in French or English or throwing back the few curses she had learnt from her jailers, '*Schwein!*' '*Dreckfink!*'[172] It was just as she had when bullies fell on her school friend Winnie: she had dived in, arms flailing, mouth swearing, scaring them off.

---

171 *Gummi* = gum, rubber in German, here means a rubber truncheon.
172 *Fink* = finch. *Dreck* = dirt, so *Dreckfink* = 'dirtyfinch', which is quite amusing, is used for 'filthy pig'. The Germans used these slang expressions towards all their prisoners. To throw such curses back at them could be rather dangerous.

Amazement and indecision washed over the faces of the '*Schläger*'.[173] Once the mistreatment ended, Violette would again become the sweet young woman with a laughing smile and maybe a silly story or even a dance to cheer everyone up, including herself. Her innate cheerfulness and lack of fear, which had been mis-interpreted as a 'suicide wish' or a 'facile attitude' in not taking things seriously enough in reports on her at the SOE training schools, was the very thing that sustained her in those dark moments. Violette reasoned that fate or the unex-pected could only be dealt with pragmatically, and so she got on with whatever fate dealt her.

‡

Finally, new groups of dirty and damaged third-class train carriages were ready. No more cattle trucks. The women were separated from the men here and were told they were going to a pretty nice camp where they would work hard, but there would be good food, books to read and hot showers. The guards had received a general order to keep the prisoners unafraid and even slightly looking forward to a labour camp where there would little or no mistreatment. This would keep the prisoners relatively docile and easy to handle over the very long distance to Ravensbrück.

The journey started out well enough.

After the starvation diet they had already suffered, there was now what the poor women considered adequate food. The soup had a few chunks of real meat sometimes, maybe half a potato. The bread was not mouldy and there were two hot drinks – one in the morning, ersatz coffee; one at night, unidentifiable but warm, if not hot.

Saarbrücken to Ravensbrück is a long distance to cover by train and took an exceedingly long time. Five hundred miles of mind-numbing clacking wheels on rail.

Ravensbrück sits on a small and lovely lake of the same name along the river Havel in eastern Mecklenburg. Today the entire area caters to everyone from youngsters and young adults to those who have retired. Boating, fishing, horse riding and many other outdoor activities in an area of growing popularity. In 1944, marshlands covered the land in grasses and, where the land was especially swampy, forests of fir trees grew tall but little vegetation arose from the mists.

Violette's world and that of her companions had reduced to endless grey railway tracks and sidings, grey stations, grey platforms and the noise of grey guards and grey dogs. Even a few of the young women turned grey with pain or fear.

---

173 *Schläger* = thug, ruffian. *Schläger* also means 'hitter' and, therefore, 'hit song'.

The long hours of the journey gave time for meditation, for discussion, gave time to weep at what had been done to humanity and their families as well as to themselves. There was time too for songs and jokes and laughter. There was time for healing but time for sinking into apathy and illness.

Counting and roll calls were a constant curse on the journey. The trains they travelled in stopped frequently and the mostly Wehrmacht guards shunted the women from one train to the next, increasingly dirty during a never-ending fortnight of fairly constant hot sun.

Occasionally, during platform '*appels*' the women were drenched from welcome summer thunderstorms, only to steam dry under the broiling sun for an hour or two, or in the stink of sweat and worse of their grimy carriage. They all stank; they could not wash. Many of the girls were already sick with dysentery.

Rarely the Wehrmacht soldiers, but always the SS and Gestapo, treated these filthy things that called themselves women as mere creatures of scorn. They were there to be used – in any way they saw fit. On this journey, thankfully, the SS and Gestapo were few and far between.

Smoke and hot steam poured in through open windows, soot settled everywhere. However, the rhythmic clattering wheels on rails did ease tensions and helped the women to doze fitfully during the day as well as at night. Sometimes at Violette's or another active woman's behest, a group of women did exercises in the passageways.

They were still shackled together in twos so that escape was made all the more difficult. However, escape was not recommended on this journey and had not been from the start of the first train in Paris; the SS warned that if anyone even tried to escape, many of their companions would be shot dead in reprisal. There was not a woman there who could accept such a direct reprisal for her action. Ideas of escape were shelved for the time being.

‡

Violette had remarked to the women with her during the never-ending journey to Fürstenberg, in their desultory conversations that they were certainly becoming well-travelled, and it wasn't costing them a penny. She watched the country change its colours and contours, she looked at the towns and villages they passed through, chatted about them with others equally fascinated, she even learnt a little German, to go with the small amount of Dutch she knew.

She was not crushed or even terribly down by the situation she found herself in. Although still in pain, she was slowly healing and took joy from new vistas during the journey, passing a little of that joy of discovery to some of the others, joy, too, in the long meandering rivers, the ponds and lakes, the fishing boats, the farms and tractors, the harvests being collected, the clothes worn by the farmers and farmhands, villagers and city folk. The livestock, horses, sheep and chickens running wild in the fields. Roosters proclaiming their territory. The sun's long golden rays delving deep into the earth as twilight rushed in.

It was, Violette decided, a fine thing to travel extensively. After the war, if she survived, she would do much more, as her brothers were already doing in the armed forces, except for young Dickie. But for her, it would always be first class, never ever again in discomfort.

She was reminded by these scenes – reluctantly to be sure and much to her surprise – that not all Germans were guttural swine, ready to bawl and shout, ready to bring down a *gummi*, pistol butt onto their soft bodies or dogs to bite on soft flesh. She also discovered that the language itself could be beautiful and despite herself was drawn to some of the songs that drifted up from one of the guards' wireless sets or from the occasional happy singsong of the guards.

She did not hate the gentle people she saw from the train window. She wondered how they could be so deluded as to follow the frantic rantings of a megalomaniac – for Hitler was that. Violette knew she could do the 'silent kill' that she had been trained to do on him, without hesitation.

She remembered Oswald Mosley who formed the British Union of Fascists in 1932 and his gangs in London. They were nothing but bullyboys, hurting and causing damage to many Jewish people in the East End of London. They pranced down the streets like idiots, she thought at the time, in black shirts and shiny black boots, thick leather belts with spikes, giving speeches and showing a mindless swagger to the world. Most people laughed at them ... And yet, there were some *8,000* English men and women who did not. Thousands who listened. Thousands who wanted to believe that democracy was waning and a new order dawning. She even remembered a friend or two, one a girl, being quite taken up with the Mosley set, currying favour, trying to persuade Violette and others to join them. So maybe you just needed the right set of circumstances, she reflected, to turn a people. She remembered laughing aloud at such crazy stuff.

The British were not partial to swagger and oration, they preferred a quieter life of individual eccentricities and freedom but ...

But Germany had been well and truly mentally infected. Would the Allies be able to rid the world of such malevolent ideology going by the name of Aryanism? Hope was in the air. Big battles were being fought and won. News filtered through. The Allies would win the war after so many devastating setbacks.

The German population knew of the camps – after all, thousands were employed in them; they were a virtual industry, sending out slave-labour to chemical plants, aircraft and weapons factories and food-processing concerns.

A German doctor reported at the trials in Nuremburg and Hamburg in December 1946 that everyone in Germany knew about *Konzentrationslagern.*[174] He had seen correspondence in 1940 from the Bishop of Bonn or Cologne, addressed to the SS-Headquarters in Berlin, complaining because the local children were using the phrase as a joke, 'I will send you to the chimney' and mothers would warn their children that if they were naughty they 'would be sent to the chimney'; the 'chimney', of course, was an extermination camp.

Violette recalled that SOE had sent agents into Germany. She remembered that there had been a German or two at the SOE schools, seen and heard only from a distance. Maybe the German, she couldn't remember his name now, but he was always very pleasant and polite, who had lived in lodgings in 18 Burnley Road had been persuaded to become an agent or a double agent for the Allies rather than live in internment camps in England. She hoped so.

Twice a day, sometimes three times, they were made to line up for perhaps an hour, often more, to be roll-called, counted, checked and double-checked. Each leg of their journey took time to organise and provision so the Wehrmacht occupied everyone's time in this useless exercise. But it did give the women a chance to stretch their legs.

A stop early in the last week of August seemed just another in the constant flow of rail beneath wheel. The train pulled slowly into Fürstenberg.

‡

---

174 *Konzentrationslagern* means concentration camps; *Lager* means camp + 'n' makes it plural, camps. Often written *KzL.*

Women forced into the camp brothels came mainly from Ravensbrück concentration camp for the benefit of *Kapos* and inmates as an inducement in camps like Mathausen (from 1942) and Sachsenhausen – established in August 1944.

37

Ravensbrück and the Final Curtain

August 1944 to February 1945

Bahnhof Fürstenberg was wonderfully located for an open-air spa but was the reception station for those about to be detrained. The air was fresh and smelt of midsummer flowers and pine. The place was invigorating and so very popular for 'cures', particularly for pneumonia and tuberculosis. But this town was unseen by the women locked in their filthy carriages. Glimpses of rail yards, trucks, tips and some construction work was all they saw.

They were ordered out onto the platform at Fürstenberg and made to stand in silent lines. Their shackles were removed and they were lined up five abreast with guards and their dogs walking up and down. They felt stiff; some stumbled but were helped up by their travelling companions.

It was all done peacefully enough. Denise Bloch thought the guards and dogs from the train were probably just as weary of the journey as they were. They had no idea where they were going but one of the older women said she thought there was a women's prison somewhere well to the north of Berlin but could not remember its name. Someone asked an SS guard from the camp who was standing nearby and was slapped so hard in the face that she fell to the ground. She lost a couple of teeth and her right jaw had been slightly cracked, but stood up again in stoic silence – eyes down, tears seeping onto her cheeks and rolling off her chin – knowing worse would follow if she did not. Violette, at the other end of the platform, bit down her outrage and stood calmly. Sometimes she smiled at a neighbour, sometimes she scowled, head to the front. She must do nothing rash, nor attract attention. In the roiling midday sun, the SS count took place. Women fainted and were manhandled until they revived or were taken to one side for recuperation or just cast aside to a grimmer destination.

Then they set off on what felt to the weary and stiff women like an interminably long walk to Ravensbrück.

‡

They marched in a straggling line of grimy, weary and weakened women. Violette, weary like the others, was dismayed to realise the soporific journey had ended. Hardly a word was spoken. Out of one hellhole into another. Hearts heavy, backs a little stooped, one step in front of the other.

Despite the ordeal, one woman pointed to a flower the colour of sunlight and smiled. Another said, 'I've just heard a bird, isn't that wonderful?'

As she marched beside the other prisoners, with her few belongings under her arm, Violette thought to herself that people suffering great mental or physical pain or with terminal illnesses would feel much as these women and herself felt, taking pleasure from the same tiny glimpses of sweet nature. A sunbeam, the caw of a raven or the chattering of a magpie, rustling leaves, a child's laugh, a song of hope, even a prayer. These pleasures usually bring smiles to the elderly and infirm; not usually to the young and vigorous, whose laughter rings out and who seek action rather than serenity.

'*Ein, zwei*! *Ein, zwei*!' screamed a young SS guard, brandishing his rifle, carried away by the power he wielded. 'One, two! One, two! It is not a stroll to a picnic; it is a march to work! *Arbeit macht frei*! Work makes you free!' He turned and grinned at a female SS guard. No longer being guarded by the Wehrmacht, the women knew things would be different now. The rosy picture painted by the Wehrmacht soldier, who probably knew no better, was mere delusion.

As she marched aimlessly along with the other women, Violette saw they were walking through woodlands. She heard the song of birds that she could not identify. She pondered that all the different kinds of birds and animals managed to live together. They would stand firm or fight if their territory were under threat, but they didn't exterminate one another.

The guards imitated their dogs, barking and snarling if some poor woman strayed too far out of line. The prisoners trudged on, one foot after the other. The tangy fresh smell of resin from the pine trees growing so well in the marshland's sandy soil gave them a lift. The air was so crisp and clear. Violette remarked to the other women what a wonderful place it was. The others nodded and plodded on. Maybe, just maybe, their situation might improve. Just maybe.

The convoy of ragged women could not remain truly sullen in this magical, mysterious and clean, clean, clean forest. Twigs cracked under their feet and old cones were still strewn where they had fallen, decaying and giving sustenance to the poor soil.

Suddenly, on the left side of the roadway, they passed some pretty two-storey houses. Fitting perfectly and snugly into their surroundings of pine forest, constructed of slatted wood, they had been painted in delightful patterns. She discovered later that their occupants were the overseers of Ravensbrück concentration camp; the fact rather marred their loveliness.

Violette trudging beside Denise, although no longer shackled at the ankles, Lilian Rolfe and a young Belgian she was next to, remained together and chatted from time to time

Although Lilian and Violette had not met in South London, as they quietly whispered together they discovered both had family there. Lilian used to visit her grandparents in Paulet Road in Brixton from time to time, not at all far from Burnley Road where the Bushells lived. The next coincidence was that Lilian, codenamed *Nadine*, landed near Orléans by Lysander on the night of 5 April, pretty well the same time that Violette had jumped out of the plane to go to Rouen–Le Havre. As they walked along, the four could not refrain from broaching the various rumours of betrayal by agents and Résistants in France and betrayal in SOE headquarters. Violette was convinced but did not mention any names. They did not arrive at a firm answer. And yet each had felt that painful emotional kick in the stomach that made them want to cry out, 'Why?'

‡

Looming up in a clearing still a few hundred yards away was something vaguely resembling an industrial zone. It soon became apparent that it was not.

The gigantic entrance dwarfed the uniformed SS guards and overseers swarming around those enormous gates and the yard beyond. Walls nearly four metres high hid something hideous and ably deterred escape. It was a women's concentration camp. Guard towers attached to tall electrified barbed wire fences bound Ravensbrück concentration camp on all sides. The walls enclosing the large parade yard were lined with barbed wire fences. Attached to fences were small boxes that nearly always gave a lethal electric shock. Black skull and crossbones squares were attached to the wire, advertising the fact. Still, many women in their desperation, especially in these latter years, ran to throw themselves onto the wire, sizzling and shaking most horribly to death in seconds. A quick if agonising release.

'*Schnell! Schnell!* Come along, you lazy scumbags, get a move on. This is not a holiday camp. You've got work to do. First, you need to be showered and deloused. Get into those shower stalls at the end of the huts. *Ein, zwei, ein, zwei!* That's more like it.'

The women obeyed mechanically.

And so began the further dehumanising process of a concentration camp. From at least autumn 1944, with the construction of gas chambers, it became an extermination camp too. Thousands had already been put to death by hanging, beating, rifle butting, medical experiments, execution by firing squad or simply shot by one of the 'officers' in the back of the neck or head. The material I have read shocks and shocks and then shocks yet again.

From towers as tall as trees SS-guards pointed rifles down at the women, hoping they would have reason to open fire. It was boring, standing up there for hours on end. A little shooting practice wouldn't go amiss.

The stench of the place floated over the group of women still outside, drifting on the pure air into the healthy forest. As Violette looked, her eyes were attracted by a flash of light. It was a tiny corner of sparkling lake. This was known as Fürstenbergsee or Schwedtsee, otherwise more aptly known as Ravensbrücksee.[175] The horrors of the camp provided an awful contrast to this scenic landscape of soft hills, forests and lakes, with a church spire standing proud above the tree tops.

SS Chief Heinrich Himmler had established Ravensbrück concentration camp as a protective custody camp for 'criminals and enemies of the state'. He owned much of the land thereabouts and received a tidy income from the toils of slave labour farmed out to factories like Siemens and others. Siemens had large workshops there in twenty-six long barracks and two other L-shaped barracks surrounded by barbed wire. Siemens' own personnel were separately housed in a further twenty barracks. This area was about 500 yards from the political barracks.

‡

Ravensbrück was the largest concentration camp in Europe, if not the world. From the lake, it sprawled to the east, the long western wall giving onto the lake itself. This wall is now known as the 'Wall of Nations' and has a plaque commemorating the courage of Violette, Denise Bloch, Lilian Rolfe and Cecily Lefort. Before it, at its unveiling, lay a long rose garden and when the ceremony of commemoration took place in May 1994, the day was glorious, the roses were red and in thick full-bloom covering the bed under which, we were informed, lay many women who had died because they would not submit.

But in 1944, this place of awful shame looked so different. Parasites, fleas, lice, vermin of every kind fostered disease such as typhus, dysentery and others that ran rife. It was huge and it was horrendous. A prison for women. And their nightmare.

The swampy marshlands had been cleared in 1939 and the prison built by 500 male prisoners to accommodate about 7,000 women in rows of long barrack huts, called *Blockhäuser*. In August 1944, it housed almost six times as many, some 40,000 women. No wonder it stank! And the numbers would increase over the next five

---

175 *Fürst* = prince, *fürsten* = royal (a common surname, like Royal in English); *Berg* = hill or mountain; *See* = lake. *Schwedt* is a derivative of an original Slavic name meaning 'hell' so *Schwedtsee* could be translated as Hell's Lake – not so inaccurate for these five or so years. Ravensbrück actually means Ravens Marsh, the 'k' having taken the place of the 'h' at the end.

months of Violette's 'stay' to 90,000! This concentration camp had one of the highest fatality rates of the many concentration camps in Germany and Poland.

‡

At first, in the early days, the procedures for registration were strict and thorough. As the women arrived via truck or having marched from Bahnhof Fürstenberg, the female SS guards struck, punched, kicked and slapped each one as she was herded into the camp.

The women prisoners were kept packed tight in small rooms until the camp medics were ready. Then they were ordered to strip off. By 1944, most were quite indifferent to their nakedness; like Violette, Denise and Lilian, they had already been subjected to treatment meant to humiliate them – without success. This was nothing.

The female guards went round checking everybody, kicking the clothes to one side, then the door opened to let two SS officers in full uniform and polished jackboots march in with great arrogance. The women were then made to run in front of the SS guards and dogs, plus a doctor and a dentist. The dogs had been trained to be ferocious, to snap and bite helping force the women to run.

The dentist was Dr Martin Hellinger. His task was to note in his records any gold teeth he found in the mouths of the women and if they died, to remove them. It was not unknown for them to be removed while they were still alive.

The doctor's job was to sort out who was 'fit for heavy work' including road-making and tree-felling; 'fit for light work' and so confined to work in the camp itself, such as sifting clothes, remaking them, all kinds of sewing, preparing meals for the camp SS personnel and the prisoners and so on; or the sinister 'no work at all' when some were used for experimentation or led to their death.

These categories had little bearing on a woman's true physical and mental condition. If a woman had swollen feet, injuries, scars or perhaps was overwhelmed, too weak or ill to run, she was compelled to take a 'recovery' period: in fact taken to the imaginary Mittweide[176] near Uckermark. This subsidiary camp about a mile from the main camp had been built around 1941 for female juvenile offenders but became gas chambers for Ravensbrück in January 1945. Before this was operational, the women were driven in the 'Green Mina',[177] a special sealed van where they were gassed. Not transported to the camp as they had been told, but transported to eternity. Simple really: the exhaust pipe was connected to the van's sealed loading compartment. The killing gas seeped in and did an effective job. It took fifteen to twenty minutes for a load of about fifty women to die.

---

176 The SS euphemism for 'gas chamber'. *Weide* = pasture; *mitt-* = mid-.
177 Nicknamed by the prisoners, perhaps because Mina is a green vale near Mecca, Saudi Arabia.

The women were given cards to indicate which category they fell in to. Receiving a yellow card either on arrival day or on routine rounds in the barracks or the sickbay – the *Revier* – meant unfit for work for three to six months. A red card meant totally unfit for work. In the latter half of 1944, a red cardholder was usually sent to the subsidiary camp. Opening it up for prisoners, the warders told them it was a 'rest camp' but in fact it was a transit camp to the gas chamber. Conditions were so dreadful that many died there from exposure and maltreatment. Very few survivors emerged.

All the possessions the women brought into the camp were taken away and sorted by two prisoners labouring in the sorting offices. Everything was docketed, sized and divided into relevant piles of goods. Even the shorn hair was gathered, the long strands collected and matched and tied in individual bundles.

By August 1944, the stream of new female prisoners overwhelmed prison capacity so the procedure had to be simplified. The women were no longer quarantined for five weeks, but they still had to undress and run around under inspection to see who needed 'recovery'. They were then showered and sprayed with disinfectant rather than quarantined, then given prison garb, which by this time, was often not the striped clothes one usually sees in photos of the women in Ravensbrück. There was no longer a sufficient supply and prisoners of category two, that is, kept in the camp to work, were not able to keep up a high enough output of garments to meet the huge influx of women from July 1944.

Instead, clothes wrested from dead prisoners and which could not be used elsewhere were dumped in the room and the new intake of women tried to choose what they wanted in the scrummage. Finally everyone had at least a pair of underpants, a dress of some sort and possibly a ragged coat or cardigan, maybe even a scarf. Hair was no longer shaved; it took too long and was considered an unnecessary expense. It was just cut in chunks to look as unattractive as possible. Sometimes, one of the female SS guards, Monika or Mohneke, would cut the scalps along with the hair – she liked to hurt, liked to humiliate. However, long hair that could be used for other purposes was cut fairly carefully. It sold well once made into wigs.

Disinfecting the women stopped too in the end. It cost money. In any case, mingling with the other women in the barrack for an hour or so would merely re-infect them. Once the women entered their hut, the foul and fetid bunk straw and the obscenely filthy blankets ensured instant infestation. So what was the point of disinfecting them on arrival?

‡

In the months between May 1939 and June 1944, an estimated 43,000 women were brought to Ravensbrück. During the next nine months, July 1944 to March 1945, an estimated *90,000* more came – to a camp originally designed for 7,000.

Regardless of the number who died, it was still hugely overcrowded. Every woman a filthy, hungry, suffering remnant of humanity.

In February 1944, Geneviève de Gaulle,[178] the niece of Charles de Gaulle, received the number 27372. She was only twenty-four when she was eventually released in April 1945. With Odette Churchill,[179] Geneviève was taken by the commandant of the camp, Fritz Sühren, to the liberators and personally handed over, with the idea that this would improve his chances. The two names de Gaulle and Churchill were a terrific bargaining chip, he thought. He must not have understood the utter degradation he had inflicted on these women and the dreadful state they were in. Geneviève said in her book *God remained Outside*, 'He looked like a fox – not very complimentary to that poor animal,' continuing that, as she was led to the car, she was accompanied by 'a terribly gaunt woman who seemed very old. A few stray hairs had grown again on her shaven head.' Perhaps Odette had thought the same thing when she saw Geneviève, who had pleurisy and was very ill. They did not dare talk but they did hold hands. Two old women who were still in their twenties!

I also met and corresponded with another ex-inmate of Ravensbrück. Christiane Césaire told me that she had been raped many times. We remained in contact and I learnt that her life had been truly difficult, so how did she retain the laughter and merriness that, to the time of our meeting, continued to fizz and effervesce into old age?

‡

All the prisoners were organised into categories, each with a distinctive colour-coded triangle, as well as by nationality. Political prisoners (including British, French and Belgian Résistance fighters, those of the eastern bloc and Germany, and Soviet prisoners of war) wore red triangles. Among them were the *Bettpolitik*,[180] there because they had had sex with a foreigner, not to be confused with the ordinary prostitutes who were among the 'asocials' category. Jehovah's Witnesses,[181] called the 'people of the book' or in German *Bibelforscherinnen*[182] wore purple

---

178 Geneviève de Gaulle wrote a small book of her time in Ravensbrück, *God remained Outside*, as well as travelling all over the world until old age prevented it to keep the flame of remembrance alive – lest we forget – at our own peril!

179 Odette Churchill (Samson, Hallowes, liaison and wife to Peter Churchill of SOE). Odette Hallowes GC.

180 *Bettpolitik* = politics of the bed.

181 Jehovah's Witnesses were imprisoned because they refused to serve the war effort, to take an oath of allegiance to the Third Reich, to make the 'Heil Hitler' salute, or to serve in the army. Their barracks were always extremely orderly and clean. They refused to try to escape, which led the SS to entrust positions of responsibility to them. At any time, they chose they could be freed by signing a document stating they would no longer practise their faith. Very few sought their freedom by signing.

182 *Forscher* = researcher, research scientist or explorer; *Bibel* = Bible.

triangles. 'Asocials' (including lesbians, prostitutes and Gypsies) wore black triangles. Criminals (common criminals and those 'criminals' who broke Nazi-imposed laws) wore green triangles. Jewish women wore yellow triangles, but if a Jewish woman was also a political prisoner, she would wear a red triangle as well as the yellow triangle, sewn on the left sleeve to form a Star of David, or a yellow stripe on top of the red triangle. To signify a prisoner's nationality, the SS made the women sew a letter of the alphabet within the triangle: F for *Französin*, French political prisoners, E for *Engländerin* and so on.

Perhaps Violette wished to sew 'E' for English and 'F' for French in a 'V' for victory shape that also represented her name. There were other coloured triangles denoting various groups of 'female subhuman species'.

Violette and her comrades were placed in one of the 'political barracks': Hausbloch N. V. (Block 5). Before being frogmarched there, they had to sit on the floor and sew on their own triangle or triangles and national letter on the left side of their jacket or blouse or dress, with the needle and thread each were given.

The political block held many highly intelligent women from several countries so the flow of conversation could be very interesting. Nanda Herbermann, whose tattooed number was 6582 (every inmate had a number tattooed on their arm), said the camp had been much more comfortable on her arrival. By the time she was transferred to the political barracks, there was still a modicum of comfort in that each woman still had a stool and cot of her own. She says it was cleaner, although fully occupied, than the admissions hut. 'Austrian social democrats, noblewomen, a mother superior over seventy years old, writers, several witty and very lively French women, representatives of different parties, bourgeois women: everything, absolutely everything could be found here,' she recollects.[183]

Twenty-three nationalities were interned in the camp and the prosecution after the war proved that at least 80,000 women had lost their lives in this camp. They died by slow starvation, hanging, shooting in the 'shooting corridor' and then thrown into the ovens, dead or alive; by medical experimentation; by hard labour and lashings, beatings on the beating block; thrown into the bunker into solitary with soup every three days; throwing themselves against the electric wire fencing or finally being shoved into the new gas chambers.

There was '*die Rolle*', '*die Walzrolle*', a large concrete roller that would normally be pulled by a tractor. Geneviève de Gaulle told me in 1994 how, as punishment, women were forced to push the roller in the nearby quarry until they died from the summer heat, thirst and exhaustion. Huge and heavy it was used to break up and pack down stone for infilling.

---

183 Nanda Herbermann's small book, *The Blessed Abyss*, is most interesting and revealing as she was bourgeois, a very careful and an obedient Nazi who found herself thrown into this underworld life after helping a priest who fled to Holland.

Eighty thousand murdered women might be considered a small number compared with the 4 million exterminated at Auschwitz, but each number was a woman, or a child. Each woman and child had a family and friends back home. It is impossible to know exactly just how many women and children were inmates and lost their lives in this appalling camp since the Nazis destroyed many of the records when their rout was imminent and fleeing was the only course open to them. We do know that some women arrived with their children or gave birth while incarcerated. We also know to some extent the horrors that were inflicted upon these youngsters and newly born.

Ravensbrück was, in actual fact, also used as a brothel. Though seldom publicly written about before the 1990s, and certainly not duly documented by the Nazi camp staff, forced sexual activities were frequent in concentration camps, including Ravensbrück. 'Women were prepared to sell their bodies for food' for their children. *Kapos*[184] seduced women and gave them food in return. Prostitution was not unknown. Male prisoners who worked in the women's sections of the camps sold food for sex, but some survivors also note that starvation causes a striking absence of any sex drive. Others confide that there was 'everlasting talk about sex and smut [which] may be considered as compensatory satisfaction.'[185]

In the summer of 1944, a section was opened up behind the cells to hold around 2,000 men, many of whom died in the same gas chambers. There had always been a few male prisoners at the camp, a couple of hundred to begin with.

Heinrich Himmler discussed an idea with Otto Pohl of the SS Economic Division in early March 1943 that he considered 'it necessary in the most liberal way to provide hard-working prisoners with women in brothels'. Pohl[186] forwarded these instructions to the camps and at Ravensbrück brothel vouchers were delivered to male prisoners of special value, but certainly not to Jews. For SS personnel who wanted a ready flow of women to satisfy their appetites, women from Ravensbrück were cleaned up and deloused for their personal use, for which 'services' they paid.

Starvation was one of the essential tools to keep the thousands of women from rioting. Just enough food to keep the women working until they dropped or died. If they collapsed and could work no longer but were not yet dead, they were still disposed of – either shot or sent to the infirmary for the doctors to experiment on. This fate was especially true for the Polish women. All kinds of vile experiments

---

184 *Kapo*, from the Italian '*capo*' meaning 'head' and 'boss', was the title given to all inmates who, in an effort to save their own lives, betrayed their fellow prisoners by becoming guards, informers or supervisors. They received extra privileges such as food or better sleeping quarters. Those who were still alive at liberation were often murdered by other prisoners.

185 Elie Cohen, *Human Behaviour in the Concentration Camp*, 1954; London Association Books 1988 p.135.

186 As witnessed by Walter Jahn, male prisoner since 1941, Otto Pohl with Camp Commander Fritz Sühren inspected the *Neue Wäscherei* – laundry – to be the new gas chambers between February and March 1945, never to see it completed.

were carried out for the professors and surgeons of the great German hospitals and German pharmaceutical companies. How interesting to have live human material to work on – all very scientific, of course, with reams of reports and controls in each group.

On 2 March 1947, a mixed inter-Allied court in the British zone tried sixteen Ravensbrück staff members and found them all guilty, except one. He died during the trial. Eleven were sentenced to death by hanging and the remainder to imprisonment. After imprisonment, they were freed and most of them lived normal lives. Conscience? Yes, for some, and, for a few, great remorse. But others didn't give a damn.

‡

The *Blockhäuser* for political prisoners were built for about 270 women, but when Violette and her friends arrived there were close on 1,000 women. In the first few years, with not too many inmates, it was well organised and the women had decent enough prison garb, food and beds, but this had grossly deteriorated by early 1944.

Women shared the infested cots with four or five others. Many did not have a bed and slept on the floor, often without a blanket, even when there was snow on the ground and the lake was frozen over. During the heatwave of the summer of 1944, there was a plague of lice and the water became contaminated. Disease was rife, especially typhus and louse-borne relapsing fever.

Violette tried to make the best of it. She was so weary and getting thinner by the day. She was thankful that her periods had stopped although she still wondered if she had fallen pregnant after Limoges and Avenue Foch. Otherwise, she remained in good health and spirits. For many women, menstruation often stopped due to stress and malnourishment. But for those for whom periods continued there was no sanitary protection to prevent the menses flowing down their legs, giving them great distress and humiliation.

Violette's surprise was joyful when, one day across the yard shortly after her arrival, she saw Marie Lecomte. They rushed into one another's arms and cried, so glad the other had survived until now. Marie was quite shocked by Violette's appearance, by the weight she had lost and the sunken look to her eyes. 'Whatever have they done to you, my little one?' she asked.

'I'm tired to death. I only want to sleep,' she told her. Violette, like most of the women, was barefoot. They were not allowed clogs until winter set in, or late autumn if it was particularly cold. The two spent a lot of time together and Violette introduced Marie to her small group of friends. 'Maman Marie, they treated us abominably. In a camp in Saarbrücken we were all in chains.'

Marie saw the marks on her ankles.

Violette met many other Frenchwomen in her allotted hut, including the communist Jeannie Rousseau, who arrived on 15 August. The papers in her SS dossier gave her name as *Madeleine Chaufeur*, evidence of her part in an espionage ring in Brittany. She was arrested in 1940. Like Violette, she had been quick to invent a reasonable story. When she was caught, she was carrying two-dozen pairs of French nylon stockings to give as a gift to her British handlers in London. On capture, she explained that they were to be sold on the black market in Brittany. When she arrived in Ravensbrück she gave her real name. For some reason, the Nazis at the camp never cleared the confusion of her dossier name, her codename, and her real name.

‡

Violette, Lilian and Denise were sent out on stone-breaking duties, as was Jeannie, and they would try to come back every day with something as a gift to Marie or one of their other friends in their *Blockhaus*; maybe only a dandelion or a piece of grass, but sometimes something they could eat or chew on. Sometimes Violette sat in on political discussions with the Englishwomen or the French – often enough in a mixed group.

All these activities were dangerous because if they were caught they would be thrashed or sent to the bunker (that prison within the prison) where they could be heavily beaten again over the 'beating block'. Many women died from the twenty-five heavy blows administered to their backs by a female criminal inmate, one of the 'asocials', bearing a green triangle. But who was this woman? Heavy-set and strong, she was clearly a sadist, probably taking nefarious pleasure from beating the women's naked backsides with all her strength, sometimes bringing the cane up under their bodies after crashing it down on their backs, using a leather-covered cane about three centimetres thick and fifty centimetres long.

Some inmates were given the task of 'elders' of the barracks, calling the prisoners to roll-call and generally governing their every movement. Some were inexplicably cruel, others helpful, others coldly efficient. They received benefits for work well done, either in small amounts of cash, or extra food rations, clothes or other benefits. In this way, the warders and other SS personnel did not have to suffer the stink, dirt and infestations of the camp, nor the early-morning calls.

Roll-call took place at half past three every morning in summer. All the women had to congregate in the large yard. There, they were to wait at attention until the *Appel* or roll-call, was completed. Sometimes it did not start for two or three hours. In winter, they were summoned into the yard at half past four in the morning, ice all around, snow on the ground, whatever the weather. A number of women died every day. They died from the suffocating heat, lack of water and food, or from the terrible cold, lack of sustenance and illness. Other prisoners had to cart them off and pile them up on top of one another, very neatly against a wall. Punishment ensued if the piles were not neat.

In the winter, snow and ice covered the ground, icicles hung from the *Blockhäuser*, the women's faces froze and they got frostbite. Violette, like many, wore summer clothes throughout her incarceration and *Kommando*[187] work in Torgau and Königsberg; they gave not a modicum of warmth. Sometimes, the roll-call would be repeated two or three times. Six hours or more could be passed in the Ravensbrück yard where hell did freeze over.

A Frenchwoman who had been a prisoner there with Violette told my friend and I that one day Violette had stepped out and danced the 'Lambeth Walk' while all the English girls joined in the singing. It gave the women who witnessed it a huge lift and there was much laughter to the furious shouts of the SS overseers. Violette found herself in the bunker in solitary for a week, during which she had soup, bread and water just once on three of those seven days. It was an airless, dark basement cell and the temperature was lower than in the *Blockhaus*. There were cockroaches crawling around, but she did have a chair, a bed and a bedcover to herself. She could hear the screams of women being beaten or tortured. She continued her exercises, more for warmth and for her brain than for her body. How else to keep sane? How to stay free from sickness, if not exactly remain healthy?

It was her second time in solitary. The first was after it was discovered that she was attempting to escape. That time she had been beaten on the thrashing block but had survived and, although the wounds took a long time to begin to heal, they did not become infected.

When she came out on both occasions, she was fussed over by all the women of her hut. They had collected minute morsels of food for her, had heated water with a few grains of ersatz coffee stolen from the canteen and they rubbed her body to warm her up and just make her feel better. It did.

The very act of searching, or scrounging from the infirmary or sewing rooms, even on occasion the kitchens, kept a spirit of adventure high. All the little plans to accomplish such things meant they had something to concentrate on.

Violette and Denise Bloch slept on their slatted wood bunk, shared by four to six other women, including Lilian. The blanket was shared by at least three women and straw on the bunk was replaced every now and then from the *Strohblock*. The new straw was soiled again immediately by women too ill with dysentery to reach the floor, never mind the filthy latrines. Every morning, fifty or more women waited their turn at each of the three latrines available.

During four years of the war, this huge hellhole had accommodated about 120,000 women, of whom only ten percent, 12,000, remained when the Russians liberated them on 29 April 1945. The Russians immediately burned to the ground every single vermin-infested *Blockhaus*. Apart from the fear of epidemics, those experienced Russian soldiers were shocked to the core by the starving, stinking

---

187 *Kommando* = work crew.

skeletons that claimed womanhood. The most recently arrived prisoners were still in reasonably good health and still had a decent covering of flesh. But the others ...

‡

In late summer 1944, as they entered their *Blockhaus* for the first time, Violette and the girls with her were speechless, unable to comprehend. A gasp, a sob, a shudder. An 'Oh no!' from here and there. When Violette looked around her, her thoughts returned with a vengeance to the possibility of escape. She was still in pretty good shape, considering. Unlike most of the women, she had kept doing exercises in prison and, to a small extent, on the journey, and maybe this helped. She could not bear to watch the suffering of so many, but she would have to bear it while she made her plans. She must not act rashly and spoil her chances of reaching the Allies, even the Russians; Violette had so much to tell them of the crimes that were being committed every day, in every place occupied by the Gestapo, the SD and the Nazis generally.

Across the lake, the church spire held a strange attraction for her. There must be a little town there, she thought. Those people must know what's going on here, surely? If that's the case, it's too dangerous to escape in that direction. She asked a woman and was told that, not only did the townsfolk know, but Arbeitkommandos or work groups of dirty, dishevelled and starving prisoners were sent into the town to do menial or construction work. Rumour had it that some large construction was taking place there, something to do with the camp – some said it was a gas chamber. The town was Fürstenberg where they had first stepped foot off the train on their arrival.

‡

On 3 September 1944, Violette, Marie, Jeannie, Lilian Rolfe and Denis Bloch with Eileen Nearne and Solange and their Kommando group were taken to Torgau, another manufacturing slave-labour camp for Siemens. Today, many call them labour camps. They were not. They were slave labour camps. No wages were forthcoming and conditions were terrible. The hours were unbelievably long and extra duties often had to be performed. The conditions in the factory where they were forced to make ammunition further eroded the prisoners' '*élan de vivre*'.

When their train arrived at Torgau, Violette and the other women were immediately set to work, but Marie Lecomte was taken to the infirmary as she was very ill, semi-conscious and they all thought she was dying. She looked green and blood ran from her mouth. She lost her memory for a while but survived. Violette talked with her many times in the hospital and outside on a patch of grass when she was not working. Gradually Marie's health improved.

Jeannie persuaded the others to refuse to work making munitions to kill 'our brothers'. They had all decided that no way would they work to support the Nazi war machine. With Jeannie were her two especially loyal friends who had worked in the Résistance with her: Countess Germaine de Renty and another communist, Marinette Curateau. Jeannie stood to the front and refused. In bad German, she made a speech to the fat-faced German chief of the camp, 'that all these women are prisoners of war and the Gestapo have no right under the Geneva Convention to force them to make ammunition that would be used to kill their own people'.

It was a gesture of pure madness, defiance of the sort that Violette was happy to take part in, loudly backed up by their friends. It raised the spirits of all the other women too. Jeannie said, 'We were so childish, you see.'

Finally, an old German doctor who was as kind as he could be advised them not to be foolish. The Torgau camp was good in comparison to others. But some would not listen. Marie says in her letter, 'all 500 of us had to be punished for a few rebels.' They were forced to obey and work or be shot out of hand. Commandant Sühren came from Ravensbrück and picked 250 women to go to Leipzig as slave labour. The other 250, including Marie, Violette and her friends were 'to suffer the command of the slow-death reprisal in Königsberg in East Prussia'. But not right away.

Violette, Lilian, Eileen Nearne and Solange were not made to return at that time. Jeannie, however, was immediately sent back to Ravensbrück, as the ringleader. She was lucky to survive. 'I would have died that time,' she said. But the Germans could not find her papers under the name of Jeannie Rousseau because, quite simply they did not exist! There were thousands of women in the camp so it would not have entered their mind that she might be registered under a pseudonym. 'They asked me why I had been sent to Ravensbrück and I said I didn't know.' Still, it was noted and recorded by the Gestapo that she was indeed a troublemaker.

The others were put back to work. There were some whippings and promises of far worse if they tried similar stunts again. SOE training came into its own for those agents who had been captured and forced to work as slave labour in the enemy manufacturing industry. Taught to feign 'stupidity, ignorance, over-caution or fear of being suspected of active sabotage', factory workers are then in a position to ask unnecessary questions, to check things frequently in order to avoid accusations of sabotage, to reject the slightest imperfections, stalling and working well but slowly, misunderstanding orders, misdirecting goods trucks and so on. 'Feigning exhaustion, workers can cause delay by slightly increased accident rate, slightly inefficient work or not correcting errors of others'. All these and more should be utterly plausible ploys.

Violette decided to employ the SOE tactics she had learned. It brought back all the skill she had had the opportunity to use in April during her very successful Rouen–Le Havre mission. She also quietly but avidly planned to escape with

Eileen and Solange. The work was not too bad and they found ways of sabotaging the manufacturing processes in tiny but damaging ways. When faults were found in the machinery or ammunition because of their sabotage, there was nothing to suggest it was sabotage. As they moved around the factory, sometimes slipping past guards, they obstructed the work in any way they could. They had decided that it was better to create small hindrances, and lots of them, rather than be caught on a big one that would soon be fixed. In fact, Violette was adamant she would do nothing to endanger their sabotage efforts and escape plans. She was cautious, planned each step precisely and would not move unless there was a high possibility of success. Being women, they could have headaches and stomach aches and generally be unco-operative – but only so far.

In this factory, the food was better. The soup had bits of cabbage and potato and once a week a tiny piece of meat. Bread rationing was increased a little from the one-tenth of a loaf they received in Ravensbrück. There was ersatz coffee in the morning and more soup for dinner in the same proportions. But they worked long hours – eleven, often twelve, hours a day.

The good spirits of the girls sustained them, as Eileen Nearne recounted to me.

Eileen told Violette many times that she thought they should get out as soon as possible. Violette's response was always that they would escape in the right damn way. No use escaping only to have the dogs jump on them, or walk straight into the arms of an informer. None of them spoke particularly good German. Violette was in very high spirits, loving every minute of planning, telling Eileen that she had been speaking to one of the chaps and that he seemed to think Violette was not bad looking and liked it when she gave him a robust kiss on the cheek. He promised to make a key for the gates.

Denise laughed as she towered over Violette's slight figure, and chided her for her deception in spite of the fact that her charms were working. Suddenly she changed subject with a frown, wondering how Lilian was doing and whether she was sickening for something. But Solange, impatient that they were getting off the subject, asked when the key would be ready. The guard had told Violette that it would be a week or so, but that he must be careful and that the key needed copying and tooling.

Violette turned to Denise saying she too was worried about Lilian but that if she were careful, she would hopefully improve and that they could all scrounge some little extras to feed her up. That seemed like a joke, though. Little extras – a few leaves of cabbage, half a potato, piece of bread that rolled under a board and got nibbled at by God knows what! And she remonstrated with Denise that she had been coughing too and must be careful!

Denise said not to worry as she would go to the infirmary the next day as they were nowhere near as bad here as they were at Ravensbrück. They would give her something. It was not too cold yet and they spent most of the time inside the factory working so she was not getting chilled to the bone, just feeling weak, nothing more.

And so they planned. The key came and still Violette would not budge. Eileen was impatient to escape but knew Violette was right when she said she would not try to escape until they had acquired some half-decent maps and warm clothing. They should keep the key safe for that time. Then they would be off like a shot. The girls going with her were thus saved from certain death lost in wintry forests or recapture if they sought help in the wrong place.

Eileen Nearne was soon moved on to another sub-camp of Ravensbrück and never saw any of them again. Eileen had parachuted in to France in February 1944 and was captured shortly afterwards. She had insisted that she was *Mademoiselle du Tort*, and the Germans decided she must be a French *réfractaire*. After spells elsewhere, she finally ended up at Torgau, where she was liberated by the Americans in 1945. She was very lucky as well as smart.

Several weeks after Eileen had left, Violette, with Denise, Lilian and Marie – who were still unwell – were trucked back to Ravensbrück. They had been considered troublesome and suspected of planning to escape. The weather was turning cold now and they were pretty short on warm clothes. The others hunted around and all found something to keep Lilian a bit warmer. Violette had nothing but the silk summer dress and now a pair of worn clogs, a couple of sizes too large for her.

‡

It was much worse when they returned to Ravensbrück this time; unbelievably more crowded and even filthier. Women were dying in their bunks or on the floor; more were throwing themselves against the electrified fences to end their torment.

Just after the girls had left to go to Torgau in September, a huge red tent had been erected in the middle of the entrance yard to accommodate the overflow of 500 Jewish women from Hungary and thousands of women from Poland's ghettos after the uprising. These women from Eastern Europe lived in unutterable filth. They starved; they fought for crumbs that fell on the muddy, stinking, rotting floor of the huge tent, awash with every form of human contaminant. They so wanted to live. They died in droves.

When Violette and her friends returned, they just could not believe their eyes, or noses. A thick, sick, putrid smell wafted thickly from its interior and instantly women vomited including Violette. Women who had been at Ravensbrück for years were shocked by this turn of events and further deeply dispirited. A jackbooted female guard pushed the returning Kommandogruppe along, with the help of three or four others, all with firearms, short whips and rubber truncheons, much as they had when Violette and her group had first arrived.

Each barrack had a stove that gave out a weak heat and so water could be boiled – but insufficient for a thousand women. However, the women all took it in turns to get hot water and Violette or Denise took the occasional hot drink over to Lilian, who was clearly desperately ill. They all spent every free moment looking for bits of food. Not one of them in this *Blockhaus* stole from another woman.

They joined the pitiful scrums when a guard for laughs would throw some small piece of dry bread or meat that had gone rotten. The kind of pride that might make them hold back would only lessen their chances of survival. Monika, a barracks guard still in her twenties, was cruel and sadistic and had been particularly fond of this pastime until she lost her young son.

‡

Violette and other women were sometimes cleaned up and forced to make a number of appallingly degrading visits to the Sachsenhausen camp brothels and its sub-camps, where a group of SS guards and officers took photographs of the sexual acts committed on Violette and other women, also making them run around, usually naked, in the snow in freezing temperatures as it was so amusing.

In December, Violette, Denise and Lilian, along with Marie Lecomte and some others of the French section, were moved far to the north, to a camp at Königsberg, as punishment for again attempting to make escape plans. Here they replaced the Russians as vital slave labour to cut down trees and stack them for transportation all over Germany. The snow frequently came up to their knees as they wielded axes on trees and logs. Violette, as testified by Marie Lecomte, wore nothing but her summer dress and clogs. She, Marie and many others had little else to keep themselves warm. Marie was livid when she saw how warmly they had dressed the women in the biographical film of Violette.[188] She kept exclaiming to us how they worked in the lightest of clothes in knee-deep snow in the bitter Königsberg winter of 1944–45. She wrote in a letter to my grandmother and me, 'The place was so terribly dirty it was frightening. What few bits of clothing were left with the palliasses were full of vermin of the worst kind. There again, Violette went to work all the time while I stayed in the camp thanks to our Corsican doctor – Maria de Pérete.'

The work was back-breakingly hard. The food hardly replenished a fifth of the energy her now-skinny body used. Violette's health was finally on the decline.

Marie continues:

My poor darling had to work in the snow, helping in the work of building an aerodrome out of forest land. It was getting colder all the time, freezing weather, with the east winds from Siberia … One night, Violette got back to camp at six o'clock. We had a fire that day. She was almost out of her mind with the cold. She had a fit of

---

188 *Carve her Name with Pride* (1958), starring Virginia McKenna and Paul Scofield, with Michael Caine in his first bit part, in the train scene.

screaming and crying. I could not quieten her for a long time. I took her in my arms, trying to warm her up a little. "I'm so cold, so cold," she said. [...] I brought her to the fire and showed her the little food I had saved from my dinner for her, a couple of thin slices of potato that I stuck to the stove to cook them. A kind of feast. She enjoyed it.

She went on to describe the arrival of Sühren, accompanied by a woman to take charge of the prisoners. She was a fiend, lashing and kicking the girls, except for Marie, as the doctor had told her she was sick in the head. Violette shared her small palliasse with Marie, saying, 'We shall keep one another warm, like this.'

They had no blankets, no fire, just their thin frocks, and it was below freezing. Marie goes on to explain that this commandant forbad the girls to make a fire, but still a fire was made. At ten o'clock that night she returned demanding through an interpreter to be told who had lit it. Nobody spoke. 'Who's in charge of the stove?' Marie replied that she was. Asked if she understood, Marie replied, 'No,' at which the woman pushed her onto the red-hot stovepipe. Next day Marie had to walk through the slush and ice to the commandant's office and caught pneumonia. When she returned, she said that they had all kept one spoon of soup for her.

The cold was so intense it was hard to keep on living. But each day they went to the forest to cut trees. Living skeletons; no strength for such hard work. Rations were just two cups of soup made of water and unwashed beet or potato peelings.

Marie concludes her account that one week they were sent to work with Austrian soldiers who were kind to Violette. She had their soup and they shared their food with the women. They felt great pity for them, especially Violette, so young and looking as she did. It was, says Marie, the first time they had had some human sympathy. There were 700 women in the camp at the time and each day their friends died in the forest, 'black from the congestion'.

After further plans to escape were discovered, Violette, Denise, Lilian and a few others, but not Marie, were all returned to Ravensbrück on direct orders from Himmler's Nazi headquarters in Berlin. The order came on 19 or 20 January for these girls to get ready to move out of the camp. They had heard from the Austrians that the Russians were getting very close and Violette was very upset at moving again as they were all hoping to celebrate liberation together.

'What does it mean?' asked Violette. 'I don't like it one bit. I have an awful feeling of foreboding.'

Marie was terribly afraid for her, not knowing how to console her, she said simply, 'You don't believe it's good, but perhaps you're being moved to a British camp where you'll be with other parachutists. You'll get chocolates, cigarettes given to you, better food perhaps. Don't get upset, *chérie*.'

Violette and the others who were leaving were given a comb and clean clothes, along with some soap. 'You see,' said Marie, 'they don't want to take you to the British in the shocking state you're now in.' Violette enjoyed having a good wash, and Marie scrubbed her down, 'Maman Marie, you must get the vermin out.' She was getting excited and feeling halfway decent again. Violette then made them promise one another that they would contact the other's family after the war and give each a kiss from the other. She wrote a note that Marie put in the hem of her thin woollen frock, remembering that there was the name Petit on it – not Petite – the feminine form:

> You will kiss them all for me and tell them everything. If we both return you will come to me in London and I will come to see you in France. We shall eat the fruits of the country, all the good things from the sea. If I return and not you, I promise to look after your family. I swear they'll never want for anything.

Then they left. Marie did not leave Königsberg until 5 February 1945.

‡

The order from Himmler's desk commanding the girls' return to Ravensbrück also instructed that the three girls were to be shot forthwith.

A similar order had been sent to all the camps with the names of the British prisoners who were to be dealt with in the same way, or simply made to disappear. No trace of their murder has been discovered.

The Germans were defeated in every quarter and were hurrying to get rid of incriminating evidence. Each of the British and French prisoners considered to be trained by SOE who were in the camp had an individual death sentence passed on them. Their evidence was too damning for them to live.

†

On returning to Ravensbrück, Violette, Lilian and Denise were thrown into the camp bunker in solitary confinement. They persuaded themselves that this was for punitive reasons. After all, Violette had made serious efforts to escape deserving of the harshest punishments like the whipping block. However, their Russian friends said it was more likely they were about to be hanged.

The same thing had happened to the Brits in Buchenwald; as Harry Peulevé said, 'seventeen of our number were taken to the bunkers'. Himmler found it easy to choose the women as there were only Violette, Lilian and Denise there, but in Buchenwald it was more difficult and 'the selection was based purely on the disorder of Himmler's filing system and the inefficiency of his girl clerks who could not find the files of the remainder.' Dr von Schuler, one of the SS camp doctors in Buchenwald, confided to his secretary that he was concerned he might be punished after the war for the unethical medical experiments he had carried out on prisoners as guinea pigs, nicknamed 'rabbits' in the camps. Yeo-Thomas, the senior officer left among the Buchenwald Brits, learned of this and made a deal with the doctor that he would put in a good word for him if he exchanged their paperwork with those of prisoners who had just died of typhus. So Yeo-Thomas and Harry Peulevé survived, deeply damaged by their years of torture and incarceration.

By January 1945, Violette was occasionally and unsurprisingly depressed and uninterested in anything, even in a younger friend, seventeen-year-old Hortense Daman, who had just come back from Block 9 after spending two days there. Violette seemed to be losing the will to live, says Hortense. It is more probable that she was by this time exhausted and very ill, possibly with pneumonia. The winter months had seen her used in brothels, condemned to the block and isolation cells and working in sub-zero temperatures. Nevertheless, Violette had given up her bed for sick Hortense and slept on the floor although she had a mass of open sores all over her legs. It was the last time they met. Several women survivors relate that Violette was always cheerful, helpful and planning to escape.

Orders arrived from the Reich main security office in Berlin towards the end of January. Only a few days later, probably on 26 January – six months to the day before Violette's twenty-fourth birthday – but no later than 5 February, Violette, Denise and Lilian were summoned to the shooting alley.

The shooting alley was about three feet wide and ran between the long Commandant's HQ building and, on the other side, the three smaller showers, kitchens and a cellblock.

Lilian and Denise could not walk and were stretchered by *Kapos* to the passage and laid on the ground. Alone, Violette walked unaided, head held high, going to her death knowing she had done her duty on every count. Her face showed her huge visible scorn for those present: the camp overseers, Commandant Sühren, Schwartzhuber and dentist Dr Hellinger, doctors and all the rest. The revolver shots rang out around the prison. Denise and Lilian were both propped up and shot in the neck. After being forced to watch her two friends die, finally Violette was pushed to the ground in a kneeling position and shot in the neck.

She smiled a little sadly.

She was dead.

‡

Marie had a gruelling journey back to Ravensbrück. Ninety of her fellow prisoners were machine-gunned en route; only 60 of the 250 women survived. More died of typhus and dysentery when they arrived. Marie begged a French nurse to give her news of Violette. Two days later the nurse reported that Violette was dead, hanged. 'I saw her clothes at the sterilisation rooms. Full of blood,' she told Marie. Marie asked what the clothes were like, and they matched those Violette had been wearing, but she said, 'There's no blood after a hanging.'

The nurse said, 'That's all I was told, but you are right.'

Violette's body was perhaps cast into the muddy waters of the lake on the left as you stand at the wall looking to the distant spire. There are reeds and plenty of strong-growing plants and water life among them. Since writing this piece, I have discovered that the ashes of the women burned in the crematoria were cast into the lake. For all the horrors committed there, it is a beautiful spot for a final resting place.

She did her duty well. She knew it. She was the victor.

‡

'Age cannot wither her.'
Shakespeare

'Thou art a monument without a tomb.'
Ben Jonson

‡

Like a star shining brightly
You are one amongst millions
But like a star shining brightly
You shine separately and brilliant

People revere you
People speak fondly of you
People are proud of you
Military and civil alike

Beautiful of face
And beautiful of spirit
Brave with grace
In pits, you had grit

You are the mother
I could not know
Except by another
I could not grow

If I could only see
The smiling face I saw …

Tania Szabó, January 1999

‡

Epilogue

December 1947: a winter so cold that ice and snow lay thick on the ground over London. For some time my grandmother, Violette's mother, has been teaching me how to curtsy. I knew, at the age of four and a half, how to curtsy perfectly and did not need to keep practising all the time. It was the word itself that gave me trouble. I called it 'skurtsy'. Everyone would laugh and then my grandfather would finally mutter, 'Can't the poor child even say the word properly? Good God, she's getting on for five.' And then he would laugh a little gruffly, give his wife a kiss on the cheek and invite me to his knee for another intriguing story about a magic princess called Tania. Try as I might, that word remained 'skurtsy' for some time to come.

The day arrives and the snow is crisp and even. My grandmother starts to tell me very carefully again about the King and curtseying and being polite. She tells me I will be able to wear the dress from Paris, and she tells me about Violette.

'You know, Tania, that your mother will never be able to come back. She is a long, long way away. She is in a place that people call Heaven.'

'Yes, but Granny, where is she? Can't I go there too?'

'No, Tania, not for a long time. But our darling Violette, your dear mother, she was very, very brave for you and for all of us. She is dead, which means that she can never come back. She must stay in Heaven, although I am sure that she will watch over you.

'And, Tania, most importantly, she wants you to do this thing for her: to go and collect her George Cross from that good and kind king, King George VI.'

And so I went to see the King.

I knew the protocol, not the word but the way to behave before the King. I had been told that he was a good man, not very strong but good, and wise. My grandparents repeated many times how brave he was in insisting that the entire royal family remain at Buckingham Palace as the bombs rained down over London. More interesting to my young mind was the fact that at last I could wear the dress that Violette had brought back for me from Paris. It still needed some alteration that my grandmother did with great care as tears glistened in her eyes.

I had been a 'sickly' child, not very tall and quite thin. When, as an adult, I returned to Australia for a brief visit in this new millennium, Rick – Dickie, as he was called when he was younger – told me that he went to Mill Hill with Mum (I too called 'Granny' 'Mum' in Australia, after asking her permission) to fetch me away. He was eleven at the time. He told me, 'Mum and I were shocked by the pervading smell of dog in the house and that you, Tania, were left alone with it. You were in a poor state of health.'

He went on, 'Maybe Vi chose Mill Hill because of some argument with Dad; why else would she have left you there?'

'I have no idea, Rick,' was my puzzled reply. 'Perhaps because they were good friends; Vera Maidment was young and Violette knew Mum needed a rest from bringing up children.'

My grandmother told Dickie on the journey home to Stockwell that I seemed to have no other companion but the dog. It is true. He was my friend and would sit next to me on a bench underneath the window that looked onto the tiny front garden. My main meal was bread and milk, which I liked very much. And just occasionally, I had a plate of chips, which tasted good. Perhaps, as I proved to be in Stockwell, I was just incredibly fussy with food. Shortly after arriving back in Stockwell, my grandmother took me to the doctor. He told her that I was seriously undernourished and would have only had another six months or so to live had I stayed in Mill Hill. But, once I had been back in Stockwell for a while, something wonderful happened: bananas arrived from a ship and a brown 'cough medicine' bottle full of the purest orange liquid was prescribed. It was orange concentrate, rationed and just for children, and I was to have a teaspoon a day in a glass of water. But it tasted so good that I would drink half the bottle before anyone could take it away.

But on this icy-cold December day there was much fuss and palaver in the Stockwell household of the Bushells. My grandparents put on their best clothes. My grandmother had had her hair done and wore her best hat. And she dressed me in my frock from Paris. She combed and brushed my hair while I squealed and fidgeted, then dressed it in shiny white ribbon bows while Dickie grumbled that the 'kid' was always kicking up a fuss. Then my coat was put on, but then, horror of horrors, because of the bitter cold wind from Siberia and my uncertain health, my grandmother started to put gaiters over my shoes and socks. Well, I knew that you just absolutely did not wear gaiters to see the King. They came up to my knees and looked horrid. So I shouted, 'No! I won't wear them!' I cried. I stamped my feet. Everyone was now in a state of high tension and red-faced with anger and frustration.

We were going to be late.

My grandmother finally gently pulled me over to her. 'Now, Violette … oh, I mean Tania. You only have to wear them to the Palace door. As soon as you're inside, I shall take them off. But you can't fall sick on the way to see the King.' Well, that made sense and knowing only too well that it was bed and not kings that I would see if I were sick, I said, 'But you must promise to take them off just inside the door. Not wait or anything, just in case the King comes in. Promise me. Promise me, or I won't go!'

Laughing by now, my grandmother promised, explaining that we would have to wait a while in the antechamber.

When we arrived, I tugged my grandmother's sleeve and said, 'Quick, quick, my gaiters. The King may come in.' And so she removed them as the courtiers smiled and asked my grandparents if they would accompany me. Before my grandfather could say a word, my grandmother said, 'Oh no, that would not be right. It is Tania's mother that is being honoured today and it is Tania who must go to the audience with the King. She has lost her mother and she must have this honour to remember all her life.'

I walked into a much larger room, but not huge. I think it was quite beautiful in a muted kind of way. And then the King came over to me – he was very tall and slim. Perhaps he had a navy-blue suit on. I curtsied as I knew so well how to do. And he leant forward and pinned the George Cross onto my right-hand side, saying that as my mother's representative I must always wear it on my right-hand side. He asked me to keep it carefully for my mother, for such a very brave lady, and I replied that I would always keep it. It is lovely: a fine massive silver cross nestling in a beautiful blue bow. And it was *his* cross. He handed me the box to keep it in and then I do not remember quite how I left, except maybe there was a lady who led me out into the antechamber to my grandparents.

I remember meeting a very well dressed gentleman who seemed very kind. He talked to my grandmother for some time. It was Philippe Liewer. He had taken the surrender of the Germans in Limoges and finally returned to England. Later, he went to live in Canada with his family.

That day we also went on the Tube, which I enjoyed very much. What I enjoyed most was how creamy and glistening the curved walls and ceilings of the Tube carriages were and, as we sat on the shiny wooden seats, I could see into each carriage and the creamy walls and creamy curved ceilings went on and on into the distance.

Some years later, when I was seven, my grandparents and I were invited to the French Embassy to meet the French Ambassador, René Massigli, KBE,[189] who would present me with Violette's Croix de Guerre with bronze star. It was not actually posthumous as it had been awarded in August 1944 in Limoges by *Colonel Rivier*, who awarded other agents, Résistants and Maquis members – including Jean-Claude Guiet, who received the same decoration for conspicuous bravery. As a prisoner of Ravensbrück concentration camp, Violette had been unable to be present.

A gala dinner had been laid on in my honour (in reality of course, in Violette's honour) and before dinner commenced I was to give a speech from the head of

---

189 René Massigli, French Ambassador in London from 1944 to 1954, whose diplomatic career ran from the First World War until 1956. Sacked by the Vichy government, he joined France libre at the beginning of 1943, becoming Commissioner of Foreign Affairs in the French Committee presided over by General de Gaulle. He was author of several books on international policy and politics.

the table to the resplendent dignitaries sitting at the long mahogany table. Crystal chandeliers glittered and glasses too, cutlery shone and dark wood gleamed. All around were servants in red wearing white gloves. They were ramrod straight, quiet and very serious. At our kitchen table in Stockwell with my grandmother, I had memorised the short speech I had been asked to give, and then been tested by my grandfather. In the great dining hall of the Embassy, I felt a little anxious but pushed those nervous thoughts away because it was important to say what I had to say. On finishing my speech, I suddenly realised the import of the words I had spoken and felt a tear or two prick my eyes. With great endeavour, I breathed in to hide the sniff and went to sit down while the table applauded. A French gentleman pulled my seat out for me and I sat down. He bent over and whispered as I gazed at all the silver knives and spoons and forks and crystal glasses set before me, 'Just start from the outside and work in.'

'Oh,' I replied.

We chatted a little, and the gentleman on my right joined in for a moment or two. Finally, as champagne was being poured, the room became very quiet and a voice boomed, 'And now, we would like to give Tania a toast.' I immediately gathered all my pride and said, politely, that I didn't want any toast, thank you. I had hoped that I, too, could sip a little champagne. After all, I had completed a very difficult task in giving a speech to all these grand people who spoke French and English to me. The only French I knew was '*Oui, Monsieur*', '*Non, Madame*' and '*Merci*'. Titters and chuckles and smiles erupted and the French gentleman on my left said that a toast was when everybody drank a tiny sip of champagne in someone's honour – mine on this occasion. After that, the toastmaster would call another toast to the French president, Charles de Gaulle and finally to our King George VI and on *both* occasions I could drink a little sip of champagne with everyone else. I was much mollified.

‡

So the years passed and many people in the English-speaking world and in France remembered the courage of one lovely young woman who had fought like a tiger and who had died with great dignity.

Today there are museums honouring Violette. In Herefordshire, owned by Rosemary Rigby MBE, is a tiny museum is dedicated to Violette at the old kennels, now called Cartref,[190] where Violette used to spend summer days roaming the lovely countryside, much as she had in France. Closest to Violette's birthday of 26 June and on the last Sunday of June since 2000, Rosemary invites people to Violette's picnic. About 200 people come to celebrate her life including French and British military, politicians, councillors, mayors, children and cadets. There is a display at

---

190 *Cartref* is Welsh for 'home'. Thanks to Cardiff School of Computer Science for this information.

the Imperial War Museum in London and in Stockwell a Blue Plaque adorns the old house at 18 Burnley Road. A block of council flats is named after her in the area and a huge circular mural opposite Stockwell Tube Station tells her story. At Stockwell Park School there is a commemorative garden dedicated to Violette and at Lambeth Town Hall and in Hans Crescent her picture is prominent. In Jersey at the Jersey War Tunnels Museum, where several million pounds were invested to develop a grand exhibition on the Occupation of the Channel Islands, is a room devoted to Violette, called the Szabó Room. In France, at Pont-Rémy, in Picardy a few miles south-east of Abbeville, there is a stele in her memory opposite the Leroy family home where she lived with Tante Marguerite. In a neighbouring village, Quevauvillers, is the street, la rue Violette Szabó, named in her honour and, in 2015, another street, this time in the Haute-Vienne, will be named for Violette. There is mention of her in the Museum of the Maquis des Diables Noirs just outside Rouen at Forges-des-Eaux. In Sussac, she is honoured each year when the people of Haute-Vienne climb to Mont Gargan to honour all the Résistants who died for France and for freedom. At a crossroads on the way, they stop at an imposing monument to commemorate Violette and are debating whether the road of the ambush should be named after her. Schools have walls covered with her story, and books and DVDs telling her tale on their shelves. In the USA, Australia and the UK, and possibly elsewhere, people have completed their degrees using Violette's heroic story to that end or have erected plaques and other memorials. Now she adorns the plinth in front of Lambeth Palace looking over the Embankment to the Houses of Parliament. The book and the film, both entitled *Carve her Name with Pride*, were translated into French for the French and Canadian French. The French title chosen was *Agent Sz* ... There have been two biographies and many short bios in collections; many articles have been written. Ohio University has compiled Violette's story for their archives of women at war.

I hope that my book has helped to breathe life into her story of enduring courage and laughing gaiety and that I have done her some small justice. Her life was short but lived to the full, with much happiness, joy, some deep sadness and great endeavour. It is we who have lost out. What a great old lady she would have made, what a contribution she would have given and what wisdom and fun she would have passed our way.

She and all those other brave souls who gave their lives for our fragile freedoms would urge us most strenuously to be ever vigilant and strive to remain free and democratic. Lest we forget. And let us beware.

‡

'All human beings are born free and equal in dignity and rights. They are endowed with reason and conscience and should act towards one another in a spirit of brotherhood.'
Universal Declaration of Human Rights (Art. 1),
adopted by General Assembly resolution 217 A (III) of 10 December 1948

Ode to Violette

a Father's Pride in Lament

FAITHFUL EVEN UNTO DEATH

by her father,
Charles George Bushell, 1946
© Tania Szabó

'Tis a glorious tale of British Pluck, of heroism grand,
The deeds of a beautiful woman, in defence of her homeland.
She stepped from a plane, high in the air, in the darkness of the night,
With a message for the Maquis, telling them where to strike.
Think of the fearful dangers, this girl had to face,
In the midst of the enemy, dropped from out of space.
Her heart beating high with courage, she knew the risks she ran;
In her head she kept the message, and complex plan –
The plan of the Allied Leaders, to land our troops in France
For the overthrow of Germany, nothing was left to chance.
How well she did her duty, the world will already know
She delivered the vital message, she had struck her blow
To avenge her soldier husband, killed in nineteen forty-two,
And countless thousands of others – when – from out of the blue
She found herself surrounded, by the dread Gestapo men.
Without a thought of surrender, she picked up a gun and then
Fighting from house to house, killing and wounding the Hun
At last she fell exhausted, her noble duty done.

Chained and thrown into prison, suffering thirst and pain,
Her little daughter in England she knew she would ne'er see again.
Atrociously tortured beyond belief, she kept locked in her heart
The secret the Nazis knew she had, and tho' they tear her apart,
She determined never to speak, that nothing should make her tell
And so this wonderful woman, bore the tortures of hell.
Her spirit still unbroken, she was sent to another camp.
The train in which she travelled, was bombed in the fields of France.
Some of the men were prisoners, wounded, without a drink.
Amid that deadly rain of bombs, again she did not shrink.
While the guards were taking cover, she staggered to their aid,
With jugs of water in her hands, she was not afraid.
And so, she came to Ravensbrück, that camp of awful fame.
Her sufferings were terrible, but 'twas all in vain.
No matter what they did, they could not make her talk,
This girl of Anglo-French descent, with face as white as chalk.
Little the Nazis knew, the courage they had to face.
And finding they could not make her speak, tied her to a stake.
Proudly she faced the firing squad, defiant to the end,
Knowing she was facing death, yet she would not bend.
The fatal shots were fired, and to the world was lost,
Madame Violette Szabó, how well she earned her Cross,
Never to be forgotten, this girl aged twenty-four
Torture could not break her, she was British to the core.

To all the women throughout the world, a pattern she has set
Of unexampled courage; and thought of the fate she met
Makes brave men and women, turn pale at the very thought.
Words fail to describe the courage, of one so frail and young,
But to the ends of the earth her praises shall be sung.
For never before in History and possibly never again,
Has a girl been so brutally tortured, tortured but all in vain.

Acknowledgements
to the First Edition (2007)

To the following people I continue to hold a debt of great gratitude. Without them the first edition could not have been written – but then nor could this second, completely revised edition. Those who are no longer among us I hold deep within my heart and those still here – again, thank you.

Phœbe Atkins, Serge Blandin, Lieutenant Colonel Bradbury, Kerrie and Annie Bushell, Roy and Rick Bushell, Sir Henry and Lady Albina Cooper, Alasdair Crosby, Huguette Deshors, Tom Ensminger, Adv. Richard Falle, Susan Foord, Clive and Annie Garner, Sylvia and William Glenn, Jean-Claude Guiet, Steven and Irene Harwood, Sarah Helms, Paul E.F. Holley, Alexander Hugh, Polly Isbey, Leslie Jackson, Steve Jepson, Roger Jones, Bob Large DFC, Ld'H, Penny and Mike Lawrence, Sahra and Trevor Le Feuvre, John and Norman Lucas, Sidney Mathews, Madame and Monsieur Montelly, Bill Morvan, Seamus Morvan, Musée de la Résistance–Forge des Eaux, Harry Patterson (Jack Higgins), Sue and Frank Prigent, Madame Renaudie, Anna Ribiéras, John-Pierre Ribiéras, the Rolfes, Rosemary Rigby MBE and her team, Patrimoine Rouen, Mark Seaman, Martin Sugarman and JSTOR, Paul Simmonds, Henry Tiarks, Albert Tisserand, Jacques Valéry, Simon Watkins, Michael Wilkins.

Tania Szabó
Island of Jersey
September 2007

Acknowledgements
to the Second Edition (2015)

So many more who have helped in individual ways, helping to correct errors, to keep the bailiff from the door and just giving their friendship and presence.

In Wales the first people to thank are those who found me a wonderful seventeenth-century cottage – Edwin and Jane Bryce.

Then those who helped with the 250 boxes of books, archives and small things – Edwin and Jane Bryce, Jane's brother Andrew and his friend Beth, Rob Clement, Ceri and Tim Hill – they were so patient and my first friends in mid-Wales.

Sandra Clipstone, cousin to Rosemary Rigby MBE – owner of the Violette Szabó Museum in Wormelow, Herefordshire. Sandra has been a source of fun and friendship during some pretty dark days, along with her friend, Carol Blackburn.

Also Rob, Dai (who strimmed beautifully), Tim and Nathan who helped in the aftermath of the devastating fire at the cottage – they moved everything at cost price, with humour in the pouring rain, snow and freezing cold over a three-month period.

The team at The History Press, with special thanks to Chrissy McMorris, freelance editor Jude John and Tom Fryer of Sparks, I thank you all for your commitment to ensuring a fine book and putting up with my concerns.

David and Bronwe Petersen, Wendy Charles and Sam, along with Rob, Ceri and Tim who kept the black dog in his place but took Mick the Magnet to their heart. The continuing support of Seamus Morvan, Robert Russell and Sylvia and William de Glenn and those whom I might have unintentionally not mentioned.

Thank you to Mark Yeats for being my generous agent and friend and introducing me to The History Press; to Jussie, Immi and Coco (Mark's three very lovely womenfolk) for putting up with my visits with Mick the Dog tagging along in happy bounds; and especially to Coco and Immi for each giving up their bed to me on each visit.

My sincere thanks to Brigitte Garin and her mother Lucette for the invaluable information and friendly hospitality they afforded me in Pony. Brigitte introduced me to municipal archives and we spent some wonderful hours talking about the Nazi occupation and the courage of Florence and Jean. Florence did survive the concentration camps and lived to have a profound impact on the people around her.

My thanks, too, to a prince among princes and many other dear people including Ian, a dear friend and mobile master.

My love and sincere thanks to all of you who kept me afloat emotionally, and as a writer, too, during a difficult few years since the death of Paul E.F. Holley, my friend and mentor and friend of Violette.

Tania Szabó

Mid-Wales

June 2015

Bibliography

This is a small fraction of the material studied by the author – books, private and public correspondence, private and public archives – but might be a guide to those wishing to research the Second World War, SOE and the Résistance in France.

Adeline, François, *Haute-Vienne la Guerre secrète*; Le Populaire du Centre
Amouroux, Henri, *Au printemps de mort et d'espoir*; Robert Laffont
Amouroux, Henri, *Le peuple du désastre*; Robert Laffont
Archives of FANY HQ
Archives of the SOE Advisor in the Foreign Office
Atkins, Phœbe, *Vera Atkins Archives*; courtesy of Sarah Helm
Binney, Marcus, *Secret War Heroes*; Hodder &Stoughton
Binney, Marcus, *The Women Who Lived for Danger*; Hodder & Stoughton
Bleicher, Hugo, *Colonel Henri's Story, The War Mémoires of Hugo Bleicher*; Kimber
Buckmaster, Maurice, *They Fought Alone*; Odhams Press
Calet, Henri, *Les Murs de Fresnes*; Viviane Hamy
Clark, Freddie, *Agents by Moonlight*; Tempus
Coiffier, Patrick, *Rouen Sous l'Occupation*; Editions Bertout
Cookridge, E.H., *Inside SOE*; Arthur Barker
Cowburn, Benjamin, *No cloak No Dagger*; The Adventurers Club
Cuningham, Cyril, *Beaulieu, The Finishing School for Secret Agents*; Leo Cooper
Deacon, Richard, *A History of the British Secret Service*; Granada
Dallot, Sébastien, *L'Indre sous l'occupation allemande*; de Borée
Dowswell, Paul, *True Stories of the Second World War*; Usborne Publishing
Ellis, Mark, *Child at War*; Mercury House
Ensminger, Thomas L., *Spies, Supplies, and Moonlit Skies, Vol II*; Xlibris Corp.
de Gaulle Anthonioz, Geneviève, *God Remained Outside*; Souvenir Press
Faramus, Anthony, *Journey into Darkness*; Grafton Books
Foot, M.R.D., *SOE 1940-46*; BBC
Foot, M.R.D., *SOE in France*; Whitehall History Publishing
Frazer-Smith, Charles, *The Secret War*; Michael Joseph

Guingouin, Georges, *Quatre Ans de Lutte sur le sol Limousin*; Lucien Souny

Gundry, Elsie, *Personal writings, diary and images*

Hamilton-Hill, Donald, *SOE Assignment*; William Kimber

Helm, Sarah, *A Life in Secrets: The Story of Vera Atkins and the Lost Agents of SOE*; Little Brown

Howarth, Patrick, *Undercover*; Phoenix Press

Hudson, Sidney, *Undercover Operator*; Leo Cooper

Hue, André, *The Next Moon*; Viking

Imperial War Museum, Archive and film archives

Jackson, Julian, *France the Dark Years*; Oxford University Press

Kartheuser, Bruno, *La France occupée, Vol II*; Editions Krautgarten

Kedward, H.R., *Occupied France: Collaboration and Resistance*; Blackwell

Lanckoronska, Countess Karolina, *Those Who Trespass Against Us*; Pimlico

Legoy, Jean, *Les Havrais dans la Guerre*; Edit par la municipalité du Havre

Loveless, Irène, *Spirit of Survivial*; Lord Mayor of Portsmouth's Charitable Fund

Luneaux, Jean, *Dans les Pas de Jean Moulin*; Editions du petit Pavé

MacKenzie, William, *Secret History of SOE*; St. Ermin's Hotel

Malraux, André, *La Corde et les Souris*; Folio

Marks, Leo, *Between Silk and Cyanide*; Harper Collins

Matthew, Adam and team, *Special Operations Executive Series 1*; Adam Matthew Publications

Maurois, André, *Rouen dévasté*; Association Le Pucheux

McCue, Paul, *SAS Operation Bulbasket*, Jedburghs; Pen & Sword

McLaughlin, Roy, *Living with the Enemy*; Channel Island Publishing

Mière, Joe, *Never to be Forgotten*; Channel Island Publishing

Miguel, Pierre, *La Seconde Guerre Mondiale*; Fayard

Millar, Georges, *Maquis*; Cassell

Minney, R.J., *Carve her Name with Pride*; Newnes

National Archives, *Personal file of Vera Atkins*

National Archives, *Personal file of Isidore Newman*

National Archives, *Personal file of Harry Peulevé*

National Archives, *Personal file of Violette Szabó*

Nicault, Maurice, *Résistance et Libération de l'Indre*; Royer

Noguères, Henri, *Histoire de la Résistance en France, Tomes 1-VI*; Robert Laffont

Overton Fuller, Jean, *The German Penetration of SOE*; George Mann

Ousby, Ian, *Occupation, the Ordeal of France*; Pimlico

Pailhès, G., *Rouen et sa région pendant la guerre*; Editions Bertout

Patrimoine Rouen *Rouen Sous L'Occupation*

Perrault, Gilles, *La longue Traque*; Jean-Claude Lattes

Place, Pascal, *Visage de la Résistance*; Éditions Lucien Souny.

Pognant, Patrick, *In Memoriam de Albert Pognant*

Poirier, Jacques, *La girafe a un long cou*; Edition du Félin

Rémy, Colonel, *La Résistance en Aquitaine*; Edition Famot

Rigden, Denis Introduction by, *SOE Syllabus*; Dundurn Group

Ringlesbach, Dorothy, *OSS: Stories that can now be told*; Authorhouse

Ruby, Marcel, *F Section SOE*; Leo Cooper

Ruffin, Raymond, *La résistance normande face à la Gestapo*; Edition Bertout

Saidel, Rachel G., *The Jewish Women of Ravensbrück Concentration Camp*; University of Wisconsin Press

Schoenbrun, David, *Soldiers of the Night*; Robert Hale

Stafford, David, *Secret Agent, Britain's Wartime Secret Service*; BBC

Stevenson, William, *A Man called Intrepid*; Macmillan

Stevenson, William, *Spymistress*; Arcade

Veillon, Dominique, *Vivre et survivre en France*; Histoire Payot

Verity, Hugh, *We Landed by Moonlight*; Air Data Publications

Vickers, Philip, *La Division Das Reich*; Lucien Souny

Ward, Dame Irene, *FANY Invicta*; Hutchinson

Weidinger, Otto, *Das Reich III*; J JFedorowicz

West, Nigel, *MI5 1945–1972, A Matter of Trust*; Coronet

Wilkinson, Peter and Bright Astley, Joan, *Gubbins & SOE*; Leo Cooper

The author also wishes to express her indebtedness to the items of private correspondence from the Bushell and Lucas families, and the Leroy family (through Madame Rolande Peletier in Pont Rémy) which has enabled her to source or verify many of the details in this book. Much other information came from public and privately owned archives, correspondence and museums in the United Kingdom, the United States, Australia, and New Zealand, France and Europe generally.

Index

Visit our website and discover thousands of other History Press books.

www.thehistorypress.co.uk